COLLECTED WORKS OF ERASMUS

VOLUME 64

ENARRATIO

VLTVM diſcriminis eſt fra/ tres unice dilecti inter ada/ mātem & uitrum,ſed multo plus diſcriminis eſt inter cor pus & animum, longe pluri/ mum uero inter res diuinas & humanas . Hoc ideo uiſũ eſt præfari,ut ſpectaculo q̃d hodie,donāte Chriſto,uobis exhibere ſtudeo,oculos atq̃ aureis dignas accómodetis. Nam ita demũ fiet, ut ex eo,quum uoluptatis plurimũ,tum utilitatem in/ æſtimabilem referatis . Qui ſedent in amphitheatris, ſpectaturi gladiatorum paria , aut hiſtriones comœ/ diam tragœdiamúe ſaltaturos, quoniam oculos & au reis adferunt talibus ſpectaculis dignas,è theatro ferè diſcedunt ſeipſis deteriores. Tales oculos,tales aureis ſi quis habet ueſtrum , oret dominum ut ipſi digne/ tur impartiri oculos mundi cordis, quibus cernuntur ſpiritualia,aureis puras,quibus percipiunt́ arcana cœ leſtis ſapiétiæ. Tales oculos,tales aureis,nec natiuitas dat,nec medicorum ars:ſolus ille cuius ſpiritu renaſci/

· aa ꒱ mur,

Enarratio pia iuxta ac docta in psalmum 33 page 5
Basel: Froben 1531
Centre for Reformation and Renaissance Studies
Victoria University, University of Toronto
This is the opening of *An Exposition of Psalm 33* page 275 below

COLLECTED WORKS OF
ERASMUS

EXPOSITIONS OF THE PSALMS

edited by Dominic Baker-Smith

CONCIONALIS INTERPRETATIO IN PSALMUM 85

IN PSALMUM 22 ENARRATIO TRIPLEX

CONSULTATIO DE BELLO TURCIS INFERENDO,
ET OBITER ENARRATUS PSALMUS 28

ENARRATIO PSALMI 33

University of Toronto Press

Toronto / Buffalo / London

The research and publication costs of the
Collected Works of Erasmus are supported by
University of Toronto Press.

ⓒ University of Toronto Press Incorporated 2005
Toronto / Buffalo / London
Printed in Canada

ISBN 0-8020-3584-1

Printed on acid-free paper

Canadian Cataloguing in Publication Data

Erasmus, Desiderius, d. 1536
[Works]
Collected works of Erasmus

Includes bibliographical references and index.
Contents: v. 64. Expositions of the Psalms / edited by Dominic Baker-Smith.
ISBN 0-8020-3584-1 (v. 64)

1. Erasmus, Desiderius, d. 1536 – Collected works.   I. Title.

PA8500 1974   199'.492   C74-006326-x rev

University of Toronto Press acknowledges the financial assistance to its
publishing program of the Canada Council and the Ontario Arts Council.

University of Toronto Press acknowledges the financial support
for its publishing activities of the Government of Canada
through the Book Publishing Industry Development Program (BPIDP).

Collected Works of Erasmus

The aim of the Collected Works of Erasmus
is to make available an accurate, readable English text
of Erasmus' correspondence and his
other principal writings. The edition is planned
and directed by an Editorial Board, an Executive Committee,
and an Advisory Committee.

Contents

Illustrations

Preface

This volume is the second of three devoted to Erasmus' expositions of the Psalms. The full range and the implications of his engagement with the Psalms is discussed in the Introduction to CWE 63. After the appearance of the 'sermon' on Psalm 4 (*In psalmum quartum concio*), which concludes the previous volume, it was three years before Erasmus turned his attention once again to a psalm text. The outcome, the *Concionalis interpretatio in psalmum 85*, was dedicated to the same patron, John Longland, bishop of Lincoln, and the title again alludes to the sermon – *concio* – as was appropriate for a preaching bishop. It was Longland who

* * * * *

Works cited frequently are referred to in the notes in abbreviated form; a list of abbreviations and full bibliographical information is given at 376 below. References to Erasmus' correspondence are to the English translation of the letters in CWE, where these have already been published, or to the Latin edition of Allen.

The following shortened titles are adopted for individual expositions of the Psalms:

Enarratio allegorica in primum psalmum: In psalmum 1
Commentarius in psalmum 2: In psalmum 2
Paraphrasis in tertium psalmum: In psalmum 3
In psalmum quartum concio: In psalmum 4
Concionalis interpretatio in psalmum 85: In psalmum 85
In psalmum 22 enarratio triplex: In psalmum 22
Consultatio de bello Turcis inferendo, et obiter enarratus psalmus 28: De bello Turcico
Enarratio psalmi 33: In psalmum 33
Enarratio in psalmum 38: In psalmum 38
De sarcienda ecclesiae concordia [in psalmum 83]: De concordia
Enarratio in psalmum 14 qui est de puritate tabernaculi: De puritate tabernaculi

Those expositions which have yet to be published in CWE volume 65 are referred to by means of the appropriate column numbers in LB V; these can easily be followed in ASD V-2 and V-3.

had urged Erasmus in 1520 to undertake a commentary on the Book of Psalms.[1] But the *Concionalis interpretatio* does mark a significant departure since, by turning to Psalm 85, Erasmus effectively put paid to the idea of a complete commentary, and the remaining expositions of individual psalms – six in all – follow no obvious principle of selection.[2] But if Erasmus reverts to the title *enarratio* in the remaining commentaries, this does not signal a change of approach: the ideal of the *concio*, an address intended to sway the hearers to action, persists as his dominant model; these are above all practical writings designed to promote a personal response to the biblical text. Even *De bello Turcico*, with its broad appraisal of the Turkish threat to Europe, gains its impact from a call to moral self-appraisal. Rather than exercises in biblical scholarship, these expositions stand as effective embodiments of the *philosophia Christi* in action.

The four works presented here were composed in the period between August 1528 and February 1531, a time of growing anxiety for Erasmus, as the bitterly contested issues of Reformation theology appeared to slip beyond any reasonable hope of reconciliation. The second part of the *Hyperaspistes*, his conclusive rejection of Luther's position on freedom of the will, had been published in the autumn of 1527, while an outbreak of mob iconoclasm at Basel in the spring of 1529 impelled Erasmus to transfer his residence to Freiburg im Breisgau. Against this background these four psalm expositions help to clarify his own fidelity to a moderate and conciliatory line of argument. It is, again, no accident that they coincide with a period of patristic study which bore fruit in editions of Irenaeus (1526), Ambrose (1527), Chrysostom (1530), and Basil (1530), as well as the revised Jerome of 1529.

Certain themes catch the attention. When dealing with the church Erasmus shows a characteristically developed sense of the mystical body of Christ, defined less by institutional features than by an attitude of mind. To enter the church is to discard your corrupt self, and no external authority can remove us from it 'unless you yourself wish it.'[3] Since the historical church will always be mixed, joining saints with sinners, the shortcomings of its ministers provide no justification for rupturing its unity; as long as

* * * * *

1 See Ep 1570 and the dedication of *In psalmum 4* CWE 63 174.
2 It is worth recalling that in addition to the quadruple psalter printed in *Hieronymi Opera* (1516; volume VIII), Erasmus edited the Psalm commentaries of Arnobius the Younger (1522) and Haymo (1533).
3 See *In psalmum 85* 17–18 and *In psalmum 22* 180 below.

you remain in charity with God and your neighbour your membership will be secure.[4] This spiritual conception of the ecclesial community, in which heresy is a self-induced condition of wilful isolation, provides a viable basis for the process of reconciliation that Erasmus never ceased to encourage. In the course of the exposition of Psalm 33 he reflects on the heterodox opinions found among the Fathers – a tactful parallel to the disputes of his own day – and concludes that intellectual error need not separate one from the church, provided that the subjective disposition (*affectus*) has not been corrupted.[5] Such an approach sought to minimize the differences between Christians without compromising the core consensus of received doctrine.

An interesting feature in these expositions is the emergence of a double-justification formula that anticipates the line adopted in the abortive efforts for reconciliation at the Colloquy of Regensberg in 1541. From the outset Erasmus is anxious to find a path between those who rely on meritorious works and those who consider that faith renders moral acts irrelevant.[6] In his treatment of Psalm 22 he adopts the actual formula, *duplex iustitia*, distinguishing between the received righteousness of faith and baptism and the synergistic operation of faith working through love.[7] One year later, writing this time on Psalm 33, he endeavours to bind the two aspects in a striking corporal image in which the bones are faith, the sinews are love, and the flesh is good works, 'which are inseparable from faith and love.'[8] While he opposes any exaggerated emphasis on human merit Erasmus does, nevertheless, insist on that assent of the will which enables grace to fulfil its operations: 'The Lord desires to rescue you, but to rescue you as you cry out.'[9]

Given his emphasis on an inner or spiritual affiliation to the church, there is a strong reaction in Erasmus against the adoption of violence in the pursuit of orthodoxy. Nowhere is this spelled out more explicitly than in *De bello Turcico*, which, for all its concern with the threat from the east, is a powerful plea for Christians to grapple first with the enemy within. It is futile to fight the Turks with the mind of a Turk. If the Turks as the scourge of God owe their success to the sins of Christians, then foremost among those

* * * * *

4 See *In psalmum* 22 180 below.
5 See *In psalmum* 33 368 below.
6 See *In psalmum* 85 21–2, 36 below.
7 See *In psalmum* 22 152 below.
8 See *In psalmum* 33 366–7 below.
9 See *In psalmum* 33 328 below.

must be the moral degeneracy of the episcopate.[10] Whether it be a case of infidels or heretics, Erasmus appeals nonetheless to the ancient clemency of the church, which sought a conversion of heart rather than coercion by violence. While Luther's case for passivity before the scourge of God is firmly rejected, so too is the kind of triumphalism that sees death in war against the infidel as instant absolution. In a proposal which was surely intended to have some bearing on the state of a divided Christendom, Erasmus even argues for a state of coexistence; this is not, of course, some anticipation of multiculturalism but an interim phase which will enable the appeal of an authentic Christianity to win over its former enemies.[11]

Behind the various themes that surface in the expositions lies Erasmus' constant preoccupation with the rediscovery of the spiritual dimension in Christian practice, the reanimation which would carry the believer through (but not beyond) outward signs and ceremonies to the personal encounter of prayer. Prayer, for him, must be the product of the whole person, requiring perhaps a bodily act but certainly a devout disposition and active charity. It is disposition (*affectus*) that elevates the act of praying into a constant awareness of God: in the remarkable elaboration of pastoral metaphor which characterizes the exposition of Psalm 22 this disposition is termed the stomach, the organ that transforms the matter of belief into vital energy.[12] Such ruminative meditation is the ultimate aim of the works presented in this volume, and it is to be hoped that their availability in English will now help to stimulate heightened interest in the writings of Erasmus' later years. His undertaking to open up the Psalms to a broad readership offers an absorbing range of nuances on the critical issues of his time, nuances that have too often been neglected or obscured by partisan accounts of the Reformation crisis.

As always in such an undertaking there is a substantial debt to the generosity of other scholars, not least to the anonymous readers of the University of Toronto Press for their careful attention to detail. Particular thanks are due to Dr J. Trapman for help with textual matters, and to Professor Hugh Williamson for guidance in Hebrew. Finally, it is a pleasure to make the by now customary acknowledgment to Mary Baldwin, Lynn Burdon, and Philippa Matheson at the Press for their patient skill in preparing the manuscript for publication.

DBS

* * * * *

10 See *De bello Turcico* 241 below.
11 See *De bello Turcico* 265 below.
12 See *In psalmum 22* 185 below.

NOTE ON BIBLICAL REFERENCES

With the decline in use of the Douai-Reims translation most English versions of the Bible now available follow the divisions and numbering of the Hebrew Bible rather than the Vulgate familiar to Erasmus. This can create difficulties for the reader, especially in the case of the Psalms. The Vulgate text of the Psalms joins Ps 9 with Ps 10 and Ps 114 with Ps 115, but it also divides Pss 116 and 147 into two parts each; consequently from 10 to 148 the Hebrew numeration is at least one figure ahead of the Vulgate. To compound the difficulty, the superscription that heads some psalms is numbered as a verse in the Vulgate but not in those versions deriving from the Hebrew. In this volume, Erasmus' treatment of Psalm 33 (34 according to the Hebrew numeration) includes an extensive discussion of the superscription, 'A Psalm of David when he changed his face before Abimelech, and he dismissed him, and he went away' (275–307 below). In the Vulgate this is numbered verse 1, but in English versions it is either placed above the numbered verses or omitted altogether. Nor is such variation confined to the Psalms. The obvious course when annotating Erasmus is to use the Vulgate, but to facilitate reference to English versions double references are given for all variable texts, first the numbers specific to the Vulgate, followed by the variant. For instance in (Vulgate) Psalm 118 where the verse numbers are common to all versions, Ps 118/119:70; but in (Vulgate) Psalm 99 where the verses differ, Ps 99:2/100:1. The same method is followed in other biblical texts where there is variation, as in John 6:61/60. Titles of some books are different in the Vulgate and modern English versions. In references where such variation might cause confusion, both titles are given.

A DEVOUT EXPLANATION OF PSALM 85
IN THE FORM OF A SERMON

Concionalis interpretatio, plena pietatis, in psalmum 85

translated and annotated by

CAROLINNE WHITE

Erasmus sent his exposition of Psalm 85 to John Longland, bishop of Lincoln,[1] in August 1528. The dedicatory letter accompanying the work makes it clear that Erasmus had written it in response to a request from Longland, to whom he had already, in 1525, dedicated his commentary on Psalm 4, and, in 1527, his translation of some of[2] Athanasius' works.[3] It is not however clear from the letter why Erasmus had selected Psalm 85 as his subject, rather than continuing with the series of commentaries on the psalms, starting with Psalm 1[4] and using a different genre for his exposition of each psalm. It may be that Longland himself asked him to treat this psalm or that its interesting tensions particularly appealed to Erasmus because it addressed some of his main concerns. Whatever the reason for his choice, Erasmus apparently completed this exposition within the space of a week, regarding it almost as a piece of light relief[5] at a time when he was busy with major projects: his edition of the works of Augustine and a new edition of the *Adagia*. His commentary on Psalm 85, of which no manuscript survives, was published by Hieronymus Froben and Johann Herwagen at Basel in 1528. This was the only edition published in Erasmus' lifetime, although he included a few emendations in his *Apologia adversus monachos* of the following year.[6] The 1528 edition was included in the 1540 publication of Erasmus' complete works and was reprinted, under the supervision of Le Maire, at Leiden in 1652. It was at Leiden, too, that the edition of the complete works of Erasmus was produced between 1703 and 1706, an edition in which the text of Erasmus' commentary on Psalm 85 differs on a number of minor points from the text of the ASD edition. While this commentary was

* * * * *

1 John Longland (1473–1547) had been a confessor to Henry VIII and became bishop of Lincoln in 1521. A member of the king's council, he was to become involved in the negotiations to arrange a divorce between Henry and Catherine of Aragon. On his career see CEBR II 341 and M. Bowker *The Henrician Reformation: The Diocese of Lincoln under John Longland* (Cambridge 1981) 4–16.

2 See Ep 1535 / CWE 63 174.

3 See Ep 1790.

4 In Ep 2315:172–7 to Sadoleto (in 1530) Erasmus would state that he had given up the idea of writing commentaries on all the psalms partly because he realized that a knowledge of Hebrew was necessary to such an enterprise and partly because he felt that there was already a surfeit of commentaries on the psalms.

5 See Allen Ep 2315:96–9 to Jacopo Sadoleto and Allen Ep 2070:11–12 to Christoph von Stadion, in which he speaks of writing the commentary hastily and rather sketchily.

6 ASD V-3 325; the ASD text, based on the 1528 edition, incorporates these corrections.

not among the best known of Erasmus' works, it was greeted favourably by his learned friends, although it would seem that Louis Berquin was somewhat critical of what he regarded as Erasmus' tolerant attitude towards the cult of the saints.[7]

Longland was well known as a preacher,[8] and it is in the form of a sermon[9] that Erasmus chose to write his expositions on both Psalm 4 and Psalm 85. Throughout the exposition of Psalm 85 Erasmus gives the impression of a live performance, addressing and exhorting his audience and referring to them as 'brothers.' After an introductory section in which he considers the nature of prayer and the proper attitude of the one who prays, and encourages his audience to listen to God so that he will listen to them, Erasmus goes on to consider the psalm verse by verse. But although the bulk of the work is a verse-by-verse commentary rather than a sermon on a single verse or on a single theme, and despite a number of digressions, Erasmus manages to provide a coherent account of the psalm, treating each of the seventeen verses in a consistent manner. At the end of the work he summarizes the message of the whole psalm by stating that it 'portrays for us the victory of Christ, the overthrow of Satan, and the destruction of idolatry. It shows how the gentiles have been welcomed into the grace of the gospel, it describes the thanksgiving of the church, tells how all who took up arms against it have been utterly defeated and put to shame, and ascribes all the credit for this to God, who fights in us and for us, giving us greater strength in battle and granting us comfort in our sufferings.'[10]

In the course of his lengthy exposition Erasmus touches on several important themes that are evident in his other works as well. He discusses the nature and purpose of prayer,[11] a subject already dealt with in the *Enchiridion* (1503) and in *Modus orandi Deum*, published in 1524 (a second, slightly longer version appeared the following year). He emphasises the paradoxes he sees as fundamental to the Christian way of life: that only those who

* * * * *

7 Reference to Berquin's criticism is made by Erasmus in Allen Ep 2077:54–6.
8 It appears that Longland gained a reputation as a preacher while in Oxford; from about 1513 he was regularly preaching at the court of Henry VIII. A few of his sermons survive, among them a series of expositions on five of the penitential psalms. See J.W. Blench *Preaching in England in the Late Fifteenth and Sixteenth Centuries* (Oxford 1964).
9 Erasmus refers to his commentary on Psalm 85 as an *expositio concionalis* and a *concionalis interpretatio*, an interpretation in the form of a sermon.
10 See 116 below.
11 Erasmus puts forward the view that 'the main aim of your prayers ought to be to possess the Lord himself'; see 58 below.

are poor are truly rich, only those who acknowledge that whatever they possess comes from God truly own what they have, only those who are foolish in the eyes of the world are truly wise, and only those who are obedient to God have true freedom. He refers to the question of the relative value of faith and works, stating that 'faith is not something ineffectual: if it is a living faith, it works through love; if it does not result in good deeds, it is dead and is not worthy of the name of faith';[12] although he does not mention Luther by name, he presumably had his views on the subject in mind in this emphasis on the need to progress along the path of faith. But if he stresses that faith is not sufficient by itself, he also states that free will is not sufficient to produce good works;[13] contrary to the Pelagian view, Erasmus believes strongly that grace is necessary at every stage of man's spiritual progress. In this work Erasmus is clearly trying to find a delicate balance between the views of the reformers regarding the primacy of faith over works and those practices of the Catholic church which put a premium on works and reflected an attitude that could be accused of Pelagianism. Erasmus also expresses criticism of contemporary religious practices, of the hypocrisy and lack of sincerity and commitment he considers to be rife among Christians.[14] Yet despite his critical, even satirical, attitude, Erasmus shows that he is also full of understanding for such weakness, for he frequently admits the difficulty of putting our trust in God alone rather than in anything this world has to offer. He is well aware of the suffering that is part of human existence and that makes it hard to be confident that Christ will indeed transform suffering into salvation. He also mentions the question of submission to human authority, stating his firm belief that we must submit even if what is demanded of us is unfair and unpleasant, as long as we are not asked to do something wicked.

On a more theological level Erasmus' commentary, in keeping with its focus on the nature of Christ and his role in man's salvation, considers the Christological issue of whether Christ possessed a human soul as well as a human body alongside his divine nature; there is also a discussion of the nature of hell. This commentary contains few specific references, however, to contemporary events or controversies: there is a brief reference

* * * * *

12 See 72 below.
13 Erasmus had discussed the problem of free will in his *De libero arbitrio* in 1524; in reply, Luther wrote his *De servo arbitrio* in 1525; Erasmus responded with *Hyperaspistes* 1 and 2 in 1526–7.
14 See 80 below.

to Turks and Muslims in the summary, but they are mentioned merely as representatives of those who are strangers to Christ.

Erasmus bases his discussion of the psalm on the text of the so-called Gallican Psalter, which was Jerome's translation into Latin of the Greek Septuagint text in the version of Origen's *Hexapla*.[15] Erasmus occasionally refers to other Latin versions, such as an Old Latin version used by Augustine and the translation made by Jerome directly from the Hebrew (which, although subsequent to the Gallican Psalter, was not adopted in the Vulgate Bible). Occasionally Erasmus will himself give an alternative Latin reading based on the Greek text: for example, where Jerome gives *confundantur* 'may they be confounded' in both the Gallican version and that according to the Hebrew, Erasmus suggests that *pudefiant* 'may they be ashamed' is a more accurate translation of the Greek.[16]

Erasmus mentions several earlier commentaries on this psalm: those of Arnobius, Augustine, and the *Breviarium in psalmos* attributed to Jerome; as in his sermon on Psalm 4, he refers most often to the last two of these.[17] His familiarity with, and interest in, Augustine's commentary is hardly surprising considering that Erasmus was involved with his edition of Augustine at the time of writing his exposition of Psalm 85.

Despite certain similarities of interpretation and even of phrasing, however, Erasmus' exposition is no mere imitation or compendium of the earlier commentators. Arnobius' commentary is an extremely brief paraphrase,[18] while the commentary on Psalm 85 in the Pseudo-Jerome *Breviar-*

* * * * *

15 Jerome made this translation at Bethlehem in the years after 386. See J.N.D. Kelly *Jerome: His Life, Writings and Controversies* (London 1975) 158–9; his versions are described in CWE 63 xx–xxi.

16 See 105 below.

17 In Allen Ep 2315:165–6 Erasmus also refers to psalm commentaries by Hilary of Poitiers, Cassiodorus, and Bruno of Carinthia, but he states that Hilary's work is fragmentary, Cassiodorus is too verbose and unfocused to be of use, while Bruno's commentary is pious but not learned. Although Erasmus does not explicitly mention Cassiodorus' *Expositio in psalmum 85* (CCL 98 779–88), their commentaries do have certain points in common, such as the reference to Apollinarianism and the interpretation of 'the whole day long' in verse 3 as referring to the span of human life. On the whole Cassiodorus appears to interpret the psalm as the prayer of Christ, relevant to Christians as an example of humility and patience.

18 Arnobius the Younger *Commentarium in psalmum 85* PL 53 448–9; Erasmus remarks in Allen Ep 2315:165–6 that Arnobius' commentary is often shorter than the psalm itself. He produced an edition of Arnobius' psalm commentaries in 1522.

ium in psalmos[19] is a short verse-by-verse exposition in which the author states that in the first few verses of this psalm Christ speaks from the cross in accordance with both his divine and human nature, but from verse 11 it is the prophet who speaks. Augustine's exposition[20] is considerably longer. He interprets the psalm verse by verse and addresses his audience as 'brothers,' as does Erasmus. Furthermore, a number of elements in Augustine's interpretation reappear in Erasmus' work, for example the idea that Christians are holy because God has made them holy and the discussion about hell. But, in many respects Erasmus' commentary differs from Augustine's: Augustine's style is more dramatic, with short sentences, anaphora, word play, and rhyme, and his piece has a strongly eschatological outlook, with frequent contrasts made between this life and the next, between the suffering experienced on earth and fulfilment in heaven. Erasmus, on the other hand, primarily emphasizes the mystical sense, as when he refers the psalm to Christ, and the tropological or moral sense, as when he applies the words of the psalm to each human individual. In fact the two senses are closely linked throughout because of the belief that Christ is the head of the church and that all Christians are the members of the body of Christ: when Christ is said to speak in accordance with the human self he adopted in the Incarnation his words become relevant to each one of us. Erasmus does not deny that there is a literal, historical interpretation of the psalm, whereby David speaks during his persecution by Saul, but he considers it sufficient to refer to this interpretation in passing before returning to what he regards as the crucial way of interpreting the psalm: the historical sense does not conflict with the mystical, which sees David as the type of Christ, but can exist side by side with it. It is of course characteristic of Erasmus to regard alternative interpretations as compatible and as essentially aiming at the same goal: this is particularly clear in this commentary at those points in the text where he considers variant readings proposed by Augustine or Jerome. On the whole Erasmus, in his emphasis on a mystical and tropolog-

* * * * *

19 PL 26 (1845) 1078–80. The *Breviarium in psalmos* is now agreed to be a spurious work which contains some genuine material; see the preface to the (genuine, but unknown to Erasmus) *Commentarioli in psalmos* by G. Morin in CSEL 72 165–7. Erasmus shows his uneasiness about the attribution in *In psalmum 2* (CWE 63 74) and *In psalmum 33* (292 and 333 below); his view that the work had been contaminated by an impostor, 'an unforgivable sacrilege,' is reiterated to Sadoleto in Allen Ep 2315:155–7. For further remarks on interpolation in the text of Jerome see his dedicatory letter and prefaces to the edition of Jerome, especially the preface to volume II part 3 CWE 61 83–97.

20 Augustine *Enarratio in psalmum 85* CCL 39 1176–97

ical or moral interpretation of the psalm, interprets those elements which concern human suffering as referring to Christ or to those Christians who have true faith and turn to God for help, while those elements referring to wickedness are taken as relevant to the Jews (especially in connection with Christ's sufferings) and to non-Christians but also to those who are Christians only in name – of whom, Erasmus is well aware, there are large numbers within the church. At times Erasmus goes one step further and interprets the references to wicked behaviour as applicable not to human agents but to desires and passions which he regards as extremely danger-ous, if often subtle and concealed, motivating forces. Not only is the church of Christ, Christ's body, corrupted from within by Christians who lead un-godly lives, but each of us is prone to corruption from within if we allow rebellious desires to distract us from God and to drag us down, away from true and lasting fulfilment.

C W

1 Inclina [Deus] Domine, aurem tuam et exaudi me, quoniam inops et pauper sum ego.

2 Custodi animam meam quoniam sanctus sum. Salvum fac servum tuum, Deus meus, sperantem in te.

3 Miserere mei, Domine, quoniam ad te clamavi tota die.

4 Laetifica animam servi tui, quoniam ad te levavi animam meam.

5 Quoniam tu, Domine, suavis et mitis, et multae misericordiae omnibus invocantibus te.

6 Auribus percipe, Domine, orationem meam, et intende voci deprecationis meae.

7 In die tribulationis clamavi ad te, quoniam tu exaudisti.

8 Non est similis tui in diis, Domine, et non est secundum opera tua.

9 Omnes gentes quascunque fecisti venient, et adorabunt coram te, Domine, et glorificabunt nomen tuum.

10 Quoniam magnus es tu et faciens mirabilia, tu es Deus solus.

11 Deduc me, Domine, in via tua, et ingrediar in veritate tua. Laetetur cor meum, ut timeat nomen tuum.

12 Confitebor tibi, Domine Deus, in toto corde meo, et glorificabo nomen tuum in aeternum.

13 Quia [Quoniam] misericordia tua magna est super me et eruisti animam meam ex inferno inferiori.

14 Deus, iniqui insurrexerunt super me, et synagoga potentium quaesierunt animam meam, et non proposuerunt te in conspectu suo.

15 Et tu, Domine Deus, miserator et misericors, patiens et multae misericordiae et verax.

16 Respice in me et miserere mei; da imperium puero tuo et salvum fac filium ancillae tuae.

17 Fac mecum signum in bonum, ut videant qui oderunt me et confundantur; quoniam tu, Domine, adiuvisti me [auxiliatus es mihi], et consolatus es me.

1 Incline your ear, O Lord [God], and listen to me, for I am poor and needy.

2 Preserve my soul, for I am holy. Save your servant, my God, who puts his hope in you.

3 Have mercy on me, O Lord, for I have cried out to you the whole day long.

4 Gladden the soul of your servant, for to you have I lifted up my soul.

5 For you, O Lord, are kind and gentle and show great mercy to all who call on you.

6 Give ear, O Lord, to my prayer and heed the words of my appeal.

7 In the day of suffering I cried out to you, for you have heard me.

8 There is none like you among the gods, O Lord, and there are no works like yours.

9 All the peoples whom you have made will come and bow down before you, O Lord. They will glorify your name.

10 For you are mighty and you do wonderful things; you alone are God.

11 Lead me, O Lord, in your way, and I shall walk in your truth. May my heart rejoice so as to fear your name.

12 I will praise you, O Lord God, with my whole heart, and I shall glorify your name for ever.

13 For your mercy towards me is great, and you have rescued my soul from the lower regions of hell.

14 O God, the wicked have risen up against me, and the synagogue of the powerful have sought my soul and have not set you in their sight.

15 But you, O Lord God, are full of pity and compassionate, patient and of great mercy and truthful.

16 Look upon me and have mercy on me. Grant power to your servant and save the son of your handmaiden.

17 Show me a sign of your favour so that they who hate me may see and be ashamed, because you, O Lord, have helped me and comforted me.

TO THE MOST REVEREND FATHER IN CHRIST JOHN LONGLAND,
LORD BISHOP OF LINCOLN IN ENGLAND, FROM ERASMUS
OF ROTTERDAM, GREETING[1]

It is an ancient saying and a true one, most honourable bishop, that 'a request from the powerful compels compliance,'[2] but a request from the deserving exerts yet greater pressure. For it is hardly safe to deny the powerful anything, but to fail to obey a deserving person is the height of shame. Ingratitude is a more detestable fault than indiscretion.

Furthermore, whenever someone who has the right to command makes a request, he commands all the more powerfully because he is not commanding but requesting. Indeed, if it is a sign of obstinacy to refuse a command, then to deny someone's request is a sign of heartlessness. Now when someone who by authority can command and by desert can exact still makes his request modestly and, in a manner, by asking does not ask, he undoubtedly makes his request with greater force. As a result modesty often obtains what importunate demands fail to achieve.

Since, then, you assail me with so many devices,[3] reverend father, with authority, with good deeds, and with a modest request, I did not want the fact that you yourself suggested an excuse to excuse me. Indeed, my excuse was neither single nor simple, and it was perhaps more just than you might wish, but I was unable to deny so great a prelate who was so deserving and who made his request in such a way. So here you have the psalm: however it has been handled, it is nevertheless a testimony to my devoted obedience, which is without limit. You should approve of my disposition even if you are less impressed by my abilities, and you cannot disdain the attempt even if the result is disappointing. I will keep you from the psalm no longer. Farewell.

* * * * *

1 The dedicatory letter is Ep 2017.
2 *Adagia* v i 46. The saying is often attributed, wrongly, to Publilius Syrus.
3 Only two letters from Longland to Erasmus survive: Ep 1570, dating from the year 1525, and Ep 2227, written in 1529. In Ep 1535 to Longland, which accompanied his exposition of Psalm 4, Erasmus writes, 'In frequent letters ... you have returned again and again to the same theme.'

A bishop, possibly John Longland, vesting;
the page is putting on the episcopal buskins.
The miniature appears in a pontifical commissioned by Longland,
and his arms are blazoned at the bottom.
MS Add 21974, folio 2 verso
Reproduced by permission of the British Library

A DEVOUT EXPLANATION OF PSALM 85
IN THE FORM OF A SERMON, BY
DESIDERIUS ERASMUS OF ROTTERDAM

In reply to the question 'What is the most delightful thing there is?' a certain philosopher answered: 'To receive,'[1] and human consensus approves this reply. May you therefore, my brothers, be keen disciples of heavenly philosophy and greedy for spiritual wealth. I bring with me what you will receive at no cost – in fact, the more greedily you take it, the more advantage you will gain from it. It is a gift from God that I bring; I myself am only here to deliver someone else's gift. If you receive with great eagerness what is offered, you will of course be expressing the desired appreciation both to the one who provides the gift and to the one who presents it. If someone offers you fine cloth or jewels or gold as a gift, does not your face suddenly light up and your feelings grow cheerful as you eagerly reach for it with clean hands? If someone offers sumptuous food, you place it on your cleanest dishes. Behold, I bring something more precious than any jewels, fine cloth, or gold, something sweeter than any cakes and also more healthy. You are doing an injustice to the gift or rather to yourselves if you receive what is freely offered as if you were sleepy, apathetic, and miserable. The Hebrew wise man has very rightly said: 'God loves a cheerful giver,'[2] but he also loves the person who receives cheerfully. A person who gives with a miserable expression robs his kind gift of some of its charm, while he who receives with a miserable expression shows ingratitude even before he receives the gift. As far as human relations are concerned, to accept cheerfully is one way to express thanks, while with regard to God such behaviour is considered as a substitute for a full payment of gratitude.

* * * * *

1 Thales of Miletus; see Diogenes Laertius *Lives of the Philosophers* 1.36. The Greek word translated by Erasmus as *accipere* 'to receive' has also been translated as 'success' or 'to obtain what you desire.'
2 Ecclus 35:11 / Sir 35:9; 2 Cor 9:7

But as I do not wish to keep you in suspense any longer with my riddles, I shall now present to you the Eighty-fifth Psalm, which begins: 'Incline your ear, O God.' Listen carefully to him so that he in turn may incline his ear to you; for what makes it possible for us to accept eagerly what he offers, to hold on to it faithfully, and to make good use of it is also a gift from him. So come now, my beloved brothers in the Lord, cleanse the ears of your heart, open the arms of your minds, and stretch out eagerly the hands of your feelings, so that this psalm may become in you a fountain of water springing up into everlasting life.[3]

Although the title 'psalm' is common to all of them and this whole work is called the Psalter, some of the psalms are nevertheless distinguished by particular titles. Some for example bear the heading 'song,' others 'song of the psalm,' some 'the psalm of the song,' others 'for the sake of teaching,' and others something else. The variety of titles is not without purpose, for to those who are possessed of a reverent curiosity each title indicates the persuasive force and the character of the theme treated in each psalm. Anyone who enters the sanctuary of the psalm must prepare his mind and spirit with reverent and careful attention to deal with these different elements. This psalm that I now present to you has the title 'A prayer of David,' as do a few others also.[4]

The psalms express nothing trivial, nothing earthly. Either men are accompanying the angels in singing the glory of God (a form that the ancient writers referred to as the doxology); or they are giving thanks to God's generosity for the benefits he has given them; or they are asking for something from God; or God is speaking to men – and he unfailingly says things which are worthy of him, either discouraging them from evil or urging them to do good, either consoling them or teaching them – not human wisdom but the heavenly philosophy. So it is absolutely inappropriate for irreverent characters to burst in here in a drunken stupor, weighed down by trivial worries. However, in the Psalms it is not the case that each of these things only occurs in one psalm at a time. Indeed, just as individual elements cling together by nature, so in the Psalms, too, they are mixed together. He who praises a powerful person does indeed deserve to receive something even if he does not expressly ask for it, and seeing that God is great, wise, and generous not only to himself but to us too, to praise

* * * * *

3 John 4:14
4 In fact only Ps 16/17 bears exactly the same title as Ps 85/86.

him is equivalent to thanking him.⁵ Furthermore if someone thanks a rich man, what is he doing by gratefully mentioning what he has received if not encouraging him to grant more? And so in this psalm too we shall find glorification, thanksgiving, and prayer.

I do not propose to torment you with a slavish adherence to the meaning of words, but I must point out that εὐχή is a prayer expressed in the mind while προσευχή refers to a prayer uttered to God:⁶ you could perhaps distinguish between them by using the words 'prayer' and 'address of prayer.' Someone who simply asks for something without worrying where it will come from can be said to pray, but the word προσεύχεται is used of someone who knows whom to approach to obtain what he wants. A person who seeks salvation does not seek it from demons or from magic spells or from himself, indeed not even from Moses or Elijah, but from God who is the only source of salvation.⁷

Now it may be that not all prayers have the same purpose. There is the prayer of Moses,⁸ which is different from the prayer of the poor and low-born man,⁹ while the prayer of David, the king and prophet who was a type of the Lord Jesus Christ in so many of his roles, is of a particular kind. Similarly, although every prayer demands a soul completely cleansed of all the filth of earthly desires, as is natural if it is to penetrate to the very throne of the divine majesty and speak to him whose exalted being makes the cherubim and seraphim tremble, it is still true that the prayer of David contains something distinctive and of a more divine nature. The king asks for nothing ignoble; the man who is after God's heart¹⁰ prays for nothing unworthy of God. But so that you may believe this more readily, this David is the only one, strong of hand,¹¹ who overcame Satan and built

* * * * *

5 See also Erasmus' annotation on 1 Cor 14:16 (*super tuam benedictionem*) LB VI 730F.
6 Erasmus also discusses the Greek words for prayer in the *Modus orandi Deum* CWE 70 154–6.
7 Cf Heb 2:10.
8 See Ps 89/90:1.
9 See Ps 101/102:1.
10 Acts 13:22
11 Jerome gives *fortis manu* 'strong of hand' as a meaning of the name David (*De nominibus Hebraicis* PL 23 [1845] 813); Erasmus adopts this (*In psalmum 4* CWE 63 213 and n224), but it is clear from its recurrent use in his other psalm commentaries (see 97 below, *In psalmum 22* 125 and 133 below, *In psalmum 33* 285 and 296 below) that he associates it with David's role as a type of Christ, as in 2 Sam 3:18, 'By the hand of my servant David I will deliver my people Israel.' On David as type of Christ see also CWE 63 Introduction xxvii.

for us the citadel of Zion, that is, the church, and fortified it. He is the only one who pleased the heart of God in all respects, obedient unto death[12] and on whose lips no guile was found,[13] a lamb without any blemish.[14] Such tributes would not be appropriate to David, the father of Solomon.

Let us therefore listen with pure and attentive ears, children of Zion, to the prayer of our king, our priest, our head. Whatever he prays, he prays for us, and if we are willing he prays in us and on our behalf and we in turn in him and through him. For the head and the limbs of the body are one, and the Lord Jesus is the head of the whole church, and the church, in accordance with the mystical union,[15] is the whole and one Christ.[16] I will put it more plainly for the sake of the less sophisticated among you: in church you hear the priest urging you to pray when he says, 'Let us pray,' and you listen carefully to what he is saying – otherwise how could you respond to his prayer with 'Amen' unless you knew what he had been praying for? He alone says the prayers aloud, but the voice of the whole church resounds through this one man; even though the voice of only one man is heard, the prayer is shared by all. Not everyone is able to pray in the proper way; it is a gift of God, just like prophecy. But it is sometimes the case that a human priest may be praying incorrectly if he prays from his heart without being in harmony with the ordinance of the church, just as Paul, when he appealed to God to free him from the sting of the flesh, was told: 'My grace is sufficient for you.'[17] By ourselves we do not know what to pray or how to pray unless this too is granted by the spirit of Christ which, according to Paul, intercedes for us and in us, with sighs too deep for words.[18]

Those who ask God to destroy their enemies, to whom we are commanded to do good,[19] do not know what to pray, and like the apostles who prayed inaptly, they will be told: 'You do not know whose spirit you are.'[20]

* * * * *

12 Phil 2:8
13 Cf 1 Pet 2:22.
14 Cf Exod 12:5 and 1 Pet 1:19.
15 Latin *conglutinatio*. On the use of the word *conglutinare* by Erasmus to describe the unity of the church created by Christ through the Holy Spirit, see *In psalmum* 22 131 n39 below.
16 For the mystical body of Christ, see Rom 12:4–8, 1 Cor 6:15–20, 10:16–17, 12:12–31, Eph 1:22–3, 4:4–16, 5:22–3, Col 1:18, 2:9–10, 19, 3:15.
17 2 Cor 12:7–9
18 Rom 8:26
19 Cf Matt 5:44 and Luke 6:27.
20 Luke 9:55

For human desire can persuade someone that whatever he has a great long-ing for is pleasing to God; as a result, when such people pray with a human spirit they believe that they are praying with a divine spirit. And those who demand wealth or physical strength or who ask to have an agreeable and impressive lifestyle in this world do not know how to pray; nor do those who ask for physical and mental health from St Christopher or St Barbara know how they should pray,[21] for they are demanding from human beings what God alone can bestow, and in fact the saints themselves received from him, freely given, what is being sought from them. But if these people are free from wicked intentions, that divine spirit forgives their human naivety and corrects the error of their prayer, not bestowing what was demanded but what is of benefit to the one who asks.

And so, if we listen carefully and pay attention to the priest as he stands at the altar and invites us to pray with the words 'Let us pray,' how much more devoutly must we not listen to the prayers uttered by the guardian of our souls,[22] the priest for ever after the order of Melchizedek?[23] He is the Lord Jesus Christ, who is already prepared for the sacred altar of the cross and will sacrifice himself, a victim most pleasing to God, for the salvation of the human race. Let us who are soldiers of Christ listen with pure and devout minds, with reverent hearts, to what our king and emperor prays, he who on our behalf will take on our enemy single-handed. It is certain that God heeds him on account of the reverence due to him,[24] but one of us could still, by his lack of attention, cause even the prayer of such a great king, such a holy priest, to be ineffectual and achieve nothing. So in order that the prayer of our priest should benefit us, let us remain within the church, for outside it there is no salvation.[25] Let us agree among

* * * * *

21 Christopher and Barbara were among the most popular saints during the High Middle Ages. Along with St George, they are often mentioned together by Erasmus as examples of the excesses and distortions involved in the contem-porary cult of the saints (cf 43 and 310 below). See, for example, *Modus orandi Deum* CWE 70 208–9; *Moria* CWE 27 114–15 and 118; *Enchiridion* CWE 66 63–4; the colloquies *Naufragium* CWE 39 355–6 (a mocking reference to the huge statue of St Christopher that stood in the church of Notre-Dame in Paris) and Ἰχθυοφαγία CWE 40 719. Erasmus defends his attitude in the *Responsio ad ex-hortationem Alberti Pii* LB IX 1095–1196.
22 Cf 1 Pet 2:25.
23 Heb 5:6, 7:17
24 Cf Heb 5:7.
25 Cf Cyprian Ep 73:21 CSEL 3 part 2 795: 'for there is no salvation outside the church'; also the colloquy Ἰχθυοφαγία CWE 40 687 and 729 n74. Erasmus fre-quently insists on membership of the church, for example *In psalmum 22* 144

ourselves, so that when our bishop says, 'Peace be with you,' his peace may remain firmly in our hearts. Let us be the living members of Christ, let us be one with Christ, so that we may pray in him and he in turn in us and for us, and we may live in him for ever, sharing in this holy sacrifice, and reign with him who alone is the source of immortality and alone possesses a kingdom that will have no end.[26]

And so, when you hear the title of the psalm, 'A prayer of David,' you should take it to mean that the Lord Jesus who is truly the highest priest is saying to all his disciples, 'Let us pray' and that the psalm is providing a brief description of what we ought to pray for and how we should do it. For each of us in his own way can be both David and Christ. There is only one whom God has anointed above his fellows,[27] but this should be taken to mean that he is the greatest, not the only one. How could he be the only one when there are people who share with him? No one should be shocked to hear me bestowing on a man the name of Christ, seeing that Scripture has given this name to holy men, for it is written: 'Do not touch my christs' (that is, my anointed ones).[28] And so, just as he is the only Son and yet has many brothers whom he has brought to the Father, so he alone has been anointed in a way that is unique, and yet he rejoices that through him many share in this same anointing. Let us therefore belong to Christ so that we may pray with Christ – otherwise we may pray for something incorrectly. He has the perfection of the spirit, and he alone knows what to pray for and how to pray. In the pagan mysteries the priest commands the profane to depart, but he himself is the most profane of all. Our priest does not make such an announcement; in fact, he actually invites those who are unclean so that by approaching this mystery they may cease to be unclean. If you are unclean (for he who is a slave to Satan is unclean), depart from yourself and you have entered into the

* * * * *

and 147 below, even stating in the *De concordia* of 1533 that it is worse to leave the church through schism or heresy than to lead an impure life within it (LB v 498B). But the thrust of his ecclesiology is to distinguish between a spiritual community which embraces all those of good will throughout history (as 51 below) and the merely juridical institution which, though a means to salvation, can hide corruption behind the trappings of authority. On the necessity of belonging to the spiritual body of Christ see the colloquy *Inquisitio de fide* ed Craig R. Thompson (New Haven 1950) 101–21 and CWE 39 429, 443–5 n108; *Explanatio symboli* CWE 70 236, 324–9.
26 Luke 1:33
27 Cf Heb 1:9 and Ps 44:8/45:7.
28 Ps 104/105:15

church; take off yourself and you have put on Christ.[29] He who has put on Christ has ceased to be unclean and has been recruited into the body of the saints. Let us then be pure as we listen to the prayers of the one who is pure and who makes everyone pure, so that we may say 'Amen' sincerely.

Nor should the fact that it is the Lord who is praying present a problem to any of us, although you may think that it is needy and inferior people who pray. Why should you be surprised that he is praying for you, he who became a baby for your sake, wailed in a cradle for your sake, and deigned to die for your sake? He prays in accordance with the manhood that he has taken upon himself, by which he became like us, but he can also grant what he prays for, in accordance with his divine nature, in which he is equal to the Father. No one should be offended by his low status; instead, all should be inspired by his amazing love. In accordance with his human nature the Lord Jesus possessed nothing that he had not received from the Father; but with regard to his divine nature, no one possesses anything good that he has not received from the Lord. Worship his exalted being and imitate his humility. We often read in the Gospels that the Lord prayed and we read that he gave thanks, and he did so in order to present us with an example. But if at times we find things in Christ's prayers which do not seem appropriate to his dignity, even with regard to his adopted nature, then let us remember that the head and body are one and the same. Is it surprising that he should adopt our words when he has taken our sins upon himself? Not that he would be defiled by them, but so as to pay the penalty for them. And when he performed that wonderful and unique sacrifice on the cross he prayed: 'Far from salvation are the words of my sins.'[30] Where did you get those sins from, Lord Jesus, you who alone are a lamb without blemish?[31] What offences caused you to despair of the salvation of your most holy soul? None of these things properly apply to Christ, but in these cases he took on our role, was burdened by our sins, and poured out his precious blood in order to expunge them. Consequently it is our words that he utters when he speaks of sins, for he committed no sin himself, nor was any guile found on his lips.[32] It is not surprising if he spoke with the voice of his members at that time, since after his ascension into heaven he still suffered persecution in his members when he called to Paul: 'Saul, Saul, why

* * * * *

29 Cf Rom 13:14 and Gal 3:27.
30 Cf Ps 21:2/22:1.
31 1 Pet 1:19
32 1 Pet 2:22

are you persecuting me?'[33] But he is revived in his members, for he allows whatever is done to any one of the least of his members to be done to him. While he still lived as a mortal on earth, he did indeed bear the likeness of sinful flesh;[34] he bore the character of a sinner when he was taken prisoner, accused, bound, whipped, beaten, condemned, and hung upon the cross, although he was free from all stain of sin. Moreover, it was without any reluctance that he shared with us those penalties that derive from sin – when he thirsted and was weary, when he endured the painful torture of his body, when he suffered mental agony, and when he was put to death. We must recognize the frailty of our human nature, which we share with him, and worship the goodness of him who willingly took upon himself our weakness out of love for us. When we hear the words of the sinner, we should understand that it is our person speaking in him, and we should give thanks to such a kind doctor who, through his own suffering, brought a cure for our disease.

But let us listen to him as he prays, not only joining our prayers to his but also paying attention to the form of the prayer and bearing in mind who is praying, to whom he is addressing his prayer, what he is praying for, and how he is praying. I have already shown you who is praying. I am aware that those who set great store by Hebrew writings interpret the subject of this psalm as the persecution of David by Saul: when, with divine help, David had been freed time and again from Saul's hands, he prays that he may progress from dangers and grief to happiness and the kingdom. That is why it is written: 'Give power to your son.' Even if the Hebrew rabbis are right in their suggestion here, it does not prejudice our interpretation in any way, for the historical sense is as it were the base and foundation, which does not exclude but rather supports the mystical sense. That is why I shall not dispute the Hebrews' conjectures, but relying on the authority of the church Fathers I shall propose certainties in place of doubtful facts, life-giving things in place of sterile ones.

Jesus Christ, who is our David, our king, our priest, is praying in this psalm, but to whom does he pray? To Abraham? He is greater than Abraham, who prayed to see his day; he saw it and was glad.[35] To Elijah? Christ is the lord of prophets and the redeemer of all the prophets. Or to Moses? Moses is a servant, but Christ is the Son. Or to one of the angels? He created the angels, and the status of his soul makes him greater than

* * * * *

33 Acts 9:4
34 Rom 8:3
35 John 8:56

the angels. To whom then does he pray? To whom if not to the greatest of all, Adonai, the father of lights, from whom every good thing flows to all men,[36] from whom Christ, even with his superior nature, derives his origin without detriment to his position of equality.

What does he pray for? Surely not for wealth or pleasures or the honours of this world or for revenge on his enemies? Not even Solomon asked for these things from the Lord, and Christ is greater than Solomon – in fact Solomon can in no way be compared with him. But as he hangs on the cross in the midst of the mysteries of this sacrifice, he prays for those who put him to death. What then does he ask for? For his church to be saved and for his Father's glory to spread far and wide (this will become clearer when I explain it).

Now as to what remains: how does he pray? Very differently from the well-known Pharisee,[37] for he does not enumerate his good deeds or exaggerate his own merits but confesses his poverty, lowliness, and his needs to God and professes his trust in God. 'For I am poor and needy,' he says, and 'the son of your handmaid,' and 'since I have trusted in you,' and 'since I have lifted up my soul to you.' He mentions God's acts of kindness, clearly showing us the pattern for our prayers, for the heavenly Father inclines his ear to people who pray in this way. The Lord, whose merits were immeasurable, does not mention his own merits: should we, then, who are mere men, enumerate our good deeds and make demands of God as if he owed us anything?

'Incline your ear, O Lord, and listen to me, for I am poor and needy.' He who in his divine aspect is equal to the Father now cries out as a suppliant in the form of a servant: 'Incline your ear, O Lord.' He is evidently adopting the role of an unimportant person, the most abject of all men, as when he says in another psalm: 'I am a worm and not a man, scorned by men and despised by the people.'[38] But how could the prayers of a wretched worm on earth reach him who sits above the seraphim, unless he inclines his ear? I do not think that I need to repeat what I have so often reminded you of, namely that since God's mind is of the most pure and simple kind, it contains nothing corporeal, nor any corporeal accident, nor any human emotions such as anger, pity, grief, joy, penitence, hatred. Instead Scripture, by lisping indistinctly with the words of men so that it may be un-

* * * * *

36 James 1:17
37 Luke 18:10–14; LB has *publicanus*, which Erasmus emended in 1529 to *pharisaeus*, the reading adopted by ASD.
38 Ps 21:7/22:6

derstood in a less forbidding way, accommodates itself to men's weakness, like a nurse or a mother using baby language to her child to make herself understood. God, then, does not move in this or that direction in a spatial sense, but the limits of human speech mean that he is said to turn away his ear when he fails to supply what we ask for and is said to incline his ear when he heeds our prayers. In the same way he is said to be angry when he punishes and merciful when he saves and forgives. It is just the same as when people who show favour to someone who is begging for something are commonly said to listen 'with well-disposed ears,' while those who are not well disposed are said to listen with their ears 'upturned' or 'turned away.' Thus when we look upon a beggar in distress, dressed in rags, covered in sores and diseased, the beggar conceives a hope that we might help him, for the sight of a wretched man stirs in us a feeling of pity. It is certainly very true that the ear of heaven hears all things and that nothing escapes the notice of God, who is seated above the cherubim and looks into the abyss,[39] and yet he says of the pious man: 'He will cry to me and I will hear him.'[40] Indeed in the Wisdom literature it is said of the wicked: 'Then they will call on me and I shall not heed them.'[41] It is fair that those who were unwilling to listen when he warned them should not be heard when they assail him with their wailing. And so 'God heeded the offering of Abel but did not heed Cain and his offering.'[42] Similarly, 'the Lord knows the way of the just,'[43] and the Lord knows who are his. But as for the foolish virgins,[44] what do they hear? 'I do not know you'; and according to Paul 'he who does not recognize will not be recognized.'[45]

My dearest brothers, let us acknowledge the Lord by obeying his commandments so that he may acknowledge us in our distress. Let us pay attention to him in all things so that he in turn may take notice of us; let us incline our ear to his precepts so that he may deign to incline his ear to our prayers; and finally, if we wish his exalted being to incline itself to us, our pride must bend down to him. He turns away from the proud, he does not listen to those who boast of their own merits, and he does not acknowledge those who make undue claims for their own righteousness. I do not

* * * * *

39 Dan 3:55 / Song of Three Children 32, Ps 98/99:1
40 Ps 90/91:15
41 Prov 1:28
42 Gen 4:4–5
43 Ps 1:6
44 Matt 25:1–13
45 1 Cor 14:38

mean that one should not accumulate good deeds, but that we should not use them to claim anything for ourselves.[46] The fact is that he who mentions his good deeds is, as it were, trying to extort something from him to whom he ought rather to give thanks. The humble publican was heeded but not the arrogant Pharisee.[47] In the Gospel Christ acknowledges those who did not know what good they had done, but those who said, 'Lord, did we not prophesy in your name and cast out devils in your name and do many mighty deeds in you name?'[48] were not recognized. What are the boastful ones told, those who mention their own deeds? 'I do not know you.' Similarly in St Luke's Gospel those who refer to their intimacy with Christ, saying, 'We ate and drank in your presence and you taught in our streets' – what are they told? Terrible are the words that they hear. What are they? 'I do not know where you come from.'[49]

If people who correctly mention the prophecies they have made in the name of Christ, the devils they have cast out, the close relationship they have had with Christ, the fact that they have given a tenth of their wealth to the poor and made fourfold compensation to a person who has lost something through fraud are not recognized, how will they be recognized who with greater arrogance boast of deeds which are less impressive than these? 'For so many years I have not tasted meat; for so many years I have worn the clothing of this or that man; for so many years I have worn a leather belt; for so many years I have not touched meat; for so many years I have not left this place.' Not that these things are bad – but they are the sort of things that can be done also by wicked people. The Lord does not acknowledge even a good deed if it is accompanied by arrogance. To be sure, all pride is hateful to God, but none is more hateful, none more dangerous than that which assumes an attitude of superiority from a show of virtue. Let us therefore bend our heads, my dearest friends, and join our humble priest in prayer, saying: 'Incline your ear, O Lord, and listen.'

Why is it surprising if he inclines his ear for our sake to listen to our prayers, when he inclined the heavens and came down to us[50] to make

* * * * *

46 Erasmus has in mind the controversy with Luther over the comparative importance of faith and good works, as discussed for example in *De libero arbitrio* and *Hyperaspistes*. In his commentary on Ps 22 he speaks of the relative worthlessness of human merit; see 193 below and also ASD V-3 341:239–41n.
47 Luke 18:10–14
48 Matt 7:22–3
49 Luke 13:26–7
50 Cf 2 Sam 22:10 and Ps 17:10/18:9.

amends for our sins – since God was in his Son, reconciling the world to himself?[51] But who is the Lord Jesus praying for at this point? He is praying for the weak, for the wicked, the ungodly: 'Incline your ear, O Lord, and listen.' For when would God hear the prayers of such men unless he inclined his ear? The justice of God makes him prick up his ears, his mercy makes him incline them. To incline is to have heard, for his goodness anticipates men's merits. When we were enemies[52] he loved us first[53] and loved us so much that he gave his only Son to die for us.[54] This Son intercedes with the Father for us and says: 'Incline your ear, O Lord, and listen.' He is not pleading the cause of one man but of all the elect who have been, are, and will exist from the creation right until the end of the world:[55] they are all in the one Christ. There was no one who had no need for God to incline his ear unless there was anyone who did not need the grace of God.

But I ask you, what right has he to demand that God should incline his ear? Surely he does not mention the sacrifices he has made, the alms he has given, his fasting, and his other good deeds? No, none of these. What reason does he then give? 'For I am poor and needy.' These words are in some way appropriate for Christ with regard to the human nature that he adopted, in accordance with which he said truly: 'Foxes have holes, and birds of the sky have nests, but the Son of Man has nowhere to lay his head.'[56] He rightly said: 'My kingdom is not of this world,'[57] and Isaiah accurately described him as 'the strangest of men, without either beauty or grace.'[58] Such was Christ when he was in this world, hated by the Scribes and Pharisees, scorned and abandoned by his brothers, mocked by Herod, spat upon by the soldiers, condemned by Pilate, deserted and rejected by those very men whom he had particularly chosen. This, I say, was what he was like in the eyes of the world, but what was he like in the eyes of the prophets? 'You are the most beautiful of the sons of men; grace is poured upon your lips.'[59] What was he like in the eyes of God? 'This is my beloved Son, in whom I am well pleased.'[60] These things are appropriate to him

* * * * *

51 Cf 2 Cor 5:19.
52 Cf Rom 5:10.
53 Cf 1 John 4:19.
54 John 3:16
55 Cf Matt 28:20.
56 Matt 8:20 and Luke 9:58
57 John 18:36
58 Isa 53:2–3
59 Ps 44:3/45:2
60 Matt 3:17, Mark 1:11

also according to his human nature. But how could he then be poor and needy, he in whom the fullness of divinity lived in bodily form,[61] he from whose fullness those whom Scripture declares to be full of grace and full of good works also derive their merits?[62] How can someone who is poor enrich so many thousands of saints? This can be answered in two ways. He is poor and needy who recognizes that whatever he possesses does not derive from himself but from someone else: whatever Christ had as a man was a gift from God. Secondly, we are without doubt really poor and needy, we in whose name he is speaking. For he speaks in the name of the church, but particularly of the church of the gentiles, which says in Psalm 39: 'But I am a poor beggar, and the Lord takes thought for me.'[63] The Jew appeared to have something which he could brag about among men, but the church of the gentiles had nothing to boast of, either among men or before God, except as a result of the redeemer's mercy. For of ourselves we have nothing but evil; if we have anything good, it is a free gift from God.

Whether these words, then, are attributed to the church as the body of Christ or to any of the members of the church, it is rightly said: 'For I am poor and needy.' We should be ashamed, my brothers, when we say in our pride: 'I have done such and such deeds.' These were the words of Abraham, Moses, all the prophets, and of John the Baptist, as well as of Peter, Paul, and all the martyrs and saints: 'I am poor and needy.' What are we in comparison with them? If we face the truth of the matter, we are all rich in evil things and poor with regard to good things; if we have acquired anything good, it belongs to someone else and only becomes ours if we admit that it belongs to someone else. For it begins to be ours only when we understand that it is not ours, and it ceases to be ours the moment we claim as our own what comes from others. There is a new law of spiritual possession: something becomes ours when the ownership is ceded to another, and we lose it when we claim it as our own. No possession is more precious or safer than one given freely to us by God, nor is anything so much ours as one that in this way is not ours.

What men sell legally they often reclaim in a lawsuit; what friends give as a gift they frequently snatch back once they have become enemies instead of friends; but God cannot repent of his generosity. The wealthiest person is he on whom God has bestowed his wealth, for God is generous

* * * * *

61 Cf Col 2:9.
62 Cf Luke 1:28, John 1:14, Acts 6:8, 9:36.
63 Ps 39:18/40:17

to all who call on him.[64] He is the poorest who acknowledges that he does not possess whatever he has as a result of his own merit but because of God's spontaneous generosity. Those who are rich with money they have borrowed from someone else are not rich – rather they are poor people making an ostentatious display of their wealth, and they are all the poorer because they use someone else's property to advertise their own merits. Anyone who boasts of virtues which he does not possess is ostentatiously poor and makes himself unworthy of receiving anything. Anyone who attributes what he has to his own talents, although it is really a gift from God, deserves to be deprived of it. 'For to him who possesses in the right way, more will be given, but anyone who does not will lose even what he seems to have.'[65] If you possess it with gratitude, you will acknowledge that you are poor and needy, and the very fact that you acknowledge your poverty will mean that you are rich.

St Paul revealed a new path to wisdom when he said: 'If anyone among you thinks that he is wise, let him become a fool that he may become wise.'[66] This psalm indicates the only path to riches: if you wish to grow rich in Christ, you should become poor in yourself. Acknowledge your poverty and the wealth of God will be ready at hand. Acknowledge your injustice and the justice of God will be at hand. Acknowledge your folly and receive the wisdom of God. Admit your wretchedness and receive the blessedness of Christ. Listen well to the words of the Apostle, who was poor: 'For I know that nothing good dwells in me, that is, in my flesh.'[67] Listen to him who was rich in Christ when he says: 'I can do all things in him who strengthens me' and 'poor ourselves, we make many rich.'[68] Who is so wealthy that he owns everything? St Paul also says in another passage: 'I am the least of the apostles and unfit to be called an apostle.'[69] In these words you hear him as a poor man reflecting on his merits. But listen to him as a rich man: 'I worked harder than any of them,'[70] he says. These are boastful words, not the words of someone who is poor but of one who is rich. But what does he add? 'But it was not I, but the grace of God that is with me.' Here you see the man who is both poor and rich, poor in himself, for he claims

* * * * *

64 Rom 10:12
65 Matt 13:12, 25:29
66 1 Cor 3:18
67 Rom 7:18
68 Phil 4:13, 2 Cor 6:10
69 1 Cor 15:9
70 1 Cor 15:10

no praise for himself, and rich in Christ, to whose grace he attributes all things.

Moreover, to make many rich is clearly a royal prerogative. But who was made rich by that most wealthy pauper? All the nations from Jerusalem as far as Illyria through which he wandered, spreading the gospel,[71] as well as those to whom he writes: 'For all things are yours, but you are Christ's.'[72] To the Corinthians he also wrote: 'In all things you have become rich in him, in all speech and in all knowledge, so that you are not lacking any spiritual gift.'[73] In himself he was poor and weak, in Christ he was strong and capable of anything. That is why he added, 'in him who strengthens me.' He made many rich, but he added, 'A commission has been entrusted to me,'[74] and 'his servant whom you believed, for neither he who plants nor he who waters is anything but only God who gives the growth.'[75] When he said, 'All things are yours,' he added, 'but you are Christ's.' But if they belonged to Christ, what did they have of their own to boast of? For fear that it might seem somewhat despicable and servile to belong to someone else, he added the phrase 'and Christ belongs to God.'[76] Woe to you, pride of the human heart! Christ did not object to belonging to God, and you want to belong to yourself? Similarly, St Paul prays for the people at Philippi so that now that they are rich they may abound more and more in all knowledge and in all discernment, filled with the fruits of righteousness.[77] These are the words of the rich, but what does he add? 'Through Jesus Christ, to the glory and praise of God.' Similarly, when he is emphasizing the wealth of the Corinthians, he does not omit the little phrase 'in him,' to make them realize that what they have is due to someone else's gift and that if they wish to boast, they should boast in the Lord, not in themselves.

But what does it mean to boast in the Lord? It means to extol his beneficence; it means to give thanks to him for his generosity towards us; it means to confess our unworthiness, to praise his bounty. We are encouraged to do this also by the words of Psalm 80: 'Sing for joy, O righteous ones.'[78] In what? In your merits? Certainly not, but in the Lord. This kind

* * * * *

71 Cf Rom 15:19.
72 Cf 1 Cor 3:22–3.
73 1 Cor 1:5 and 7
74 1 Cor 9:17
75 1 Cor 3:5, 7
76 1 Cor 3:23
77 Phil 1:9 and 11
78 The phrase 'Sing for joy, O righteous ones' occurs at Ps 32/33:1; in Ps 80:2/81:1 the phrase is 'Sing for joy to God our strength.'

of boasting by the poor is not reprehensible and is most pleasing to God. However, because some of the people at Corinth did not boast in this way, St Paul writes to them that their boasting is not good.[79] Why? Because they did not boast in the Lord but in themselves. But Paul knew how they should boast, he who writes to the people of Thessalonica: 'What is our hope or joy or crown of glory? Is it not you?' These are boastful words, yet listen to what he adds: 'before our Lord Jesus Christ at his coming.'[80] He who boasts in Christ boasts in safety, but he was making a dangerous boast whom Paul attacked with the words 'What have you that you did not receive? If you received it, why do you boast as if you had not received it?'[81] But a more foolish boast was made by that bishop of Laodicea who was told in the book of Revelation: 'And you say, "I am rich and I prospered and I need nothing," and you are unaware that you are wretched, miserable, poor, blind, and naked.'[82] God hates nothing more than a poor man who is proud – for the book of Ecclesiasticus indicates that this is one of the three things which the Lord's soul hates and detests.[83]

My dear friends, if we turn our eyes to look at those who are motivated by the spirit of this world,[84] what tricks and crimes they perform, what labours and difficulties they undergo in their quest for wealth, which soon, at their death, will pass to other men, even if no accident snatches it away before then! What sleepless nights, hard work, and dangers they endure as they struggle for a glory which is not only worthless but will soon disappear, for all flesh is as grass and all its beauty is as the flower of the field![85] On account of these things they sail even beyond Phasis, beyond Gades and the Ganges;[86] on account of these things they wage war, and people's lives are thrown into confusion and turned upside down.[87] Why then do we not use all our energies to win a lasting glory for ourselves, one that will remain with us for ever? This will happen if we glory in the Lord. Why do we not try to gain for ourselves genuine and everlasting riches?

* * * * *

79 1 Cor 5:6
80 1 Thess 2:19
81 1 Cor 4:7
82 Rev 3:17
83 Ecclus 25:3–4 / Sir 25:2
84 Cf 1 Cor 2:12.
85 Isa 40:6
86 For Phasis, see *Adagia* II iv 49: *Ad Phasim usque navigavit* 'He has sailed as far as Phasis'; for Gades and Ganges, cf Pindar *Nemean Ode* 4.69, Juvenal *Satires* 10.2, and Erasmus *Adagia* III v 24: *Ad Herculis columnas.*
87 Cf Erasmus *Adagia* I iii 85: *Sursum et deorsum* 'Up and down.'

This will happen if, though poor in ourselves, we have learned to grow rich in the Lord.

One person can say to another: 'I am yours. Whatever I am, whatever I am capable of, whatever I have, it is thanks to you.' The grateful servant says this to his master, the son says it to his thrifty father. The courtier says it to his prince, by whose favour he has attained a high position; the bishop or cardinal says it to the pope, who enabled him to obtain his high rank. Is it not far more just that we should say this to God – indeed, will we not reap much greater benefit from saying it to him, as long as we say it sincerely? But where do you find people who are so far from professing themselves to be poor and needy that their merits are stacked high for their private use, as it were, while they distribute them grudgingly to others?

We have seen in Christ the perfect example of a poor man, and we have seen in Paul what each of us should emulate. Now let us consider the person of the church, which is poor in itself but rich in Christ. The Gospel has presented us with the following scene which, so we read, delighted the Lord.[88] His aim was to give us an example, and our aim must be to imitate it. What could be poorer than that widow who put everything she owned into the collection box? And yet her whole wealth hardly amounted to anything at all. How much was it? Two mites, the equivalent of one farthing. Is there anyone so indigent nowadays that he does not own more than this? Even so she was willing to be still poorer. What did she have left when she had cast this away? Nothing but complete poverty. She subjected her natural reason to faith, her will to love. If anyone possesses some talent as a result of nature's generosity (though God is the creator of this, too), he should cast it all into the collection box and dedicate it all to the Lord so that it may remain safe and increase in value. This kind of poverty is the only path to true riches.

Now consider this same woman, deprived of her possessions but made rich with the wealth of Christ. The Forty-fourth Psalm presents her to us when it says: 'The queen stood at your right hand in golden robes, surrounded by variety; all her beauty comes from within, in fringes of gold.'[89] Nothing lies deeper within a devout person than the spirit of Christ, and this is the source of all glory in good men. Nevertheless, this widow did not cease to cry: 'Incline your ear, O Lord, and listen, for I am poor and needy,' however rich she had become through the generosity of her new bridegroom. Wealthy people, however generous they are, tend to find this

* * * * *

88 Cf Mark 12:41–4, Luke 21:1–4.
89 Ps 44:10–14 / 45:9–14

irritating: if they hand out flour today, the beggars return tomorrow with a bag, the next day with a jar, and then with a barrel. Then the wealthy man exclaims: 'Oh dear, is there no limit? It is as if I were pouring all that I give into a leaking bucket; now I understand how very true the Greek proverb is which says that the purses of beggars are always empty.'[90] For just as human generosity can be exhausted, so it can also become tired out; but to God, who is so very generous, such an importunate and shameless approach on the part of beggars is most welcome. How could this fail to be the case, seeing that his goodness is natural and his generosity cannot be exhausted by giving in abundance?

But you will find God all the more open to your prayers, the more your ears are open to the poor. In God's eyes there is no one who is not in dire need, while among men some are rich, others poor. Those who are oppressed by poverty besiege the gates of the powerful and assail the ears of the rich crying, 'Incline your ear, for I am poor and needy.' What the rich possess in this world they possess as a gift from God, and yet the man who is rich and possesses abundant wealth does not incline his ear to his poor brother – but he dares to say to God: 'Incline your ear.' He who is deaf to the cries of the poor will find God deaf to his wailing, for God only listens to the poor. But how poor is he who, when his neighbour is dying, keeps for himself what he possesses! The poor man cries out to you, indeed Christ himself cries out to you in the poor man, and do you walk past without taking any notice? Your neighbour has sinned against you and cries out: 'Forgive me, I have done wrong,' but you refuse to lay aside your anger. Then in vain will you cry out to God: 'Incline your ear.' Acknowledge the agreement God has made: 'Give and it will be given to you'[91] and 'Blessed are the merciful for they shall obtain mercy.'[92] Another psalm accords with this when it says: 'Blessed is he who considers the poor and the needy; the Lord will deliver him in the day of evil.'[93] What is the day of evil? The day of temptation, the day of suffering, the day of wrath and judgment, not of mercy. On that day of evil, the Lord will incline his ear to him because he did not refuse to listen when his neighbours were suffering. That rich man in the Gospel did not incline his ear to the beggar Lazarus, and on

* * * * *

90 Cf *Adagia* II x 11: *Mendicorum loculi semper inanes* 'Beggars' wallets are always empty' and *Adagia* II v 24: *Mendici pera non impletur* 'A beggar's satchel is never filled.'
91 Luke 6:38
92 Matt 5:7
93 Ps 40:2/41:1

the day of evil, when he was tortured in hell, he found no one to heed his cries.[94]

Now because it did not simply say, 'for I am poor,' but used two words – 'poor' and 'needy,' either the repetition of a word with the same meaning is intended to emphasise his poverty or, if there is some difference between them, then πτωχός is used of someone who professes his poverty by begging, πένης of the man who lacks the bare necessities. For the beggar is not always poor, nor is the poor man always a beggar. Furthermore, πτωχός (here translated as 'needy') is sometimes translated as 'poor,' as in the Ninth Psalm: 'The poor man is left to you,'[95] but then in Psalm 39 it is translated as 'beggar'[96] – 'I am a beggar and a poor man' – as if there were very little or no difference between them.

Many people say to the Lord: 'I am poor and needy,' but the Lord does not incline his ear to them because they do not say it sincerely. Let us cry out in earnest: 'For I am poor and needy,' and he will listen to us, he who shows favour to the poor throughout the Holy Scriptures. In Psalm 10 it is written: 'His eyes take notice of the poor,'[97] in Psalm 21 we read: 'He has not scorned or despised the appeal of the poor,'[98] and in Psalm 67: 'In his sweetness God has prepared for the poor man,'[99] and in Psalm 106: 'He hears the poor man in his need.'[100] In Psalm 108 it is written: 'He even stands at the right hand of the poor man,'[101] and in the Ninth Psalm: 'The Lord has hearkened to the desire of the poor.'[102] Do we need to give any more examples? The whole of Scripture represents God as being favourably disposed to the poor. And finally in the Gospel it is stated: 'Blessed are the poor in spirit, for theirs is the kingdom of heaven.'[103]

The world has poor of its own, but it is a source of great joy to be the poor man of God – unless perhaps you believe that to have God favourably disposed to you is an ordinary sort of happiness. God only listens to the poor. What except everlasting death awaits the person whom God does not hear? No one is excepted, neither king nor emperor, neither eastern poten-

* * * * *

94 Luke 16:19–31
95 Ps 9B/10:14
96 Ps 39:18/40:17
97 Ps 10:5/11:4
98 Ps 21:25/22:24
99 Ps 67:11/68:10
100 Ps 106/107:41
101 Ps 108/109:31
102 Ps 9B/10:17
103 Matt 5:3

tate nor cardinal, not even the pope himself: unless they cry out as poor men, they will not be heard. They should not be ashamed of this name; David was not ashamed of it, although he was such an outstanding king, so great a prophet, and such a friend of God. Rather they should do what is as necessary as it is difficult so that they may be worthy of this name.

In fact, even the added pronoun[104] conveys a certain emphasis – 'I am poor and needy' – indicating that he himself is poor but that he is dealing with one who alone is rich with regard to all men and whose wealth overcomes all poverty. If you consider the common people, how many faults are present in each of them, how rare virtues are (and how imperfect even these are), and how corrupted they are in so many ways! Then consider how weak nature is, how many dangers beset us who have this treasure in earthen vessels,[105] for we are always worried that what we have will be snatched away. Even the saints have many defects, and there is not one of them in whom there is no room for progress and who cannot exert himself further, forgetting what lies in the past.[106] And so every man is poor and needy, however devout he may be in this life, ever hungering and thirsting after righteousness[107] until he finds satisfaction at the resurrection.

But it is worth noticing what the poor man asks for. It is no ordinary thing for which he assails the divine ears with his cries: 'Preserve my soul, for I am holy.' If you apply this to the head, he was indeed the holy of holies by whom all things were sanctified, and he alone was free from sin.[108] So as to sanctify all those who believe in him, he gave his body to die and be buried, and his soul descended into hell. Immediately before doing this he commends his soul to God, just as we read that he also called out on the cross: 'Father, into your hands I commend my spirit.'[109] Did this holy of holies have some fear for his soul? Not at all. He had confidence in the Father's promise and was confident that his soul could not be held captive in hell.[110] But by means of these figures of speech, Scripture shows us that whatever happens here in this life is done with the Father's authority and the Son's obedience, at least according to the nature he adopted. The

* * * * *

104 The pronoun *ego* 'I,' is not strictly necessary in the Latin phrase in verse 1, 'inops et pauper sum ego.'
105 Cf 2 Cor 4:7.
106 Cf Phil 3:13.
107 Matt 5:6
108 Heb 4:15
109 Luke 23:46
110 Cf Ps 15/16:10.

salvation of all souls depended on the soul of this one man; for if the Lord
had not risen again, everything else would have been to no purpose and
would not have been believed.[111] That is why he says: 'Father, according to
your will, I lay down my life for my sheep'[112] (that life which the enemy
tries to attack in a thousand ways and which death gapes wide to swallow
up), 'but I commend it, Father, to your safe keeping, even if it has to suffer torture and grief, even if it must leave the body or descend into the
kingdom of death. With you to protect it, it will be safe and will not fear
to walk through the shadow of death.[113] Death will swallow it up, just as
the whale swallowed Jonah, but in three days it will return it alive.[114] And
since you, my Father, have sanctified me, your Son, whom you sent into
the world to sanctify all men according to your promise, you will not allow
your holy one to see corruption,[115] either in body or in soul. Reveal in me
what those who are to believe in you through me ought to hope for. You
sent me into the world to save souls, not to destroy them. One is given for
the sake of all;[116] in the one preserve all those whom you have given to me.
You alone are more powerful than all, and if you preserve them, no one
will snatch from my hand those whom you have entrusted to me once and
for all according to your eternal plan.' Christ's soul was in no danger, and
yet he often cries out as if it were: 'Bring my soul out of prison that I might
praise your name;'[117] 'O God, save my soul from the sword and my precious life from the power of the dog;'[118] 'Do not abandon my soul in hell.'[119]
The souls of all men are protected by means of the one innocent soul.

The head forms one person, so to speak, with the whole church of the
saints who have existed from the beginning of the world right to the very
end. This person never ceases to cry out: 'Preserve my soul, for I am holy.'
The head cries out on behalf of the members, the members cry out in the
person of their head, the members cry out on behalf of other members. Just
as those who put on Christ become one flesh with him, one spirit, according
to the law of the mystical body, so all who have been pervaded by the spirit

* * * * *

111 Cf 1 Cor 15:14; Erasmus treats this theme in *Explanatio symboli* CWE 70 306–10
as well as in the colloquy *Inquisitio de fide* CWE 39 426.
112 John 10:15
113 Cf Ps 22/23:4.
114 Cf Jon 2, Matt 12:39–40, 16:4, and Luke 11:30.
115 Ps 15/16:10
116 Cf John 11:50.
117 Cf Ps 141:8/142:7.
118 Ps 21:21/22:20
119 Cf Ps 15/16:10.

of Christ have one soul. This is what Luke declared about the newly formed church when he said that the multitude of the believers had one heart and one soul.[120] The poor man who puts all his confidence in the goodness and mercy of the Father entrusts this soul to him who cares for the poor and who alone assists the orphan and the poor man according to the words of the psalm: 'I am a beggar and a poor man, but the Lord cares for me.'[121] It is this soul for which the world sets so many traps and against which the devil, stalking about like a roaring lion seeking whom he may devour,[122] plots so many secret attacks, but with your watchful protection this wicked robber can achieve nothing. Satan attacked Peter and the other apostles to sift them like wheat.[123] And then think how often the world attacks the souls of the devout with death, with tricks, and with flattery, but it has been unable to destroy any of the souls of the holy, that is, of those who put all their trust in your mercy. This is exactly what we pray for in the Lord's Prayer: 'Lead us not into temptation, but deliver us from evil,'[124] in other words, 'Preserve our soul.'

The soul is our most precious possession, and it cannot be compensated for by the life of this body, as the Gospel says.[125] He is considered fortunate who by losing everything gains life, although it will soon pass away. The body disintegrates if the soul departs from it, but the soul is destroyed if God departs from it. How anxiously we say to someone: 'Keep a watch on the food store, look after the clothing, guard the money because we do not want to lose any of it!' We appeal to the doctor: 'Save my life!' So why do we not call to God: 'Preserve my soul'? For unless the soul is safe, all other things are preserved in vain, and it cannot be saved unless God protects it. Now if each of us were to look inside himself and consider how poor and needy he is in every respect and how he lives surrounded by great dangers, how could he not cry out to God without ceasing: 'Preserve my soul'? But perhaps he will not dare to add: 'Because I am holy,' conscious as he is of having committed so many offences, especially in God's eyes. As this is the case, who could be called holy? Which of us, standing before God who sees everything,[126] would dare to say: 'I am holy'? Peter

* * * * *

120 Acts 4:32
121 Ps 39:18/40:17
122 1 Pet 5:8
123 Cf Luke 22:31.
124 Matt 6:13
125 Cf Matt 16:26, Mark 8:36–7, Luke 9:25.
126 Cf Heb 4:13.

shuddered at Christ's presence, although he did not yet, I think, really believe that Christ was God. 'Go away from me, O Lord,' he said, 'for I am a sinful man.'[127] He had not yet denied the Lord, and we read of no crime that he had previously committed. But not even the heavens are pure in the sight of God, who detected wickedness even among his own angels.[128] How will anyone, then, have the audacity to say to God, 'because I am holy'? One person alone is holy, the one who sanctifies all the saints, the Lord Jesus, the only one who was pleasing to the Father in all things without exception. Far be it for any other man to claim for himself the honour of this title.

There is however a lesser kind of holy person whom the apostle Paul repeatedly refers to in his letters, as when he greets those working in Rome as those called to be saints,[129] not because they were free from all sin but because they had been cleansed from the sins of their former life through Christ's death and their Christian faith, and by means of God's gratuitous goodness they were called to holiness of life. Elsewhere he calls them those who are called to be saints according to his purpose,[130] in other words, not according to man's purpose but God's, by whom those who are holy have been sanctified, but not because of any merit on their part. And we call the Catholic church holy although it is not completely free from sin as long as it exists in this mortal world, bearing a body that weighs down the soul,[131] burdened as it is by the flesh, which lusts against the spirit.[132] Otherwise why does it cry out each day: 'Forgive us our trespasses'?[133] (For there is no doubt that 'trespasses' refers to our sins.) He is holy according to his own limitations not in whom there is no sin but in whom sin is not dominant, 'for the righteous man falls seven times a day and gets up again,'[134] and yet he does not cease to be called righteous.

We should therefore make a distinction between different uses of the word 'holy' and should also distinguish between our own weakness and the sublime being of our head; nor should we arrogate to ourselves what belongs to him or refuse what is given by his munificence. He is completely

* * * * *

127 Luke 5:8
128 Cf Job 4:18.
129 Rom 1:7
130 Cf Rom 8:28.
131 Cf Wisd 9:15.
132 Cf Gal 5:17.
133 Matt 6:12
134 Prov 24:16

holy according to the nature he has adopted, and according to his divine nature he is also the sanctifier of all men. A man is wicked if he claims for himself the esteem due to our head, but he is ungrateful and unjust if he denies that he is holy after Christ's blood has washed him clean of original sin and after all his sins have been forgiven, either through baptism or penitence,[135] both those sins that he incurred through his birth and those that he added as evil interest, so to speak, to his evil capital by leading an immoral life. He sanctified you, but not because of any merit on your part: why do you ungratefully conceal the fact of the Lord's kindness? You have put on Christ[136] and have thus become a member of Christ: why do you wrong Christ by denying that his members are holy? You have holiness, but you do not have it by your own merit, so you must not become puffed up with arrogance. Nor did you obtain it by your own merits, so do not try to conceal the redeemer's grace. And so you should say to God: 'Since I am by nature a son of wrath,[137] it is by your spontaneous goodness that I have been made holy.' Then you will not be lacking in piety or gratitude.

So far our discussion has primarily been concerned with the sins of holy men, sins that human nature in its weakness commits through carelessness. But what about the person who is polluted by such sins as hatred of his neighbour, adultery, drunkenness, jealousy, bitterness, murder, or the use of poison? Will even he dare to say: 'Preserve my soul, for I am holy'? Or will he instead cry out from afar: 'Heal my soul, for I have sinned against you; have mercy on me, O God, according to your great mercy'?[138] And yet, when he says this and says it sincerely, he is already holy, because he has rid himself of his wicked inclination. Perhaps even those people who have not yet given up their attachment to sin may not inappropriately be called holy ones as long as the seed of faith remains in them, since they have been baptized and participate in the church's sacraments, albeit unworthily. In the same way, vessels are called holy once they have been consecrated for sacred purposes. But it is better for them to refer, not to this psalm, which is on such a sublime level, but to other psalms that are more suited to the penitent.[139] When they have washed themselves with tears,

* * * * *

135 See J.B. Payne *Erasmus: His Theology of the Sacraments* (Richmond, VA 1970) 164 and 181.
136 Cf Rom 13:14 and Gal 3:27.
137 Cf Eph 2:3.
138 Ps 40:5/41:4 and Ps 50:3/51:1
139 Psalms 6, 31/32, 37/38, 50/51, 101/102, 129/130, and 142/143 were traditionally regarded as the seven penitential psalms.

when they have begun to be living members of Christ, then each of them can unite with our head in singing: 'Preserve my soul, for I am holy.' And he who protected Christ's most holy soul from all sin, protected it in death, and protected it at the gates of hell will also protect the souls of his holy ones so that in them sin may not reign supreme. Even if he should allow them to suffer temptation so as to make them grow in virtue, he will make it possible for them to bear the temptation he has created[140] and protect them from a second death,[141] restoring each to his own body at the resurrection of the just.[142]

But let no one allow this wicked thought to suggest itself: 'I have God to protect my soul; once I have entrusted it to him, with such a guardian it cannot come to any harm. I can live free from anxieties and there is no reason for me to torture myself with good works.'[143] Alas, what a preposterous idea! We hear such remarks nowadays tossed off by certain people who boast of their confidence in God – based on what I have no idea! They seem to believe that living faith is to be found in the company of wicked deeds. These people are undoubtedly pitifully deceiving themselves. God does indeed protect souls, but only of those who are themselves also keeping watch as best they can.[144] That is why Solomon advises us to protect our heart with all vigilance, for from it life proceeds.[145] It is pointless for you to keep watch if the Lord does not protect your soul, but he will not protect it unless you take care of it to the best of your ability. His protection is a result of his kindness, but your vigilance is a question of duty. Assist the poor, instruct the ignorant, encourage those who doubt, console those who suffer, forgive those who do wrong, wear down your body by fasting, and amidst all this, cry out: 'Preserve my soul.'

'On what merits do you base your confidence in demanding that I should preserve your soul?' 'I am confident because by your mercy I have been cleansed of my sins with the blood of your Son; I have been trans-

* * * * *

140 1 Cor 10:13
141 Rev 2:11
142 Luke 14:14
143 Cf *Epistola contra pseudevangelicos* ASD IX-1 295, where Erasmus similarly reproaches those who put too much confidence in their faith and are not concerned with good works.
144 Erasmus is concerned to steer a delicate middle course between the crude Pelagianism of some Christians who emphasized the ability to gain salvation by means of good works and the extreme views on justification by faith alone held by the Reformers.
145 Prov 4:23

formed from a sinner into someone holy; from now on I shall live not for myself but for you.[146] It is as a result of your generosity that I am holy. Protect the object of your goodness. For not only was I unable of my own accord to set my soul free but I am also unable to protect it without you now that it is free. May your grace accomplish in me what it has begun. You allowed me to become holy, not through my own righteousness but through that of your Son, and if you protect me I shall continue resolutely in the hope of becoming perfect. But I shall not be perfect unless you keep the whole of me safe and restore my whole self at the resurrection.'

There are some people who profess the resurrection of the soul but deny that of the body:[147] they reduce the blessedness of the saints by half. No, it is just and fitting that he who has surrendered his whole self to God's commands should be kept wholly safe. This is what Paul prays for on behalf of the people of Thessalonica: 'May the God of peace himself sanctify you wholly, so that your spirit and soul and body may be preserved without harm or grievance at the coming of our Lord Jesus Christ.'[148] Concern for the soul was placed first because that part of man has the higher priority; now the body, too, which was as it were the partner and the assistant in the struggle, wishes to share in the glory.

'Save your servant, my God, who puts his hope in you.' In the first verse he called on the Lord, confessing his poverty – for a servant has nothing, and if he does have anything, he has it for his master by whose kindness he possesses it. For what can he possess of his own, he who does not even own himself? Here he calls himself a servant, not of men but of God. 'Servant of God' is an illustrious title, and to be a servant of God is a source of great happiness. Unless you have been the servant of God, you will not reign with God. Let no man delude himself, whether he holds the power of a king or the papacy or any other human dignity, he will not be saved unless he is the servant of God. Anyone can be the servant of God even amidst the splendour of the highest positions, and similarly no one is in a position of such abject slavery among men that he cannot be the servant of God. Anyone who possesses his wealth for God, anyone who holds and wields his power for God may be a king before men, but before God he is a servant, and he is truly a king for the very reason that he is God's servant.

* * * * *

146 Cf 2 Cor 5:15.
147 The theory that man would undergo spiritual but not bodily resurrection was apparently first put forward by Valentinus, the founder of a Gnostic sect in the second century. See *Explanatio symboli* CWE 70 310.
148 1 Thess 5:23

Anyone who commits a sin is a slave to sin,[149] and no one can serve two masters.[150] He who is ruled by lust, greed, anger, ambition, even if he governs ten kingdoms, is a despicable slave, belonging not to God but to his own desires.

The shrewdest of the philosophers, known as Stoics, held the false belief that there was a certain kind of freedom in which the sum total of happiness could be found; on the other hand, they believed there was a kind of slavery that was the source of utter misery.[151] But they were deluded by dreams of this kind, ignorant as they were of true freedom. Such an attitude on the part of the wise man, recommended, praised, and boasted of by these Stoics, does not bring with it true freedom.[152] What does, then? The grace of God, for they are truly free men whom the Son has set free. How does he set them free? We were slaves to sin, free from righteousness[153] but Christ took away our sins and thus set us free from the slavery of Satan and bestowed on us his own righteousness, which we did not possess of our own accord – nor could we possess it. In this way our position was happily changed. We ceased to be the devil's slaves and began to be the sons and servants of God – sons on account of our love, servants on account of our obedience.

A servant is completely dependent on his master's will and does not act according to his own inclinations. Instead, his master's wishes are binding on him, for a servant is merely the living instrument of his master. Similarly, those in whom human desires are dead and who do not now live for themselves but in whom Christ lives and acts,[154] these are true servants of God. The apostle Paul boasts of this title throughout his writings, calling himself the servant of Jesus Christ, seeking not the things which belong to him but what belongs to Jesus Christ, striving to please not men but God. For what is it he says? 'If I were still pleasing men, I would not be a servant of Christ.'[155] But what does it mean to please men? It means to seek

* * * * *

149 John 8:34
150 Matt 6:24, Luke 16:13
151 See Cicero *Paradoxa Stoicorum* 5; Seneca *Epistulae morales* 47.17. The Stoics believed that a person dominated by his own desires is a wretched slave; only the person who is detached from passion and desires what is truly good can be free and happy.
152 In the colloquy Ἰχθυοφαγία CWE 40 702 Erasmus puts forward the idea that true freedom can only exist in Christ.
153 Rom 6:20
154 Cf Gal 2:20.
155 Gal 1:10

praise and profit from men rather than from God. But he who is a proper servant never moves his eyes from his master's face, is always attentive to his wishes, accommodates all the actions of his own life to his master's will, not working out what profit he himself can gain, not fearing the threats of men or imminent death. He eagerly undertakes whatever he sees is pleasing to his master. Only Christ, who did not carry out his own wishes but those of his Father,[156] was in every respect a perfect servant like this, for he carried them out not with bitterness and defiance but gladly, willingly, and with eagerness. For when the hour of death was at hand, he rejoiced in the Spirit and gave thanks to the Father.[157]

I shall not at this point raise the question of whether the word 'servant' is appropriate to Christ. Those who make much of his high status prefer him to be called 'Son' rather than 'servant,' while those who are more concerned to emphasize his humility and obedience unto death[158] do not find the word 'servant' repugnant. The sacred writings prefer the name 'Son,' and the Lord himself more often addresses his Father by this name than as his Lord or his God; and yet Paul writes that the Lord took the form of a servant – in other words, of a man, according to some people's interpretation – and not only of a servant but even of a wicked servant who deserved to be beaten, for it is said of him that he came in the likeness of sinful flesh.[159] But God forbid that this should be a matter for argument between fellow servants: those who are happy to use the term 'servant' should imitate his obedience, while those who prefer the term 'Son' should imitate his love, and those who acknowledge the Lord Jesus with both names should insist as much as possible upon both aspects. For in spiritual matters there is nothing to prevent the same person being sometimes called a servant, sometimes a son. In fact, as I said before, only those who are truly poor are really rich, and in the same way one might say that no one is really free unless he is the servant of God.

Slavery is a distasteful word, and there is no one to whom freedom is not dear. But there are many different kinds of slavery, and only servitude to God can liberate us from all of them. Every day we hear men complaining: some lament that they are being harshly treated by their masters, others

* * * * *

156 Cf Luke 22:42, John 6:38.
157 Cf Luke 10:21.
158 Cf Phil 2:8. These contrasted perceptions of Christ underlay Erasmus' clash with Jacques Lefèvre d'Etaples in his *Apologia ad Fabrum* (1517); see CWE 83 36.
159 Rom 8:3

are oppressed by the yoke of their rulers, many declare that the decrees of men are intolerable. There are also sons who object to parental authority, and wives who are oppressed by the domineering behaviour of their husbands; but the most real slavery is slavery to sin. There is no kind of slavery, however, from which servitude to God does not set us free. It is to this freedom that Paul calls us when he writes in the seventh chapter of his first letter to the Corinthians: 'You were bought at a price; do not become slaves of men.'[160] You have a master and you must serve him sincerely, not motivated by fear of beatings but by love of God, who commanded this through the apostle Paul. If you serve God in the person of your master, you have already ceased to be the slave of a man; but if you pay no heed to God and would deceive your master and steal from him if you did not fear punishment, then you are not really the servant of God but of man, ignoring God and fearing man. This is Christian freedom, to which the Apostle often calls us. To shake off the yoke of men in this way is an act of piety pleasing to God. Otherwise, if religious observance could free one from the condition of slavery, Paul would not have sent Onesimus, the runaway slave, back to his master Philemon.[161]

If the orders given by rulers are just, they must be obeyed with alacrity, because they require us to do something good. But if they are unjust, obey the Lord in them as long as they are not wicked, for he ordered us to obey those who have been put in charge not only when they are agreeable but even when they are hard to please and capricious. 'Where does he bid us do this?' you may ask. He orders it through the mouth and the pen of Peter, who writes: 'Be subject to every creature.'[162] You will undoubtedly object that this is wretched slavery, but he shows that it is freedom when he adds, 'for the sake of God.' He who is subject to man for the sake of God is not a servant to a man but to God. And then Peter adds: 'For it is God's will that by doing right you should put to silence the ignorance of foolish men, living as free men and not using your freedom as a pretext for evil but living as servants of God.'[163] It is a false liberty to be a slave to one's own feelings while using Christianity as a front. Be a servant of God truly and totally and you have shaken off the yoke of men. If a friend advises you what is in your own interest, you listen to him willingly and thank him; you do not consider yourself to be a slave for complying with

* * * * *

160 1 Cor 7:23
161 Philem 12
162 1 Pet 2:13
163 1 Pet 2:15–16

someone else's wishes but are glad to be given the chance to feather your own nest. Similarly, if the laws of the rulers urge you to do honourable things, you are not being dragged along against your will but being encouraged; but if they are unjust and harsh, endure them in the way a martyr endures a wicked tyrant. If the latter orders him to be put in chains, he puts up with it, if he orders that he be stretched on the rack, he submits to that, in obedience not to the commands of the tyrant but to the will of the Lord: he is subject to God but superior to man. However, one should not obey either a man or an angel if they order one to do things that are wicked. The tyrant says to the martyr: 'Lay your neck on the block,' and he lays it down, but if the tyrant says: 'Burn incense to Jupiter,' he refuses. And so if a husband or father tells you to do things that are good, consider that it is God who is ordering you through these men; if they tell you to do things that are unpleasant, gratify God in doing them and your freedom will remain intact; but if they order wicked things, there is no reason for you to accept them as if God had given the order and no reason to endure them for love of God, in the hope that you may be praised here for your long-suffering and there for your obedience. By this path we progress towards true freedom, ceasing to be the servants of men when we become the servants of God. For to serve God is to have power, but they who throw off the yoke of men in such a way that they find their neck trapped beneath the yoke of the devil strive in vain after freedom. Let love eagerly perform what the law enjoins and then you are free from the authority of the law.

But I do not want my digression to lead you in circles any longer so I shall return to the discussion of the psalm itself. The Lord Jesus Christ, together with his whole body, which is the church, is as it were one servant, and as he does not wish him to be destroyed, he cries out: 'Save your servant.' It should also be noted that he addresses the Father as 'my God.' For God, according to his omnipotence, is the God of all men, but according to what is appropriate to the Scriptures, he is only called the God of the pious – those who worship him as God, who esteem nothing more highly than him, who love him with all their heart, with all their soul, and with all their strength, as for example when he is called the God of Abraham, the God of Isaac, and the God of Jacob.[164] Shameless is the man who addresses him as 'my God' if his god is his stomach,[165] if his god is Mammon[166] or

* * * * *

164 Deut 6:5, referred to at Matt 22:37; Exod 3:16, referred to at Matt 22:32 and Mark 12:26
165 Cf Phil 3:19.
166 Cf Matt 6:24 and Luke 16:13.

pleasure[167] or anything else for the sake of which he ignores God. It is
equally shameless for people to call him 'Father' if their father is the devil
– for whoever hates his neighbour is the devil's child[168] – and shameless is
he who calls him 'Lord' if he does not obey his commandments. By far the
most shameless, however, are those who call him their God but who are enslaved to many gods of their own. Nor is he the God of the heretics who
separate themselves off from Christ and the church. Let us therefore be in
Christ, let us be in the church, so that we can say with one voice: 'Save your
servant, my God.'

Notice how many arguments this sinner uses to make his importunate
demands, putting pressure on God's goodness, so to speak. In the first verse
he said: 'For I am poor and needy,' as if God only listened to such people
and as if to be poor and needy meant that you had merited divine favour.
In the next verse he says: 'For I am holy.' It is contrary to God's mercy not
to listen to the poor, and it is contrary to the constancy of his divine nature
not to protect what he himself has sanctified through the death of his only-
begotten Son. The poor cry out that they may be heard, and it is unlawful
to violate what is holy. Now what does he add in support of his plea? 'Your
servant.' Even wicked men help any servants of theirs who are in danger,
for no other reason than that they are servants. But there are also slaves
who are scoundrels, that is, 'false slaves'; in order to make a distinction
between himself and these he added, 'who puts his hope in you.' The Lord
is the source of all the pride of a true servant, and all his hope is in the
Lord. Whatever he has the servant possesses with the Lord's approval, and
his hope is of things that are not yet visible, as St Paul teaches.[169] And so
while the servant of God remains in this life he performs everything with
alacrity and bears everything with resignation, prepared to meet death and
relying on nothing but the promises made by the Lord, whom he knows
cannot deceive, since he is truth itself.

I think, however, that 'hope' has been used here for 'trust,' or if there
is any difference between the two words, it is that hope waits in expectation
while trust entertains no doubts and that the word 'trust' has a broader application than 'hope.' For 'blessed are all who put their trust in the Lord.'[170]
On the other hand: 'Cursed is he who puts his trust in man.'[171] What then

* * * * *

167 Cf 2 Tim 3:4.
168 Cf 1 John 3:8–10.
169 Cf Rom 8:24, Heb 11:1.
170 Ps 2:13/12, Ps 117/118:8–9
171 Jer 17:5

should we say about those who put their trust in uncertain riches,[172] who have confidence in their own strength or talents or merits, that is, those who put their trust in themselves like that wicked slave in the comedy who says: 'I put all my hope in myself'?[173] There exists a human hope that applies to human affairs, whereby men hope for certain things from other people. But cursed is he who places the anchor of his hope[174] – whereby we hope for eternal salvation – in man. So true is this that it would not be right for us to put our hope even in Christ if he were only a man, for only God can keep us safe for ever. In him alone, then, should all those who are glad to be called his servants put their hope. Other hopes often cause men shame, but the hope that is firmly set in God disappoints no one. Even if they are disappointed for the moment this does not last, because they are set free from shame, and disgrace is turned into glory, not through their own righteousness but through God's. In the words of another psalm: 'In you, O Lord, have I hoped; I shall not be put to shame for ever; in your righteousness deliver me.'[175] But what is this righteousness of God? It means that he has promised his assistance to all who set their hope firmly in him, for anyone who carries out what he has undertaken to do is righteous. Does he then help his servants because he owes it to them rather than as a result of grace? It would be so if his promise had not been made freely. It was in this way that the Lord of glory was put to shame for a while when he was scorned by men and abandoned by the mob,[176] but his disgrace turned to glory.

But if the church ought not to rest its hopes even in Christ as man, how wrong they are who lead corrupt lives and put their hope of salvation in St Barbara, St Christopher, or St George, convinced that they will not perish no matter what kind of lives they have led as long as they worship these saints according to certain definite rituals.[177] Moreover, while the church out of indulgence for the feelings of simple people turns a blind eye to things like the fact that what was once a sailor's song (in which we call the most holy Virgin *spes nostra*) is now sung even in some churches[178] –

* * * * *

172 1 Tim 6:17
173 Terence *Phormio* 139
174 Cf Heb 6:19.
175 Ps 30:2/31:1
176 See Ps 21:7–8/22:6–7; Matt 27:22–3 and 28–31.
177 On Erasmus' view of devotion to these saints, see n21 above.
178 The song to which Erasmus refers here is the antiphon *Salve regina* (*Analecta Hymnica* 1 318 no 245) in which the Virgin Mary is addressed as *spes nostra*. Erasmus mentions this popular hymn frequently in his writings, for example

and devout men make plausible excuses for it – nonetheless, the spiritually-minded ought to regard as more precious that which is so commonly found in Holy Scripture that no room is left for anything else.

However, it should not be inferred that this sermon is intended to condemn the worship of the saints.[179] Instead its aim is to make us see where Scripture teaches us to fix the anchor of all our hope. Although the influence of the saints is very strong, we should certainly not fix the sacred anchor of our salvation anywhere except in God, for whatever we receive – from whatever source or in whatever way – is a gift from him. Some people place their hopes in the prayers of monks or nuns: they give food and arrange a lucrative partnership, and relying on this hope they live at the whim of their desires. I commend the fact that they help the poor and I approve of the fact that they realize that the prayers of the devout are most effective in influencing God, but who can condone the fact that they have more confidence in men than in God?

At this point you may say: 'But I do hope in the Lord.'[180] If you hope, then change your way of life, for anyone who hopes in the Lord fears the Lord, loves the Lord. It is a foolish hope that leads one to expect from God something which he has not promised. He has given assurance of his mercy, but only to those who have repented, to those who fear him, to those who call to him, to those who love him. Make use also of the appeals of the devout as secondary supports, but you yourself should beg for the Lord's mercy, so that having prevailed over your passions you may place your hope in God. No one truly hopes in the Lord unless he despises all forms of protection which the world provides.

All men everywhere cry out that they hope in God, but the fire of temptation reveals those who really have placed their hope firmly in God. We see many people who, when they lose their children or have no re-sources left or are deprived of their privileges, react with complaints and cries of anguish and by making a great commotion. They tear their hair, beat their breast, scratch their cheeks, and some go so far as to hang them-

* * * * *

in the colloquies Ἰχθυοφαγία CWE 40 719 and *Naufragium* CWE 39 355 and in the *Modus orandi Deum* CWE 70 200; he also rendered it in hexameters (CWE 85 338). Luther, too, criticized what he saw as the excessive devotion shown to the Virgin Mary exemplified in this antiphon.

179 See the tolerant attitude expressed in the *Modus orandi Deum* CWE 70 194–5, where Erasmus defends the proper invocation of the saints, an attitude for which he was criticized by some of the Reformers.

180 Cf Phil 2:19.

selves; others do not even refrain from blaspheming against God. If you were to ask these people in calmer circumstances whether they put their hope in God, they would answer without hesitation: 'Of course.' But the storm of suffering reveals very clearly where they had fixed their hopes. He who, on losing a son, cries out: 'I am in despair, I am lost,' had placed his hope in his son, not in God. He who, on the death of his wife, despairs and cries out against life's harshness had placed his hope in his wife, not in God. He who has lost his source of income and seeks to put an end to his grief by killing himself had put his hope in money, not in the Lord. They who have truly fixed their hope in God can say along with the blessed Job: 'The Lord gave, the Lord has taken away, it has been done as it pleases the Lord; blessed be the name of the Lord,'[181] and they join Paul in saying: 'For me to live is Christ and to die is gain.'[182] It is not for anyone whatsoever to say: 'I hope in the Lord.' The principal qualification for piety is contained in this statement, and St Paul includes it among the claims to distinction of the true widow when he says: 'If she has set her hope in the Lord.'[183]

Some of you may perhaps consider what follows a minor point and unworthy of a sermon, but it should nevertheless be made to help the less sophisticated ones; the learned must listen patiently out of love to what is directed towards the needs of the uneducated. In Latin, if someone says, 'I cried out,' he implies that he has finished crying out; if someone says, 'he stood' or 'he hoped,' he implies that it is in the past. The same is not the case in Greek: instead there are many words which indicate that an action has indeed begun but is still continuing. For example, when they say: 'I have set my hope in you,' they do not mean that they have given up hope but that their hope is firmly established; when they say: 'I was glad,' they do not mean that their joy is over but that it remains firm within; similarly, when they say: 'I have cried out,' they are not implying that there is silence but rather a continuous cry.[184] This is the case also with a few Latin words in the active voice. For example, when *novit* [he knew] is used of someone it does not mean that he has ceased to know but that he keeps the knowledge

* * * * *

181 Job 1:21
182 Phil 1:21
183 Cf 1 Tim 5:5.
184 Erasmus is alluding to the use of the aorist tense in Greek, which does not have the limitations as to continuance and completion that other tenses have and which therefore can give the sense of a state or condition resulting from a past action and continuing in the present. In Latin on the other hand, only a few defective verbs such as *novit* or *odit* have a past form but a present sense.

firmly in mind; when *odit* [he hated] is used, it does not imply that someone has stopped hating but that the hatred is strongly rooted in his heart; the word *meminit* [he remembered] is used not of a person who has ceased to retain something in his memory but of him who keeps it firmly impressed on his memory. Accordingly, to have hoped in the Lord is to have set one's hope firmly in the Lord; and to have cried out to the Lord is to entreat him without ceasing. This is the word used in the following verse, for the psalm continues: 'Have mercy on me, O Lord, for I have cried out to you the whole day long.'

What did Christ have that was pitiable except that he had taken on our pitiful condition so as to transform it for us into blessedness? And so the head cries out on behalf of his whole body: 'Have mercy on me, O Lord.' Strictly speaking there is no misery where there is no sin, for he alone is really wretched who is the object of God's anger: sin alone separates God from men. By nature we were all sons of wrath[185] and the enemies of God, and so our Priest prays that through his death God may pardon the sins of all who believe in him.[186] He does not call on God's righteousness here, but his mercy, for we have been set free by grace – at great cost,[187] to be sure, but it is someone else who has paid the price.

In fact, in the divine writings the word 'evil' does not always denote an offence; occasionally it means suffering, as in the Gospel: 'The day's own evil is sufficient for it.'[188] Similarly, the psalm uses the phrase 'day of evil' to denote a day of dread and danger,[189] and the patriarch Jacob says in Genesis 47 that the days of his life are few and evil,[190] not because they are particularly steeped in wickedness, but because they are full of suffering. St Paul, writing to the Ephesians, orders them to make the most of the time because the days are evil,[191] and in Ecclesiastes we are told to enjoy the good day and to beware the evil one in a passage where 'good' is used to signify prosperity and 'evil' to denote disaster.[192] In the same way the word 'misery' also sometimes denotes suffering, which tends particularly to beset the holy in this world, as we read in Psalm 11: 'Because of the misery

* * * * *

185 Eph 2:3
186 Cf Luke 23:34.
187 Cf 1 Cor 6:20.
188 Matt 6:34
189 Cf Ps 26/27:5.
190 Gen 47:9
191 Eph 5:16
192 Eccles 7:14

of the needy and the groans of the poor, I will arise.'[193] Here the Greek word is ταλαιπωρία, which is used of enduring troubles, not sins. Paul made use of this word in chapter 7 of his letter to the Romans: 'Wretched man that I am! Who will deliver me?'[194] Moreover, the Hebrew books, as befits the idiom of that language, occasionally refer to a gift given out of piety without asking anything in return as a 'mercy.' In Latin, too, we do the same, using the Greek word when we call it *eleemosyna*. There is therefore room for mercy even where there is no sin but where there is suffering and danger. Wherever there is mercy there is misery, which attends everyone as long as he is oppressed by this mortal body. And so as long as we live in this world, we must cry out to the Lord: 'Have mercy on me, O Lord.'

A cry is an expression of strong emotion, not just a projection of the voice like the shouts of the priests of Baal, whose commotion the prophet rightly mocked because they wished with their shouts to rouse God as if he were fast asleep or had gone on a journey or was focusing his attention on others.[195] It is not that it is reprehensible to pray aloud, for it is fitting for the whole man to pray, but the physical voice is ineffectual unless the emotions cry out; nor should the shouting be done with the voice but with the feelings, which even in silence strike God's ears. The physical voice should be restrained, but nowadays some people in church who wish to show off their voices can be said to thunder rather than sing, without their thoughts being engaged. Works of piety also have an effective voice, for just as love is articulate and faith has a loud voice which reaches God's ears even if the tongue is silent, so mercy produces a sound of its own – in short, all the good deeds which spring from love for God cry out, and cry out to God, while the things done for the sake of honour cry out to men and are silent before God. Do you want a proof that good deeds have a voice of their own? Listen to the Lord speaking through the mouth of Isaiah: 'Let the oppressed go free and break every yoke asunder. Share your bread with the hungry and bring the poor and homeless into your house; when you see someone naked, clothe him, and do not despise your own flesh.' How does he go on? 'Then you will call and the Lord will listen; you will cry out and he will say, "Here I am, for I the Lord your God am merciful."'[196] To do this is undoubtedly to cry out. The writer of Ecclesiasticus confirms this when he says: 'Perform acts of charity in the heart of the poor man and these will

* * * * *

193 Ps 11:6/12:5
194 Rom 7:24
195 1 Kings 18:26–8
196 Cf Isa 58:6–7 and 9.

intercede for you to keep you from all evil.'[197] Things which are kept out of sight tend not to be easily heard, but the more mercy is concealed, the more powerfully it assails the divine ears with its cries. To God the most pleasing cry is that when the works of love and the physical voice, together with a pious attitude, produce a sweet-sounding harmony in God's ears as the situation demands. However the Lord has no need of the physical voice: the blood of Abel cried out to God from the earth, although Abel was not saying anything.[198] Moses was told by God: 'Why do you call to me?'[199] when he was lying prostrate and praying in silence; and Hannah, the wife of Elkanah, cried out and was heard although she uttered no sound.[200]

Let us cry out with these people, my brothers, that we may be heard, but we must cry out to the Lord, not against the Lord. In distressing circumstances many people cry out, but against the Lord, for they shout that God has wronged them because they suffer such things; but those who have set their hopes firmly in the Lord cry out to the Lord. Those who have put their trust in the powerful cry out to their leaders when trouble is impending, and they who have confidence in riches call out to these when they are in danger, but the sheep of God cannot cry out, cannot bleat, except to God who is their shepherd. But what do they cry? 'Have mercy.' They do not pray for anything specifically but are content that God should have mercy. He himself knows best how he should have mercy. Sometimes he has mercy when he inflicts suffering, and I would even go so far as to say that he has mercy when he allows his people to fall into error and commit serious offences. He has mercy when he alleviates suffering and grants relief so that our weakness can endure it. He has mercy when he delivers us from evil and grants more joyful circumstances in place of distress. He has mercy when he bestows grace, when he strengthens, and when he saves. Whatever favour we receive from God is mercy because it is not owed to us and is given without anything being asked in return. And so not only is the earth filled with the mercy of the Lord,[201] but his mercy is also above the heavens[202] and down in hell. Nor is the Lord's mercy of one kind only, for his mercies are manifold, available to all who cry out to him. One kind of mercy sets free, another anticipates; one accompanies, another follows; one

* * * * *

197 Ecclus 29:15 / Sir 29:12
198 Cf Gen 4:10.
199 Exod 14:15
200 1 Sam 1:13
201 Ps 32/33:5
202 Pss 56:11/57:10, 85/86:13, 107:5/108:4

protects, another consoles; one beats in order to correct, another bestows in order to enrich. Need I say more? As his wisdom is beyond measure, so is his mercy.[203]

The rich men of this world remove from their entrances vociferous and noisy beggars because they disturb their enjoyment. But God is well disposed to such beggars, not because he derives pleasure from them but because they are useful to us. Look at the audacity of this beggar: all day he cries out and expects that just because he does not cease to cry out, he should command favourable attention. But what does 'all day' mean, if not throughout one's whole life? The day begins with the sunrise and ends at sunset; similarly, each man's day begins at his birth and draws to a close with his death, for birth is our sunrise, old age is our evening, and death our sunset. However, our setting is not always preceded by an evening to warn us of its approach, nor can any man number the hours of his day as we measure the day with water-clocks and timepieces: we all know that we shall die, but no one knows when he is to die. We are allowed to know what is useful to us, but what is not useful is kept secret. We should expect death at each moment and must not postpone turning to the Lord. If a traveller has no sundial or clock to tell him the time, how anxiously he watches the shadows made by the trees and scrutinizes the sky; but if a dense layer of cloud makes this impossible, the more uncertain he is, the more he hurries on his way in case nightfall should take him by surprise. But for us, just as nothing is more certain than death, so nothing is more uncertain than the hour of our death. We believe that we are only at the entrance,[204] although death can occur at any moment. We must not stop on our journey, we must hurry, we must quicken our pace in case eternal night should take us by surprise. The traveller overtaken by nightfall finds solace during the tedium of the night in waiting for the light that will return; but everlasting is the night that follows on our day if we have spent the time in idleness.

Let us cry out to the Lord, my dear brothers, let us cry out unceasingly, and let us cry out while the day is still with us. Once night has fallen our cries will be useless. In vain did the foolish virgins cry out, for they cried at night;[205] in vain did the rich man in the Gospel cry out, for he did so after his sunset;[206] in vain did they cry out who uttered prophecies in the name

* * * * *

203 Cf Ps 146/147:5.
204 Cf *Adagia* II ii 85: *In foribus adesse* 'To be at the door.'
205 Cf Matt 25:6.
206 Cf Luke 16:24.

of Jesus, for they cried out at night.[207] There is a time for everything, my brothers, as it is written in Ecclesiastes: there is a time for speaking, there is a time for keeping quiet.[208] The time to speak is while we remain in this life, but when we have moved on from here, it will be time to keep quiet. There our enemy will speak, accusing us before God; there the judge will speak, giving judgment to each person according to what he has done in the body. What shall we say there or whom shall we appeal to? To mercy? We shall be told: 'The time for mercy is past; now is the time for judgment. You should have made your appeal while it was still day.' Shall we call on justice? We shall be told: 'Examine yourself before the judgment.'[209] It is not safe to appeal to the justice of God, however, unless his mercy, which triumphs over judgment,[210] is also present. In the next world it will be the turn of justice to hold the stage, but in this world we appeal to the Lord's mercy, and by means of it we prepare our righteousness so that it may precede us to that seat of judgment and so that the glory of the Lord may be our rear guard, in accordance with the prophecy of Isaiah.[211]

We should cry out the whole day long; but anyone who has not cried out at dawn, who was silent at midday, who did not cry out at evening should at least cry out to the Lord as nightfall approaches. We must not despair: while there is life there is hope.[212] As soon as someone has breathed his last, night has fallen. Perhaps others can cry out on your behalf, but you cannot cry out for yourself. And yet we read in the mystical writings that they who were holy cried out to the Lord in the middle of the night, for it was night when Christ cried out to the Father in the garden.[213] But anyone who calls to the Lord while he is alive is calling out during the day, even if profound darkness covers the sky.

There is also a night of suffering and temptation: it is during this time especially that one must cry out to the Lord. It was night (in both senses) when the apostles ran away and when Peter denied the Lord;[214] it was night even at the sixth hour, in bright daylight, when the Lord was crucified,[215] so

* * * * *

207 Cf Matt 7:22–3.
208 Eccles 3:1, 7
209 Cf Ecclus 18:19 / Sir 18:20.
210 James 2:13
211 Isa 58:8
212 Cf *Adagia* ii iv 12: *Aegroto dum anima est, spes est* 'While there's life in a sick man there's hope.'
213 Cf Matt 26:36–46.
214 Cf Matt 26:56 and 69–75.
215 Mark 15:25

great was the power of darkness. Then he repeated the words of Psalm 21 in which he speaks thus: 'I cried out by day and you do not listen and by night and not to my confusion.'[216] One must cry out to God both in prosperity and in adversity, even if he does not immediately grant what we seek; we must not cease our cries, for if he did not heed us when we cried in the daytime he will hear us when we cry at night. He will hear, I say, even if he does not grant what you asked for in your prayers. This should be your principal desire: you wish for eternal salvation; and if prosperity is not conducive to this, God inflicts suffering so that hardship may allow him to hear you.[217] Whenever this happens, if you are not heard when you cry out in the day you are heard in the night. You have gained the most important things you could wish for even if what your human desires demanded has been denied.

Now there is also a night of ignorance, in which the Jews lived, keeping to the letter of the Law; this is even more true of the pagans, who had no knowledge of God and worshipped dumb idols as their gods. When the light of the gospel appeared, it dispelled this darkness, it dispersed the shadows of the Law and exposed the errors of the pagans, sending forth the rays of brightest truth throughout the world. This is what the Apostle means when he writes: 'The night is far gone, the day is at hand. Let us then cast off the works of darkness.'[218] This was the day which the Lord made,[219] so that we who were first the sons of darkness should now exult and rejoice in the light of the Lord our God.[220] But the whole period of time that runs its course in the passing of years, months, and days from the revelation of the gospel until the end of the world[221] is one day, as we learn from Paul.[222] Indeed, the whole period from the creation of the world right down to the day of judgment is one single day. For although before the grace of Christ was revealed the gospel was in many ways hidden, no one who was pious was without the daylight of the gospel as far as was sufficient to that age.[223] And this whole day long the church never ceases to cry out to the Lord with one voice: 'Have mercy on me.' Some have not

* * * * *

216 Ps 21:3/22:2
217 Cf Isa 28:19.
218 Cf Rom 13:12.
219 Ps 117/118:24, adopted as the Gradual for Easter Sunday mass
220 Cf Ps 117/118:24.
221 Cf Matt 28:20.
222 Cf 2 Pet 3:8.
223 See n25 above on the spiritual church.

yet been born, others have departed this life, and yet the church's cry continues unceasingly among those who are here; nor is it silent on behalf of those who are in torment but whose offences, being of a less serious nature, give hope of respite.

Since he who begs for mercy is confessing his wretched state and his distress, he adds: 'Gladden the soul of your servant, for to you have I lifted up my soul.' The mystical Scriptures often mention Christ's soul, and so what grounds do the followers of Apollinaris – who try to deny that Christ had a human soul, stating falsely that his divine nature took the place of a soul[224] – have to stand on? There were three different things or substances in Christ: a real human body subject to suffering and death or at least capable of these conditions; the divine nature, which took upon itself a human nature; and finally a human soul, free from sin, to be sure, but subject to the same conditions as ours. And all these things were the one and the same Christ, to whom be glory for ever. He took upon himself the whole man so that he might restore the whole man. His body suffered death and his soul was tormented, but these things did not affect the divine nature. Furthermore, he experienced grief in his soul, he who asks that his soul be gladdened. The soul of Christ was sorrowful even unto death,[225] when he trembled and was in such anguish that drops of blood fell to the ground from his most sacred body.[226] He took this pain upon himself, not in pretence but truly, partly to provide us with proof that he had taken our weakness upon himself, partly to set his martyrs an example from which they should seek solace in similar circumstances.[227] The thought of imminent death did not grieve him as much as his realization that so many people who stumbled as a result of the weakness of the flesh would suffer everlasting death. He longed for men's salvation with an indescribable longing – and he was not the only one who was sorrowful, but the hearts of all his chosen ones, whom he wished to share in his death, were also oppressed with grief. In fact, even after his resurrection two of the disciples who were talking to-

* * * * *

224 Apollinaris, bishop of Laodicea in the fourth century, was a supporter of Athanasius against Arianism but denied that Christ had a human soul; instead he adopted the formula 'one nature of the Logos made flesh.' Although his views were condemned, they continued to find support and were developed by the so-called Monophysites.

225 Cf Matt 26:38 and Mark 14:34.

226 Cf Luke 22:44.

227 Erasmus discusses the question of Christ's suffering in his debate with Colet entitled *De taedio Iesu* CWE 70 13–67, of which 64–5 are particularly relevant here.

gether about Jesus on their way to Emmaus felt sad and were almost in despair.[228]

The head prays for his members when they are in danger, so that those who were devastated by the Lord's death should be gladdened by his resurrection. Although the Lord Jesus died once and for all for our sins[229] and will never again die, and although he rose from the dead once and for all and will live in heaven for ever, yet after his death has been recalled during the forty days of Lent and when that day of resurrection shines forth, how cheerful the whole church becomes, how it rejoices, how triumphant it feels, and what joyful songs it produces, shouting 'Alleluia' again and again and continually repeating the verse 'This is the day that the Lord has made; let us rejoice and be glad in it.'[230] But for many people this joy is inappropriate and for some it is useless, unless they also have spiritual liveliness. Some people welcome the fact that at last Lent is over in the wrong way. They are glad that they can stop fasting, that meat has reappeared; they cast off their drab clothes and put on colourful ones. The tables are spread with sumptuous banquets, splendour returns, luxuries are brought back, as are dances – not that they gave them up during Lent, they just concealed their existence. In short, they cease to lament in such a way that they once again commit deplorable deeds. My brothers, this is not the gladness which the psalm asks for with such a loud cry, for the psalmist does not cry out, 'Gladden my stomach' or 'my gullet' or 'the flesh of your servant,' but 'Gladden the soul of your servant.' No one is really made happy by the resurrection of Christ unless he rises up with Christ from his sins, in newness of life.[231] What is the point of putting on a white robe if your soul is even dirtier than before? What is the good of crying loudly 'Alleluia' with your mouth, if your wretched mind has a guilty conscience and sings to itself of lamentation and distress?

Do you wish to acquire true spiritual joy? Consider what follows: 'For to you have I lifted up my soul.' Unless you lift up your soul to God you will not experience that true Easter joy. Christ has risen; you too must rise. The world occupies a low position, and the Lord says that in the world you will have sorrow.[232] But where is the joy? He himself indicates it when he says: 'I will see you again, and your heart will rejoice, and no one will take

* * * * *

228 Luke 24:17
229 Cf 1 Pet 3:18.
230 Ps 117/118:24. See n219 above.
231 Cf Rom 6:4.
232 John 16:22

your joy from you.'[233] Would that Christ might rise in us all and deign to
see us again, so that not our tongue might rejoice, not our gullet, not our
stomach or our flesh, but our heart. There is no one who does not seek joy,
and there are many devices whereby men try to acquire it for themselves,
but the joy of the heart is not to be found in this world, believe me, the
joy of the heart is not to be found in this world. In Christ is true joy, in
Christ is the joy of the heart, in Christ is the joy which is never lost. But
Christ has gone up into heaven, and if we cannot lift our bodies up as far as
heaven, let us at least lift up our hearts, let us raise our souls to that place,
being wise not with regard to things on earth but to things in heaven.[234]
Where your love is, there your soul has its home, so that you can say with
the Apostle: 'But our home is in heaven.'[235] When the soul has its home
there, it experiences the things that no eye has seen and no ear has heard,
nor has the heart of man conceived, and which God has prepared for those
who love him.[236] There are men who set their minds on the things of the
flesh,[237] for flesh is an earthly thing, but one should rise above the human
if one wishes to experience this joy. Many people lift their souls against
God and involve themselves in numerous sufferings, but anyone who lifts
his soul to God realizes the truth of what the Hebrew wise man said: 'An
untroubled mind is like a continual feast.'[238] When we pray we lift up our
heads and hands and raise our eyes towards heaven, and we do well if at
the same time we also lift up our soul to God.

Our minds become like the things we love, and since nothing is heavier than sin, how can the soul that is weighed down by sin lift itself up
to God? In the book of the prophet Zechariah, the woman is sitting in the
leaden vessel and a lump of lead is pushed into her mouth.[239] The leaden
container represents wickedness, the woman evil desire: she was attached to
the container and swallowed the lump of lead. This is an image of the soul
weighed down by sin. Now consider carefully how insignificant are those
things the desire for which obsesses those who are devoted to this world.
Gold, silver, jewels are produced in the darkest recesses of the earth: there
dwells the soul of the greedy man. Physical lust is relegated to the extrem-

* * * * *

233 John 16:22
234 Cf Col 3:2.
235 Phil 3:20; cf Matt 6:21, Mark 10:21, Luke 12:34, 18:22.
236 1 Cor 2:9
237 Cf Rom 8:5.
238 Prov 15:15
239 Zech 5:7–8

ities of the body: there dwells the soul of the lecher, and in the wine cellars lives the soul of the drunkard. Do not such people live in holes in the earth like foxes and bears? Do they not roll in the muck like pigs? Do they not wriggle around in the mud like eels and crawl along the ground like slugs?

How can such people lift their souls up to heaven unless they become doves instead of foxes and pigs, so that flying up to the holes in the rock (for the rock is Christ),[240] they may find rest, they may find the true joy which they cannot find in themselves? The prophet, worn out by the burden of this body, longed to become a dove when he says in another psalm: 'Who will give me the wings of a dove and I may fly and find rest?'[241] Flying involves great effort, but it is followed by rest. It is hard for human nature to turn away from the things that produce present pleasure or torment to the love and hope of heavenly things; but unless you fly upwards you will not find rest, you will not have joy of heart. Everything contained by this visible world is lowly, everyone is lowly, and unless he flies above himself his soul will not be filled with joy. It is not enough to say that base pleasures and sordid gain are lowly things; even if you attain the heights of human dignity, human wisdom, human justice, these are all worthless, and they cannot gladden a man's soul unless it is raised up on high.

You may say, in the words of the Greek proverb: 'How can a donkey become a bird?'[242] It happens because the Lord draws us towards him so that we are raised up to him. He removes the burden of our sins, he attaches the wings of faith, bestows the fire of love and the longing of hope, and by these means the soul is transported up to the Lord. But Jeremiah teaches us the way when he writes: 'It is good for a man to bear the yoke from his youth. He will sit alone and be silent because he has raised himself above himself.'[243] At this point some people might think to themselves: 'What good is a yoke for flying? It forces things down rather than raising them up.' But the yoke of the Lord is so light[244] that it can even carry things up to heaven. And so anyone who desires to fly up to the Lord should throw off the yoke of Satan and this world and put on the yoke of Christ, which is comfortable and light, and he should do this from his youth, that is, when his childhood is past and he begins to make spiritual progress. For piety,

* * * * *

240 1 Cor 10:4, Song of Sol 2:14; cf the combination of these texts in *In psalmum 1* CWE 63 54 nn262, 264.
241 Ps 54:7/55:6; cf *Enchiridion* CWE 66 84.
242 *Adagia* III vii 24: *Asinus avis*
243 Lam 3:27–8
244 Cf Matt 11:30.

too, has a period of infancy, of adolescence, of youth, and of manhood, but it has no old age – for old age is the mark of sinners. However, he who has put off the old man and his way of life[245] regains his youth in Christ. He will sit – now that the desires of the flesh which weighed his soul down have been controlled. And he will sit alone – when he has rejected all those sources of protection which press themselves upon him and when he neither looks for help to his father or mother or wife or children or to princes or people in high office nor relies on the youthfulness of his body or his strength or his wealth, or the wisdom of this world or death or life, and finally not even on the saints or angels. He will sit in silence – not making murmurs of protest in adversity, not exulting in prosperity, but behaving in accordance with the words of the preceding verse written by the same prophet: 'He will wait in silence for the salvation of the Lord.'[246] You will say: 'How can an earthly creature do such a difficult thing?' Because he has raised himself above himself. With his feet he touches the earth, but his heart is with God. Let us pray to the Lord, my brothers, that he may transform those who cannot yet lift their souls to the Lord from reptiles into doves. He flew down from heaven, he crawled with us on earth so that he might make us birds of the air instead of creatures of the earth and might gradually lift our desires up towards heavenly things like an eagle encouraging its chicks to fly. He often prayed on the mountain, and it was on a mountain that he was transfigured; he was raised up on a cross and died closer to heaven; it was from a mountain that he was raised up to heaven. What is this but a challenge to his as yet unfledged chicks to fly? He sent the fiery spirit and thus transformed earthly creatures into fiery men, for fire always moves up towards heaven. How base, how stupid were the disciples before they raised themselves up above themselves! And how different they became, as the prophet Isaiah recognized when he said with admiration: 'Who are these who fly like a cloud and like doves to their windows?'[247] Do the letters of Peter or of Paul contain anything base, anything earthly? Their speech is pure flame, it flashes with lightning and its thunder resounds through the heavens. Roused by their example, we should entreat the Lord to draw our souls to him, so that with his assistance we may lift our souls to him and obtain true joy from him who is the source of all joy. As I said, let us lift up our souls to him, putting our confidence in his kindness, not in our own merits.

* * * * *

245 Cf Col 3:9.
246 Lam 3:26
247 Isa 60:8

That is why the psalmist added: 'For you, O Lord, are kind and gentle and show great mercy to all who call on you.' Gladden the soul of your servant, not because I deserve it, but because you are by nature kind and gentle. The Latin reading, *suavis*, is χρηστός in Greek, which signifies something like 'good,' 'obliging,' and 'generous.' The Latin reading, *mitis*, is ἐπιεικής in Greek, which you could translate as 'humane.' Similarly, when we read in the Gospel that the yoke of the Lord is easy, the Greek word is χρηστόν to distinguish it from the tyrannical yoke of Satan, which is heavy and uncomfortable. And ἐπιεικής is properly used of one who does not use his ultimate authority but rather acts in accordance with humane feelings. To take on the yoke of the Lord is to lift the soul up to the Lord, but no one can take on the yoke of God unless he has first thrown off the yoke of the devil, which pitifully oppresses those who are enslaved to sin. There is no reason to fear the yoke of the Lord: he is obliging and kind, and by granting charity he makes his commandments easy to bear and is fair and humane in his judgment of our deeds. He recognizes our inadequacies and forgives our weakness if we have been unable to raise up our hearts to him as far as we should; he gives assistance to our slender resources and pardons us for our indifference, giving support and relief while we make progress; he is not only kind and humane but also πολυέλεος, in other words, very merciful.

To be merciful means to forgive sins, but to be very merciful means also to enrich with spiritual grace those whose sins you have forgiven. Let us therefore in our weakness approach the Lord with confidence,[248] for he is kind and gentle; let us in our imperfection draw near to the Lord, who is humane and sympathetic to less serious faults; let us draw near in penitence to him who is great in his mercy – for this is the meaning of the Hebrew phrase that is translated 'very merciful' in the Septuagint. If you tremble at the extent of his power, think of the extent of his mercy. Just call on him, acknowledge your faults, and beg for forgiveness. He shows no partiality and is very merciful to all who call on him. The Jews attempted to exclude the gentiles from the grace of the gospel, for they did not recognize the greatness and the extent of the divine mercy; but the Lord has debarred no one from his grace, neither Jew nor Greek, neither Asian nor barbarian.[249] The Scythian called to him and he was heard; the Dane called to him and he was not rejected; the Spaniard called to him and he was granted access; the Irishman called to him and he experienced his mercy; the Indian cried out and he was heard; the Ethiopian cried out and his cry was heeded. Peoples

* * * * *

248 Cf Heb 4:16.
249 Cf Col 3:11, Rom 1:14, 10:12.

with such savage habits that you might wonder whether they are human beings or wild animals call on the name of the Lord and have experienced the abundance of his mercy. Nor is anyone debarred by sex or age from the mercy of the Lord, which was first restricted to the Jews but was later extended to all the nations of the earth. This is what the Lord prayed to the Father for as he was about to go to his sacrifice, that the name of the Lord should be invoked and that all men should experience his kindness, his humane character and his mercy, not only in the corner of the world which is Judea but in all nations throughout the world. Even today, anyone who invokes the name of the Lord is saved.[250]

Call on the Lord, in other words, as a servant recognize your master and call on him not only with your voice but also in your hearts. For he pays no attention to those who cry out 'Lord, Lord' with their lips but who express something very different in their heart. Moreover, the man who asks for something that is useless for eternal salvation is not calling on the Lord; he who asks for the death of his enemy does not call on the Lord, for he is demanding something that displeases the Lord. The Lord has commanded you to love your enemy – and do you seek his destruction? It is a bad servant who prescribes to his master what he should do. He who asks to be cured of his illness does not know whether he is calling on the Lord, seeing that he is not sure whether what he asks for is conducive to salvation. If the illness continues, he must not mutter: 'What has become of the Lord who is kind, humane, and most merciful to those who call upon him? Look how often I have called to him, but my cry has not been heeded.' If you have really called to him, you will be heard. You have not been granted what you asked for, but it is a sign of greater mercy to refuse than to grant what you wanted. The main aim of your prayers ought to be to possess the Lord himself, and so you have been granted what is more conducive to this aim. Let us call on the Lord with Christ and in Christ, who has taught us to pray, who has prayed for us, and who prays in us, as long as we are led by his spirit and are heeded by means of it. And if the granting of what we ask for is postponed, we should not immediately give up hope.

Let us imitate the importunate widow who is held up as an example to us in the Gospel.[251] We should imitate the man making his request at night, who by his insistence forces his neighbour to get out of bed and give him three loaves of bread.[252] Let us knock at the door again and again,

* * * * *

250 Cf Acts 2:21.
251 Luke 18:1–8
252 Luke 11:5–10

shouting out: 'Give ear, O Lord, to my prayer, and heed the words of my appeal.' This beggar cries out with greater confidence when he has reflected on the Lord's kindness, humane attitude, and great compassion. First of all he cried out: 'Incline your ear,' but now he has become bolder and prays that the Lord will allow his supplication to reach his ears and will not make light of it but show himself closely attentive to his prayer.

You can discern the tongue of the Scriptures speaking to men as if to a child, using certain human figures of speech. God inclines his ear when he does not reject our prayers; he is said to listen (or to give ear, if I follow the Greek word, which is ἐνώτισαι) when he deigns to bestow what we ask for; he pays close attention to our prayer when he bestows what is most conducive to our eternal salvation. When a man is asked for something, he sometimes gives it but later regrets that he gave it because it was harmful to the one who asked for it; but he who listens to prayers with close attention can judge the prayer of the one who is demanding something and make better provision for him than he can for himself.

People sometimes deign to listen to prayers but do not allow them to impinge on their thoughts; God's ear, however, is identical with his thoughts. And if they do admit the prayer into their thoughts, they then forget it, with the result that they have to be appealed to repeatedly; but God forgets nothing once he has heard it, although he is pleased by our appeals, not because he needs to be reminded but because our desire for him thereby increases. We should therefore ask for things that are worthy of him if we wish him to pay attention to our words. Many people ask God for things that they would not dare to ask for from a good human ruler, and yet they dare to say: 'Heed the words of my appeal.' This is not the way to earn compassion but to provoke the Lord's anger. If you pray for the destruction of your neighbour, your prayer is cruel – and yet you then beg the Lord to have mercy on you! How can you say to the Lord: 'For you are kind and gentle,' when you are so pitiless and harsh in your treatment of your brother? How can you hope to make the Lord favourably disposed if you offend him in trying to placate him? How will your sacrifice propitiate him if your sacrifice is sinful? How can you impudently demand that the Lord attend to your prayers when you are deaf to your neighbour's appeals? Or with what audacity do you ask him to give ear to your supplication when your ears are deaf to his commandments? Indeed, if we are to be able to ask for these things boldly, my brothers, and if our words are to be profitable, we must not move our eyes from our leader, Jesus Christ. He always listened attentively to the Father's orders, even to the point of death; his ears were always open to the cry of the wretched. Let us imitate him to the best of our ability, so that we may be heard with him. He cried out on the cross and he was heard. Let each of us also ascend his own cross and from it let us cry out to the Lord: 'In the day of suffering I cried out to you, for you have heard me.'

Notice how his confidence increases as he prays. In the preceding verse he proclaimed the kindness, the humane character, and the compassion of the Lord. How did he know about it? 'I have experienced it,' he says, and in another psalm he says: 'See and taste that the Lord is sweet.'[253] Once this poor man has experienced the Lord's kindness he appeals to it again with greater confidence; many people, however, do the opposite, for although they have experienced the Lord's goodness, they forget his kindnesses and turn elsewhere.

In the phrase 'the day of suffering' the Greek word is θλιψέως, which is sometimes translated 'pressure,' sometimes 'affliction.' We have already said that the whole of a man's life is one day and this is indeed a day of suffering. The church's translators were very fond of this word, for according to the Greek proverb, man's life really is full of thorns:[254] he is born of woman, lives for a short time, and is engulfed in many troubles.[255] After we have been driven from paradise and banished to this place of exile, what does our earth produce for us but thorns and spikes? Everywhere we are pricked by thorns, on all sides we are scratched. It is not only sufferings that are full of thorns: riches, too, have thorns of their own,[256] high office has thorns of its own, and pleasures also have thorns of their own. It was this life, so full of thorns, that the Lord took up for our sake: poor, mocked, harassed, and finally crowned with thorns, he took upon himself our thorns so as to restore us to paradise. He prayed at his baptism and he was heard. Do you want proofs of this? The heavens opened, the dove came down, the Father's voice was heard saying: 'This is my beloved Son.'[257] This was the beginning of his suffering. For what did Christ's life consist of subsequently, according to what you read? Fasting, wandering, nights spent in prayer, the task of teaching, thirst, hunger, weariness, insults that he endured, persecution, abuse, floggings, crucifixion. At the end he cried out and was heard. Similarly in St John's Gospel he says: 'Now my soul is troubled; and what shall I say? Father, save me from this hour. But it was for this purpose that

* * * * *

253 Ps 33:9/34:8
254 *Adagia* IV vii 56: *Victus spinosus*
255 Job 14:1
256 Cf Matt 13:22, Mark 4:19, and Luke 8:14.
257 Matt 3:16–7, Mark 1:10–11, and Luke 3:21–2

I have come to this hour. Father, glorify thy name.'[258] When you hear that his spirit was troubled, you know that this was a day of suffering, for he bore our griefs.[259] But he was heard, for it goes on: 'A voice came from heaven, "And I have glorified it and I shall glorify it again."'

Christ prayed after the mystical supper and he was heard: he prayed in the garden and he was heard, for the angels came and ministered to him;[260] he cried out on the altar of the cross;[261] and finally, he cried out as he gave up the ghost.[262] We notice here a kind of image of our own mass: there are prayers that precede the consecration, some that are performed during the sacred mysteries themselves, and some that bring the mysteries to an end. In the same way, when his sacrificial rite had been completed, Christ said: 'It is finished,'[263] and with his last words he cried out to the Lord, saying: 'Father, into your hands I commend my spirit.'[264] The sun, which withdrew its light from the world, the curtain in the temple, torn from top to bottom, the rocks, split open, the opened tombs, and the dead who came to life[265] witness to the fact that Christ was heard. And so, just as he is about to make this very last prayer he says: 'In the day of suffering I cried out to you, for you heard me when I cried before, knowing that you always hear me.'

But whatever the head did in this world, he did on behalf of his body, which is the church. He has shown it the way and given it an example to follow. Has not the church been afflicted with innumerable troubles? Has it not been battered by endless waves of persecution and repeatedly tested by torture and death? The cruelty of rulers, the stubborn wickedness of the Jews, the impiety of heretics, and the whole world have risen up against it and used every kind of device to attack it. But did the church, bearing in mind the Lord's example, resort to arms in its day of suffering? Did it rely on the support of kings? Or on the protection offered by philosophy? No, none of these. What then? In the day of suffering it cried out to the Lord – and its cry was heard, was it not? For what else did its brutal persecutors achieve but that the grace of the gospel and the glory of Jesus shone out over

* * * * *

258 John 12:27–8
259 Cf Isa 53:4–5.
260 Cf Matt 26:39–42, Mark 14:35–9, Luke 22:41–3.
261 Cf Matt 27:46, Mark 15:34.
262 See nn263 and 264 below.
263 John 19:30
264 Luke 23:46
265 Matt 27:51–3, Mark 15:38, Luke 23:45

a wider area? This was what those preachers of the gospel sought to achieve, and what they sought has been granted. The martyrs were put to death, but the gospel triumphed. Although there are not always men like Annas and Caiaphas or Nero and Diocletian, nevertheless, from the beginning of the world right until its end what St Paul wrote holds true: all who wish to live a godly life in Christ Jesus will suffer persecution.[266]

In short, each person has more than enough thorns of his own in this life. Amidst these thorns we must cry out to the Lord, not to Baal, not to magic tricks, and not to men, either living or dead. Let us cry out to him who is both more merciful and more powerful than anything else. He heard us when we cried out in the person of our head, when he set us free from the tyranny of Belial, and he will hear us again when we cry out, suffering for righteousness' sake, as long as we remain in him. He will transform our suffering into salvation for us and for many and into the glory of his name. We see the whole world subject to the gospel; we see that there is no nation where the trophy of the cross has not been set up and so, in accordance with God's wonderful plan, a great change in the world has been brought about by disgrace, by death, and by the apostles, who were few in number, of low status, and idiots in the eyes of the world.[267] The highest monarchs bow their heads at the name of Jesus; the idols of the pagans, together with their hordes of gods, have been laid low – what is better, they have been annihilated; all seek salvation from the one God. While preparing for his sacrifice Christ prayed that this might happen,[268] and even today all who are living members of Christ cry out that all nations may be reborn through Christ, they cry that out of love for him they may endure all things for the sake of righteousness and be crucified to this world[269] through Christ and that walking in newness of life[270] in the footsteps of Christ they may deserve to reign with him and be glorified.

'There is none like you among the gods, O Lord, and there are no works like yours.' He prayed for the conversion of the gentiles, and when his prayer had been heard, he said: 'There is none like you among the gods, O Lord.' By the light of your gospel the pagans will recognize the truth of this and will cast aside the objects of their blasphemous worship. For what

* * * * *

266 2 Tim 3:12
267 In *Adagia* III iii 1: *Sileni Alcibiadis* 'The Sileni of Alcibiades' Erasmus refers to the apostles as Sileni (CWE 34 265).
268 Conceivably a reference to Christ's discourse in John 17
269 Cf Gal 6:14.
270 Cf Rom 6:4.

are the gods of the pagans but abominable monsters? They worship snakes, crocodiles, bulls, and monkeys as their gods. What could be more insane? But even more ridiculous is the way in which they worship dumb stones and pieces of wood as gods, so that in comparison with these people, the behaviour of those who have conferred divine honours on certain humans seems excusable. But more abominable than all these practices is the fact that they venerate as gods wicked demons who are fraudulent and inimical to the human race. From such ancestors we are descended, from these abominable evils we have been delivered by Christ. Those who worship the sun and moon and the rest of the heavenly host as their gods certainly worship magnificent objects – but what about God who created them when they did not exist? Imagine a creature, however sublime, imagine powers and principalities, imagine the highest angel from the order of the seraphim – nothing created can be compared to the creator. The angels are God's assistants, serving in fear the majesty of him whose sublime nature is inconceivable to us. When the splendour of his great majesty appeared, all the fictitious names of the gods vanished, with good cause, and now the whole world cries out with one voice: 'There is none like you among the gods, O Lord.'

How is this evident? The facts themselves prove it, for he adds: 'And there are no works like yours.' The gods of the pagans are demons, but God made the heavens.[271] God's power, wisdom, and goodness shine forth for us everywhere in the things that he himself has created. Now this is the first step towards acknowledging God. Is not this world a marvellous piece of work? Does not great authority, power, goodness, and wisdom shine forth in this creation? In contemplating it, certain wise men of the world perceived God's strength and his everlasting divinity; how much more would they have perceived had they contemplated it with the eyes of faith! God made not only the heavens but also the angels – in short, nothing has been made which was not made by him.[272] How admirably he watches over and governs this creation of his, but how much greater an achievement it was to restore the human race! With what an incomprehensible plan he has redeemed, established, enriched, and promoted his church! God himself took on human nature, and by his death he reconciled men to God. Have the gods of the pagans done anything similar? They have deluded wretched men so that they might have companions in death, while God has healed all men with the truth that he revealed. They seduced men to wickedness,

* * * * *

271 Ps 95/96:5
272 Cf John 1:3.

while God has taken away the sins of the world. They plunged their followers into hell, while God has taken them up to heaven. What is the point
of seeking other gods when there is one who is so far superior to the rest
that there is none like him, neither in heaven nor on earth?

At this point, if we turn to consider contemporary rituals, it may be
true that we do not find any temples in which offerings of incense are made
to Jupiter, Mercury, or Venus, but I am afraid many people make sacrifices
to gods of this kind in their hearts, as if in temples. Whatever you value
more highly than God you have made your god, and in some way you
have denied the one true God. For if the bodies of good people are temples
of God, which Paul says must not be desecrated,[273] then the heart of an
avaricious man is a temple of Mammon, the body of a lustful person is a
temple of Venus, the heart of the ambitious person is a temple of Jupiter, the
heart of an astrologer is a temple of Apollo, the heart of one who lives a life
of idleness and luxury is a temple of Comus or, if you prefer, of Silenus.[274]
Whenever you disregard God's commands and comply with desires of this
kind you are offering a sacrifice, not to God but to the demons. There is no
reason for you to shudder when you hear such shocking words; your mind
should rather dread the thing itself, which is far more abominable. If at this
point someone should seriously wish to express the enormous difference
between things that the gods of our desires bestow on us and those that
our God grants, he will cry out with his whole soul: 'There is none like you
among the gods, O Lord, and there are no works like yours.'

If you seek honour, our God bestows everlasting glory. If you want to
gain power in government, he admits you to his kingdom, which will have
no end. Compare with this the things promised by that Jupiter of yours – if
he is capable of promising anything at all. He may promise wealth, but you
possess everything in him who alone is Lord of all. Similarly, what does
that Mercury of yours lead you to expect? He may promise oracular pronouncements, but you have Scripture, which has the most assured credibil-
ity, in which God speaks to you from his sanctuary whenever you wish. He
may promise pleasure, but God alone gives that complete joy which no one
can take away. Do Venus and Comus grant anything similar to those who
worship them? Brothers, to your devout selves one may speak the truth
frankly. What is the good of having cast out the gods from pagan temples if we make sacrifices to them in our hearts? There are many nominal
Christians who in fact worship demons.

* * * * *

273 1 Cor 3:16–17
274 Comus was a minor Greek god associated with drunkenness; Silenus the satyr
     was the foster-father and companion of Bacchus, the god of wine.

And so we must cast out, we must drive away the useless gods from our hearts and place all our confidence in the one God who made heaven and earth;[275] and mindful of the many kind gifts that he has lavishly bestowed on us, we must say, and say sincerely: 'There is none like you among the gods, O Lord, and there are no works like yours. All the nations that you have made will come and bow down before you, O Lord.'

The Jews worshipped at Jerusalem, the Samaritans on the mountains, while the pagans worshipped a number of different gods with countless different superstitions and rituals. But the death of Christ caused the name of the one true God to become known to all nations throughout the whole world. Not all men have believed in the gospel, but there is no country that has not received the teaching of Christ. Is it surprising that he who created all the nations should restore all the nations? In his kindness the creator did not allow his creation to be destroyed, but through the death of his Son he recreated what he had created through him. For by his word he created all things. He had made them in the first instance, but they turned away from their creator and worshipped what was created, setting it above him who created everything. He made them again, creating them once more by the word of life[276] so that they might be a new creation. The Jews crucified the Lord, thereby proclaiming themselves unworthy of the kingdom of God; their lack of faith opened the door to all nations so that people who had withdrawn from God by their impiety might approach by faith and worship him, paying no heed to their idols. They will all come – why do you protest, you malevolent Jew? All nations without distinction will come, for in the amplitude of the people lies the glory of the king.[277] He invites everyone to the wedding,[278] and he wishes his house to be filled with people summoned from everywhere. Previously they sang: 'Praise the Lord, O Jerusalem; praise your God, O Zion,'[279] but now the time for another psalm has come: 'Sing unto the Lord a new song. Sing to the Lord all the earth,'[280] and 'Praise him, all you peoples.'[281]

They will come, then, but only because they have been called; they will come, but because they have been brought there – for no one comes

* * * * *

275 Cf Isa 37:16.
276 Cf Phil 2:16.
277 Cf Prov 14:28.
278 Cf Matt 22:1–14.
279 Ps 147:12
280 Ps 95/96:1
281 Ps 116/117:1

to Christ unless he is brought by the Father. God first came to them so that they could come to him.[282] Where will they come from? From the dark depths of ignorance, from enslavement to demons, from the most immoral way of life. Where will they come? To the light of the gospel, to the worship of the true God, to the holiness of life. Where will they come? To Moses or to the cherubim or to the place of atonement? Certainly not. So where? To the home of their host, which is the church. Here they will be reborn in the sacred font, putting off the old nature with its practices and putting on the new one.[283] Here they will receive the Holy Spirit when the hands of the priests have been laid upon their heads, and so they will begin to speak with new tongues, not of their own acts of righteousness, which they do not have, but of God's wonderful works.[284]

The old tongue used to celebrate Jupiter, Mercury, and Bacchus; it used to shout: 'Great is the Diana of the Ephesians'[285] and hurl blasphemous utterances against the Lord and against his Christ. With the new tongue they will all with one accord glorify the name of the Lord, who will be the sole object of their veneration. Where? There is no specific place, but 'they will bow down before you, O Lord.' Formerly they used to prostrate themselves before dumb statues of Jupiter, asking for life from one who himself lacked life; they used to fall down before a crocodile, a serpent, or a bull, not having yet come to the light; but afterwards they will bow down before you, O Lord. What is the meaning of 'before you'? God is spirit, and the new worshippers worship him in the spirit.[286] God is in your heart: worship him there. The church has spread its tents, and instead of the small Jewish nation it has admitted all nations, and everywhere offerings are made to his name[287] – a pure sacrifice in the spirit, made not with slaughtered beasts but with repentant minds. When we read about the impious religions of our ancestors, we are shocked; abhorring the idols and their demons, we glorify the name of the Lord, whose power, wisdom, and goodness have delivered us from that most shameful servitude and admitted us into the kingdom of the Son of God. This is what our priest longed for, this is what he prayed for: that raised up from the earth he might draw everything to

* * * * *

282 Cf John 6:44.
283 Cf Tit 3:5, Col 3:9–10.
284 Cf Acts 2:4, 11; after the rebirth of baptism, the reference here is to the sacrament of confirmation.
285 Acts 19:28 and 34
286 Cf John 4:24.
287 Cf Mal 1:11.

himself and that out of the infinite diversity of errors might be made one shepherd and one flock.[288]

And not only will they worship the Lord but they will also worship in the Lord's presence, convinced as they are that there is nowhere where he is not present and contemplating him with the eyes of faith and with a pure heart – as far as it is possible to perceive him in this mortal life. But if you are to bow down before the Lord you must dispel from the mind all human fantasies arising from the senses. You can in no way describe or imagine what God is, he who alone is to be worshipped. When you have transcended all the heights of the angelic minds, you will still be infinitely far from the heights of God, who inhabits light inaccessible.[289] But when you worship him, you look upon a representation of God. You can look upon it, but see it as a piece of wood or stone, crafted by human hands. God is best seen with your eyes closed but with your heart raised up. I will not object if you gaze at the statue with the eyes of the body as long as your mind is with God, but it is a sign of gross insensitivity in a Christian if he cannot contemplate God except by means of a picture – if indeed it is possible to make any picture of God. A representation that gives a false impression is misleading. How far even a true likeness of someone is from being really representative of the person! Do you then demand a picture of God? (I am not saying this because I approve of the destructive behaviour of the iconoclasts but because I consider it to be more fitting for Christian churches not to contain numerous pictures of any kind whatever; instead churches should in general be unadorned and excite a feeling of devotion by their very plainness).[290]

Moreover, the act of worship has gestures of its own. The hands are clasped together and lifted up towards heaven, the knees are bent, kisses are given, and the posture of the whole body made to conform to a feeling of devotion. These things are done with propriety if they are also done within, if they are done before the Lord. If you pour forth words, you should at the same time pour out your heart before the Lord. But consider, my brothers, what great purity and reverence are needed if one is to worship in the sight of God; then consider how far removed from this feeling

* * * * *

288 Cf John 12:32, 10:16.
289 1 Tim 6:16
290 Cf *Modus orandi Deum* CWE 70 156; the iconoclasts to whom Erasmus refers here are the Protestant reformers of his time who believed that churches must be completely stripped of any ornamentation. On Erasmus' attitude, see Carlos M.N. Eire *War against the Idols* (Cambridge 1986) 28–53.

of devotion in worship they are who, while they stand during the act of divine worship or even next to the sacred altars, meditate on things that are not only trivial but also shameful and whose minds are as uncontrolled as their bodies. Such people do not yet belong to those peoples whom the Lord has made; although they bear the sign of God, they are still ignorant of the Lord and do not bow down before him. We must pray that the Lord will recreate these people, too, that they may come again with the others and together may bow down before the Lord and glorify his name.

For the psalm continues: 'They will glorify his name.' When the Jew in his pride boasts of his acts of righteousness, he is not glorifying God's name but his own. But since the gentiles had no merits of their own to mention and were called by grace away from great evils to become partners in the church, what else can they do but glorify the name of the Lord, to whose mercy they owe whatever they have? If they reflect on their own merits, they shudder at what they have deserved. When they reflect on the magnitude of the honour and happiness to which they are called without any merit on their part, they confess to the Lord that he is good and his mercy is everlasting.[291] Anyone who acknowledges the wretchedness of his own state and gives thanks for God's mercy is glorifying the name of the Lord. God does not wish man's salvation to be to man's glory but to his own, for he does not grant it to anyone else, as he himself says in the book of Isaiah.[292] And so, when they have received new tongues, they will sing the new song of God whose praise is in the assembly of the faithful.[293]

What song is this? 'For you are mighty and you do wonderful things; you alone are God.' Whatever this world contains, however sublime and exalted, is worthless, indeed it is nonexistent, in comparison with God. He alone by his very nature is truly great; he alone does wonderful things and he alone is truly good and truly holy. He created the world in a wonderful way, he restored it in a more wonderful way, and he will bring it to its end in the most wonderful way. He is wonderful not only in himself but also in his saints,[294] through whom he accomplishes whatever he wants by means of his immeasurable power and his inscrutable plan, to show that transcendent power belongs to God.[295] God alone has accomplished all that

* * * * *

291 Cf Ps 106/107:1.
292 Isa 42:8
293 Ps 149:1; cf Rev 5:9, 14:3.
294 Cf Ps 67:36 in the Vulgate rendering.
295 Cf 2 Cor 4:7.

he wished in heaven and on earth.[296] What miraculous things we see in animals, fountains, streams, trees, grass, precious stones, in the stars and the sun, and especially in man himself! God alone is the cause of all these. Whatever miracles have been proclaimed through the prophets, apostles, martyrs, or other saints have been achieved by God alone. What about the miracles performed by other gods? They are tricks and shams – pure fraud, if you consider them more closely. Indeed, whatever miracles they perform before men are undoubtedly harmful, but God's miracles are beneficial to men. Magicians appeared to turn a rod into a serpent,[297] but does not God every day miraculously transform many things for man's benefit, as when he makes a tree from a tiny seed or creates human beings and other creatures from a small amount of fluid? It is no great miracle to turn a rod into a serpent or to make a camel out of a flea;[298] the greatest miracle is to transform an impious and idolatrous man into a devout worshipper of God. There is nothing miraculous about destroying some city or other with missiles, but it was a great miracle to renew the whole world by the word alone for the religion of the gospel. What man or god could have done this?

When they have given due consideration to these things, the people say with one accord: 'You alone are God.' (Augustine reads 'You alone are mighty,' no doubt with devout intentions but misled by a textual error.)[299] This is the new tongue you are hearing. Earlier the psalmist said: 'There is none like you among the gods, O Lord, and there are no works like yours.' There he gives precedence to God, but he still mentions other gods, too. Here, after his attention has been drawn to God's many miracles, he confesses openly: 'You alone are God.' The wording of these verses represents for us the steps of progress. At first the pagans laughed at the preaching of the gospel, which Paul refers to as 'folly to the gentiles,'[300] but when they saw that by invoking the name of Jesus the poor and humble apostles

* * * * *

296 Cf Ps 134/135:6.
297 Exod 7:11–12
298 Cf Matt 23:24.
299 Augustine, in writing his *Enarrationes*, was using a different text of the Psalms from the one which later became the accepted version in the Vulgate. In *Enarratio in psalmum 85* 14 (on verse 10) CCL 39 1187–8 the text he used here, 'tu es Deus solus magnus,' is the same as that found in two early psalters, the Verona Psalter and the Psalter of Saint-Germain; see R.Weber *Le Psautier Romain et les autres anciens Psautiers* (Rome 1953) and CWE 63 xxi. Erasmus mentions the existence of different versions of the psalms in Ep 456:98–102.
300 1 Cor 1:23

were able to defeat demons, get rid of incurable illnesses, and bring the dead back to life – things which the gods and their prophets, magicians, and seers were unable to do – they said in fear: 'Who is like you among the gods, O Lord?' This was the beginning of a change of mind. Then when they learned in the catechism that Father, Son, and Holy Spirit form the one and only true God and there is no other apart from him, in heaven or on earth, they repudiated their former gods, cursed their statues, abandoned their shrines, and ran to the church, where, on receiving the gift of tongues, they confess: 'For you alone are God.'

In this way the head of the church glorified the Father: 'that they might recognize you as the only true God and Jesus Christ whom you sent.'[301] The Jew acknowledges the Father but denies the Son and refuses to worship the Holy Spirit; he therefore does not say: 'You alone are God' but mutilates God. Similarly Arius, in making the Son and Holy Spirit a created being, tears the divine being apart, although it cannot be divided up.[302] Where God is, there the whole Trinity is, but Sabellius fails to maintain the distinctions in it and Arius chops it up.[303]The church, however, has been taught to distinguish between the persons of the Trinity but not to pull to pieces the divine nature, which cannot be cut up, and so it cries out with Christ: 'You alone are God.' Although I believe that this confession is made by all who are reborn in Christ, nevertheless no one can honestly say: 'You alone are God,' if he values man more than God or if he loves something in such a way that in his eagerness to obtain it he fails to observe God's commands. A man who is obsessed with a prostitute has found for himself another god; if the same man is a slave to drink or to pride and the other sins, how can he dare to say: 'You alone are God,' since he is enslaved to several gods?

* * * * *

301 John 17:3
302 Arius (256–336) believed that the second and third persons of the Trinity were created and denied that Christ was divine and that the Son was of one substance with the Father. Cf Erasmus *In psalmum 1* CWE 63 16–17 and *Explanatio symboli* CWE 70 344–5.
303 Sabellius, in the third century, stressed the unity of the three persons of the Trinity. This view, while protecting the oneness of God against the charge that Christians worshipped more than one God, was regarded as refusing sufficient reality to the Son's individual divine existence. In his poem 'Concerning his own life,' written at the height of the Christological controversies of the fourth century, Gregory of Nazianzus defines the Sabellians and Arians thus: 'Some merge the Trinity, which cannot be made to coalesce, or take apart the nature which cannot be divided'; *De Vita Sua* 1176–7 trans Carolinne White in *Gregory of Nazianzus, Autobiographical Poems* (Cambridge 1996).

This psalm appears to conflict with an earlier one, namely Psalm 82, for there he prays for the destruction of all the nations, while in this one he pleads the cause of all nations. But if we look more closely, we shall see that he is praying for the same thing in both cases, for the nations could not glorify God if the wicked peoples had not first been put to death. For God puts to death in such a way that he restores to life.[304] He puts an impious man to death and raises up a pious man, in the same way as he brought Saul to the ground and raised up Paul, put the wolf to death and raised up a shepherd of the flock.[305] For in baptism our old nature dies and a new one arises.[306] Furthermore, the names of those enemies, Moab, Agar, Gebal, Ammon, Amelech, and the others mentioned in that psalm,[307] exist in our hearts, for they evidently represent impious desires; when they have been destroyed, the nations glorify God. The Lord seeks to destroy such impious feelings by praying: 'My God, make them like whirling dust and like chaff before the wind; like fire that consumes the forest, like the flame consuming the mountains. Pursue them thus in your storm.'[308] It is a harsh prayer, but listen to the positive outcome: 'Fill their faces with shame.' Why? So that they might die in disgrace? No. What then? 'And they will seek your name, O Lord.'[309]

The first words spoken in the Gospels are: 'Repent, for the kingdom of heaven is at hand,'[310] and 'The axe is laid to the root of the tree,'[311] and 'The wrath of God is revealed from heaven against all unrighteousness.'[312] They were terrified, then they were taught, then they became ashamed and came to their senses. This applies to the Romans, to whom Paul writes: 'But then what did you gain from the things of which you are now ashamed?'[313] This proves that these threats are not aimed at destruction but at salvation. But what follows is harsher. 'Let them be put to shame and dismayed for ever, and let them be ruined and destroyed.[314] May their impiety be destroyed and may they come to their senses and acknowledge that your name is Lord

* * * * *

304 Cf Deut 32:39, 1 Cor 15:36.
305 Acts 9:1–9
306 Cf Rom 6:4.
307 Ps 82:7–9/83:6–8
308 Ps 82:14–16/83:13–15
309 Ps 82:17/83:16
310 Matt 3:2
311 Luke 3:9
312 Rom 1:18
313 Rom 6:21
314 Ps 82:18/83:17

and that you alone are the most high over all the earth.[315] God puts to death in such a way that he is really a kindly murderer, in the words of the Greek proverb.[316] To be put to death by him is to be brought to life.

We have here an account of the beginnings of the church, which started with the Jews, and also an account of its expansion, when the nations everywhere flocked to it. Now he prays for progress, that the church might stand firm in faith and love and might ever progress towards better things. He has redeemed and cleansed his bride,[317] but without God's protection no one is able to stand firm in what is good, unless God's grace, which has called the undeserving, directs and guides those who have been called. The bitter struggle against the powers of the air, against the princes of this world,[318] against the unbelieving and stubborn continues. On all sides they are harassed by terrifying things or seduced from the path of truth by attractive things. He prays, therefore, for Peter, in other words, for the church, to prevent its faith growing weak: 'Lead me, O Lord, in your way, and I shall walk in your truth.'

By means of faith and baptism they have been led away from their wicked ways and brought to the path that leads to life. What remains? For them to progress along the way of the Lord. If we are to take the first steps along this path we need grace to lead us; if we are to proceed along it diligently, we need grace to accompany us. Christ is the door, and through him we enter on this path. He is also the path which leads to life: it is admittedly a narrow one, but it is also very safe and short.[319] The pagans have been led to it in a miraculous way; they have died to their sins and risen with Christ, and it remains for them to walk in newness of life[320] according to his teaching and his example.

Faith is not something ineffectual: if it is a living faith, it works through love; if it does not result in good deeds, it is dead and is not worthy of the name of faith. So let no one say: 'I have been justified by grace,[321] I have been grafted on to the members of Christ, I will be saved.' You have been grafted on, but so that you should bear fruit, not out of

* * * * *

315 Ps 82:19/83:18
316 *Adagia* III ii 7: *Benevolus trucidator*
317 Cf Eph 5:25–7.
318 Cf Eph 6:12.
319 Cf John 10:7 and 9, 14:6, Matt 7:13–14.
320 Cf Rom 6:2–4.
321 Cf Rom 3:24.

yourself but out of the sap of the root.[322] Grace has brought you back
to the path from the error which led you astray, but why should it be
called a path if it does not lead you anywhere? How can it take you anywhere if you do not walk along it? We have no home in this world, for
we are on a journey. But if you are to walk on the path of the Lord, you
need his grace to lead you, you need the grace which came first also to accompany you until you reach life.[323] Unless you bear fruit when you are
grafted on to Christ, take care that you are not cut out. The Lord threatens this in St John's Gospel when he says: 'The Father will remove every branch of mine that bears no fruit.'[324] You have been made a good
tree, but it remains for you to produce good fruit, for the fig tree which
was covered with leaves but bore no fruit was cursed by the Lord.[325] As
long as the gentiles were carnal, they produced carnal fruit; once they
have drawn in the spirit of Christ, they produce the fruit of the spirit.
For the fruits are good works, by means of which a tree is judged to
be good.

The Pelagian ascribes this fruit to free will set free by grace once and
for all,[326] and he refuses to sing this verse: 'Lead me, O Lord, in your way.'
The law reveals the path, the law lights the way for the traveller, according
to the psalm which says: 'Your word is a lantern to my feet,'[327] but grace
enables you to proceed along the path. Who granted this if not he who
said in the Gospel: 'Without me you can do nothing'?[328] If you begin to
have confidence in your own resources and fail to consider grace, you have
already left the path, for Christ himself is the way,[329] and whoever remains
in him proceeds without danger along the way of the Lord. What he prays

* * * * *

322 Cf John 15:1–6, Rom 11:17–24; see also *In psalmum* 4 CWE 63 258–9, where
   Erasmus uses the image of the fruit tree of which faith is the root.
323 This form of grace, termed prevenient grace, is believed to precede the free determination of the will: it can be rejected, but without it no spiritual progress
   is possible.
324 John 15:2
325 Matt 21:18–9, Mark 11:13–4.
326 Pelagius (c 350–c 425) believed that God's grace was a natural gift possessed
   by every individual. His views were combatted by Augustine and Jerome,
   among others. The Reformers of Erasmus' time often view as Pelagian the
   Catholic church's apparent belief that man could gain salvation by means of
   good works.
327 Ps 118/119:105
328 John 15:5
329 Cf John 14:6.

for in this passage he prays for also in St John's Gospel, although there he uses different words: 'Holy Father, keep those in my name whom you have given me, that they may be one just as we are one.'[330]

So many people slip from the way of the Lord and fall back into their former errors even after they have repented.[331] To prevent this happening to any of us, each one must cry out: 'Lead me, O Lord in your way.' For blessed are they whose way is blameless, who walk in the law of the Lord.[332] Your way is hedged in by the Lord's precepts: do not turn off to the right or the left.[333] The perfection of the gospel made this path narrower, but do not be deterred by the narrowness of the path, for it has been widened by grace and your heart has been enlarged[334] to allow you to enter on it and even to run eagerly along this path, as it says in Psalm 118: 'I have run the path of your commandments, when you enlarged my heart.'[335]

In the psalm under discussion, the word 'enter' is not used as if some-one outside is entering a house or someone undertaking a journey is tak-ing the first steps along the road – this would be εἰσελθεῖν or εἰσέρχεσθαι in Greek – but it is used as a synonym for 'walk,' for the Greek manuscripts have the word πορεύσομαι which means: 'I shall move on.'

Impiety also has a path of its own, along which it is dangerous to walk, but it is more dangerous to stop along it and most dangerous of all to sit down, as we see from the first psalm.[336] Again, one must not stop or sit on the path of the Lord, but must either walk or run along it. People of average goodness walk along it and gradually progress towards a bet-ter state, while those who are perfect run along it, and this is what Paul was encouraging his readers to do when he wrote: 'So run that you may obtain it.'[337] He showed himself to be such a person when he said: 'I have finished the race.'[338] But in this psalm, concerned as it is with the begin-nings of the church, the prophet uses the language of modest achievement, not of perfection. For as regards Christ, clearly he was the most energetic of

* * * * *

330 John 17:11
331 On the idea of progress in the way of the Lord, see also Erasmus *In psalmum* 14 LB V 301–2.
332 Ps 118/119:1
333 Cf Prov 4:27.
334 Cf 2 Cor 6:11.
335 Ps 118/119:32
336 Ps 1:1; see *In psalmum* 1 CWE 63 19. This psalm is also cited in a similar context in Erasmus' commentary on Psalm 14 LB V 301D.
337 1 Cor 9:24
338 2 Tim 4:7

all runners on this course, as we are told in Psalm 38:[339] 'Like a strong man he rejoiced to run the course.' We must walk, my brothers, along the narrow path if we cannot yet run, always striving to remove vices and add to our virtues until we become agile runners and even, if possible, fast ones. With Christ as our leader and our protector, we must not give up hope of anything.[340] Do not look round at your own resources lest the steep drop down on either side make you dizzy; keep your eyes on your guide so that you may walk safely.

Furthermore, what Christ prayed for on behalf of the church, the church prays for every day on behalf of its own sons whom it brings forth for Christ: 'Lead me, O Lord, in your way.' No one must say to free will: 'Lead me in the way of the Lord'; no one must say to human wisdom, which is the work of men: 'Lead me in the way of the Lord.' You must say to the Lord himself: 'Lead me' – not in the ways of men but 'in your way.' This way alone knows no error. The ways of the philosophers are many and varied, and so are those of the Jews and heretics, but there is only one way to salvation – and that is the way not of man but of God. Similarly there is a human truth, but it is not reliable and often misleads because of the errors it contains, while the truth of the Lord that endures for ever is unique. If you agree to be my guide I shall walk in your truth, proceeding by faith and hope, for in these two lie God's truth; we believe in his words and hope for what he has promised – with regard to both things he alone is trustworthy.

He who lives according to the gospel teachings, trusting in the gospel promises, and who does not put his hope in this life but in the life to come proceeds without fear in the truth of God. For there is no risk of the teaching containing falsehood or of the promises being empty. Walk without fear, do what is good unceasingly. You have a teacher who does not lead you astray and is not himself led astray; you have someone to reward you who cannot refuse to give himself, since he is by nature the truth. Admittedly, the attempt to achieve a virtuous life does contain some bitterness at the beginning, while sinful habits try again and again to take control once more and while the flesh wars against the spirit,[341] but that most merciful guide alleviates this distress with spiritual consolation, inspiring us with the eagerness of a good conscience, which not only prevents us from

* * * * *

339 Both LB and ASD contain the erroneous reference to Ps 38, based on an error in the original 1528 edition; in fact this phrase comes from Ps 18:6/19:5.
340 Cf *Adagia* II v 100: *Mopso Nysa datur* 'Nisa is Mopsus' bride.'
341 Cf Gal 5:17.

becoming dissatisfied and sick of life but also enables us to live out our lives in joy.

The psalm continues: 'May my heart rejoice so as to fear your name.' On the face of it these words have a rather absurd meaning if they are taken in the normal way. For who rejoices so that he might fear, seeing that joy and fear are opposites? Joy expands the soul, fear constricts it, and if one emotion is produced by the other, joy is surely born from fear, not fear from joy, seeing that fear of the Lord is the beginning of wisdom.[342] But the Greek text gives this sense instead: 'May my heart rejoice in that it fears your name': εὐφρανθήτω ἡ καρδία μου τοῦ φοβεῖσθαι τὸ ὄνομά σου. Previously the gentiles used to sin with impunity, as it were, because they did not fear the Lord, partly because they did not know him, partly because they rejected him with scorn. Then when the gospel had revealed God's justice towards all impiety they learned to fear the name of the Lord, and by means of this fear they came to their senses and led a reformed life, following God's commandments. And just as a man rejoices after taking unpleasant medicine because he has been restored to health, so the sinner rejoices when fear of the Lord drives him to lead a life of purity. What then does Christ our priest pray for? That the joy of a good conscience might succeed the sorrow of repentance.

I must make it clear to you that the Latin word *deduc* is ὁδήγησον in Greek, which really refers to someone who is a leader or guide on a journey. For the Latin word *deduco* has a double meaning. Sometimes it is used of the person who out of courtesy accompanies his guest or friend when he sets off somewhere. But St Jerome, following the original Hebrew text, translates it in this way: 'Teach me, O Lord, your way.'[343] Let no one be shocked at the use of different words, for this actually serves to clarify our understanding to some degree. The meaning is in fact the same in both cases.

Observe, my dear friends, how the order is beautifully preserved. The first step to salvation is to recognize God's power from created things and from miracles and thereby to come to fear him, since he is the avenger of wrongs. That is why the psalmist says: 'There is none like you among the gods, O Lord,' and then: 'You alone are God.' The Jews proclaim these words with us, and anyone who has learned that there is only one God and

* * * * *

342 Cf Ps 110/111:10.
343 This version of verse 11 was given by Jerome only in his *Psalterium iuxta Hebraeos* PL 28 (1890) 1258B.

that he is the creator, ruler, and judge of all things both on earth and in heaven has made some progress. The next step is catechism, baptism, and dedication to a life of fighting for Christ, for these things are so to speak the basics of our religion. But the teaching is of two kinds: there is the more simple one, contained in a few articles and passed on to the catechumens; and there is the more perfect kind, which is revealed to those who have already been initiated. This more perfect kind consists of two parts, one of which reveals some of the secret mysteries of the Christian philosophy, while the other prescribes a pattern of life. For mother church has a milk of her own with which she nourishes infants and she also provides solid food to those who are already mature in Christ.[344]

Is it my imagination or does St Matthew's Gospel declare this explicitly? 'Go therefore and teach all nations, baptizing them in the name of the Father and of the Son and of the Holy Spirit, teaching them to observe all that I have commanded you.'[345] Does this passage not tell you of both kinds of teaching, the one before baptism, the other, which involves keeping the commandments, after baptism? There is no doubt that the Gospel is referring to those who are mature. Now since the ancient authority of the church allows infants, who can be dipped into water but who cannot yet be taught, to be baptized,[346] I wish that after baptism they would at least learn those things which it is an offence for a Christian not to know. In fact, this secondary teaching must never be neglected, but one must always advance along it, as also in performing good works and in the practice of piety. Now error has been cast away, now the first lessons of faith have been given. After this the path is revealed which, if we follow Christ's example, leads to life, and we are brought to this path when our head begs on our behalf: 'Teach me, O Lord, your way.'

We are now standing on the second step. What remains but for us to walk according to what we have learned, advancing from understanding to understanding, from virtue to virtue? This is the third step in the progress of those who are at last beginning to find the yoke of the Lord pleasant, although in the beginning it seemed rather harsh; and they say: 'May my heart rejoice because it fears your name.' They have at last

* * * * *

344 Cf 1 Cor 3:1–2.
345 Matt 28:19–20
346 Erasmus discusses the tradition of infant baptism in his commentary on Psalm 83 (*De concordia*) LB V 505B and in the colloquy *Convivium Religiosum* CWE 39 196 and n221. Cf Augustine *De baptismo* 4.24 CSEL 51 259.

reached such a point of perfection that they can rejoice with Paul even in their sufferings,[347] because God has considered them worthy of this honour: that they might suffer reproach for the name of Jesus.[348] This is the fourth step along the way and belongs to those who are perfect. Such were those whose piety Paul praised when he said: 'You joyfully accepted the plundering of your property, since you knew that you had a better possession and an abiding one.'[349] It is this state that St James encourages us to achieve when he writes: 'Count it all joy, my brothers, when you encounter many different temptations.'[350] Indeed, even the Lord himself tells his disciples in the Gospel to rejoice and be glad when they are persecuted.[351] How can there be joy in such a grim situation? Because of one's confident expectation of future reward, 'for your reward is great in heaven.'[352]

It should also be noted that it was said: 'May my heart rejoice.' Not all joy is joy of the heart. In anger there is a joy that comes from vengeance, in lust there is a joy dependent on the shameful act, in the stomach there is a joy that comes from indulgence, and in the eyes there is a joy deriving from privileges conferred; but no one possesses joy of the heart unless he fears the name of the Lord. Indeed, no one has a heart unless he fears this name. How can someone who has no heart possess joy of the heart? Such were the people whom the Lord addresses through Jeremiah: 'Hear, you foolish people who have no heart,'[353] and again through Hosea: 'Ephraim has become like a dove that has gone astray and has no heart.'[354] Some people return to their own vomit[355] and cast off the fear of the Lord, but far from this evil are those who rejoice because they have conceived a fear of the Lord as a result of a gift from heaven. Who are they who praise the Lord, if not those who fear the Lord, according to Psalm 21?[356]

It is certainly true, as St John writes in his epistle, that love drives out fear,[357] and there is equal truth in what is said in Psalm 18: 'The fear

* * * * *

347 Cf 2 Cor 7:4, 12:10.
348 Cf 1 Pet 4:14.
349 Heb 10:34
350 James 1:2
351 Cf Matt 5:11–12, Luke 6:22–3.
352 Matt 5:12, Luke 6:23
353 Jer 5:21
354 Hos 7:11
355 Cf Prov 26:11 and 2 Pet 2:22.
356 Ps 21:24/22:23
357 1 John 4:18

of the Lord is holy, enduring for ever and ever.'[358] In fact, there is a fear that is called servile, which restrains a man from sin but in such a way that the soul says: 'I would do it if I could do it with impunity.' A bad slave fears the rod rather than his master. And yet even this implies some kind of progress in correcting one's way of life. But this fear is driven out by love, which leads us to do what God commands eagerly and willingly, no longer from a fear of hell but from love of God. First is what is natural, then comes what is spiritual.[359] But holy fear, the fear that combines a kind of reverence with love and brings it about that if possible we do not wish to offend our gracious Lord even in the smallest matters, endures for ever and ever. From this fear a spirit is conceived, and the more it flourishes in us, the more that dismal dread, the fear that is anxious rather than holy, vanishes. But sons who have conceived the spirit of love[360] know how to exult with trembling, and the more passionately they love the Father, the more they fear to offend him. The teacher withdraws when the rational faculties have been sharpened and can persuade the will what must be done more effectively than the teacher himself could do by coercion.

However at this point there is something of a discrepancy between the original Hebrew text and what is sung by both the Latin church and the Greek one. Instead of 'May my heart rejoice,' Jerome gives the translation 'Make my heart one,' while others believe the reading to be 'Unite my heart.'[361] With regard to the physical nature of the body, nothing is more compact and, so to speak, more united than the heart of a living creature; it is gathered up in to a mass of fibres folded back on themselves. No animal has more than one heart. But with regard to the tropological sense, are there not many people who have a number of hearts, and many whose hearts are torn in two and pulled apart? Those who are said by Scripture to have spoken with double heart did not have one heart.[362] Those who used to say: 'I belong to Apollo, I belong to Cephas, I belong to Paul, I belong to Christ,'[363] did not have a unified heart. The heretics who agree neither with the church nor among themselves do not have one either. Those who make

* * * * *

358 Ps 18:10 / 19:9
359 Cf 1 Cor 15:46.
360 Cf 2 Tim 1:7.
361 Although Jerome gives the version 'May my heart rejoice' in the Roman and Gallican psalters, in his *Psalterium iuxta Hebraeos* PL 28 (1890) 1258B he gives the version 'Make my heart one.'
362 Ps 11:3 / 12:2
363 1 Cor 1:12

pretence of piety in their words and actions, although inside they are very different, do not have a unified heart, nor do people who are distracted by the cares of this world and who worry about wealth, about pleasures, about their status: their interests are divided and they are distracted in their hearts, as Paul said with reference to the married woman.[364]

But how can a heart of this kind become unified? Fear of the Lord acts as a bonding agent by means of which the sinner returns to his senses and pulls himself together. An animal will by nature contract itself when it experiences fear. The joys of the flesh are driven out so that the joy of the spirit can take their place. Our heart is not capable of holding this joy unless it becomes a single unit, restored to unity and made to cohere in the simplicity of the spirit, after rejecting a multiplicity of gods, many and various desires, different philosophical theories, the vast number of heretical beliefs, disputes, and sources of discord, a faith that vacillates, and the distraction of worldly cares. All this is a gift from God: he causes our heart to contract through fear of him and causes it to expand with love of him. If you confess your sins and do not hope for grace except from God alone, then you have a heart that is single and unified. It was a heart of this kind that David, who had earlier been divided in his heart when he dealt deceitfully with Uriah, when he devised his death by trickery, and when he gave his heart to another man's wife, prayed for.[365] He says: 'Create in me a clean heart.'[366] What joy can there be in an unclean heart? No heart is clean unless God has created it, and he creates by means of his spirit, to which one of the psalms refers when it says: 'Send forth your spirit and they will be created.'[367] Those who have one spirit have also one heart; the church has many different gifts but in one and the same spirit.[368]

God speaks to the unified heart in order to gladden it, for in the book of Hosea he says: 'I shall speak to her heart, and she shall sing according to the days of her youth.'[369] Jerusalem, our mother, speaks to the unified heart, and this is the kind of heart that the Lord promises to his people, according to Jeremiah chapter 32: 'I shall give them one heart and one way that they may fear me for ever.'[370] He makes the same promise in Ezekiel,

* * * * *

364 1 Cor 7:34
365 2 Sam 11
366 Ps 50:12/51:10
367 Ps 103/104:30
368 Cf 1 Cor 12:14.
369 Hos 2:14–5
370 Jer 32:39

chapter 11, when he says: 'I shall give them one heart and put a new spirit within them.'[371] St Paul exhorts his readers with a very vehement appeal to unify their hearts: 'So if there is any consolation in Christ Jesus, any comfort in love, if there is any participation in the spirit, any sincere compassion, complete my joy so that you may be of one mind, having the same love, being in full accord and of one mind.'[372]

And so he who unites the heart also makes it one; he who cleans the heart also makes it rejoice. This is why he prays: 'May my heart rejoice.' Our head, who joyfully brought back the lost sheep on his shoulders and was more pleased about the one that was recovered than about the ninety-nine that had not gone astray,[373] prays for this. Mother church, whose greatest joy is to see her children walking in the truth[374] and working out their salvation in fear of the Lord,[375] prays for the same thing. The church desires peace, and when the believers have one heart and one soul,[376] then the church is filled with the joy of a united heart. Even ordinary people call those who are in this state united and like-minded. Is not the most pleasurable fear that which makes us not fear anything? If you fear God, there is no reason for you to fear Satan or hell; if you truly fear God, you will not fear what man may do to you, you will not fear poverty, bereavement, exile, or even death. Only one thing is to be feared with joy, lest we fear many things with sorrow.

People who ask somebody for something usually promise to do some favour in return so that they may obtain more easily what they desire. But this poor man who demands so many things – that God should incline his ear, that his soul be protected, that his soul be made joyful, that he be guided along the path – what on earth can he promise in return for all this? What can he promise to one who lacks nothing? He can only promise a sacrifice of praise, which the Lord delights in, not because we can add anything to his glory but because we are made better by praising him. 'I shall praise you, O Lord God, with my whole heart, and I shall glorify your name for ever.' If you preserve my soul so that it is not swallowed up by death, and if through resurrection you make the soul of your servant rejoice, I shall make you an offering of praise before all the nations,

* * * * *

371 Ezek 11:19
372 Phil 2:1–2
373 Cf Luke 15:3–7.
374 2 John 4
375 Cf Phil 2:12.
376 Acts 4:32

and I shall do this with all my heart, not just with my lips, and I shall glorify your name for ever. For I shall not ascribe to myself any of the things that you wanted to be done through me, but I shall transfer all glory to your name; just as the church will have no end, so I shall never cease to praise your glory. By my death and resurrection you wished your name to become well known to all nations. You wish your ineffable mercy to be recognized by all, and you desire to be glorified by men for your mercy. When I have returned from hell, been delivered from the hands of the Jews, and brought back to life from death, and when Satan has been overthrown, I shall praise you, because 'great is your mercy towards me, and you have delivered my soul from the lower regions of hell.' The more notorious their cruelty, the more famous will your mercy be; the more terrible the danger, the more celebrated the kindness of the one who saved us. 'You have snatched my soul from the lower regions of hell.' Here you are being told of extreme suffering from which no one can be delivered except by God's mercy, his great mercy. For where sin abounded, there grace also abounded.[377]

With regard to Christ our head, at the time when the Lord's body was lying lifeless in the tomb his soul descended into hell, and when he had put an end to death's dominion he preached the gospel to the spirits imprisoned there,[378] announcing to them that by his death he had overthrown Satan and opened the way to heaven. They had believed that this would happen and by their faith in this they had lived, by their expectation of this they had died, and by their hope they had been nourished in hell, longing to see the Christ of the Lord. They saw and were glad.[379] There was no redemption in hell before the arrival of that soul over which the prince of this world had no power whatsoever.[380] Tartarus opened its jaws in the belief that some plunder was on its way, but instead of plunder there came a plunderer who entered the home of the strong man and plundered his goods.[381] And so the song is reversed: those who sat in darkness and in the shadow of death have been gladdened by a new light[382] and acknowledge the one redeemer, saying: 'For the Lord has mercy, and with him is abundant redemption.'[383]

* * * * *

377 Rom 5:20
378 1 Pet 3:19
379 Cf John 8:56.
380 Cf John 12:31, 14:30, 16:11.
381 Cf Matt 12:29, Mark 3:27.
382 Luke 1:79, Isa 9:2; cf Ps 106/107:10.
383 Ps 129/130:7

Never had a soul like it descended to this kingdom: all other souls were held prisoner, although not in equal hope or in the same condition. Just as the Lord came down in the form of a body to us who are clothed with bodies, so also he descended to the spirits in the form of a spirit. In this world it seemed that death had swallowed up his body once it was hidden in the tomb, and yet death was unable to hold it fast; the monster spewed our Jonah up again on the third day[384] – in fact it found it so impossible to hold fast him whom it had swallowed that it was actually forced by the one body to spew up many bodies once more. In the same way, the soul descended into hell, the prison of death from which no one was allowed to return, but so impossible was it to keep him prisoner that when he ascended from there he actually took captivity captive with him.[385] This was not as a result of human strength but of divine mercy. You see how powerful fear of the Lord is, since it makes us not even fear hell!

And so, in accordance with the human nature he has adopted, Christ gives thanks to God the Father, by whose power the kingdom of hell was conquered. For Christ is reporting what he knows will definitely happen in the future as if it had already taken place. He sometimes sees with prophetic sight things that will occur in the distant future as if they have happened or are taking place in the present. And so it is the case that in the divine writings things that are to happen in the future are occasionally reported as if they are happening now or have already happened. With the eyes of faith we perceive Christ returning from hell in triumph, but the psalmist saw this with prophetic sight as if it had taken place, for it was so inevitable that it might as well already have happened.

It was a great achievement to be snatched out of hell, but he seems to be revealing something greater when he says 'from the lower regions of hell.' Certainly it is not without reason that the words 'from the lower regions' are added. St Augustine got into difficulties at this point[386] and begged his readers to pardon him for not putting forward more definite explanations of problems that bore no easy solution. He says it is very difficult to give a definite explanation of things that we have not seen ourselves and that the Scriptures do not provide us with a clear account of. None of us has spent any time in hell, so I cannot be accused of lying – nor could I obtain more reliable information from anyone else! And yet difficult passages like this one are very common in the Bible; one must avoid

* * * * *

384 Cf Jon 2:10, Matt 12:40.
385 Eph 4:8, where Paul quotes Ps 67:19/68:18
386 *Enarratio in psalmum 85* 17–18 (on verses 12–13) CCL 39 1189–91

rash pronouncements, but a painstaking investigation is justified. And so you must please forgive me, just as Augustine's audience, barbarian though they were, forgave that great man.

It is not absurd to believe that hell is divided into three regions:[387] one which, before the coming of Christ, held the souls of the pious awaiting their redeemer in a state of sleep; another containing the souls of those who did indeed fall asleep in faith but who brought with them something of the flesh's impurity to be removed by the fires of purgatory; and the third containing the souls of the wicked, condemned to eternal torment by God's just judgment. It seems that Lazarus and Abraham were to be found in the first region, undoubtedly in a state of rest. In the third was that pleasure-loving rich man, tormented amid the flames. It makes no difference to me if someone wishes to distinguish souls due for temporal purgation from those tormented without hope of redemption not by place but rather by circumstance, not tortured by a different fire but to a different end. This would mean that there are two regions of Tartarus, one higher up and the other lower down – this is more or less obvious from the words of the Gospel, which relate that when the rich man raised his eyes he saw Lazarus, apparently above him. The Gospel also states that a huge abyss separated the region of torment from that of rest so that no one could climb up from the lower region or descend to the other one.[388]

It is probable that the soul of Christ penetrated both parts of hell, both the higher one, which he emptied completely, and the lower one, from which he delivered all the souls being purged by torments. And indeed, if the pope at Rome can free so many souls from hell,[389] is it not much more likely that the supreme leader of the church, trusting in the fullness of God's power, should have delivered all souls from torment, apart from those whom the divine justice consigned to eternal punishment, not to be purged but tormented? There were those who supposed that Christ's soul had experienced the suffering of hell on our behalf,[390] in the same way

* * * * *

387 That is, limbo, purgatory, and hell
388 Cf the story of the beggar Lazarus and the rich man in Luke 16:19–26.
389 Erasmus is here alluding to the practice prevalent in the Catholic church in the later Middle Ages whereby indulgences were granted in exchange for good works or acts of piety. Such indulgences, by virtue of the merits of Christ and the saints, might remit the temporal penalty due to sin, and by extension, the pains of purgatory. In its extreme form the doctrine led to claims that the pope had jurisdiction over purgatory; see In psalmum 22 177 n354 below.
390 Cf Explanatio symboli CWE 70 305, where mention is made of those Christians who conjectured that Christ's soul suffered among the dead for the souls

that he suffered death, but the church does not acknowledge this belief. Christ's soul went down to subdue, not to suffer, to plunder, not to be tormented. How can someone who has not been captive be said to be set free? Sometimes even the person who is saved from danger is said to be set free: for example, we say to a doctor who has given us advice on how to avoid a disease: 'You have set me free from death.' Or the person who lights a fire for the ship's captain to see from afar to prevent him dashing against the rocks is said to have delivered him from shipwreck. In this way God snatched Christ's soul from the lower regions of hell because it could not be held captive there but returned victorious, bringing the supreme spoils of battle.

Now if someone says that the story told about Lazarus in the Gospel is designated a parable, he may perhaps look for a different meaning for this passage; I do not think he should be discouraged, as long as it does not interfere with other people's pious and plausible belief.

St Augustine divides the whole universe into three levels, so that those who live in heaven, where there is neither death nor sin, neither suffering nor temptation, but only everlasting happiness, are referred to as 'those above.' Even though we long for that level, nevertheless, while our souls live in this dwelling that Paul calls the body of death,[391] and while they sorrow and rejoice, desire and fear, struggle against concupiscence, are in danger, and are sometimes overcome whether they like it or not, they are (so to speak) down in hell. Where there is sin, there is death; where there is death, there is hell. Consider the wretchedness of this life and compare it with the life of the heavenly beings: you will admit that Tartarus is here, but if you compare it with the place down to which the souls of the wicked go, you can say it is a higher level, for just as we call those in heaven 'those above,' so those who are held captive down there call us 'those above.' Augustine seems to have derived this scheme from the Platonists, but he turned a blind eye to their error, for it is not part of our religion to believe that souls are sent into human bodies to expiate the offences they committed elsewhere.

It is, however, neither blasphemous nor absurd to say that souls have suffered because of their nature, corrupted by Adam's sin, which is almost

* * * * *

detained there, and the colloquy *Inquisitio de fide* CWE 39 426, where it is stated that Christ descended into hell but did not suffer there. Cf Calvin's work, published in 1535, *Institutio christianae religionis* II 16.10–12, where Calvin discussed the need for Christ to suffer in hell.
391 Rom 7:24

exactly what Plato, and following him, Virgil recorded about hell.[392] Each person has his own Rhadamanthus in his heart,[393] and the mind is a victim of its own Furies when it is racked by a guilty conscience. There are some people who are held prisoner in that bottomless pit without hope of return, although we, to whom the hearts of men are incomprehensible, should not despair of anyone as long as he lives; there are some whose faults are expiated by certain torments; and there are some who have progressed to the point where they have been, as it were, transported to the Elysian fields: having subdued the passions of the flesh, they live in peace of spirit, having already some foretaste of the joys of heaven, even before they are released from the body and fly up to the Lord.[394] It was from these lower regions that God snatched Christ's soul: he did not allow it to be stained by any sin and he restored it from the hardships of this world, from torment, and from death, bringing it back unscathed from the lowest regions of Tartarus to these lower regions. But he raised it free from all mortality, glorious and immortal, with an immortal body, up to heaven, where those who are truly higher beings live. All these things, I believe, have been suggested with some plausibility.

I am not worried by the fact that the phrase used in the psalm is not 'the lower regions' but 'the lowest regions.'[395] For if you make a distinction in this life between the grades of sinners, you will find many lower than others and, as we have shown, hell itself, after death, is not uniform. Even heaven has its own levels. And so, while God is the highest being, more sublime than all else, Tartarus is on the lowest level, further removed from God than any other place. For nothing can lie further away from the supreme good than the ultimate evil. Anyone leading the life of a criminal is undoubtedly living in the lower region, is in the devil's power, has been swallowed up by death, and has withdrawn far from God. But since in this life we should not, as I said, despair of anyone, to us he is not yet in the lowest part of hell, where there is nothing good and nothing that is not evil; but to God he is. It was from all the lower regions that God snatched the soul of Jesus.

* * * * *

392 Plato *Phaedo* 113D–14C; Virgil *Aeneid* 6.566–9
393 Cf *Adagia* II ix 30: *Rhadamantheum iudicium* 'The verdict of Rhadamanthys.'
394 Cf 2 Cor 12:2–4, the *locus classicus* for such Christian rapture; the condition described here matches the ecstatic folly at the climax of the *Moria* CWE 27 152.
395 Erasmus quotes the Greek (ἐξ ᾅδου κατωτάτου) of the Septuagint text.

Now let us consider the whole person consisting as it were of head and body together: according to the mystical explanation, just as all the pious form one flesh, so they all form one soul, which God's great mercy delivered from all the many lower regions when he forgave our sins without asking anything in return, redeemed us from the slavery of Satan, prevented us from being overwhelmed by temptations, and allowed us to prevail in torment. Although he allowed us to die, he did not allow death to be everlasting, intending to bring even these mortal bodies to the glory of immortality. Christ's soul experienced the kindness that is bestowed on each individual soul, just as even now it is, so to speak, cherished and comforted in his members.

The gentiles were far removed from God as long as they believed that there was no God or worshipped beasts and dumb statues as their god, leading lives that were as corrupt as was their unholy religion. Were we not living at that time in the deepest hell? The Jews who seemed to be closer to God – did they not fall into the deepest pit when they put the Son of God to death? And yet, so great was the Lord's mercy that he delivered many thousands of souls from these lower regions. What shall I say about us, we who after baptism often fall back into the pit of sin, committing adultery or murder, and yet by means of repentance, the Lord's mercy sets our souls free from the lower regions of hell despite their frequent relapses. He who acknowledges that he has been in great darkness praises the Lord's mercy, reciting these verses: 'I shall praise you, O Lord God, with my whole heart, and I shall glorify your name for ever; for your mercy towards me is great, and you have snatched my soul from the lower regions of hell' (or as St Jerome translates it, 'the outermost regions,'[396] for in the Gospel, too, some people are said to be cast into the outer darkness).[397]

Christ our head fought on our behalf and prevailed for us, he showed us hope and showed us what our reward would be, but he left to his church cause for perpetual struggle. He passed on to it the burden of his cross, but he also gave the church his support, gave it an example of how to conduct the fight, broke the enemy's power but did not eliminate it, revealed to the church the victory, and showed it the crown. Faced with such a struggle, the Lord prays for the victory of his bride: 'O God, the wicked have risen up against me, and the synagogue of the powerful have sought my soul and have not set you in their sight.' These things had occurred earlier, at

*　*　*　*　*

396 Again, this is Jerome's version of verse 13 in his *Psalterium iuxta Hebraeos* PL 28 (1890) 1258B.
397 Matt 8:12

the very beginning, when the nations were roaring in anger and the people conspired against the Lord and against his anointed one.[398] What did Satan not attempt, using as his instruments the Scribes and Pharisees, the elders and the people, Annas and Caiaphas, Pilate and Herod, the guards and soldiers, to put the Lord to death? Was this not enough for these wicked people that they had also to try to expunge completely the name of him whom they had murdered? But this was the name in which all men who are saved seek salvation. Did those who had attacked the Lord spare his disciples? If they call the master of the house Beelzebub,[399] the sons cannot hope for more merciful treatment. The Lord says: 'If the world hates you, know that it has hated me first,'[400] but he also says: 'Fear not, little flock, for yours is the kingdom of heaven,'[401] and 'Be confident, for I have overcome the world.'[402] With what arrogance the world rose up against Jesus' disciples, what tricks and threats it used! How loud was the muttering of the Jews and the uproar of the gentiles!

The Latin word *iniqui* [unjust] here is a translation of the Greek word παράνομοι [transgressing the law] rather than of ἄνομοι [lawless]. Ἄνομοι, which is more appropriately applied to the gentiles, is said of those who are not bound by the Law, while παράνομοι, which refers rather to the Jews, means those who transgress the Law. This is why St Augustine gives the reading: 'Those who pay no heed to the Law have risen up against me.' St Jerome, working from the original Hebrew text, gives the translation 'the proud,'[403] a word that suits what follows: 'and the synagogue of the powerful (or "the strong") sought my soul.'

Pride is the source of all wickedness,[404] and the Law is a yoke which the proud cast off and refuse to bear. The gentiles possessed natural law implanted in their hearts, and after they had cast this aside they broke out in every kind of wicked behaviour. The Jews did not cast aside this law but transgressed it, fighting against this law in their devotion to the Law and conspiring against the one whom the Law had promised and described. This was undoubtedly the synagogue of the powerful or of the strong and therefore of the proud. These people were swollen with pride in the Law

* * * * *

398 Cf Ps 2:1–2.
399 Matt 10:25
400 Cf John 15:18.
401 Luke 12:32
402 John 16:33
403 Jerome *Psalterium iuxta Hebraeos* PL 28 (1890) 1258c
404 Cf Ecclus 10:15 / Sir 10:13.

that God had given them, the citadel of religion belonged to them, their knowledge of the Law and the prophets was a source of pride, and they prided themselves on their deeds of righteousness and their rituals. Their arrogance was increased by their pride in the temple built at God's command, the priesthood, and the sacrifices. From these things the synagogue drew its strength and behaved arrogantly towards the church of God, which was humble and weak in itself but strong and powerful in God who gives it strength. And the synagogue had not only strength but also unity: whatever the Scribes were able to do by their cunning, the Pharisees by their skill, the elders by their authority, Annas and Caiaphas because of their high position, and the people by their shouts and uproar, all this was directed against Christ and later against the disciples. A person who commits manslaughter accidentally is usually given a less severe punishment, but how many secret devices did the Pharisees – who for a long time concealed the wickedness of their character – use in plotting Jesus' death![405] They sought to kill him in secret, but when their passionate anger made this plan impossible, they sought a pretext that would make it seem that they had driven the Lord to his death out of devotion and reverence. In the same way Nero used the Christians as scapegoats for the anger felt at the burning of Rome, and similarly the Christians were accused of sorcery and infanticide. This is presumably what is meant by 'seeking the soul' of the righteous.

But what follows refers rather to the Jews: 'And they did not set you up in their sight.' For the gentiles did not know God, while the Jews, although they knew him, did not set him up in their sight; instead they turned their backs on him when he called, inviting them to come; they turned away their eyes and stopped up their ears. For if they had set God the Father up in their sight, why did they not fear to put his Son to death? But wicked desires got in their eyes like sties, preventing them from seeing God. Greed obscured their vision, as did the authority they had with the people, the impressiveness of their lifestyle (in which they were superior to others), and other benefits that they preferred to look to rather than looking at God. Anyone who fixes his gaze on God cannot sin for long, but he who has turned away from God and gives himself up to his own desires at last falls into the pit of extreme wickedness, so blinded that he can convince himself that things he does in the most criminal way are actually motivated by religious devotion.

* * * * *

405 Cf *Adagia* IV vii 61: *Cuniculis oppugnare.*

The Jews say: 'We killed a man; we did not know that he was God.' To be sure, it was a man you killed, but one who was innocent and who deserved to be treated well, and you did not tremble at what Pilate, who wanted to find a way of releasing the innocent man, feared to do and what Pilate's wife, who was but a woman and a gentile, feared to do. Your wickedness prevailed, and if it had not completely blinded you, you would have been able to perceive in Jesus something greater than man. If you had spared the man, through the man you would have reached God. They say: 'We were not the ones who put him to death.' No indeed, but it was your voices that put him to death, and this was all the more criminal because by your treachery you sought his life for a long time and by your persistent cries you forced a just governor to commit an ungodly crime.

This was the lament of Christ our head, this was the lament of the infant church, which was cruelly persecuted not only by the barbarity of the emperors, who used exile, torture, and death, but also by the Jews, who tried to drag the church back to servitude to the Law, by the heretics, who with their many different beliefs broke the net holding the church together, by the false brothers,[406] whose persecution of the church was all the more cruel because they were loved and protected by it. And so although people do not always act in the same way, nevertheless, from the beginning of the world right until its end, the body of Christ cries out to God: 'O God, the wicked have risen up against me, and the synagogue of the powerful have sought my soul and have not set you in their sight.'

No age is without its Herods, who massacre infants, none which does not have its Annas and Caiaphas, its own Scribes and Pharisees; this is the case even during the church's most peaceful periods, not only in this most turbulent century when the nets are so torn by differences of opinion and character that they can hardly be mended even by those who are in the apostolic succession – although we read in the Gospels that the disciples did manage it. But to make this storm abate, the church is compelled to tolerate always in its heart those who are nominally Christians but pagans in their lifestyle. These people, who corrupt good behaviour with their deadly talk and wicked examples, kill many more people than Herod or Nero did, and more cruelly. What could the cruelty of these rulers achieve even in its most extreme form? Only the death of the body, but these so-called Christians send many souls down to hell. That is why the church does not weep at the deaths of martyrs, celebrating them instead with joy and referring to

* * * * *

406 Cf 2 Cor 11:26, Gal 2:4.

them as birthdays; but it laments with bitter tears that the little children in its embrace, whom it bore for Christ, are slaughtered. Weeping over them, lamenting and wailing, it finds no consolation, because they are no more.[407] For anyone who is guilty of a crime, a crime that is mortal to the soul[408] and deprives it of God its life, perishes completely and truly, as far as that is possible.[409]

All those who are the living members of the church and rejoice whenever one member is glorified but suffer torment whenever any member is persecuted or vilified will understand what I mean, for in a living body all the members are in agreement or – to use the more accurate Greek term – in sympathy. How then can it be that such things do not torment the mind of a man who is truly devout? Paul, who was in travail again and again, cries out: 'Am I not indignant whenever anyone is made to fall?'[410] How many are torn away from Christ by those who are drunkards, gamblers, harlots, or ambitious and wicked men! Is it impossible for you to see what is everywhere before your eyes? If you see it but are not upset by it, then Christian love is not alive in you. In fact, each of us can perceive this anguish in himself unless he is completely dead. St Paul admits no hope of relaxation in this life and exempts no one from this struggle, but warns all who wish to live devoutly in Christ Jesus that they will suffer persecution.[411] If you do perceive it, then cry out again and again; if you do not perceive it, you are not living devoutly in Christ.

I appeal to your individual consciences – which of us is not tormented whenever wicked desires rise up against our good intentions? These desires transgress the law, for they do not submit to the law but produce a new law in our members that conflicts with the law of our mind.[412] If someone denies that he experiences anything of this kind, what does he gain but the reputation of being shameless, since even Paul, admitting this struggle and overcome by weariness, as it were, cries out: 'Wretched man that I am! Who will deliver me from the body of this death?'[413] The law of God says: 'Share your property with the poor,'[414] but greed rebels against this,

* * * * *

407 Cf Matt 2:18, where Jer 31:15 is quoted.
408 Cf Matt 10:28.
409 The meaning of this sentence is not wholly clear.
410 2 Cor 11:29
411 Cf 2 Tim 3:12.
412 Rom 7:23
413 Rom 7:24
414 Cf 1 John 3:17.

crying out in protest: 'No! Increase your property in whatever way you can.' The law of God calls: 'Do not resist evil at all,'[415] but anger calls out: 'Destroy your enemy that you may enjoy revenge.' The law of God tells us to watch and pray,[416] but a mind that is eager to do this is seriously hindered by a decadent lifestyle and its companion, lack of energy. The law of God urges us to be chaste and self-controlled, but lust rebels, urging us on in a completely different direction. Who could enumerate all the passions which conspire, as it were, to cause Christ's death in us? The desires that spurn God and entice us away from God's teachings are proud and transgress the law; they are the synagogue, because one desire encourages another; they are powerful, because they sometimes strike down even the strongest men. What powerful missiles the lust of the flesh uses to disturb our minds! What violent assaults are made by anger! 'To what lengths is the heart of man driven by the accursed craving for gold!'[417] What battering rams ambition brings into operation! It is hard to do battle against even one such powerful enemy; how much harder is it to fight against a whole troop of such enemies – or rather, a whole army! But let no one despair in such circumstances; he should instead rejoice, realizing that he is in the same situation as all devout people. Equipped with spiritual arms[418] and fighting bravely, he cries out to the Lord the verse which we are at present discussing. He who granted Christ victory over death and did not allow his church to be submerged when dashed by so many waves will not permit any of us to be overwhelmed by rebellious desires, as long as we put our trust in his mercy and not in our own abilities and have not turned our eyes away from God but have in all matters set him in our sight, making to him an offering of our hearts and controlling all our actions in the awareness that we are constantly before God's eyes. What we have explained with regard to the Jews and kings and wicked desires can also be applied to impious spirits who fight a continual battle against all devout people, while we serve as soldiers in this tent.[419]

But what does this person, who is oppressed by so many enemies conspiring against him, ask for when he shouts? Does he ask for the destruction of his enemy? Nowhere in the Gospels or in the Epistles do we read that the church prayed for the death of those who persecuted it; rather,

* * * * *

415 Cf Matt 5:39.
416 Matt 26:41
417 Virgil *Aeneid* 3.57
418 Cf Eph 6:11–17.
419 That is, in the body; cf 2 Cor 5:4, 2 Pet 1:13.

it follows the example of its head and prays that its persecutors may be converted and live.[420] He does not pray for the devil, because he can neither die nor be converted. Instead he struggles with great difficulty against the passions of the flesh, succeeding in preventing himself becoming enslaved to them but not in destroying them, for he knows that this is only granted after this life; that is why he longs to depart and be with Christ.[421] He does however pray for men, however wicked they are, while they are alive, that they may escape from the devil's snares.[422] He prays for victory, but if possible a victory involving no bloodshed. A victory is only successful when the victor is released from persecution and the vanquished one is delivered from wickedness. For so great is the Lord's mercy that it also draws the persecutor to it by means of those who are the victims of the persecution.

It is this ineffable mercy that our priest, the Lord Jesus, earnestly prays for when he says: 'But you, O Lord God, are full of pity and compassionate, patient and of great mercy and reliable.' Mercy ought to be great and many-sided if it is to overcome such great wickedness and replace great evil with good. At the beginning he calls on the Lord God, who can destroy those whom he wishes to, but in accordance with his immense goodness he does not wish for the death of a sinner but rather desires all men to be saved,[423] although he owes salvation to no one, of course, because the whole mass of the human race has been corrupted by Adam's sin.[424]

I do not think that any of the five expressions he here applies to God is superfluous: full of pity, compassionate, patient, of great mercy, and truthful. The Latin word *miserator* [full of pity] is οἰκτήρμων in Greek; this word applies to those who bring relief to the wretched and pitiable. The Latin word *misericors* [compassionate] is ἐλεήμων in Greek, while the Latin *patiens* [patient] is μακρόθυμος in Greek, a word denoting mildness of character and one who shows forbearance and is slow to take revenge. The Latin phrase *multum misericors* [of great mercy] is rendered by the Greek word πολυέλεος. Should someone argue that this piling up of words serves no purpose other than to magnify the greatness of God's mercy, his claim would not in my opinion be absurd. On the other hand, it would not be a

* * * * *

420 Ezek 33:11
421 Phil 1:23
422 2 Tim 2:26
423 Cf 1 Tim 2:4.
424 Cf 1 Cor 15:22. Augustine frequently used the phrase *massa damnata* or *massa peccati* of the human race corrupted by original sin and thus deserving death.

matter of reprehensible pedantry if one were to distinguish between them in such a way that 'full of pity' was said to refer to the remission of original sin. For original sin is really more a matter of wretchedness than of wickedness; it is a sin, but it is someone else's sin, and those who are subject to it are as pitiable as they are wretched. Infants cry and by means of their cries call for someone to pity them, and God's pity brings relief to their misery, through circumcision under the law of Moses and through baptism under the law of the gospel. They had died through no fault of their own, and now they are saved, but not by their own efforts; they died because of another's sin but are brought back to life by another's faith.[425]

God is full of pity [*miserator*] to infants and merciful [*misericors*] to those who are baptized as adults, burdened more by their own sins than by that of Adam. Now although baptism is available to all, many people still postpone it until the very end of their lives, in the meantime remaining enslaved to their desires,[426] and although God invited all men to accept the grace of the gospel, yet his generosity was for the most part rejected with scorn by the Jews and the gospel mocked by the gentiles. What did such people deserve if not utter destruction? But for a long time God's gentleness [*lenitas*] tolerated these people, too, in the hope that they should at long last see reason and come to their senses. He does admittedly have foreknowledge of which people will change their mind and which will not, and yet he puts up with them partly to make his righteousness shine more brightly and partly to teach us gentleness towards sinners, for we do not know for sure when they might be turned into good fruit.

For many centuries the Jews persisted in their blindness, and yet the Lord tolerated them, calling on them each day to accept regeneration through his church. Christians tolerate them, too, when they blaspheme against Christ and curse us all, although they could utterly annihilate the Jews if they wished. The Jews are far fewer in number than Christians, they have no state, no laws, no magistrates or ruler, no military capability and no resources; they could all be massacred in one day, but they are tolerated in the hope that the apostle Paul gave us when he wrote to the Christians at Rome. For he denies that the Jews have become so weak that they will be overthrown, and he reveals a mystery, announcing to his friends that there will come a time when, after the full number of gentiles has entered, the Jews will come to their senses again and all Israel will be saved, for

* * * * *

425 Cf 1 Cor 15:21–2.
426 Cf Titus 3:3.

according to the prophecy of Isaiah: 'He will come from Zion and he will remove iniquity and banish it from Jacob.'[427]

Is this not an admirable example of the Lord's gentleness? If someone hurls insults at a human ruler and as a result is hurried away to be punished, what cruel methods are used to kill him! And yet such things are sometimes justly and rightly said to the ruler. But God, to whom is owed all glory, tolerates the Jews, the pagans, and heretics with such gentleness, encouraging them to repent. This is no doubt a wonderful example of gentleness, but it is more remarkable that by this means he every day tolerates Christians who, after receiving baptism and experiencing the good word of God, often relapse into all kinds of offences, holding the Son of God in contempt and treating his blood as if it were not holy,[428] and they crucify once again the one who is undoubtedly within them.[429] Not even at such people does he hurl the thunderbolt of his righteous anger, but instead he calls them back when they turn away and receives them, applying the remedy of penitence, when they turn back to him. He does not just receive them once or twice, but whenever a sinner sighs he receives him and restores him. Here is an example of God's remarkable patience – a word given in the Septuagint as μακροθυμία and which some have rendered as 'longanimitas' [long-suffering]: μακρός means long and θυμός sometimes signifies the onrush or ardour of a passionate soul. Some people, translating from the Hebrew, have preferred to give the reading 'slow to anger' [lentus furore] instead of 'patient' [patiens], for however placid a person may be, 'oft-wounded patience will to madness turn,'[430] but God's patience cannot be worn down. As long as this life lasts, his mercy is at hand, and if ever in this life he inflicts suffering on sinners, it is really a medicine rather than a punishment.

God is not only full of pity towards the young, merciful to the mature and those who are corrupted also by their own sins, and long-suffering with regard to those who transgress repeatedly and relapse again and again, but he is also very merciful [πολυέλεος, that is, multum misericors] to those who come to their senses, whether they are Jews, pagans, or sinning Christians. He not only forgives them all their sins, but in addition he enriches them with many gifts of spiritual graces, giving back a hundredfold at this time

* * * * *

427 Rom 11:25–6, quoting Isa 59:20
428 Cf Heb 10:29.
429 Cf Heb 6:4–6.
430 Erasmus quotes Publilius Syrus' well-known maxim in *Adagia* I v 67: *Funem abrumpere nimium tendendo* 'To stretch the rope till it breaks.'

as well as eternal life in the age to come.[431] My dearest brothers, is this not mercy of a most generous kind? Is anything similar found among men, however peaceable and compassionate they may be? Bear in mind at this point what I have often declared, that whatever God grants us, whatever he bestows on us, is a product of his mercy, for we do not wish to lose the gift by failing to acknowledge the source of the gift.

The word 'reliable' [verax] is placed last in the list and refers to God's promises. For he does not bestow all these things on us in response to our merits but has assigned them thus in accordance with his eternal plan, before the world began, and promised them many thousands of years ago through the prophets;[432] so far he has not failed to fulfil any of the things he promised, and there is no doubt that he will as reliably fulfil what he promised concerning the end of the world, the Last Judgment, the resurrection and the beatitude of the righteous. But God gave promises to increase our trust, since indeed he never changes his mind about his promises or his gifts.[433] He is by nature reliable, and even if we have denied him by our sins, he who has promised mercy to all who repent cannot deny himself[434] by withdrawing his compassion.

And so, my God, since your natural goodness makes you like this; and since you have, by means of your prophets, attested your faithfulness to all; since you have thus far begun to fulfil your promises and have sent me into the world to restore the human race by my death: 'Look upon me and have mercy on me.' The Jews in their persistent wickedness struggle against your goodness, and soon the whole world will seek to destroy the kingdom of heaven, using every device to rebel against the gospel. Do not look upon their blindness, O God, but look upon me, for you have promised that I shall inherit all the nations and that my kingdom will reach to the ends of the earth.[435] You said: 'Go forth with success, proceed, and reign.'[436] Look, here I am about to do battle with the enemy for the sake of your kingdom, which you wanted me to liberate for you. Help me as I go into battle, grant me victory, 'grant power to your servant' – or 'give strength to your son,' for κράτος can mean both strength and power: strength is appropriate for one who fights, power for the one who has conquered.

* * * * *

431 Cf Mark 10:30, Luke 18:30, Matt 19:29.
432 Cf Rom 1:2.
433 Cf Rom 11:29; Tit 1:2.
434 Cf 2 Tim 2:13.
435 Cf Ps 2:8, Ps 110:7/111:6.
436 Ps 44:5/45:4

This is that David, strong of hand,[437] who tore apart both the lion and the bear for the glory of all Israel,[438] who met the arrogant Goliath in an extraordinary battle.[439] Goliath trusted in his sword, his spear, and his shield, but David put aside Saul's sword, bronze helmet, and coat of mail, for our leader was not accustomed to such weapons and he did not come to win himself a kingdom of this world by use of arms but marched forward, armed with confidence in the name of the Lord. Our David is therefore praying as he goes into battle, desiring that all the glory of the victory should be ascribed to God. 'Look upon me and have mercy; grant power to your servant' (or 'your son,' for the Greek word παιδί is ambiguous, signifying someone young, whether a son or a servant.)

Whichever of these translations you accept, there is nothing incongruous in its meaning. We read that David was a young man when he attacked Goliath, for this is what the account in the Book of Kings says: 'He was but a youth, ruddy and very good-looking.'[440] The Lord was also in the flower of his youth according to the flesh when he was crucified. According to the mystical sense he was a green tree, as he himself declares;[441] and according to Paul's testimony he was that second Adam who took away the weariness and old age of the whole world, reinvigorating every creature;[442] and finally, he was a child in that he was free from all fault and all deceit. He was also the Son of God, not only by adoption but even by nature, and in accordance with the dispensation entrusted to him[443] he was an assistant and a servant, the envoy of the Father, the minister of the New Testament, and the one who performed the sacrifice ordained by his Father. As a child he is free from all sin, as a son there is nothing he refuses to do, as minister he neglects nothing that the Father has commanded. He was ruddy in the sense that his whole being burned with the fire of love; bold, but in the Lord's name; and good-looking because he was full of grace, as it says in another psalm: 'You are more handsome than the children of men, and grace is spread on your lips.'[444] He was most lovely in the eyes of the Father, who several times declared that he was well pleased with

* * * * *

437 See n11 above.
438 1 Sam 17:34–7
439 Cf 1 Sam 17:38–58.
440 1 Sam 17:42; in the Latin Bible, 1 Samuel and 2 Samuel are also called the first and second books of Kings.
441 Cf Luke 23:31.
442 Cf 1 Cor 15:45.
443 Cf Col 1:25.
444 Ps 44:3 / 45:2

him.[445] But he was lovely not only in the eyes of God but also in the eyes of men and of devils, for the Jews in their madness could find no sin in him and the prince of this world[446] could detect nothing to find fault with; Pilate, too, although he was a pagan, perceived his innocence,[447] and even Judas, who betrayed, him declared that he was innocent.[448]

At the beginning of the psalm he cried out that God should incline his ear to investigate his case; here he also asks him to turn his eyes to this struggle so that what is done on God's orders should be done in his sight. Blessed are they whom God deigns to look at, for his eyes are only on the righteous.[449] Anyone who can say to God with heart and soul: 'Look upon me,' has already ceased to be wicked. Someone may perhaps be prompted to ask: 'How does it fit that after begging for mercy, he then asks for power and goes on to say: "And save the son of your handmaiden"'? He who prays for mercy acknowledges his wretchedness, while he who asks to be saved recognizes that he is in great danger. But if you look more closely you will see that his words are not contradictory: he prays for mercy so that praise for the victory may be ascribed to the one God. He asks for power so that after the destruction of the kingdom of Satan the kingdom of the church might be born. Once again he asks to be saved, in other words, he asks that the kingdom of the church may be everlasting and that the gates of hell may not prevail against it.[450] But if at this point you remember that one man comprises the head and all the members, you will find nothing shocking. For he is delivered by God's mercy, chosen to enter the kingdom of heaven, and saved so that he might win the prize of immortality.[451] For when Christ hands over the kingdom to God the Father[452] and all his members have been united into one whole, then salvation will be a definite reality, but in this world there is neither security nor perfection.

You may perhaps also inquire what is meant by the fact that it was not enough for him to say once, 'to your child,' but that he needed to add: 'Save the son of your handmaiden.' This phrase seems to imply that he had used 'child' to mean servant and that by the repetition of 'the son of your

* * * * *

445 Cf Matt 3:17, 17:5, Mark 1:11, and Luke 3:22.
446 Cf John 12:31, 14:30, 16:11.
447 Cf Matt 27:23–4, Mark 15:14, Luke 23:22, and John 19:4–6.
448 Cf Matt 27:4.
449 Cf Ps 33:16/34:15.
450 Matt 16:18
451 Cf 1 Cor 9:24–5, Phil 3:14.
452 1 Cor 15:24

handmaiden' he wished to emphasize his meaning, such repetition being a common scriptural device. In the eyes of the world there is a difference between one servant and another, as is indicated by the Greek proverb δοῦλος πρὸ δούλου [one slave before another],[453] and you can have a servant who is not the son of your handmaiden. Bought slaves are not highly valued, while family slaves are more dear and are loved almost as your own children. If you accept that the device of repetition is being used here, then you should understand that it is used to indicate the supreme obedience in Christ; if you favour the idea of a progression, then you should understand it as meaning that Christ was a servant, but also the Father's beloved and uniquely dear Son.

Some people take 'maidservant' to refer to the most holy Virgin Mary, who conceived Jesus according to the flesh when she declared that she was the handmaiden of the Lord.[454] This interpretation was approved by Augustine and Arnobius,[455] and I do not see any reason to reject it, since it is both reverent and true. Others,[456] however, prefer to take it as referring to the church, but I do not know whether Christ can be said to be the son of the church – he appears to be the bridegroom of the church rather than its son. For it was not the church that gave birth to him but rather he himself who gave birth to and created the church. It would not be incongruous to call him the son of the synagogue, seeing that according to his human body he had his origin in Judaea, under Judaism, as even Paul bears witness when he says of the Jews that Christ came from them according to the flesh.[457] For a time the law of Moses also served the divine will, when it acted as a teacher, leading men to Christ and preparing them for him who is the bridegroom of the church. But the term 'handmaiden' is better suited to the synagogue than to the church, which is honoured by the titles of 'bride' and 'daughter.' Fear coerced the synagogue, but grace supports the church. John the Baptist said: 'He who has the bride is the bridegroom,'[458] and the Lord himself refers to himself occasionally in the parables as 'bridegroom.'[459] In the person of the bridegroom, the Song of Solomon describes the mystical

* * * * *

453 *Adagia* II iii 61: *Servus servo praestat*
454 Luke 1:38
455 Arnobius the Younger *Commentarium in psalmum 85* PL 53 449; Augustine *Enarratio in psalmum 85* 22 (on verse 16) CCL 39 1194
456 For example, Pseudo-Jerome *Breviarium in psalmos* PL 26 (1845) 1079; Eusebius of Caesarea *Commentarium in psalmum 85* PG 23 1037
457 Rom 9:5
458 John 3:29
459 For example, Matt 9:15, Mark 2:19–20, Luke 5:34–5

love between Christ and the church, and in Psalm 44 the church is told: 'Hear, O daughter, and consider, and incline your ear, and the king will desire your beauty.'[460]

Our Lord also called his church the kingdom of heaven,[461] and we read that Christ was entrusted with supreme power over it. He himself says in the Gospels that all power in heaven and on earth is given to him.[462] But when was power entrusted to the mystical body? Was it not a great power that he gave to his disciples when he granted them power to cast out devils, expel poisons, and cure any disease? Was not the Lord entrusting great power when he said: 'Whatever you loose on earth shall be loosed in heaven; whatever you bind on earth shall be bound in heaven'?[463] And again when he breathed on[464] them and said: 'Receive the Holy Spirit; the sins of those whose sins you forgive are forgiven, and the sins of those whose sins you retain will be retained'?[465] All this he granted them in this life. Did the monarchs of this world ever possess as much power? But what the Lord promised for the future is a mark of even greater authority: 'When the Son of Man shall sit on his throne in glory, you also will sit on twelve thrones, judging the twelve tribes of Israel.'[466] And Paul writes: 'And shall we not judge the angels?'[467] And so Christ reigns in his church and his church reigns in him, and it is so strong that not even the gates of hell can prevail against it,[468] nor can the wickedness of the Jews or the cruelty of tyrants or the arrogance of the philosophers or the stubbornness of heretics. Through Christ the church overcomes all things, is triumphant, and reigns supreme.

Since this kingdom is not yet peaceful and complete in every respect, the church, wishing that it may be extended and brought to perfection, cries out each day: 'Your kingdom come, your will be done on earth as in heaven.'[469] And so the fact that Christ prayed for it and the whole body of Christ prays for it in no way prevents each Christian from praying: 'Give

* * * * *

460 Ps 44:11–12/45:10–11
461 John 3:3–5
462 Matt 28:18
463 Matt 16:19
464 ASD mistakenly reads *instans* for *inflans*, the LB reading.
465 John 20:22–3
466 Matt 19:28
467 1 Cor 6:3
468 Matt 16:18
469 Matt 6:10

power' – or 'strength' – 'to your servant and save the son of your hand-maiden.' What handmaiden if not the church? The church has borne us a second time for her bridegroom, by means of the water of rebirth in the word of life.[470] Each individual who has been reborn in Christ becomes David, strong in faith, handsome in his innocence, a young man in the newness of life. Each individual engages in the battle against Goliath and defeats him when he overcomes the devil's temptation; and when he has subdued the lust of the flesh, he is led by the spirit. But the devil reigns supreme in someone who is dominated by the carnal passions, while Christ reigns in the one who is led by the spirit of God. Does one not rule over a splendid kingdom if one can control lust, crush greed, subdue indulgence, cast down pride, and despise death? Not the one who kills but rather the one who overcomes is the more powerful: the martyrs were put to death, but by dying they proved victorious and celebrated a triumph over those who had put them to death.

'You will rule,' writes one of the pagans, 'if you are ruled by rea-son,'[471] but every Christian will be a king if he is ruled by the spirit of Christ. What can we achieve by our own efforts if we cannot even think of anything good by ourselves?[472] Accordingly, if you ever manage through the spirit to mortify the deeds of the flesh,[473] do not praise yourself but give thanks to the Lord. For if you possess this power of your own accord, why should you need to cry out each day: 'Grant power to your servant'? When David asked for power, he was praying that Christ, who had been promised by the prophets, might come; and when the church makes the same prayer to receive power, it is praying that Christ may be victorious and reign throughout his whole body. When each of us prays for this, he is asking that his carnal passions be controlled and that he be led by the spirit of Christ; and when he prays that the son of the handmaiden be saved, he is praying that he might continue firmly within the church, finish his life in Christ, and attain that life where he who competes no longer faces any danger but is crowned as victor.

But the Lord is so determined that his victory should be a splendid one that he makes his splendour dazzle the eyes of those who resist him, making them come to their senses against their will at last and acknowledge their

* * * * *

470 Cf Titus 3:5, Phil 2:16.
471 Cf Seneca *Epistulae morales* 37.4, Horace *Epistles* 1.1.59.
472 Cf 2 Cor 3:5.
473 Rom 8:13

madness or be stricken with everlasting shame. But in order to strengthen the confidence of his church, David asks the Lord to make with him a sign for its benefit (for many people ask for a sign but to their detriment). He does not say: 'Show me a sign,' but 'Make with me a sign,' so that you might understand that it is a sign which confirms the promise and the agreement they made. In the same way we read that the Lord placed his rainbow as a sign of the covenant between him and the earth, so that when the people saw it they would not expect a similar flood again.[474] If this had not been granted, people who had been told about the previous flood would have trembled at the sight of every cloud and every drop of rain. Abraham, too, sought a sign in his favour from God so that he could be more confident of the promise made to him that his seed would be multiplied until it equalled the number of stars in the heavens.[475] Moses also asked for a sign and received many, but they were unable to prevent him from failing to observe God's commandments.[476] He said: 'I beg you, Lord, to send the one whom you will send.'[477] The Lord was angry with Moses because of his lack of trust.[478] Ahaz was told to ask for a sign from the Lord, and even when he refused to do so, a sign was granted to him.[479] Gideon asked for a similar sign and was granted it, but he was not satisfied with just one. A first sign was given by the angel when the sacrificial meat was consumed by the fire which terrified Gideon; when he was about to do battle with the enemy he demanded from the Lord a second sign and another slightly different miracle occurred to make him more confident of victory.[480] Circumcision was also granted to Abraham as a sign of faith, for in Genesis the Lord calls circumcision a sign of the covenant.[481] Not only did Moses produce many signs in the presence of Pharaoh but the fact that he parted the sea with his rod[482] was also a sign, as were the cloud that went before him by day and the column of fire by night,[483] the water that leapt from the rock and

* * * * *

474 Gen 9:8–17
475 Gen 15:5
476 Exod 3:11–4:9
477 Exod 4:13
478 Exod 4:14
479 Isa 7:10–14
480 An account of the first sign is given in Judg 6:17–21 and of the second in 6:36–40.
481 Gen 17:10–11
482 Exod 14:15–21
483 Exod 13:21–2

accompanied them on their way,[484] the manna falling from heaven,[485] and the serpent in the desert raised on a pole.[486]

In short, all the miraculous events of the Old Testament are signs and figures of our own times. Satan, too, has signs of his own, but his signs work to our detriment even when they seem to be granted for our benefit. God, however, grants only beneficial signs, although we sometimes turn them into harmful ones. The Lord set a mark on Cain,[487] a wicked man, and yet it was to Cain's advantage, for it prevented anyone from killing him; the wicked man was granted a period of life in the hope that he might come to his senses.

The Jews require signs, as the apostle writes,[488] but even after having been given so many visible signs they have not learned to trust in the Lord, for they even say to him: 'What sign do you show us, that you do these things?'[489] And they demanded a sign from heaven, as if all the miracles that the Lord gave them every day were not signs enough! Since therefore a great number of signs did not prove effective in the case of the Jews, who lacked faith, and the gentiles, who mocked them, our high priest and leader, on the point of going into battle against the enemy, asks for only one sign but a sign that is extraordinary, a sign that is beneficial, at least to those who believe in it, a sign that is clear and effective, which will draw the whole world to himself when he is raised up.[490] 'Show me a sign of your favour,' he says. 'Give me a sign that will encourage my friends and put my enemies to shame.' God alone was able to provide this sign. What sign was it? What sign if not that of the prophet Jonah? The Lord himself promises this sign in the Gospel: 'As Jonah was in the belly of the whale for three days and three nights, so shall the Son of Man be three days in

* * * * *

484 Exod 17:6, Num 20:11. In 1 Cor 10:4 Paul gives a spiritual interpretation of these passages and alludes to a legend that the rock from which Moses made water flow accompanied the Israelites through the wilderness; in his note on 1 Cor 10:4 (*consequente eos*) *Annotationes in Novum Testamentum* LB VI 710C–D Erasmus refers to Origen's interpretation in the Fifth Homily on Exodus, but he puts forwards the view that the rock that accompanied the Israelites was not the cloud that went before them but the water that sprang from the rock.
485 Exod 16:14–15
486 Num 21:8–9
487 Gen 4:15
488 1 Cor 1:22
489 John 2:18
490 John 12:32

the heart of the earth.'[491] He gave them this sign in these words, but they did not understand it. He put forward the same sign in different words: 'Destroy this temple, and in three days I shall restore it.'[492]

Since the faith of the whole church has been confirmed once and for all by this sign, there is no reason for us to expect other signs. We have the sign of Jonah, which signifies Christ's death according to the weakness of the flesh and his resurrection according to the power of the spirit; we have the sign of the cross, the trophy of our leader; we have in the Eucharist the pledge of the eternal covenant between the head and his members.[493] But all these things are one sign, namely the Lord Jesus himself, who was given as a sign for the destruction and the resurrection of many, a sign which is spoken against by many even to this day.[494] All the signs of the Old Testament have been fulfilled in this sign. The Word was made flesh and dwelt among us;[495] he was seen, heard, and touched by men;[496] he was put to death publicly, he rose from the dead and was taken up into glory; he was preached to all the nations and believed by the world; he shines brightly, he appears clearly, he flashes forth to bring all men to salvation. Nowhere in the Old Testament do we read that such a sign was produced. No one is ever destroyed unless he turns his eyes away from this sign. It was given for your benefit. Do not, by your lack of faith, make it work to your disadvantage, as was the case with the Jews, regarding whom the Lord testifies: 'If I had not come and spoken to them, they would not have had sin.'[497] This is the sign that the Lord, desiring the salvation of the human race, wished to be set up even as he was going to the cross; this is the sign he wished to shine brightly throughout the whole world, 'that they may see,' he says; 'I mean not only those who love me' (among whom was counted the old man Simeon) 'but also those who hate me, so that they who are unwilling to believe what I say may see this sign whether they like it or not (for the sign is too clear to be ignored); and so that they may at least be ashamed at having rejected this sign for so long and so obstinately. Let the former see that they may be strengthened, the latter that they may be converted.

* * * * *

491 Matt 12:40
492 John 2:19
493 See Matt 26:28.
494 Luke 2:34
495 John 1:14
496 Cf 1 John 1:1.
497 John 15:22

For the word which we read as 'may be confounded' is αἰσχυνθήτωσαν in Greek, which has the meaning 'may be ashamed.' That blush of shame is beneficial if it calls one back from a life of impiety – 'He blushed, it is all right,' says the old man in the comedy.[498] This was the blush which suffused the publican's face when he stood apart, not daring to raise his eyes to heaven;[499] this was how the exiled son blushed when he saw the error of his ways and voluntarily renounced his claim to be called son, confessing that he was not worthy of it, and who sought a place among the hired servants.[500] Many Jews blushed in this way after they had crucified the Lord in their ignorance,[501] and the gentiles also blushed when they turned away from their idols and corrupt habits towards the light of the gospel (which St Paul refers to when he writes, 'things of which you are now ashamed').[502] Paul himself blushed when he said that he was not worthy to be called an apostle because he had persecuted the church of God.[503] And so they who blush out of repentance are fortunate to feel shame.

However, shame does not cure all men; some people, if it leads them to show effrontery, are hardened by it instead. For the Greek word is ambiguous and can refer both to someone overcome with shame and to someone who feels disgraced when he is refuted and proved wrong. The Scribes and Pharisees often withdrew from the Lord in disgrace when they were unable to answer him, but they did not blush, though this might have brought them to their senses; instead, they shamelessly adopted the brazenness of a harlot, in their obstinacy using wicked devices to resist the obvious truth. They did not even blush for shame when they saw him risen from the dead or when, after the sending of the Holy Spirit, they witnessed the lame being healed in the name of him who had been crucified, or demons put to flight, diseases expelled, and the dead awakened; or even when the splendour of the gospel spread throughout the world and they saw all their efforts frustrated and proving counter-productive. What extraordinarily stubborn shamelessness! For many years now the name of Christ has held sway throughout the world, but the Jews still do not blush for shame. They are overwhelmed by disgrace, but shame does not cure them. 'That they may see,' the psalmist says, 'and be ashamed.' If only they would be ashamed in this life so that

* * * * *

498 Terence *Adelphi* 643
499 Luke 18:13
500 Luke 15:17–21; Erasmus is alluding to the parable of the prodigal son.
501 Cf Acts 3:17.
502 Rom 6:21
503 1 Cor 15:9

they need not be ashamed for ever. They can see this sign whether they like it or not, for it is present to the eyes of all men. If they see it and blush for shame, the sign will benefit them, but if they see it and mock at it, in the way their ancestors mocked Christ as he hung on the cross, reviling him and shaking their heads,[504] then the sign will cause them harm. They will see this sign once more in heaven when the Lord comes to judge;[505] they will see him whom they taunted, they will see him whom they assaulted with every kind of insult in this world in the majesty of the Father. In the next world they will become ashamed in the sight of all nations and the angels, but they will be ashamed for ever, because they turned to their disadvantage the sign which had been given for their benefit.

Nor will it be the Jews alone who will be ashamed in the next world: so will all the rulers and all the philosophers who used their resources and talents to fight against this sign. In the next world nothing will be hidden. They will see their wickedness brought to nothing, they will see the victor's glory, they will witness the triumphs of the martyrs whom they put to death in this life by means of ingenious tortures: they will be ashamed, but it will be too late. All the heresiarchs, along with their flocks of disciples, who while they lived refused to blush for shame although this would have saved them, will feel shame. However, even nowadays, have those who attempted to undermine the house of God gained anything but disgrace? Where is Simon Magus, that zealous seeker after divinity?[506] Where is Cerinthus, who denied Christ's divine nature?[507] Where is Montanus, that pseudo-paraclete?[508] Where is Valentinus,[509] who invented monstrous tales, and where is Marcion,[510] where is Basilides?[511] Have they

* * * * *

504 Cf Ps 21:8 / 22:7.
505 Cf Matt 24:30.
506 Acts 8:9–24. Simon Magus came to be regarded as the father of all heresies.
507 Cerinthus was a Jewish Christian Gnostic teacher of the early second century, to whom various heretical cosmological and Christological doctrines are attributed. Cf In psalmum 1 CWE 63 16–17, where Erasmus mentions the erroneous Christological views of various early heresies.
508 Montanus, the founder of the Montanist sect in the second century, claimed to be the living incarnation of the Holy Spirit. Tertullian was a convert to Montanism.
509 Valentinus was a teacher of Gnostic doctrines in the second century.
510 Marcion was the founder of one of the most popular heresies. He taught a fundamental dichotomy between the Old and New Testaments, between the inferior creator of the old order and the supreme God of the new. Cf Ep 1738:169–72 for a definition of the Marcionite heresy.
511 Basilides was also a second century Gnostic teacher who held heretical views on creation and cosmology.

not been overthrown and rendered speechless? Where is Arius,[512] who chopped the Holy Trinity in pieces, and where is Sabellius,[513] who failed to respect its distinctions? Have they not been made ashamed, cast out and utterly defeated? Where is Apollinaris,[514] who deprived the human nature of Christ of its better element? What has happened to the portents of the Manichees,[515] to the riots of the Donatists?[516] Have they not all been made ashamed and speechless? Where is that blasphemer Porphyry,[517] and Celsus,[518] equally blasphemous? There have been many kinds of heresy – armed with philosophy and trained in rhetoric and often formidable because they have had the rulers' support, these heresies have caused many storms to assail the church. But what, I ask you, have their great disturbances managed to accomplish? They are all ashamed and have grown silent and all those that exist today or that will arise in the future will also be ashamed.

Similarly, bad Christians will feel shame unless they hasten to blush with shame in this life. We have no pagans among us, and as for the Jews, they are either nonexistent or cause very little trouble, behaving like madmen in their own caves.[519] And yet the wheat of the church has so many weeds and tares mixed in with it[520] that everywhere there are people who mock, cheat, rob, and oppress anyone who wishes to live piously and simply in Christ Jesus. If Christ's cross once seemed folly to the gentiles and

* * * * *

512 See n302 above.
513 See n303 above.
514 Apollinaris, bishop of Laodicea in the fourth century, was accused of denying that Christ had a human soul.
515 The Manichees (Manichaeans) were the followers of the third century Persian Mani, who taught an elaborate dualistic cosmology which claimed to explain the existence of evil in the universe. This heresy spread throughout the Roman Empire in the fourth century and was for a time a serious threat to Christianity.
516 The Donatists were a schismatic sect flourishing in North Africa in the fourth century. They refused to accept that the Catholic church was the true church because certain Catholics had betrayed the Scriptures to the authorities or even apostasized during the persecutions of Diocletian: Donatists held that consecrations performed by such people were invalid.
517 Porphyry was a fourth century Neoplatonist, a pupil of Plotinus, who in his book *Against the Christians* (now lost) attacked Christianity by applying historical criticism to biblical texts.
518 Celsus of Alexandria was a Platonist of the second century whose attacks on Christianity Origen countered in a major work, *Contra Celsum*.
519 Probably an allusion to Plato's cave-myth in *Republic* 7.514–17; cf *In psalmum* 4 CWE 63 180.
520 Matt 13:24–43

was a stumbling block to the Jews,[521] that had to be endured by whatever means possible; but it is a source of great sorrow that a person who has been redeemed through the cross, has been marked by the sign of the cross, and has acknowledged the cross should deride the cross. Those who weaken their body by fasting are called insane; those who live simply are called wretched; those who do not strive for wealth and who give what they have to the poor are called crazy; those who shun the honours bestowed by this world are called foolish; those who do not wish to cheat anyone for the sake of profit they call naive; those who avoid illicit pleasures are said to be un-happy; those who are keen to obey the orders of their superiors they call idiots; while those who do not take revenge for wrongs done to them they call cowards; those who despise the world and who place all their hope in God they call madmen. Those who mock Christians are confident and ap-pear to live a pleasant life in comfortable circumstances, while Christians are regarded as miserable, downtrodden, and despised.

If only they would examine more closely the characters of those they despise! If they could also look more deeply into themselves they would see what a Lerna of wicked thoughts[522] controls their minds, while those pleasures – which are as illusory as they are short-lived – will soon be suc-ceeded by torments. If they were to do this, they would no doubt be deeply ashamed – but how could they perceive in a way that made them blush with shame if God did not open their eyes, just as he opened the eyes of Adam and Eve? As soon as they had tasted of the forbidden tree, their eyes were opened, evidently by God, who was leading them to repentance. For so it is written in Genesis: 'Their eyes were opened, and they saw that they were naked and they blushed with shame.'[523] Is it not much more fitting that people should blush before God when they have cast off the robe of innocence given them at their baptism and wander around naked, not only unclothed by any virtues but disfigured by innumerable vices?

My brothers, I hope that there are no such people, or only a few, among you; if there are any, I urge and implore them for the love of Christ to blush with shame soon, while it is still profitable to blush, and not to put off reforming their life until their last breath. Death catches many people off their guard so that there is no time for repentance. How do you know whether God will open your eyes at the moment of death? Though none should be despaired of until they have breathed their last, nobody recovers

* * * * *

521 1 Cor 1:23
522 *Adagia* I iii 27: *Lerna malorum* 'A Lerna of troubles'
523 Gen 3:7

their senses of their own volition. If you are not willing to be converted, why do you delude yourself that you will repent at a later stage? If you do wish to be converted, and it is important to you, why do you put it off? Why do you not allow something so important to happen this year rather than next? Why do you think it better next month than this? Why not today rather than tomorrow? If your body is in danger, you do not put off taking medicine, but when the whole person is in danger of being destroyed for ever, you postpone it for days, months, or even years. We should examine ourselves in the mirror of Christ's teaching, of his life and that of the other saints, and we should be ashamed of ourselves.

'Let those who hate us see,' and those who plot everlasting destruction for us, 'let them blush for shame.' Who are they, you may ask, who hate us? Are not our principal enemies envy, hatred of our neighbours, greed, pride, self-indulgence and lust – in other words, the carnal passions? What else do they strive to achieve, what do they work at night and day, but to kill Christ in us? Let us be led by the spirit of Christ so that all such desires are put to shame, together with their fruits. The evil spirits, too, will blush for shame, they that apply thorns to our flesh[524] like oil to the furnace.[525] Those who refuse in this life to blush for shame before God and a few men, which would benefit them, will be ashamed in the next life in the presence of all the saints, but to no purpose and to their own detriment. Some people are frightened to confess because of a misplaced sense of shame, for they stand more in awe of man than of God. If they are ashamed to make their confession to a priest, their reverence for God ought to make them all the more afraid to sin. Are you ashamed to tell a man what you dared to do before God's very eyes? In the case of physical illness, the desire for health casts out shame; should this not be all the more true in the case of spiritual danger? One should blush with shame not only for serious offences but also for more trivial ones, for every sin is horrid and loathsome and therefore shameful. You are embarrassed by a swelling on the forehead or a wart on the nose, but you are not ashamed of idle chatter, or uncontrolled laughter, or the slightest moment of wasted time that could be put to good use.

But what will they see, how will they blush for shame, those who wish to harm Christ? 'Because you, O Lord, have helped me and comforted me.' The Jews shouted at Christ as if he had been despaired of and abandoned by God and man alike: 'If he is the Son of God, let him come down from the cross now. He trusted in the Lord, let God deliver him now if he desires

* * * * *

524 Cf 2 Cor 12:7.
525 Cf Horace *Satires* 2.3.321.

him.'[526] They mocked him, as the victorious mock the vanquished, but in fact things have been turned the other way round, and the conquered one triumphs while the conqueror weeps. You have helped me in my struggle, you have comforted me with victory. There can only be comfort where there has been distress. A double sense of shame has seized the Jews, for they see God helping him whom they thought God had abandoned and they see in glory the one whom they thought had been consigned to eternal disgrace. Then they also see that their own hopes have misled them, according to the saying: 'Their wickedness has led them astray.'[527]

But they will blush for shame even more when the Son of Man comes in majesty to judge the living and the dead.[528] What will Annas and Caiaphas say then? What will the Scribes and Pharisees, what will the elders say, who shouted: 'Away with him, away with him, crucify him'?[529] How ashamed they will be when they are told: 'Go, you cursed ones, into the eternal fires.'[530] What will Nero say then, and the others who spared no brutality in their treatment of the apostles and martyrs of Christ, when they see that their victories are more radiant than the sun and that they have become associates and partners in Christ's kingdom? 'When they see them they will be seized by terror and confusion and they will be shocked by the suddenness of their unexpected salvation. They will groan in anguish of spirit and will say to one another in repentance,"These are the people whom we once held in derision and made a target of our contempt. Fools that we were, we considered their life madness and their end dishonourable. Look! they have been numbered among the sons of God and their lot is among the saints."'[531]

You hear these words, which are an expression of profound shame – but one that is useless; you hear these words, which are a sign of repentance – but it comes too late; these words are a confession – but one that is fruitless. In the words of the common proverb: 'It is useless to give medicine to a dead man.'[532] We must blush for shame here in this life, my friends; we must repent here, we must confess here; a greater shame drives out a

* * * * *

526 Matt 27:40–3
527 Ps 26/27:12
528 Matt 25:31; for the phrase 'to judge the living and the dead' see 2 Tim 4:1 and the Nicene and Apostles' Creeds. Cf *In psalmum* 22 170 below.
529 John 19:15
530 Matt 25:41
531 Wisd 5:2–5
532 Cf *Adagia* III vi 17: *Post bellum auxilium*

lesser, as one nail drives out another,[533] and it is better to blush for a time in this life than to be ashamed for eternity.[534] The time is short, life passes quickly, death hurries on and is closer to each of us than we suspect. That day will come like a thief in the night[535] – we should therefore keep watch for it so that it does not take us by surprise.

It ought also to be noted, I think, that when the prophet says: 'Because you, O Lord, have helped me and comforted me' he is not assuming credit for the victory but attributing it to God. 'You alone are God, you who alone do marvellous things, you alone have helped me; you have helped me because you are full of pity, and you have comforted me because you are kind and very merciful and trustworthy. All these things are your gift, and to you is owed all glory. Sometimes your help and your comfort, too, whereby you secretly relieve the harshness of suffering by means of the anointing of your Spirit, is hidden; but the outcome of the struggle teaches us that man's protection and comfort lies not in this world but with you, and that with you as our protector we can overcome the flesh, the world, and the devil.' For the time being, the devout can see this, but the wicked do not; the time will come, however, when they will see and will blush, realizing that there is no help except from the Lord and that blessed are they who mourn in this life, for they will enjoy everlasting comfort[536] when God wipes away every tear from their eyes.[537] Then there will be nothing to fear or to grieve for; instead there will be perpetual freedom from anxiety and perfect joy, a joy of the heart and a joy of the body that can never be taken away.

But in the meantime, while we walk along the path, happy in hope rather than in possession, each of us must be careful that we are not deprived of divine help and comfort. Instead we must cooperate with God's grace and strive to the best of our ability to make our good works shine before men, so that they may see them and glorify our Father who is in heaven.[538] For the name of God is either brought into disrepute or glorified by the way we live.

What I am saying is nothing new, my brothers. Paul said this to the people at Corinth who had already professed the name of Christ: 'You were

* * * * *

533 *Adagia* I ii 4: *Clavum clavo pellere*
534 Ps 70/71:1
535 1 Thess 5:2, Rev 3:3
536 Cf Matt 5:5.
537 Isa 25:8, Rev 7:17 and 21:4
538 Matt 5:16

bought at a great price, so glorify God and bear him in your body.'[539] Similarly in Leviticus it is written of him who had given one of his children to Moloch: 'Because he had defiled my sanctuary and profaned my holy name.'[540] Do not people who lead shameful lives within the church of God defile God's sanctuary? In the same way, the holy name of God is profaned by those whose whole way of life contradicts Christ although they are nominally Christians. What Paul wrote against the Jews who led impious lives is much more suitably applied to those who are Christians in name but who in fact live like pagans. 'You who boast in the law of the gospel, do you dishonour God by breaking the law? For the name of God is blasphemed among the gentiles because of you.'[541] In fact, because of us God's name is blasphemed among Jews, among pagans, and among Christians. For what do the Jews and pagans say when they see certain Christians leading a life almost more wicked than that led by the gentiles at that time? 'Look what kind of worshipper that God has. Look at Christ's disciples. Look what kind of sons that bride of Christ gives birth to. If God is merciful, why does he not correct them? If he is just, why does he allow them to sin with impunity?' The holy name of God, of Christ, and of the church is brought into disrepute by those who are Christians in name but who in their lives and thoughts are more like pagans. There is no crime more shocking than blasphemy, but their blasphemy will redound on the heads of those who provoked it. In fact, they themselves hurl blasphemies at God, if not verbally, then certainly by their deeds, which is more wicked.

This is true of all Christians but especially of those who occupy the highest positions in the church, for the Lord set them like a light on a stand that they might give light to all in the house of God,[542] which is the church; or rather, that they might provide light also for those who are outside the house to enable them to enter. Paul is not satisfied with a bishop who has a good reputation among those who are inside if he does not also have one among those outside.[543] You are said to be a Christian: glorify the name you bear and make sure that it can take pride in you so that you can take pride in it. You are a bishop, the vicar of Christ: do not disgrace the name of the one whose title you take pride in, but glorify his holy name. You will

* * * * *

539 1 Cor 6:20
540 Lev 20:3
541 Rom 2:23–4
542 Matt 5:15
543 1 Tim 3:7

glorify it if the people can see from your way of life that Christ lives in you, if they perceive that you are untiring in your labours, that you cannot be overcome by temptation, that you are zealous in the face of persecution and even prepared to lay down your life for his flock.[544] Then the shameless, too, who used to hate you, will see and blush for shame, since the Lord has helped you in the fight against evil and has comforted you with a sure hope of future reward. Who has the strength to endure such things on his own? Who in such circumstances could be not only resolute and brave but also enthusiastic, unless the Spirit and the hope which does not make one ashamed were there to comfort him? Let us overcome evil with good[545] and, according to the teaching of St Peter, by doing good let us silence the foolishness of shameless men,[546] so that they may either see reason and turn from their wickedness or at least grow ashamed of themselves.

One of you might perhaps ask me: 'How should we glorify God and drive wicked men to a sense of shame?' Paul reveals this to us concisely and clearly when he writes to the Christians at Rome: 'If he gives let him do it with simplicity, if he rules let him do so with diligence, if he is compassionate let him be so with cheerfulness. Let love be free from pretence, hate what is evil, hold fast to what is good, love one another with brotherly affection, outdo one another in showing honour; do not be lazy when it comes to concern for others, be fervent in spirit, serve the Lord, rejoice in hope, be patient in suffering and insistent in prayer. Contribute to the needs of the saints, practise hospitality. Bless those who persecute you, bless them and do not curse them. Rejoice with those who rejoice, weep with those who weep. Live in harmony with one another. Do not be haughty, but be sympathetic to the lowly. Do not keep your wisdom to yourselves; repay no man evil for evil, but take thought for what is good not only before God but also in the sight of men. If possible, live in peace with all men as far as you can; do not avenge yourselves, my beloved, but make way for God's anger. For it is written, "Vengeance is mine and I shall repay, says the Lord." "If your enemy is hungry, feed him; if he is thirsty, give him a drink, for by doing this you will heap burning coals on his head." Do not be overcome by evil, but overcome evil with good.'[547] Here you have the likeness of a Christian man, a picture, as it were, painted by Paul but with the inspiration of the Holy Spirit. This is not written specifically for bishops

* * * * *

544 Cf John 10:11.
545 Rom 12:21
546 1 Pet 2:15
547 Rom 12:8–21, citing Deut 32:35, Prov 25:21–2

or priests or monks; it is written for all Christians without discrimination, for the highest as well as the lowest.

Now since we have been made a spectacle to God, to angels, and to men, according to what this same Paul wrote to the Christians at Corinth,[548] let us picture a theatre[549] and pretend that in one part of the theatre are seated the Jewish people, in another the pagans or Turks or Muslims or any other people who are strangers to Christ. In the third part are seated the schismatics and the heretics; in the fourth section are seated those who are attached to the world, corrupted by their passions rather than by their beliefs. In the fifth section are the weak, in other words, those who are as yet infants in Christ or who have lost their resolve. In the sixth are seated the perfect, in the seventh, on a higher level, our Lord Jesus Christ is seated together with the angels and the souls of the devout, as he watches the drama of our lives unfold before him.[550] In the eighth, on a lower level, is Satan and his bodyguard of wicked demons, watching to see the outcome of the contest. At centre stage we can put the true Christian, who fulfils with determination and enthusiasm all the things that Paul encouraged us to do. Will not all the wicked ones in the audience be dissatisfied and feel ashamed, acknowledging that in him the sign had a beneficial effect? Will they not recognize God's help and the Spirit as comforter? And, as if burning coals had been heaped on the heads of all, will not those among them who are curable be inflamed with a love of God when they see that he has servants of this calibre? The weak will be encouraged in their desire for piety, while those who are perfect will enjoy spiritual happiness, glorifying the name of the Lord in this Christian. Satan will burst with jealousy when he sees that Christ is working and prevailing even in his servants. Christ, the judge of the contest,[551] together with all the saints whom he has already received into a position of security, will be joyful in heaven as if the triumph of his own death has been repeated, just as God, in the mystical writings, boasted to Satan of his servant Job.[552] For the glory of Christ, the head, has not yet been completed, and he wishes it to be made perfect

* * * * *

548 1 Cor 4:9
549 Cf Cicero *Tusculan Disputations* 2.26.64; Erasmus uses this idea several times in his commentary on Psalm 33; see 275, 282, 330 below.
550 On the idea of Christ as the *choragus* of the drama of salvation, see also Allen Ep 2483 and Bietenholz *History and Biography* 26–8.
551 On the idea of Christ as the *agonotheta* used here and below, see also *De Concordia* LB V 491C. Cf Tertullian *Ad martyres* 3 CCL 1 5 and *De fuga* CCL 2 1136, Jerome Ep 71.2 CSEL 55 3, and Aldhelm *De laudibus virginitatis* 18 PL 89 116.
552 Cf Job 1:8, 2:3.

by the whole body together. This is what the church militant desires, this is what the church triumphant desires, and so the joy is shared by all.

Then place in this same theatre any bishop, priest, monk, or Christian who leads an ungodly life, who worships Mammon, covets special privileges, indulges in extravagant and wanton living, is proud, takes revenge, is prone to anger, implacable, or hostile to all that is characteristic of true piety. Will you not see here a completely different audience reaction? You will see the pagans and Jews hurling blasphemous insults at Christ, and the heretics and schismatics being confirmed in their perverse beliefs, saying: 'What have we to do with a church like this, which does not possess Christ? They excommunicate us and hand us over to Satan, but they themselves are completely devoted to Satan.' What effect will it have on those who are bad Christians if not to incite them to sin more recklessly, especially if the one on the stage holds a high-ranking office in the church? And what about the weak? Are they not seriously harmed and drawn to their destruction? In short, the enemies of the spirit will exult and mock, the company of the saints will mourn, and Christ will, so to speak, become ashamed when Satan triumphs in us. Away with any carping critic of my words! If you consider Christ as a whole, he still groans, sighs, is troubled, blushes for shame, and grieves, and since this is so, beloved brothers, we must endeavour with the help of God's grace to glorify the name of the Lord we profess, lest the sign that God gave us for our good should be turned to our disadvantage through our own fault.

We must be a pleasant fragrance to God in every place[553] and continue to stand on God's foundation, which, according to Paul, 'stands firm, bearing this inscription: "The Lord knows those who are his," and "Whoever calls on the name of the Lord departs from iniquity"';[554] and anyone who is a true Christian calls on it. Anyone who is said to be a Christian but does not attempt to withdraw from iniquity is not standing on the foundation and bears a misleading inscription; or if he does not have a misleading inscription, he certainly bears it deceitfully, because he takes pride in the name of one whom he dishonours (in so far as it depends on him) by the way he lives, and he holds God and his only Son Jesus Christ up to contempt.[555] Let us fight bravely, armed with faith, for we have God to support us; let us fight eagerly, for the judge of our contest[556] is also our

* * * * *

553 Cf 2 Cor 2:14–5.
554 2 Tim 2:19, with allusions to Num 16:5 and Isa 26:13
555 Cf Heb 6:6.
556 *agonotheta*; see n551 above.

comforter. Let us hold our battle standard firmly, for it is a good standard, a triumphant standard, and one that terrifies the enemy if we bear it not only as an outward sign but also in our hearts. The cross should be visible on your forehead,[557] but it should be more apparent in your way of life – that is where it will terrify the enemy, that is where it will put him to flight, that is where it will defeat him.

If we are to fight more confidently, we must remain in our fighting unit, we must remain within the walls, we must remain inside the citadel. This is the impregnable city of the church, to which the psalm that follows this one refers when it says: 'Its foundations are on the holy mountains,'[558] and to which the prophecy of Isaiah is referring when it promises a new song to be sung not in the land of Babylon but in the land of Judah,[559] in other words, the land of those who declare that the whole of man's salvation depends on God. What song is this? 'Zion is the city of our strength; a saviour will be placed in her as a wall and a bulwark.'[560] Zion is situated high up, which is why the name signifies 'lookout post' in Hebrew.[561] Our David built this city for us, and he is its wall and bulwark – a wall when he helps us in battle, a bulwark when he strengthens us with his grace before the battle.

It is extraordinary how the whole theme of this song[562] is in harmony with the present psalm, which, as you already know, portrays for us the victory of Christ, the overthrow of Satan, and the destruction of idolatry. It shows how the gentiles have been welcomed into the grace of the gospel, it describes the thanksgiving of the church, tells how all who took up arms against it have been utterly defeated and put to shame, and ascribes all the credit for this to God, who fights in us and for us, giving us greater strength in battle and granting us comfort in our sufferings. This psalm says: 'They will come and bow down before you, O Lord,'[563] while the song in Isaiah says: 'Open the gates and the righteous nation will enter, guarding the truth.'[564] This city is called Zion, in other words, lookout post, and the psalm says: 'For I have lifted up my soul to you.'[565] The psalm contains

* * * * *

557 Cf Arnobius the Younger *Commentarium in psalmum 85* PL 53 449.
558 Ps 86/87:1
559 Isa 26:1
560 Isa 26:1
561 Jerome *De nominibus Hebraicis* PL 23 (1845) 822
562 That is, Isa 26
563 Ps 85/86:9
564 Isa 26:2
565 Ps 85/86:4

the words: 'There is none like you among the gods, O Lord,'[566] while the song says: 'Ancient error has departed,'[567] and in the psalm the people who have been justified by Christ's blood sing in Judah a song to God: 'You are mighty and you do wonderful things. You alone are God.'[568] The psalm says: 'Lead me, O Lord, along your way, and I shall walk in your truth,'[569] and the song gives the corresponding line: 'The way of the righteous is straight, the path of the righteous is straight for walking on.'[570] The psalm says: 'May my heart rejoice so as to fear your name,'[571] while the song has the corresponding line: 'And in the path of your judgments, O Lord, we have held with you; your name and your remembrance are the desire of our soul.'[572] The psalm says: 'Save your servant who trusts in you,'[573] while the words of the song are: 'You will keep peace, peace because we have trusted in you; you trust in the Lord for ever, in the Lord God who is eternally strong.'[574] The psalm says: 'Give me a sign for my benefit that those who hate me may see and be confounded.'[575] What does the song say? 'O Lord, raise your hand, so that they shall not see; let those who are jealous of the people see and be confounded, and let fire destroy your enemies.'[576] The psalm says: 'Give power to your servant,'[577] while the song contains the corresponding line: 'Because the Lord will bend those who live on the heights, he will lay low the lofty city, he will lay it low right to the ground, he will cast it right to the dust, the foot will trample it, the foot of the poor, the steps of the needy.'[578] In the psalm, too, the one who asks for power admits that he is poor and needy.[579] You see how the whole psalm is in harmony with the song. Is it surprising, seeing that they were both dictated by the same spirit?

* * * * *

566 Ps 85/86:8
567 Isa 26:10
568 Ps 85/86:10
569 Ps 85/86:11
570 Isa 26:7
571 Ps 85/86:11
572 Isa 26:8
573 Ps 85/86:2
574 Isa 26:3–4
575 Ps 85/86:17
576 Isa 26:11; the Latin text of this verse differs from the Greek of the Septuagint and the Hebrew version and it is unclear in what sense Erasmus interpreted it.
577 Ps 85/86:16
578 Isa 26:5
579 Ps 85/86:1

I should like to dwell longer on spiritual delights of this kind, but I shall not burden the weaker ones among you any further. Let us trust sincerely in God, let us put our hope firmly in Christ, let us lift our souls to God, let us walk in the way of God, let us advance in the truth of God with joyful awe and trembling joy, in eagerness of spirit but with care and caution lest we slip back into the things that we renounced. Let us remain in Christ, let us fight beneath his banner, and with his help we shall overcome the enemy; but we must not ascribe anything to our own abilities but give all credit to God's mercy. In our life and actions we must show forth Christ, so that those who formerly hated his name may through us become ashamed and if possible also be converted to Christ, to whom, with the Father and the Holy Spirit, is owed all praise, honour, glory, and power for ever and ever, Amen.

A THREEFOLD EXPOSITION OF PSALM 22

In psalmum 22 enarratio triplex

translated and annotated by

EMILY KEARNS

Towards the end of 1529, Erasmus received a letter from one 'Gerard the Frisian,' in the employ of Thomas Boleyn, the English nobleman and courtier, requesting that his master might receive an exposition of Psalm 22/3, 'The Lord is my shepherd.'[1] Though Boleyn was later described by Erasmus as 'among the foremost in learning,'[2] we may doubt whether he would have found a lengthy Latin text easy reading; to Gerard's letter he appends the following: 'I pray yow gyff credyt to thys, and pardon me thow I wryt nat at thys tyme to yow my selff.' Though he wrote with his own hand, he had evidently so little linguistic expertise that the composition of one simple Latin sentence was beyond him: would such a man really have enjoyed reading the text he later received?

Thomas Boleyn was the father of Anne: that was the real reason for the request. Later, Erasmus described his thoughts on the matter to Jacopo Sadoleto.[3] In 1526 he had written the *Institutio christiani matrimonii* for Catherine of Aragon, not then knowing that her request for such a work from one of Europe's leading scholars was connected with the threat to her marriage with Henry VIII of England. But by the time Gerard's letter arrived, the 'king's great matter' was common knowledge, and it was not hard to see that the pro-divorce party wished for their own Erasmian work to add lustre to their cause. Erasmus agonized whether to accept the commission, but finally decided that since the psalm was short and contained nothing that could be relevant to the dispute, there was no harm in the undertaking. The work was quickly produced: it was in progress in January 1530 and published at the latest by April, the date of the letter to Sadoleto with which he sent a copy. With Erasmus, speed of composition does not necessarily indicate a perfunctory approach, but in this case he seems to have been less than enthusiastic about the work: 'Our studies languish,' he writes in January to Haio Herman, 'we have nothing new under way except a homily on Psalm 22.'[4]

Indeed, despite the fact that the text Erasmus is commenting on has become the most popular of the psalms, his treatment does not stand out among the psalm expositions; nor (as he hoped) does it reflect the interesting background to its composition. The chief interest in the work must be found in its method of exegesis. The hermeneutic principles adopted here are not radically different from those Erasmus uses elsewhere, but the

* * * * *

1 Allen Ep 2232
2 Allen Ep 2315:131
3 Allen Ep 2315:129–47
4 Allen Ep 2261:38–42

enarratio triplex is a unique form; nowhere else does he give three different and systematic interpretations of the same text. Scripture may be interpreted in four ways, he tells us at the outset, which would sound familiar
enough to his readers, who would think of the literal, allegorical, tropological, and anagogical senses of traditional exegesis; but he defeats his readers'
expectations by tacitly rejecting a division he regards as over-schematized
and post-classical. Instead, he refuses altogether to treat the literal sense
and divides the remaining figurative applications in a quite different way,
though one that has patristic antecedents, taking the 'I' of the psalm – in
the literal sense, David – as first Christ, then the church, and finally the
individual.

Once embarked with this framework on his undertaking, Erasmus produced little to surprise us. There are philological discussions (132, 169–70,
172–3, 190), attacks on hypocritical churchmen (134–5, 174–5), and praise of
piety in whatever walk of life it occurs (191–2), all common enough features: this is not Erasmus in controversial mood. On one occasion (152–3)
the 'paths of righteousness' induce him to glance at the central Reformation
controversy over justification, but his formula is bland and he will not become involved. Despite its length, the work is one of the closest in style and
feeling to the patristic texts which were the ultimate model for the genre of
the *enarratio*. This is perhaps unexpected in view of Erasmus' claim in the
prefatory letter that he depended largely upon his own resources in com-
posing it, a claim modified slightly in the letter to Sadoleto by the statement
that his debts are to Jerome and Augustine alone.[5] Yet the fact that in both
places Erasmus lists the major Latin authors of psalm commentaries ought
to put us on our guard; he has at least glanced at most of these authors
(in fact he has edited several) and can scarcely have absorbed nothing. He
may well consider Jerome and Augustine the most valuable of the group,
despite his view that the text of Jerome is vitiated by interpolations,[6] but he
has demonstrably used Arnobius, and not only for censure (126, 160, 171,
194). And although he does not refer directly to the Greek Fathers in his
letters to Boleyn and Sadoleto, he appears in his commentary to allude to
Origen, Athanasius, and Chrysostom (146, 159; 157; 146). But he is nonetheless right to stress his independence from any single source, for the work
is very far from a paraphrase of any one earlier commentary on the psalm;

* * * * *

5 Allen Ep 2315:167–8
6 On Erasmus' doubts about the authenticity of the *Breviarium in psalmos* attributed to Jerome see *In psalmum 85* introductory note 6 n19 above and Allen
   Ep 2315:155–7.

the sources for much of Erasmus' lore lie in classical authors as well as in the other writings of the Fathers, but above all in the Bible.

As with so many of Erasmus' works on the Scriptures, the text of this commentary is interwoven with scriptural phrases, sometimes in such a dense, complex, and allusive manner that it is almost impossible to disentangle them. This is one of several problems presented to the translator, not the least of which is the text of the psalm itself: even more than in most cases, the psalm as given in the Vulgate – substantially the text as first quoted by Erasmus – differs very considerably from the familiar English versions, and it has therefore often been impossible even to modify the standard biblical translations. Another, not unrelated, difficulty lies in Erasmus' detailed discussion of particular words and variant translations. It is obviously impossible to find exact equivalents for these Latin (and sometimes Greek) words in English, and I have therefore been forced to disfigure the translation with a higher than usual incidence of words in square brackets. I hope the reader will forgive these inconveniences.

The history of the text is simple: there were no reprintings between the first edition and the Basel *Opera Omnia* of 1540. The text used for this translation is substantially that of ASD v-2, collated throughout with that of LB.

EK

PSALM 22

1 Dominus regit me, et nihil mihi deerit.

2 In loco pascuae, ibi me collocavit; super aquas refectionis educavit me.

3 Animam meam convertit; deduxit me super semitas iustitiae propter nomen suum.

4 Nam et si ambulavero in medio umbrae mortis non timebo mala, quoniam tu mecum es; virga tua et baculus, ipsa me consolata sunt.

5 Parasti in conspectu meo mensam adversus eos qui affligunt me; impinguasti oleo caput meum, et calix meus inebrians quam praeclarus est.

6 Et misericordia tua subsequetur me, omnibus diebus vitae meae, et ut inhabitem in domo Domini in longitudinem dierum.

1 The Lord directs me, and I shall lack nothing.

2 In the place of pasture, there he has put me; over the waters of refreshment he has led me.

3 He has turned my soul; he has led me over the paths of righteousness, for his name's sake.

4 For even if I walk in the midst of the shadow of death, I will not fear evil, since you are with me; your rod and your staff, they have comforted me.

5 You have prepared in my sight a table against those who afflict me; you have anointed my head with oil, and how wonderful is the cup that intoxicates me.

6 And your mercy shall follow me all the days of my life, and that I may dwell in the house of the Lord through the length of days.

TO THE MOST NOBLE BARON OF ENGLAND, SIR THOMAS
ROCHEFORD, DESIDERIUS ERASMUS OF ROTTERDAM, GREETINGS[1]

Noble sir, you have already long since furnished clear evidence of an
exceptional disposition, through your perception that the likenesses of your
ancestors, the family trees, the gold chains, and rings (which both the ancient nobility of your line and your own character, truly worthy of such
a descent, entitle you to display) would be insufficient ornament unless
you could also deck out your mind with a more precious sort of chain, of
which the links, as it were, would be the most upright teachings of philosophy. But now I am even more impressed by your happy state because
I see that a man of influence, a layman and a courtier, is attached to sacred as well as to secular learning and that you are captivated by a longing for that pearl of great price.[2] For this reason I was all the readier to
comply with your most devout wish. The psalm which you selected I have
expounded in three ways – how successfully, I leave to your judgment.
But certainly I myself have gained no little fruit from this small piece,
since while working on it I experienced an extraordinary sense of delight and comfort. If you too are pleased in like measure, then I congratulate myself on obeying your wishes. But if you will consent to in-
form me of what you do not like, then I shall thank you for increasing my
learning.

St Jerome has written about this psalm, but briefly, as is his wont,[3]
and Arnobius is even briefer.[4] St Augustine's work is not an exposition but
consists of the shortest of notes,[5] which I suspect he composed as an aid
to his memory when about to give a sermon, and I am at a loss to know
how his commentary has perished. Cassiodorus I did not have to hand, but
he does not usually contain much of importance.[6] Consequently the work
had to be done to a great extent 'with my own Mars,'[7] as they say. Still,
if it contains anything good, it is absolutely due to Christ alone. And now
please accept the psalm.

* * * * *

1 The dedicatory letter is Ep 2266.
2 Matt 13:46
3 The commentary attributed to Jerome (PL 26 [1845] 884–6), is part of the
  Pseudo-Jerome *Breviarium in psalmos*; see introductory note 121 and n6 above.
4 Arnobius the Younger *Commentarium in psalmum* 22 PL 53 354–5.
5 *Enarratio in psalmum* 22 PL 36 182
6 It is true that the work does not seem to owe anything to this commentary
  (*Expositio in psalmum* 22 PL 70 167–71), although Erasmus does make use of
  Cassiodorus elsewhere; see for instance CWE 63 93, 207.
7 *Adagia* I vi 19

Dear friends,[1] the psalm that I bring before you contains a limited number of words but an abundant harvest of spiritual joys. Count the verses, and you will find the piece very short; but reckon the joys promised in it, and you will find them everlasting, knowing no bounds and no end. Now may the Lord bring together your hearts in one, that you may listen attentively; may he open out your spirits, that you may be able to receive the mysteries.

The psalm is ascribed in the heading to David himself, and its subject is pastoral. Here you will recall that famous prophecy in Ezekiel 34, which speaks of David as the one and only shepherd, who rescues the Lord's flock from all the outrages of the enemy and leads it to graze in fertile pastures abounding in all sorts of foods.[2] History relates a number of facts about King David. He came from a flock to a kingdom, and from a shepherd of sheep he became a shepherd of men.[3] He was known as a man according to God's heart,[4] but the fullness of the mystery refers to our own David, the 'strong of hand,' the slayer of Goliath, that fierce enemy of God's people.[5] He alone it is who was strong enough to rescue his sheep, and who having saved them preserves them faithfully from the tyranny of Satan; nor can any prevail to snatch them from his hands. This is our Lord Jesus Christ, the true living head of the church, the merciful redeemer, wise governor, and unvanquished protector, to whom is given all authority on heaven and

* * * * *

1 Following patristic models, Erasmus adopts for this written work some of the conventions of the orally delivered sermon; this feature occurs sporadically throughout the psalm commentaries but is particularly marked in the treatment of Psalm 22.
2 Much of the following passage is indebted to this chapter.
3 1 Sam 16:11–13, 2 Sam 1–2
4 1 Sam 13:14
5 1 Sam 17:41–51; see also *In psalmum 85* 14 n11 above.

in earth, whose kingdom will have no end, to whom be glory, honour, and power for all time, Amen.[6]

And yet, although in many respects King David prefigured Christ, he held sway over only one portion of the Jewish race. He was not consistently a man close to God's heart, for he killed Uriah and defiled Bathsheba, combining adultery with murder.[7] Again, when he proclaimed a levy of the people, he gravely offended against the Lord,[8] and he could not always protect his people against the enemy. But the Father's witness to Christ was for eternity, and completely true: 'This is my beloved Son, in whom I am pleased.'[9] Consequently we may ignore the historical aspects if we wish, especially since the title gives no clear indication of a subject to which the psalm's literal meaning might refer, and we may attempt to expound the allegorical sense, if your prayers will join with mine to ask the help of the Holy Spirit, and if your eager and attentive concentration encourages me to speak. The art of rhetoric demands that the speaker obtain the good will of his audience and make it more attentive and ready to hear.[10] But this function should be mutual; nothing gives a speaker more assistance in his exposition than a listener who is enthusiastic, attentive, and eager to learn. So it is through your agency that the Lord will consent to give me eloquence.

To begin with, it may be asked how it can be appropriate that while the preceding psalm (which our Lord recited on the cross, so demonstrating the prophecy's fulfilment)[11] depicts the sorrows of death and crucifixion, here all of a sudden there is such rejoicing and happiness.[12] To me this seems a very appropriate sequence, since Christ's death is the source of all our happiness, and it is to him that we owe all the benefits of which the present psalm speaks. Through death there is the way to life, and through the affliction of the cross is the road to joys which have no end.

You are of course quite well aware that whenever one departs from the historical or literal sense the Sacred Scriptures may be interpreted in

* * * * *

6 Cf Rev 5:12–13.
7 2 Samuel 11
8 2 Sam 24:1–10
9 Cf Matt 3:17, Mark 1:11, Luke 3:22.
10 The need for the orator, especially at the opening of his speech, to capture the audience's sympathetic attention (*captatio benevolentiae*), is mentioned in most of the ancient rhetorical treatises; this passage is particularly close to Cicero *De oratore* 2.79.323.
11 That is, Ps 21:2/22:1; cf Matt 27:46, Mark 15:34.
12 Arnobius also comments on the change of mood between the two psalms; *Commentarium in psalmum 22* PL 53 354.

four ways.[13] They may be applied most appropriately to Christ as the head of the church, or to his mystical body the church, or to both together, or to each separately. It deals with each separately when the whole prophetic passage applies equally well to head and body, and with both together when one part of the passage applies to Christ but cannot have reference to his body, while another will fit the body but cannot properly be spoken of the head. There is also a distinction to be made in the use of the word 'church.' Sometimes this word signifies the whole gathering of those who profess the name of Christ, which like the net in the gospel draws in good and bad without distinction while we remain on earth, until the end of time, when the angels of him who alone knows human hearts will separate the good from the wicked.[14] On other occasions 'church' means that uniquely loved bride, without spot or blemish,[15] in whom we believe by faith, whom we do not discern with our eyes, and who is known only by him who makes her clean. Again, the word refers sometimes to the assembly now triumphant in heaven, and sometimes to the assembly here, which is divided, being physically on earth but spiritually in heaven, where Jerusalem, contemplating true and perfect peace, is the mother of all the devout. On occasion a biblical passage may refer to both these entities jointly. Such, my friends, is the fertility of Holy Scripture, at once feeding children with milk, giving adults more solid food, and nourishing with higher learning those who are grown.[16] Scripture possesses an inexhaustible vein of resources; the further you reach into it, the more wonderful are the riches it displays. This is not true of the works of philosophers or poets or of the laws of men. Each of these has its measure of utility, but Scripture, from whatever point of view you contemplate it, bears fruit in abundance. It is impious to laugh at scriptural allegories but fruitful to examine them in a religious spirit; and there is no danger if we err, provided that there is nothing outrageous or impious in our interpretation.[17] I know that it is rather awkward to refer this present psalm to Christ, in a way that abandons the physical sense, but nevertheless, with the Lord's favour, I shall attempt it.

* * * * *

13 Erasmus has taken the idea of the four senses in which a biblical passage may be interpreted (on which see CWE 63 Introduction xxvii–xxx) and applied the traditional number to a quite different division, in which, characteristically, the literal sense is altogether omitted. See Chomarat *Grammaire et rhétorique* 683–7.

14 Cf Matt 13:47–50, Acts 1:24.

15 Cf Eph 5:27.

16 The metaphor derives from 1 Cor 3:1–2 and, especially, Heb 5:12–14, whence it became commonplace in the Fathers.

17 A similar point is made by Augustine in *De doctrina christiana* 3.27 PL 34 80.

The preceding psalm portrays the bitterness of the cross and places before our eyes the struggle in all its difficulty. For this reason one can almost take some of its words as those of a man in despair, who recognizes the vast extent of the evils around him. Such are: 'My God, my God, why have you forsaken me? The words of my sins are far from my salvation,' and 'I am a worm and no man, rejected of men and despised of the people,' and 'I am poured out like water,' and 'My strength is dried up like a potsherd.' But even that psalm ends by showing Christ's victory: 'And my soul shall live for him, and my seed shall serve him.'[18] So this psalm follows very well on such a conclusion, since it shows that when the conflict with Satan is over, everything is safe and peaceful for us; our shepherd's victory is not for himself but for us. Christ, then, speaks according to the human nature he has assumed, assigning all the victory to his Father and saying, 'The Lord directs me' (or 'The Lord feeds me')[19] and it is by his authority that I take on this role, by his protection that I remain undefeated, and by his power that all the prophecies regarding me have been fulfilled. 'He has placed me in fields of pasture': this pasture is the church, to which Christ was sent to perform the redemption of the human race. He continues: When my soul was sorrowful unto death,[20] he sent his angels to restore it with solace from heaven. When I hungered and thirsted after men's salvation, he looked on with favour and refreshed[21] my soul, granting that through my teaching and death all my people should have that for which I so desperately hungered and thirsted. For this was the thirst that tormented me when I was weary at the well and said to the woman of Samaria, 'Give me water to drink'; this was the thirst that made me cry out on the cross, 'I thirst.'[22] These waters alone, where my Father gave me to drink, could cool

* * * * *

18 Ps 21:2, 7, 15, 16, 31 / 22:1, 6, 14, 15, 29–30

19 The translation *Dominus regit me* 'The Lord directs (or rules) me' is that of the Vulgate and was therefore the most familiar; Jerome's rendering in the *Psalterium iuxta Hebraeos* (PL 28 [1890] 1205C), *Dominus pascit me*, 'The Lord pastures me,' was by now widely known to be a more literal rendition (though 'shepherd' is sometimes used metaphorically in Hebrew to mean 'ruler'). Erasmus discusses the different versions of this verse 132 below.

20 Cf Matt 26:38, Mark 14:34.

21 Again Erasmus is following the *Psalterium iuxta Hebraeos* PL 28 (1890) 1206A. *Reficere*, literally 'to remake,' along with its close synonym *recreare*, very frequently carries the connotation 'to refresh.' I have translated these words sometimes as 'refresh,' sometimes as 'refashion,' according as each meaning seems uppermost in the context, but the reader should bear in mind that both meanings may be implied.

22 John 4:7; 19:28

that burning thirst. Then my Father was appeased and overturned the walls, opening heaven to those who believe in me, and 'turned my soul' (or 're- freshed my soul,' as the Hebrew says)[23] from the grief of the cross to rejoic- ing for those redeemed through the cross. When he had refreshed me with this hope, he led me by the paths of righteousness, as I alone can walk the narrow path of the gospel's righteousness without straying, neglecting none of my Father's instructions and speaking nothing apart from the office allot- ted me.[24] I performed the works of my Father, in whose name I was sent, in all things seeking the glory of him who sent me.[25] Following him, therefore, I brought the Law to completion, fulfilling all righteousness,[26] and I con- sidered I had nothing to fear from wicked men or from evil spirits. I lived among the dead, for sin is death, and I went willingly to death on the cross. My soul descended to hell, but took no fright at any kind of ill, for you were always with me, and you never deprived my soul of your divine protection. The pains of death surrounded me,[27] yet by my death I conquered death.[28] I descended into the realm of Hades, and Tartarus opened its jaws, but the everlasting darkness yielded before my light. I threw open the adamantine gates, broke the iron bars, cast the tyrant into chains, and with my spoils I re- turned in triumph above. No human resources could have achieved this, but you, O God, were present in your Son, reconciling the world to you, and by your power, your guidance, and your favour all this was achieved. For you I won the kingdom, and with you as protector I cast down the enemy, and yours was the rod. For the rod that directs the way is the rod of your king- dom; yours was the staff with which I crushed the serpent's head.[29] All this not only made me trust in you, but even in the midst of my afflictions these things were my consolation, so that I endured everything not only bravely, but eagerly. The Pharisees jeered over me as though I were defeated, say- ing, 'Ha, you who destroy the temple of God! If he is the son of God, let him come down now from the cross.'[30] Satan was fitting out his triumph, but you were preparing a triumphal feast for me, for the time when you would bring back my soul from hell and awaken my body from the tomb,

* * * * *

23 See n21 above.
24 Cf John 7:16, 8:28, 12:49, 14:24.
25 Cf John 8:50.
26 Matt 3:15
27 Ps 114/116:3
28 A reminiscence of a phrase in the eucharistic preface for the Easter season ('who in dying has destroyed our death')
29 Cf Gen 3:14, Ps 73/74:14.
30 Matt 27:40

when you would send out your spirit and bring the world under your laws, when you would destroy the idols and change the whole irreligious worship of demons into pious honour paid to your name, and when you would turn the shame of the cross into the highest glory. This is the table of victory which you have prepared for me against those who trouble me and mine, so that they might see him whom they wished dead, and whose name they thought extinguished, exalted above all worldly heights and crowned with the glory of immortality and with everlasting honour. You have washed away the sorrow of the cross, Father, and have changed the sadness of death into the glory of resurrection. My head, which was once spat upon, swollen with blows, and crowned with thorns, 'having neither form nor beauty,'[31] you have anointed with the oil of gladness,[32] and I have drained the cup which you gave me to drink. This cup was not useless, but noble, illustrious, and powerful; many have become drunk from it, to the point where they can despise riches, family, blows, fire, torture, and even life itself. For it did not contain the water of the letter, which the Jews drank before my death, but new wine, the must of the spirit. Babylon too has its cup, and so do the philosophers, but only the cup that is yours causes this drunkenness. This kindness of yours, Father, did not stop short at me alone, but you wished your kindness to be perpetual towards your bride the church, for whom I drank the cup. Your goodness went before me, it accompanied me as I performed the act of redemption in accordance with your commands, and it will persist among my members until the end of time. So I dwell, not in the temple of Jerusalem, which was made with hands, but in the house of the Lord, a house built from living stones[33] and prey to no tempests, in which you hear simultaneously the prayers of those who cry to you from every part of the earth. This is the house which your wisdom built for herself;[34] this is the house which alone I asked for and sought out, so that I might live there all the days of my life and 'through length of days,' that is for ever – nothing being long which has an end at some point in time. Moses dwelt in your tabernacle,[35] but because he was a slave, he did not live there for ever, for the synagogue gave way to the church: only the Son remains in this house for ever. My delight is to be with the sons of men;[36] the head

* * * * *

31 Cf Isa 53:2.
32 Ps 44:8/45:7, Heb 1:9
33 Cf 1 Pet 2:5.
34 Cf Prov 9:1.
35 Perhaps a reference to Exod 33.7–11
36 Prov 8:31

longs for the body to be complete, all members gathered together, so that after I have brought everything under your sway and handed over to you a kingdom now pacified and quiet, I may be complete and perfect as I feast in that heavenly abode, praising your name for all eternity, Amen.

Here, then, is the whole extent of the psalm applied to the person of Christ. It contains, I think, no impiety, as long as you remember that whatever was present in Christ as man was due to the good will of God, which the Bible sometimes calls 'mercy.' Again, all the qualities that pertain to his divine nature derive from the Father, not by his gift but by nature, so that the most complete authority belongs to the Father, who alone is the source of everything, in such a way that he himself derives from none. In the Bible, the Father instructs and the Son performs, following the example 'Let there be light: and there was light'; for it was through the Son that he created the world also, as Paul bears witness.[37] 'Let there be light,' then, are the words of the Father to the Son, while 'and there was light' are the words of the prophetically inspired writer, referring to the Son. Yet this seniority does not lessen the equal status of the Persons of the Trinity, nor does it cause a separation of functions.

Now if in your charity you so desire, we shall with equal brevity apply this same psalm to Christ's body, the church.[38] The church extends far and wide across the world, but since it is bound together with love, through the same Spirit, it speaks as one human being. For it is a greater thing to be unified than to be one.[39] If the same spirit were to animate a thousand bodies, you would have one person, not a thousand, since the same spirit would give life to all these dwellings. In the same way, all those who are animated and directed by the same spirit of Christ form in a sense one person. Thus there were philosophers not lacking in lofty thoughts who maintained that

* * * * *

37 Gen 1:3, Heb 1:2
38 'The church speaking to Christ' is Augustine's interpretation of this psalm; *Enarratio in psalmum* 22 PL 36 182.
39 The unity of the church is a strong and literal concept for Erasmus (see CWE 63 lxxi), and he tends to express it through the Pauline concept of the mystical body of Christ. 'Bound together with love' is literally 'glued into one by love,' *caritate conglutinatur in unum*. The verb *conglutino* is repeated in a similar context 165 below and *In psalmum* 33 321 below. The following sentence is in Latin *plus est unum esse quam unus*, opposing 'one thing' or 'a unity' to 'one person,' with a glance at John 17:11, 21, 22. See also J.K. McConica 'Erasmus and the Grammar of Consent' in *Scrinium Erasmianum* ed J. Coppens, 2 vols (Leiden 1969) II 77–99; H.M. Pabel 'The Peaceful People of Christ' in *Erasmus' Vision of the Church* ed Pabel (Kirksville, MO 1995) 57–93.

the whole of this world, composed as it is of so many diverse and even mu-
tually hostile elements, is together with all it contains just one living creature.[40] Their reason was simply that they thought a single soul gave life to
it, even though it might function in different ways, just as our own soul
does in the various parts of the body, according to the difference in substance; it does not effect understanding in the stomach, sight in the hand,
smell in the tongue, touch in the nails or hair, and in different parts of the
body it has a more or less acute perception. I mention this example not because I agree with the opinion, but to show by analogy how we can think
of the universal church as one human being. This person, then, who is composed of countless thousands, speaks to himself of the Lord's mercy and
says, rejoicing in the benefits bestowed by his head, 'The Lord directs me,
and I shall lack nothing.' Our common reading 'directs' is rendered 'feeds'
in Jerome's version from the Hebrew original, and Augustine also has this
reading.[41] But neither word really corresponds to the sense of the Greek
ποιμαίνει [acts as shepherd]. Any kind of giving of food is expressed in 'he
feeds' [pascit], while the man who sits at the rudder 'directs' [regit] the ship;
ποιμαίνει, however, is properly said of a shepherd who looks after his flock.
The duties of a shepherd are manifold: to gather the scattered flock, to find
fertile and healthy pastures, to recover sheep that have strayed, to heal the
sick, to remain awake guarding against thieves, to be armed against rav-
aging wolves, to lead the flock out, and to lead it back. All these, and anything else belonging to the office of a faithful and courageous shepherd, are
implied in the Greek word ποιμαίνειν. But what is this flock, which is so
much one in soul that although it is in number incalculable and dispersed
through regions of the globe, yet all its members speak with one voice? It is,
of course, the flock that says in another psalm: 'We are your people and the
sheep of your pasture.'[42] What is the sheepfold? What else but the church,
the house of God? Who is the shepherd and also the master (for he is no
hired herdsman)? It is Jesus Christ, the head, redeemer, and leader of his
most dear bride. He is her head,[43] because she lives by his spirit; her Lord,
because he redeemed her from Satan's tyranny with his blood; her leader,

* * * * *

40 It was the Stoics who were particularly associated with the idea of the 'world-
soul' (anima mundi), but the idea is already present in Plato (Timaeus 30A, Phile-
bus 30–7).
41 Jerome Psalterium iuxta Hebraeos PL 28 (1890) 1205C (see n19 above); Augustine
Enarratio in psalmum 22 PL 36 182.
42 Ps 78/79:13
43 Cf Eph 5:23.

for he said himself: 'I am with you until the end of the world.'[44] This flock had once been separated: one part was in servitude to a robber, the devil, through whose agency its members were led into every kind of impiety, to the point that they worshipped human beings, snakes, cattle, monkeys, and other animals, even wood and stone; while the other part, led by the Pharisees and false prophets, was labouring under the letter of the Law and regulations of human origin. The whole flock was all the while sick and ill cared for and had wolves for shepherds: arrogant philosophers, idolatrous kings, profane legislators, Scribes, Pharisees, and false prophets, masters of errors, teachers of a foolish wisdom, and priests of an irreligious religion. About them the Lord wove his long complaint in Ezekiel, saying that they fed themselves and not their flock, consuming milk, clothing themselves in wool, and slaughtering the fat sheep, but had no care for the Lord's flock, neither strengthening the weak, healing the sick, binding the broken, leading back those that had strayed, nor seeking those that had perished. They ruled with harshness and exercised a tyranny over those whom they should have cherished with a fatherly affection.[45] Through their negligence came about what follows in that passage: 'The sheep have been scattered; they are exposed as a prey to be devoured by all the beasts of the field.' They strayed over all the mountains, over every lofty hill, over all the face of the earth,[46] for although they had many masters they had no shepherd. The Lord in his great mercy refused to tolerate this and promised that he would come himself to deliver his sheep, now labouring under the tyranny of robbers, and that though they were divided by their differing beliefs and had gone astray he would lead them back into their own land, to the mountains of Israel, so that there they might graze by streams and lie down in plentiful pastures,[47] in the lush meadows of spiritual and heavenly philosophy. And finally he promised that he would send his servant David, that great shepherd who was called from his sheep to a kingdom;[48] David 'strong of hand' who slew Goliath and delivered God's people from shame, who alone in his wisdom can make a true and certain judgment between sheep and goats, between a healthy, active flock and the languid and sickly,[49] between the

* * * * *

44 Matt 28:20
45 Ezek 34:2–4; cf 125 and n2 above.
46 Ezek 34:5–8
47 Ezek 34:11–16
48 Ezek 34:23–4, 1 Chron 17:7, 2 Sam 7:8
49 Cf Matt 25:32–3, Ezek 34:17–22; on 'strong of hand' see *In psalmum 85* 14 n11 above.

real sheep and those who clothe their wolf's nature with a sheep's fleece.[50] God kept his word, and the Father came in his son David – that is, our Lord Jesus Christ. He called back the lost sheep of the house of Israel, freed them from the tyranny of the Pharisees and the slavery of the Law, and led them away from the barren and savourless letter, opening the living springs of the spirit. But he also brought together the sheep scattered throughout the entire world, separated as they were in so many sects, erroneous beliefs, human requirements, and religious demands, and led them back into one fold, making all these races with all these languages associates in the same truth of the gospel. 'His voice went out in every land.'[51] Before this God was known only in Judaea, but once the voice of the true shepherd had been heard people began to rush together from Scythia, from the furthest parts of Spain, from among the Goths, the Irish, and the Britons, from India and Ethiopia. In the end there was no corner of the world from which a flock was not gathered by this best of shepherds, who gave his life to free his sheep.[52]

All those before him who had not come through him, and all those who will come, were and will be thieves and robbers.[53] The Lord came only to save, whence he was called Σωτήρ or Saviour. But what of a thief? He comes solely to steal, to slaughter, and to destroy. You know the meaning of the proverb 'a wolf guarding the sheep.'[54] 'Thief' and 'robber' are harsh words, dear friends, which no one could hear with equanimity, but what the truth has declared cannot be rejected as groundless. Those who loathe the reproof should avoid incurring it and be filled with as much revulsion for the deed as for the word. If a bishop performs his office for his own glory and gain, having no concern for the Lord's flock, not feeding them with health-giving teaching but rather by his own wicked life inciting them to sin, the titles with which he is graced by men are of no significance. He may be called 'thrice and four times reverend,' but the greatest and most holy Lord, who neither deceives nor is deceived, proclaims out loud that he is a thief and a robber. Such are those who rule with harshness, who have nothing but the

* * * * *

50 Cf Matt 7:15.
51 Cf Ps 18/19:5.
52 Cf John 10:11; in this powerful section Erasmus follows the pastoral tropes of the Old Testament, notably Ezekiel 34 and Psalm 22/23, through to their culmination in the good shepherd of John 10.
53 Cf John 10:8.
54 *Adagia* I iv 10

thunderbolt of excommunication,[55] nothing but prisons, cannons, and the insignia of power; they have none of the teaching that nourishes. But that true shepherd is not like this. He tends the sick sheep, he brings back on his shoulders those that have strayed,[56] and in the words of Isaiah's prophecy 'he does not call out, and his voice is not heard abroad; he does not break a bruised reed, nor extinguish a smouldering wick.'[57] He is not severe or quarrelsome, but gathers and tends his sheep as a hen gathers her chicks under her wing and tends them.[58] You see the terrible consequences with which the Lord through Ezekiel threatens evil shepherds, and the appalling fate he predicts to the Scribes and Pharisees.[59] Those who call themselves shepherds but who behave like wolves and then become the rams that walk at the head of the Lord's flock should tremble to think how they will render account to him who will demand his sheep from their hands; for the Lord's words cannot remain unfulfilled.[60] All these words about evil bishops apply equally to princes. They too are shepherds, as we see from Homer, who so many thousands of years ago called Agamemnon 'shepherd of the peoples.'[61] Consequently, although when kings hold power for their own benefit rather than that of their country no man would be bold enough to say of them that they are thieves and robbers, the Lord has dared to say this; he cannot lie, and he holds no one in fear. And what profit is it for the name to remain unspoken among men if the reality persists in the sight of God?

But let us now return to the good shepherd. If you wish to behold the sad dispersion of the Lord's sheep, then ponder in your hearts the many sects among the Jews: the Pharisees, the Sadducees, the Herodians, the Essenes, and the Samaritans; and among the pagans, the many schools of philosophy, each alike promising a kind of beatitude, and yet, in seeking the source of the highest good, all in violent disagreement with each other – since none followed the true source. Ponder the innumerable and

* * * * *

55 The 'thunderbolt of excommunication' is referred to also in *Julius Exclusus* CWE 27 170. With this passage compare also *In psalmum 1* CWE 63 27.
56 Cf Ezek 34:16, Matt 18:12–14, Luke 15:4–6; these examples of pastoral care embody Erasmus' ideal of authority as service.
57 Isa 42:2–4
58 Cf Isa 40:11, Matt 23:37.
59 Ezek 34:7–10, 17–22, Matt 23:13–38
60 The identification of the rams of the flock with the leaders of church and state is further developed in *De bello Turcico* 217–18 below and *In psalmum 33* 306 below.
61 For example at *Iliad* 1.263

monstrous different religions, or rather superstitions, the different deities, different forms of worship, religious laws, and stories about the gods. Ponder the great mass of regulations of human origin, among the Jews quite as much as among the gentiles – the rabbis were no less at variance with one another than were the philosophers. Now consider the diversity of localities, languages, laws, dispositions, customs, and appearances. The German considers the Saracen or Moor to be scarcely human; a Tartar, you would say, growls like a beast rather than speaking with a human voice. Who was it, then, who brought together all these so disparate peoples? Who restored to their original condition these sheep, reduced to such a miserable state? It was the good shepherd, who by his voice gathered them all together. Straightaway those who belonged to his fold recognized their true shepherd's voice.[62] The shepherds heard angels singing and ran towards the child displayed to them. The Magi heard their shepherd bringing them some message through a star and from distant lands they hurried to the fold. Herod, who was a wolf not a sheep, began to plot his massacre, while the priests, the Scribes, and the Pharisees heard without hearing and saw without seeing.[63] They saw when the king asked them where Christ would be born and they replied correctly, using the prophets; they did not see when they cried out in protest at his teaching and his miracles. They heard in giving their approval to Moses, and they did not hear when they rejected and crucified him of whom Moses spoke.[64]

As Jesus was walking by the sea of Galilee, he called Simon and Andrew, apparently casually.[65] Since they were sheep, they at once heard the voice of their shepherd. What were the words which were so compelling? 'Follow me.' For what reward? 'I will make you fishers of men.' He did not promise high office, or riches, or a kingdom, or honours; he promised nothing but the burden of preaching the gospel. And yet on hearing these words, they asked no questions but left their nets and followed the Lord. They abandoned the sea in withdrawing themselves from the world; they abandoned their nets in renouncing all desires of the flesh. Among them was Simon, who had a wife and mother-in-law at home,[66] yet deaf to their words he heard only the voice of his shepherd. This shepherd did not wander over land and sea to entice his hosts into the net of the Pharisees, but

* * * * *

62 John 10:3–5
63 Cf Matt 13:13, Mark 4:12, Luke 8:10, and John 12:40, all alluding to Isa 6:9–10.
64 Cf John 5:46.
65 Matt 4:18–20, Mark 1:16–18
66 Cf Mark 1:30.

going a little further on, he said to John and James: 'Follow me.'[67] They were sheep, and knew the voice of their shepherd. They abandoned not only the nets that were their family's livelihood but also the father whom they were bound to honour, and followed him who is of greater worth than all attachments. Then who would have believed that Matthew, seated in the custom-house, was a sheep? Yet he at once heard the voice of his shepherd. The words? 'Follow me.'[68] The promised reward? A sheep has no need of promises. It is enough to hear 'Follow me.' For the happiness of the sheep consists in following their shepherd, and while they remain with him they can lack nothing. He called on sheep to become shepherds because only those who are sheep and who follow their shepherd Jesus can be good shepherds. So when Peter, whose concern was still in part the things of the flesh,[69] began to lead his shepherd, saying, 'May heaven favour you, that will not happen,' he heard the words 'Get you behind me, Satan; you do not know the things that are God's.'[70] Zachaeus, despite being chief of the tax-collectors, was a sheep, since on hearing the voice of his shepherd he hurried down from the barren, proud sycamore and hastened towards the faith of the gospel.[71] But the priests and Scribes and Pharisees, although called to the fold in so many different ways, paid no heed to the shepherd's voice. Why did they fail to recognize him? Because they were not among his sheep but heard the voice of their own shepherd, Satan. And what is Satan's call? 'Follow me, and I will make you rich and respected and powerful.'

No one can come to Christ unless he is called by him; and yet there are many whom he draws to himself,[72] not by a bodily voice, but by a silent call only, as he called the thief on the cross.[73] There are many who have heard the Lord's voice with the ears of the body, but they have heard without hearing,[74] because they have not believed what they have heard. As for us, let us hear within, and abandoning the attachments of the world, let us follow him who calls us with all our hearts. Let us hear, my friends, that voice which gathers the scattered sheep, and let anyone who may have

* * * * *

67 Matt 4:21–2, Mark 1:19–20
68 Matt 9:9; cf Mark 2:14, Luke 5:27
69 Rom 8:5
70 Matt 16:22–3
71 Luke 19:1–10
72 Cf John 12:32.
73 Luke 20:42–3
74 Matt 13:13, Luke 8:10; cf n63 above.

strayed come running back to him. In the Gospel he proclaims: 'Come to me, all you who labour and are heavy-laden, and I will refresh you. Take my yoke upon you, and learn from me that I am gentle and humble of heart, and you will find rest for your soul. For my yoke is easy and my burden light.'[75] Dearly beloved, let us too be sheep; let us hear the voice of our most kind shepherd and not stop up our ears. For still today he calls to us all: 'Come to me.' Let us leave the Pharisees, who are the servants of their own bellies, not of Jesus Christ; they are the blind leading the blind, and we should take care lest we fall with them into the pit.[76] Further, let us not be sheep that go astray, but let us keep to him to whom we have turned once and for all, the shepherd and guardian of our souls,[77] our Lord Jesus Christ, who is blessed throughout all ages, Amen.

As I contemplate the Lord's flock, however, another occasion for wonder occurs to me. Christ speaks of a 'little flock,'[78] and this phrase does not apply to the time of our Lord's earthly life alone. The Lord's sheep always were and always will be very few in number when compared with the great mass that remains apart from them. The blessed apostle Paul, writing to the Corinthians, says: 'Consider, my brothers, your calling; not many of you are wise according to the flesh, not many are powerful, not many well-born.'[79] The sheep is a harmless, unaggressive animal; it is not armed with horns or teeth, not equipped to defend itself with hooves or claws or poison. And that first flock and its leaders were chosen from fishermen, from those of humble rank, the poor, and the unknown. They passed their lives in need, amid dangers, betrayals, hardships, mockery, tortures, and deaths – things that are always present for those who wish to live a pious life in Christ Jesus. So whence come those majestic words of the little afflicted flock: 'I shall lack nothing'? Where is the king or emperor, however rich or powerful he may be, who would dare to say 'I lack nothing'? – yet it is bolder still to say 'I shall lack nothing.' How do such bold words come from such a small and lowly flock of sheep? Let those who know nothing but the world marvel at this; for us initiates in Christ's mysteries, there should be no cause for wonder. For faith is a bold and unvanquished thing, against which not even the gates of hell prevail.[80] But this is not trust in

* * * * *

75 Matt 11:28–30
76 Cf Luke 6:39.
77 Cf Isa 53:6, 1 Pet 2:25.
78 Luke 12:32
79 1 Cor 1:26
80 Cf Matt 16:18.

men, which often fails; it is trust in God, which is given by him to his elect
and does not retreat even before the power and ill-will of evil spirits, so
far is it from quailing before the threats of men. It is this, of course, which
enables that bold flock, however small, however lowly and despised, to say
in the midst of confusion and death: 'I shall lack nothing.' What does it rely
on – on its numbers? No. On cunning? Scarcely. On wealth? God forbid.
On arms and power? Nothing could be further from the truth. Different
people rely on different supports, and sometimes one man relies on several, but the flock says 'I am simple, and lean on one anchor'[81] – and that
anchor is, that the Lord my shepherd has taken my care upon him, and I
have once and for all given myself to him with all my heart. Since he is
all-powerful and the source of all good things, I have no fear lest anything
be lacking, as long as he is there; and he has promised that he would be
present until the end of time.[82] This is the unbreakable faith to which Christ
committed the keys of the kingdom of heaven and on which he built his
church,[83] the church which no storms and gales, no sea-surges will overcome. How many persecutions, how many schisms and armies of heretics
have shaken the church right from its beginning, and how many shake it
now! And yet the church trusts in her shepherd, and in joy never ceases to
proclaim: 'The Lord directs me, and I shall lack nothing.' Everything that
is truly good and necessary to salvation flows to me from such a source.

　　'In the place of pasture, there he has put me,' or according to the actual Hebrew, 'in pastures of grass, there he has made me lie down.'[84] The
presence of the adverb 'there' is explained by the idiosyncrasies of Hebrew syntax:[85] the Septuagint translates the phrase 'in the place of grass,'
by which is meant a grassy place, suitable for pasturing. The word that
Jerome renders 'has made to lie down' is translated as κατεσκήνωσεν in the
Septuagint, which is to say 'has given me shade' or 'has put me under a
canopy.' All the while that the sheep were straying among the thorn bushes

* * * * *

81 The one anchor is hope; Heb 6:19. The proverbially prudent use two anchors;
　　cf *Adagia* I i 13: *Duabus ancoris fultis*, and IV viii 72: *Bonum est duabus niti ancoris*.
　　The Christian has no need of worldly precautions.
82 Matt 62:20
83 Cf Matt 16:18–19.
84 'Made me lie down' is Jerome's version in the *Psalterium iuxta Hebraeos* PL 28
　　(1890) 1205C.
85 This is simply a guess, reasonable but in fact wrong. No word for 'there'
　　appears in the Hebrew, or indeed in either Latin version; Erasmus deduces
　　its presence in the original from its unidiomatic and unexplained appearance
　　in the Septuagint.

of the philosophers and the barren sands of the Pharisees, they had no place in which they could obtain relief from the desires of the flesh. Yet shepherds generally make sure that their pastures contain a glade, a cave, or a canopy, or some sort of shady place to which the sheep may retreat so that the sun's heat does not cause them to lose weight or become diseased. These shepherds' canopies are mentioned both in the Song of Songs and in Isaiah.[86] There are two things that moderate excessive heat: shade and a nearby stream of water. So with grassy pastures all about, what more can a flock desire? What can prevent the sheep from lying down in comfort? As for the 'waters of refreshment,' the phrase corresponds to the Hebrew idiom and means refreshing or pleasant waters, which by their coolness restore him who is weary, which when looked on refresh the eyes, and when drunk put an end to the discomfort of thirst. So the true shepherd makes his sheep lie down in pastures that are green with plentiful grass, in the shade near calm and pleasant waters, and here, freed from all desire for worldly things, they may rest in safety and need not seek comfort elsewhere. They could not find such pastures with their own resources; rather, the shepherd guided his sheep, which previously had gone astray, to this place, and there he placed them in the shade and led them to the waters which refreshed wearied souls. Some, I know, interpret the place as the life of blessedness:[87] here, when they are purified by the water of baptism, Christ has made his sheep lie down, not yet in actuality but by virtue of the most certain of expectations. In the midst of the troubles of this mortal life, this hope gives them such nourishment that they derive from it great spiritual strength, such shade that no fleshly desires cause them to sweat, and such refreshment and renewal that those things too are sweet to them which seem bitter to those who only know this world. The world brings sultry weather of various kinds – ambition, greed, lust, and envy – and it, too, has its pastures, but they are barren, filthy, and full of poisonous and deadly grass. The Lord has taken his flock away from such pastures in removing his chosen from the world, and so, having put to death everything in them that belongs to earthly life,[88] they have converse in heaven.[89] They keep their heart where their treasure is,[90] and there they find their comfort

* * * * *

86 Song of Sol 1:7, Isa 4:6
87 No doubt Erasmus has chiefly in mind Pseudo-Jerome, who gives this interpretation of the psalm in *Breviarium in psalmos* PL 26 (1845) 884.
88 Col 3:5
89 Cf Phil 3:20.
90 Cf Matt 6:21, Luke 12:34.

and their cool refuge, as their shepherd prophesied: 'In the world you will have sorrow, in me peace.'[91] All those who have imbibed the spirit of Christ may creep about on earth in the flesh, but their minds are touched by the fire of love and made pure from earthly infections, and are borne only to heaven, its source.[92] God has poured out his spirit upon his church abundantly, or, as Paul's Greek better expresses it, πλουσίως, or 'richly.'[93] Paul says that 'those who do not have the spirit of Christ are not his,'[94] but it is the spirit of Christ that is the motive force in Christ's flock. This is the bride of Christ, at whom the heavenly spirits marvel as she is borne upwards in the Song of Songs: 'Who is she who comes up through the wilderness like a pillar of smoke, with odour of myrrh and frankincense and all the powders of the spice-merchant?'[95] But the souls of those who are driven not by God but by the spirit of this world do not dwell in heaven, where they have laid up no treasure.[96] Where then are they? They live among veins of gold and of other metals, in mines where wealth lies buried – 'unenviable wealth' as the proverb has it[97] – in granaries and wine cellars: in short, either they live under the earth, or at least they do not take wing above it. Such people do not belong to the church but to the synagogue of Satan;[98] for he too has his mystical body and his spirit. But those who are destined to the inheritance of the heavenly Jerusalem through faith, hope, and charity enjoy here on earth, so far as is possible, all the purity, the quiet, the joys, and good things that exist there.

No one should think it out of place that in the midst of that heavenly beatitude we put a shepherd, pastures, shepherds' canopies, and cooling waters. Indeed, some liberty is allowed in expounding allegories, but the exposition ought not to conflict with Holy Scripture. And John in the Apocalypse makes plain the presence of the shepherd, the canopy, and the waters: 'These are they who have come from great tribulation and have washed their garments and made them white in the blood of the lamb. Therefore

* * * * *

91 Cf John 16:33.
92 It was a common belief in the Graeco-Roman world, not confined to any philosophical school, that since the soul's substance is fire it will naturally (as at death, its separation from the body) tend towards the cosmic fire, the *aether* (upper air). See for instance Cicero *De natura deorum* 2.36.91, 3.3.36.
93 Titus 3:6
94 Rom 8:9
95 Song of Sol 3:6
96 Cf Matt 6:20, Luke 12:33.
97 *Adagia* III iii 6, quoted in Greek
98 Rev 2:9

they are before the throne of God and serve him day and night in his temple, and he who sits on the throne will dwell over them. They will not hunger or thirst any more, neither shall the sun beat on them, nor any heat, for the lamb who is in the midst of the throne shall rule them (or, shall be their shepherd).'[99] Here, too, the Greek word is ποιμανεῖ [he will shepherd],[100] and he will lead them down to the springs of life, and God will wipe every tear from their eyes.[101] Here he feeds them with faith and with grace; there he will feed them with his presence. Here he renews them with the pledge of the Spirit; there he will bring them cool and refreshment with eternal glory. They drink from the spiritual rock which is the companion of the pious in the wilderness of this world and which refreshes them;[102] they drink of rivers of living water which flow from within the shepherd,[103] of which our Lord spoke to the woman of Samaria: 'There will be in him a spring of living water welling up to everlasting life.'[104] And the theme of Psalm 41 is related: 'As the hart longs for springs of water, so my soul longs for you, O God.'[105] As springs of water are to a stag on fire with the poison of serpents, so is God to the soul in this its earthly habitation of the body, wearied by cares and troubles and temptations. And Psalm 35 is in agreement: 'Since the fountain of life, O God, is with you.'[106] The canopies are mentioned in Psalm 83: 'How lovely are your tabernacles, O Lord of hosts; my soul feels longing in the courts of the Lord,' and again in Psalm 45: 'The onrush of a river makes the city glad, and the most high has made his tabernacle holy.'[107] There both river and canopy are mentioned. Moreover, it is simple to prove that the peace and happiness of eternal life are called by the name of 'paradise.'[108] And our Lord on the cross said to the thief 'Today you will be with me in paradise'[109] – meaning, of course, that everlast-

* * * * *

99 Rev 7:14–16
100 The word ποιμαίνει means 'acts as shepherd,' and like the familiar English 'The Lord is my shepherd' is a close rendition of the Hebrew. The Latin *pascit* is more limited, referring to feeding only.
101 Rev 7:17
102 Cf Exod 17:2–6, 1 Cor 10:4.
103 Cf John 7:38.
104 John 4:14
105 Ps 41:2/42:1
106 Ps 35:10/36:9
107 Pss 83:2–3/84:1–2 and 45:5/46:4
108 *Paradeisos*, literally 'a pleasure garden,' properly refers in a biblical context to the garden of Eden.
109 Luke 23:43

ing blessedness which no trouble or fear of evil can mar, a taste of which was vouchsafed to Paul when he was snatched up to God's paradise.[110] And where paradise is, there is no lack of pleasant pastures or of living waters, so that now they neither hunger nor thirst,[111] for all their wants are sated by the presence of him who is the limitless source of all that either men or angels could desire. So Psalm 35: 'They shall be made drunk with the plenty of your house, and you shall give them to drink of the river of your pleasures.'[112]

There are many other scriptural passages from which we can see that the life everlasting has a shepherd and pastures and shade and waters; these passages, like numerous others, can also be applied to this church on earth. This should cause no surprise; the church is one and the same, and the essential difference is that whereas the church beyond has already completed her struggle and awaits nothing but the resurrection of the bodies which sleep on earth and the arrival of those brothers who remain soldiers on earth, this church here is still engaged in the struggle against the world, the flesh, and the devil[113] and hastens eagerly towards its heavenly prize.[114] There the church contemplates her shepherd face to face, as he is; here she perceives him in a mirror and a riddle.[115] There she possesses in full those things which in a certain sense our shepherd offers us here: the pastures, the canopies, and the waters. But here the shepherd rules his sheep. He directs their path to prevent them from straying or brings them back when they have strayed already, and though he feeds them on pastures, they have been hungry and are likely to faint if they are given no food; though he protects them with shade, they are hot and worn out; and though he refreshes them with water, they have thirsted after justice[116] and would otherwise waste away. So now, my brothers, let us pray to our most kindly shepherd that he will stoop to guide us in expounding the sense of these words, so that our souls may understand their mystical truth and so be nourished and refreshed.

* * * * *

110 2 Cor 12:2–4
111 Rev 7:16
112 Ps 35:9/36:8
113 A traditional formula derived from Christ's threefold temptation in Matt 4:1–11 and Luke 4:1–13; cf also 1 John 2:16.
114 Erasmus is here drawing on the imagery of contests and prizes used by Paul, for instance at 1 Cor 9:24, Phil 3:14, and 2 Tim 4:7.
115 Cf 1 Cor 13:12.
116 Matt 5:6

Error[117] can take many different forms, and falsehood is often opposed to falsehood; but truth is one, and truth can never oppose truth.[118]
So this prince of shepherds has led us away from the countless paths of error and brought us to the knowledge of truth through his gospel. He has
led us away from the barren letter of the law of Moses, from the thirst and
hunger of temporal things – which can never satisfy the human spirit but
torture it all the more – and made us part of his body, so that we may live
by his spirit and lack no spiritual resource or delight. 'All things are yours,'
says Paul, 'but you are Christ's.'[119] He has made us lie down in the grassy
meadows of the church and has placed us among his snow-white flock.
There our minds first began to grow quiet after the tumult of wrongdoing
and errors, for outside the enclosure of the church there is no peace.[120] He
has made us lie down in the grassy meadows of spiritual teaching, which is
the food of the soul just as bread is the food of the body. So our Lord said:
'Man cannot live by bread alone, but by every word that comes from the
mouth of God.'[121] And he has given us the promise of his Spirit[122] so that,
dead to the world, we might not be tortured by any love of worldly things
– this is the canopy which shelters us from the heat of desire. He has led us
to the waters of refreshment – that is, to the source of regeneration where
we cast off the old man with his deeds and are reborn into the new man,
created in the likeness of God and formed to recognize God in accordance
with the image of his creator.[123] See what a heavy burden weighs on the
person laden with sin, making him a slave of Satan and heir to Gehenna.
Consider the tardy confession of the wicked: 'We have grown weary in the
way of wickedness and of perdition, we have walked through paths that
are hard, and we have not known the way of the Lord.'[124] You will have no
difficulty in realizing what comfort and refreshment it gives us to be received through instruction and through the sacrament of baptism into the
unity of the church, whose strength is in the innocence she has received,
freely given, from her shepherd. The church contains so many sacramental

* * * * *

117 *Error* in Latin covers both literally 'going astray' (like sheep) and figuratively
     'making a mistake' (morally or intellectually).
118 A patristic commonplace, as in Leo Ep 172 PL 54 1216; compare *In psalmum 4*
     CWE 63 264.
119 1 Cor 3:22–3
120 Cf *In psalmum 85* 16 n25 above.
121 Matt 4:4, Luke 4:4
122 John 14:16, 26; cf Gal 3:14.
123 Cf Col 3:9–10.
124 Wisd 5:7

benefits to fill our souls with spiritual grace; it contains the differing gifts of the Spirit, varying in accordance with each recipient's measure of faith; it contains the milk of simple teaching to sustain children and the food of higher learning with which adults mature;[125] and it contains ever ready the remedy of penance, which will restore any who may be snatched from the flock's fellowship by the devil, who is always on the attack like a roaring lion, searching for one to devour.[126] In the first place, the shepherd breathed into her the gift of faith, which gives us a sure knowledge of those things we cannot see. He added the gift of hope, through which we await in complete confidence the fulfilment of all that God has promised us. And he has added finally the gift of love, which sweetens all things, however harsh. Now consider, my dear friends. Is it without cause that those who possess all these in such measure rejoice in their good fortune – not indeed one individual, but one body speaking as one man, and give thanks to their shepherd: 'The Lord gives me pasture, and I shall lack nothing. He has put me in a place of pasture; he has led me by the waters of refreshment' (or, in Jerome's version, 'he has fed me')?[127] This may be taken as particularly appropriate to those under instruction in the faith, but is relevant to all Christians, since no one in this life has reached the point at which no further progress is possible. And by 'the waters of refreshment' some understand the teaching that we find in Scripture,[128] which is in truth a paradise nourishing, sustaining, and fashioning anew the souls of the pious who grow weary in this vale of miseries. In the darkness of this world it is this that shines before us as a bright lantern in a dark place, until the day grows bright in our hearts;[129] it is this that comforts us in our troubles with the hope of heavenly rewards, as Paul points out: 'Whatever things were written were written for our instruction, so that through patience and the comfort of the Scriptures we may have hope.'[130] Scripture reproves those in error, rebuts the obstinate, and improves those who are making progress and brings them to perfection. As Paul writes to Timothy: 'All Scripture inspired by God is useful for teaching, for refutation, for correction, and for

* * * * *

125 Cf 1 Cor 3:1, Heb 5:12.

126 1 Pet 5:8

127 Jerome's version is in the *Psalterium iuxta Hebraeos* (see nn19, 41 above) and also in the paraphrase in Pseudo-Jerome *Breviarium in psalmos* PL 26 (1845) 884.

128 Pseudo-Jerome *Breviarium in psalmos* PL 26 (1845) 884–5 gives this interpretation as an alternative to that which identifies the 'waters of refreshment' with baptism.

129 Cf 2 Pet 1:19.

130 Rom 15:4

instruction in righteousness, so that the man of God may be perfect and fitted for every good work.'[131] Lastly, it has the two-edged sword which can pierce even to the place where soul and spirit divide,[132] and it has the body and blood of the Lord, that food and that drink which give those who partake of them eternal life.[133] For in the interpretation of the ancients our Lord spoke the words 'My flesh is truly food, and my blood is truly drink' primarily with reference to his teaching.[134] This discourse is living and effective; it can even call those who are dead and buried back to life, as we read in John chapter 5: 'The dead will hear the voice of the Son of God, and those who hear will live.'[135] The apostles experienced this re-creation when the Lord asked them if they too wished to go away: 'Lord,' they said 'where shall we go? You have the words of life.'[136]

It is not out of place to take the grassy pastures and the waters of refreshment as referring to the same thing, since it is quite in keeping with scriptural usage to express the same sentiment with several different images, so that it may make a deeper impression on the mind. Dear brothers, let us be sheep; let us follow our shepherd Jesus, who will lead us to the common pasture of the church, feed us with wholesome grass, and take us down to the waters that wash away all stains, bestow heavenly wisdom, comfort the afflicted, and refresh the weary – the clear, living waters that well up towards everlasting life.[137] No one reaches such waters except by the guidance of our shepherd, no one drinks them except through his spirit, and no one is revived unless he drinks. They are drained in faith and drunk with feeling, and you may search in vain for this water outside the unity of the church.[138] Outside the dwelling of the church one may be baptized,

* * * * *

131 2 Tim 3:16–17
132 Heb 4:12
133 John 6:54–5/53–4
134 John 6:56/55. The most common explanation of Christ's words relates them to the Eucharist, as in Augustine *Tractatus in Ioannis evangelium* 26.6.17 PL 35 1613; an alternative reading identifies the food and drink with Christ's teaching, as in Origen *De principiis* PG 11 244–7 and Chrysostom *In Ioannem homilia* 46 PG 59 259. It is the latter tradition that Erasmus invokes here in his claim that the Scriptures possess the body and blood of Christ; compare his appeal to 'the earliest commentators' in *In psalmum 4* CWE 63 209 and n208. On the Scriptures as food see D. Baker-Smith 'Erasmus as Reader of the Psalms' ERSY 20 (2000) 10–11.
135 John 5:25
136 John 6:68–9/67–8
137 John 4:14
138 Cf *In psalmum 85* 16 n25 above.

but the fruits of baptism may be enjoyed only within the church. And the Scriptures, which were given to us through the Spirit of Christ, can be understood correctly only through the same spirit. As the Spirit once came from heaven to those gathered together in the same chamber,[139] so it flees from those who shun the companionship of this house. Outside it, the Jews have their own water, the skin of water that was exhausted in the wilderness and the well from which Hagar, as best she could, gave her son Ishmael to drink[140] – that is, the inactive letter of the Law by which the Jews were constrained until the appointed time. They have the waters of Marah, too bitter to drink,[141] which for us have been made sweet by Christ's cross. They have the six old pitchers full of water, which Christ has changed for us by his spirit into the best of wines.[142] They drink death – for 'the letter kills'[143] – but we drink life everlasting. The heretics, too, have their broken cisterns, which can hold no water;[144] they were not dug by Abraham and restored by our own Isaac, [145] but by the heretics themselves for their own use. The enemies of the church have a torrent of arrogance, but the Lord will not allow it to overwhelm his sheep, as we learn from Psalm 123: 'When their fury was hot against us, perhaps the water might have swallowed us; the torrent might have passed over our soul, the waters of pride might have gone over our soul.' (This is Jerome's version, keeping close to the actual Hebrew words, because the proud are swollen and savage, like rapids).[146] Philosophers too have streams of water, but they are deadly in part and in part unhealthy, and always made muddy and turbulent by manifold errors. Poets have their own springs, but such as may turn men into women, as in the old myth of the spring of Salmacis.[147] The Sirens' lovely song, the sweetness of their voices, seduce the ears,[148] but the lack

* * * * *

139 Acts 2:1–4
140 Gen 21:14–19
141 Exod 15:23
142 Cf John 2:1–11.
143 2 Cor 3:6
144 Jer 2:13
145 Cf Gen 26:15, 18.
146 Ps 123/124:3–5. Erasmus quotes a mixed version of these verses: up to 'might have swallowed us' he gives the familiar Vulgate words, and for what follows he quotes Jerome's *Psalterium iuxta Hebraeos* PL 28 (1890) 1292 (where the Vulgate is close to incoherence).
147 See Ovid *Metamorphoses* 4.286–388.
148 See Homer *Odyssey* 12.39–55, 166–200. The allegorical interpretation of the Sirens was current in antiquity; Plutarch *Moralia* 745D–E (*Quaestiones conviviales* 9.14.6), and see R. Lamberton *Homer the Theologian* (Berkeley and Los Ange-

of virility in the sentiment makes minds effeminate. (I am speaking here of those poets who wrote frivolous verse). Then there are the Philistines, who attempt to throw earth into the wells dug by Isaac and to destroy them.[149] Who are these Philistines? They are those who give a strained interpretation to the heavenly Scriptures, referring them to human emotions, and so, by a 'Lesbian rule'[150] bending them to fit our habits, when in fact our life ought to be ruled by their standard. Perhaps one should also number among the Philistines those who add an excessive amount of secular philosophy and vast mounds of human reasoning, and so do not allow Scripture to flow forth in its full purity. At every turn a philosopher is quoted – but however ingenious he may be in every way, this is not enough for some people. We hear much of Averroës, but he is insufficient for our intellectual pride, and we have added an obscure and problematic system of philosophy.[151] There are also the pools represented by those doctors whose books have been accepted in the church as being in accordance with canonical Scripture; no one is prevented from drinking from these, provided that he does so with discrimination. For none of them has managed to avoid error completely, even though this can be pardoned because of human frailty.[152] It is only canonical Scripture that has springs from which you may safely drink your fill, provided that he who has the key of David is with you, he who closes so that none may open and opens so that none may close.[153]

And so, my friends, if we desire to be truly cleansed and truly refashioned, let us not search for waters outside the pastures of the church, but remaining among them let us joyfully drink the waters from the wells of

* * * * *

les 1986) 7, 10. On Christian interpretations of the theme, see H. Rahner *Greek Myths and Christian Mystery* (London 1963; German original 1957) 328–86. In the *Enchiridion* CWE 66 33 Erasmus states that the allegorical reading of Homer in general is well established and useful.

149 Gen 26:15; the allegorical interpretation was common.

150 *Adagia* I v 93

151 Erasmus is referring to his favourite target, scholastic philosophy, which he attacks for what he takes to be its inappropriately heavy and obfuscating use of Aristotle and other non-Christian thinkers. The views of Averroës, the twelfth-century Arab philosopher and commentator on Aristotle, though several times condemned by ecclesiastical authority, remained influential throughout the late Middle Ages. The point seems to have been particularly on Erasmus' mind at this time; he uses very similar words in his letter to Sadoleto of May 1530, Ep 2315:68–9.

152 This idea is developed at length in a slightly different context in *In psalmum 38* LB V 432A–435B; cf also *In psalmum 33* 367–8 below.

153 Cf Isa 22:22, Rev 3:7.

Isaac, from the springs of Jesus our saviour.[154] ('Isaac' signifies 'joy,' and Jesus is the name of salvation).[155] The church of Christ drinks faithfully from these springs, filling itself in the joy of the spirit with the joy of salvation. This paradise possesses a most copious spring, whence flow four rivers to irrigate the earth.[156] Here are the waters of the Jordan, where Naaman the Syrian was cured of his leprosy at his seventh immersion and came out clean as a little child;[157] later, our Lord made them sacred for us by his baptism.[158] Here are the waters of Shiloah, which flow in silence[159] – the silence, of course, of spiritual wisdom, which according to St James is peaceable and restrained.[160] It is shunned by the obstinate heretics, avoided by those who are puffed up with belief in human wisdom,[161] and mocked by those who are drunk with the cup of Babylon.[162] Here is the pool of Siloam, where the man who was born blind straight away gains his sight when he washes his eyes.[163] Here is the sea made red by the blood of Christ, which drowns the whole multitude of black sins and allows the people of God to escape freely.[164] Here is the sheep-pool, which when stirred by an angel heals every kind of ill;[165] here the stream that flows from the right-hand side of the temple,[166] which the child in Christ crosses and the water only reaches his ankles – this is the water of forgiveness. The same water is deeper at another point, so that it reaches the knees, and in still another place it is too deep for a man to cross, since the judgments of God are a great abyss.[167] (Indeed it has been said, not without point, that the Scriptures are a river in which the sheep walks and the elephant swims).[168] And

* * * * *

154 Cf *In psalmum 85* 16 n25 above.
155 The source is Jerome *De nominibus Hebraicis* 91 PL 23 (1845) 841.
156 Cf Gen 2:10–14.
157 2 Kings 5:14, Luke 4:27
158 Matt 3:13–17, Mark 1:9–11, Luke 3:3, 21–2
159 Isa 8:6
160 James 3:17
161 Cf 1 Cor 8:1.
162 Cf Rev 17:2.
163 John 9:1–7
164 An allusion to Christ's redemptive act as the fulfilment of the symbol of the Israelites crossing the Red Sea, a favourite patristic theme deriving ultimately from Rev 15:2–4
165 John 5:2–7
166 Ezek 47:1–5, a passage that Erasmus continues to draw on in the following description.
167 Cf Ps 35/36:7.
168 Gregory, in his letter to Leander prefacing the Commentary on Job PL 75 515A

according to the same prophecy every creature reached by this stream of water is alive and safe, though if it left the banks it would die.[169] Along the banks of the stream are trees which bear fruit; that is, the doctors and saints of both Testaments, to which the First Psalm refers in imitation of this passage of the prophet: 'And he shall be like a tree planted by the waterside, which will yield its fruit in its season, and its leaf will not wither; and everything he does shall prosper.'[170] The fruit of these trees is useful for food and their leaves for healing medicines, since they are nourished by no ordinary waters but by the water which flows from the sanctuary of the heavenly temple.[171] The Jews do not possess this river, but rather they have the waters of Marah,[172] on whose banks grow fig trees which vaunt their foliage of words and turns of phrase but bear no fruit, and for this reason are hateful to the Lord, just like the fig tree in Luke, which the Lord threatens to cut down.[173] The infertile race of the Jews has persisted to our own days in being such a tree; although it has been manured throughout the ages, and for so long tolerated by the Lord in his mildness, in case at length it might come to its senses, it has produced nothing up to now but the leaves and the foliage of the Law.[174] But Jesus does not hunger for leaves; he seeks in humankind the sweet-tasting fruit of faith.[175] And a tree cannot be fruitful unless its roots are watered by the river which flows from the sanctuary of the Spirit. But let us proceed, and contemplate the fertile waters contained in the paradise-garden of the church. There is the river of peace, the stream of glory in flood,[176] which Isaiah mentions again elsewhere, saying 'There will appear in Zion a rushing river, glorious in a parched land.'[177] There is the stream of pleasures and delight, which makes the pious drunk, so that they despise all those things held precious by the world.[178] And so that the sheep may lack nothing, there is also water containing soda, somewhat bitter to the taste, but able to wash away the stain of sin. This water is recommended to us in Psalm 6: 'Each night I shall wash my bed, and with

* * * * *

169 Cf Ezek 47:9–11.
170 Ps 1:3
171 Cf Ezek 47:7, 12.
172 Exod 15:23
173 Luke 13:6–9
174 On Erasmus' attitude to Jews, see CWE 63 Introduction xlviii–lvi. The word *infelix* means both 'infertile' and 'unfortunate.'
175 Cf Matt 21:18–19, Mark 11:12–14, and see CWE 63 44–5.
176 Isa 48:18, 6:12
177 Cf Isa 44:3.
178 Cf Ps 35:9/36:8.

my tears I shall water my pallet.'[179] There are two kinds of penitential water. One is that of baptism, which freely washes everything clean, and the
other is the water of reconciliation, which is like a second baptism; it also
cleanses, but not without the acrid quality of soda.

Now whether we take the 'waters of refreshment' to be the washing of
rebirth,[180] or spiritual teaching, or a gift of the Spirit, what effect do these
waters have? 'He has turned my soul,' or (with St Jerome) 'he has refreshed
my soul,'[181] or, as some prefer, 'he has restored my soul.' You should not be
worried by these alternative versions, since they serve to clarify the point
rather than to obscure it.[182] When you taste the spiritual joys of the church,
your mind begins to be revolted by what it used to delight in; what you
once thought sweet you find bitter, what seemed precious you reckon as
filth and rubbish, what seemed exalted you think worthless,[183] and turning away from all of these you are completely caught up in wonder and
love of the things of heaven, and you say with the psalmist: 'Lord, I have
loved the beauty of your house and the dwelling place of your glory.'[184]
When the disciples still knew only the flesh, they marvelled at the temple in Jerusalem,[185] although it was made with hands[186] and was in effect a
filthy hovel compared with the spiritual building that is the house of God;
but that cannot be seen except with the eyes of a pure heart, since all the
glory of the bride of Christ is within.[187] Now the Greek does not say simply
'turned,' but ἐπέστρεψεν, that is, 'turned towards him.'[188] He has turned us
away from the empty shadows of things and towards the truth itself, beautiful beyond measure, that is, towards the highest good, which is none other
than our shepherd. When this happens, everything else immediately grows
worthless; for once the mind attains that pearl whose price cannot be reck-
oned,[189] it not only disposes of all it possesses but reckons life itself as of
no value as long as it can possess that other. My brothers, what I am saying

* * * * *

179 Ps 6:7/6
180 Titus 3:5
181 See n21 above.
182 Cf In psalmum 33 294–5 and n107 below.
183 Similar sentiments and expressions are found in De puero Iesu CWE 29 69.
184 Ps 25/26:8
185 Matt 24:1, Mark 13:1, Luke 21:5
186 Cf Mark 14:58.
187 Cf Ps 44:14/45:13.
188 Similarly, convertit in Latin means both physically 'turned' and figuratively
'converted.'
189 Cf Matt 13:45–6.

will be understood by those to whom it is given to taste and see how sweet
is the Lord.[190] Even now they are aware of the misery of those who are
slaves to ambition, lust, luxurious living, avarice, and all the other vices,
and on the other hand 'how happy are all who put their trust in the Lord'[191]
and whose Lord and master is truly God.[192] And so whoever turns to God
is completely refreshed, and in fact restored. But from what and to what
is he restored? He is restored from darkness to light, from the death into
which he had sunk through his own and Adam's sins back to his first origins and the innocence in which Adam was set before the Fall; indeed he is
more happily restored to that state by grace than Adam was placed in it by
nature.[193] For God in his mercy so disposed things that Adam's downfall
should result in gain to the pious, to the glory of God.

I think it is not accidental that the text says 'he has turned my soul'
rather than 'he has turned me.' A human being may turn a body, but only
God can turn a soul. There is no benefit in baptism, in learning, in professing Christianity, in sharing in the sacraments, if God has not turned the
soul with invisible grace. Sometimes the soul is taken up with human emotions, which lead sometimes to the flesh, sometimes to the spirit – but more
of this later.

What still remains? Listen to the words that follow: 'He has led me
over the paths of righteousness.' Righteousness is of two kinds, the first
being the innocence to which we are restored through faith and baptism
and the second the righteousness of faith working through love.[194] For we

* * * * *

190 Ps 33:9/34:8
191 Cf Ps 2:13/12.
192 *Dominus* is the appropriate word both for 'Lord' (in a religious context) and
     'master' (of a slave).
193 Compare *De puero Iesu* CWE 25 59; Erasmus' words echo both the proclamation
     of the Easter vigil, with its reference to the 'necessary sin of Adam,' and the
     blessing of the water in the offertory of the mass, 'O God, by whom the dig-
     nity of human nature was wondrously established and yet more wondrously
     restored.' Cf also n318 below.
194 The formula of a 'double righteousness' (*iustitia duplex*) derives from Aris-
     totle, who in *Magna moralia* 1.33 1195a distinguishes between 'natural' and
     'conventional' justice. It is used by Erasmus, following the exegesis of Origen
     (*Commentarii in epistolam ad Romanos* 8.2 PG 14 1160C–1161A), in his *Paraphrase
     on Romans* (CWE 42 60) to express the distinction between the righteousness
     of Moses and of Christ, the Old Testament and the New. Here it is used in
     a third sense, covering what was normally seen as the distinction between
     righteousness attained through faith and that attained through works. Thus
     Erasmus touches upon a central Reformation debate (see CWE 63 Introduction

are reborn by a holy washing which is so powerful that just as while we lived in the 'old man'[195] and with the flesh we gave our members – that is, our emotions – to serve wrongdoing upon wrongdoing,[196] so too when we have 'put on the new man'[197] we go forward in the paths of the Lord from virtue to virtue[198] until we reach the perfection of manhood and the fullness of Christ Jesus.[199] The word 'paths' occurs for two reasons, the shortness of the way and its narrow breadth. Those who travel in coaches, on horseback, or in litters are entering by the broad highway that leads to death; but narrow is the way that leads to life[200] – narrow because it is a path trodden by few. On the other point, our Lord has compressed the whole labyrinth of the Law into a short compass (as Scripture says, 'the Lord will complete his word in brevity upon earth'),[201] showing that the whole of the Law is contained in love alone.[202] Perhaps the author preferred to say 'paths' rather than 'roads' because the teaching of the gospel constrains more closely than that of the Law; more is demanded from us than from those under the Law, because we have received more and therefore we are more in debt. Do you wish to hear the paths of righteousness according to the gospel? 'He who is angry with his brother will be brought to judgment; he who says to his brother, "Raca," must answer for it to the court; he who says to his brother, "Fool," must answer for it in the fires of hell. He who sees a woman and desires her has committed adultery with her in his heart. Let no one put away his wife except for the fault of adultery. Do not swear any oath, neither by heaven nor by earth. If someone strikes you on the right cheek, offer him the other one as well. Love your enemies and do good to them that hate you; pray for your prosecutors and those who malign you'[203] – and there are very many other injunctions given by our Lord in Matthew 5 and 6. But the narrow paths need not frighten you as you contemplate human weakness; it is the Lord who will lead you along these paths, and however narrow the way it will be easy when your

* * * * *

lxiii) but attempts to avoid controversy by using the word 'faith' in connexion with both types of righteousness.
195 Rom 6:6, Col 3:9
196 Cf Rom 6:13, 19.
197 Eph 4:24, Col 3:10
198 Ps 83:8/84:7
199 Cf Eph 4:13.
200 Cf Matt 7:14.
201 Rom 9:28, citing Isa 10:23
202 Matt 7:12, Luke 10:25–8, and cf Rom 13:10, Gal 5:14.
203 Cf Matt 5:22, 28, 32, 34–5, 39, 44.

heart is enlarged. The man who said 'I have run the way of your commandments, when you enlarged my heart'[204] was not afraid. Where the spirit of
the Lord is there is freedom. The road has been widened for us by the re-
duction of those rites through which the Jews would timidly make their
way, and it has been narrowed towards perfect piety.

At this point, in order that the psalm may run freely, let us review in
conclusion the bountiful deeds of our shepherd. He has led us away from
the world, he has made us lie down in fertile pastures, he has cleansed us
from our sins with his blood, he has refreshed us with the water of the
spirit, he has captivated our soul with longing for eternal life, he has led us
by the paths of good works. And what merit of ours brought us so many
benefits? What good had we performed, what service made us deserve so
well of God? We were by nature sons of anger,[205] we were enslaved to
idols and to our own desires, and we lived without law and without God.
Then what explains our shepherd's great liberality towards us? The reply is
brief: 'for his name's sake.' What does this mean, for his name's sake? All
these things he has given us freely, though we deserved nothing, so that
he might use us to display to all the glory of his name and the faith of his
promises. The Lord wished his mercy to be recognized, so that we might
'acknowledge that he is good, that his mercy endures for ever.'[206] Take away
from me, you Jew, the righteousness of your works; 'all have sinned and
have been wanting in the glory of God.'[207] He does not give this glory of
his to any other, lest you should claim any part of it as your own. My dear
friends, everything Christ has done for his church was done of his mercy;
but it can in a sense be called justice, since what he gave he had promised.
(This too is a kind of justice, to perform what you have promised.)[208] And
the words 'for his name's sake' refer to each of the preceding clauses: 'The
Lord directs me, for his name's sake; he allows me to lack nothing, for his
name's sake. He has made me lie down in pastures, for his name's sake. He
has led me to the waters of refreshment, for his name's sake. He has led me
by the paths of righteousness, for his name's sake.' And so, my brothers,
whatever good things we also may do, let us do them for his name's sake
and not for our own; let us indeed acknowledge the grace of the Lord, but
in such a way that our own efforts may be its servant.

* * * * *

204 Ps 118/119:32
205 Eph 2:3
206 Ps 105/106:1, 106/107:1, 117/118:1
207 Rom 3:23
208 A point made in patristic writers, for instance Ambrose in his *Commentarium
     in epistolam ad Romanos* (on Rom 1:17) PL 17 (1845) 56B

Those who enter on the straight paths of the Lord must await tribulation, temptation, and persecution by evil men in whom Satan exercises his strength. To grasp this more clearly, think of the fate suffered by Abel, by the prophets, by John the Baptist, by Christ himself, by the apostles and the martyrs – and what the small and lowly flock[209] continues to suffer today at the hands of its enemies, both without and within. Yet still it cannot be deflected from the paths of righteousness, and this is because it depends on the might of its leader, the same to whom, moving on, it now addresses the following words: 'For even if I walk in the midst of the shadow of death, I will not fear evil, since you are with me.' Christ is the light of his church, while ignorance and sin are the shadow of death, that is, the uttermost obscurity, in which the prince of darkness is lord. The bride of Christ passes these terrors as she makes her way through the paths of righteousness, hastening towards everlasting felicity, but she is not afraid. Whence comes this extraordinary confidence? It does not derive from her own strength. She looks around her, and when she finds no resources in herself she throws herself on her spouse, embraces him and says, 'Since you are with me.' Where he is, there is light, there is righteousness, there the prince of darkness[210] is powerless, since he who takes our side is stronger than all our adversaries. Meanwhile the church advances through the midst of this darkness and these terrors, secure through the leadership of its shepherd, for according to the promise in the Gospel 'the gates of hell will not prevail against it.'[211] But at the same time, until the ending of the world, she is shaken by every kind of device; yet protected by her spouse she emerges victorious over every attack and cunning plot and 'every high thing that raises itself against the knowledge of God.'[212] The church once moved amidst this darkness, when it was subject to Pharaoh in Egypt, but as Moses led the people of Israel into the wilderness, so Christ has called his sheep away from ignorance of God, out of the utter darkness of sin into his wonderful light.[213] He freed them into his keeping, so that now they do not fear death's shadow since their shepherd has truly[214] conquered death by his own death. The church does not fear the world, since it puts its trust in him who said, 'Be of good cheer, I have overcome the

* * * * *

209 Cf Luke 12:32.
210 The common title derives from Eph 6:12.
211 Matt 16:18
212 2 Cor 10:5
213 1 Pet 2:9
214 Reading *vere* for *veram*. The emendation improves the sense, and the slip would have been an easy one.

world.'[215] It does not fear the flesh which fights against the spirit,[216] because although it walks now in the flesh it does not walk according to the flesh.[217] It does not fear the theft of its property, since it has laid up its treasure in heaven;[218] it does not fear the death of the body, since it has a sure hope of resurrection.[219] But meanwhile the tyrant tries ceaselessly to recover the prey that has been snatched from him; he exercises all his craft and brings all his devices to bear, he turns himself into every possible shape, even at times metamorphosing himself into an angel of light[220] in order to lay his hands on some of the sheep – or rather to destroy the whole fold. For this reason it has been said quite rightly that the life of the faithful is soldiering on earth,[221] and it is essential, as the church continues to advance along the paths of righteousness, that it should march in military style, arms at the ready, drawn up in ranks, sober and alert and ready to receive every enemy attack. It is in this way that the apostle Paul, writing to the Ephesians, exhorts the church to advance: 'For the rest, my brothers, be strong in the Lord, and in the power of his might. Put on the armour of God, so that you may be able to stand firm against the wiles of the devil. For our fight is not against flesh and blood, but against princes and powers, against the rulers of this world of darkness, against the spiritual powers of evil in the heavens. Therefore receive the armour of God' – and so on.[222] Do even sheep, then, have weapons that will be effective against so many and such evil enemies? They do; but the weapons are powerful in God, and so they may say with Paul, 'We can do all things in him who gives us strength.'[223] The prophet uttered a brave sentiment when he said 'The Lord is my helper: I shall not fear what man may do to me';[224] but the shepherd has given greater trust to his sheep, so that they can say: The Lord is with me, I shall not fear anything that the princes of darkness may do to me. 'The Lord is my light and my salvation: whom shall I fear? The Lord is the guardian of my life: of whom shall I be afraid?'[225] When men

* * * * *

215 John 16:33
216 Cf 1 Pet 2:11, Rom 7:21–3.
217 Cf 2 Cor 10:3.
218 Cf Matt 6:19–20, 19:21, Mark 10:2, Luke 12:33, 18:22.
219 Cf 1 Pet 1:3.
220 2 Cor 11:14
221 Cf Job 7:1, also quoted at the opening of the *Enchiridion* CWE 66 24.
222 Eph 6:10–13
223 Cf Phil 4:13.
224 Ps 117/118:6
225 Ps 26/27:1

make war on each other they rely on all sorts of defences and like foxes make use of many different artifices. But the church, like the hedgehog,[226] has only one defence, yet that one is most sure: 'For you are with me.' The man who possesses Christ is safe even in hell, while he who has lost Christ may go up to heaven but will be no safer than before. At this point someone may ask the point of such laborious warfare, when the shepherd has it in his power to leave the sheep undisturbed and repel every evil. 'O man, who are you to reply to God?'[227] Victory is assured, but Christ desired to overcome in this way, in this way to triumph through his own, and he wished his own to reach the fellowship of the heavenly kingdom by treading in the footsteps with which he went before us. The work is ours in part, but the victor's praise belongs entirely to him, from whom comes all our ability.

I shall now move on to the next verse, if first I may briefly examine the significance of one syllable, 'for,' which connects this verse with those preceding. Jerome gives instead the translation 'but,' and another scholar considers that it should be omitted.[228] Still, in my view, it was not needlessly added in the Septuagint, nor should it be alien to your devotion to deal with these details in passing, since you are aware that in Holy Scripture there is not one letter that is insignificant.[229] Those who are skilled in dialectic reason in both directions, sometimes deducing cause from effect, sometimes effect from cause. You can say, 'The sun is above the earth, for it is day' or else, 'It is day, for the sun is above the earth'; both present equally correct reasoning. This example refers to necessary consequences, but it is the same with probable consequences: 'This picture ought to be very fine, for Apelles painted it.' 'Apelles painted this picture, for it is excellent.'[230] It is more usual, however, to deduce effect from cause; yet is seems that the psalmist is using the effects to establish the cause. He has already said much: the Lord directs me, he has made me lie down, he has refreshed me, he has led me along the paths of righteousness. At this point it is as though someone were to ask 'But what evidence is there that what you say is true?'

* * * * *

226 Cf *Adagia* I v 18.
227 Rom 9:20
228 'For' is omitted in the text quoted by Athanasius in his *Expositio in psalmum 22* PG 27 140C, and in Felice da Prato *Psalterium* 14 recto. For Erasmus' acquaintance with the latter see Ep 456:103. On Jerome's translation see n231 below.
229 Cf Matt 5:18.
230 Apelles was considered the most eminent of Greek painters.

He replies: 'For even if I walk in the midst of the shadow of death I shall
not fear evil, since my shepherd is with me.' For it is his good will alone
that provides this security. But the church does not say this to an inquirer,
but rather to its own shepherd, as though calling him to witness that she
has said nothing that is not true. For no one can make his way through the
dangers of this world unless he is governed, refashioned, and led by the all-
powerful shepherd, our Lord Jesus Christ. And Christ cannot deny himself
so that his promises fail, nor can any power overcome the all-powerful.

No less plain is the sentiment in St Jerome's version: 'But even if I
walk in the valley of the shadow of death ...'[231] 'But even if' carries increased emphasis, implying 'I have said little in that he feeds me, he has refreshed me, he has led me along the paths of righteousness; he has given me
something more generous, enabling me to go safely upon my ways.' He has
not only snatched me away from the power of darkness, but he has given
me so much strength that I may be fearless in the face of all the tyrant's
assaults, relying on the presence of my shepherd who has cast down the
prince of this world,[232] who has overcome the world[233] – has overcome it
for us and overcomes it in us.

I want now to say something else of an equally detailed nature, but
not without its usefulness. This verse can be applied to everything which
has gone before, just as we have shown how the phrase 'for his name's
sake' in the previous line can refer to what precedes. For the great confidence which the church has derives from this: that whatever her spouse offers her or has promised her is not attributed to her own merits, of which
she has none – or if she has any she does not acknowledge them, or if she
acknowledges them she does not count them either as originating in herself
or as worthy of such rewards. But because that good shepherd gives everything to his chosen ones for the sake of his name's glory (that is, to confer
renown on his wonderful mercy towards the human race), there is no danger that he will change his views, since in a sense it is his own business
which is being transacted. His name remains for ever.[234] What does this
mean? 'I am who I am.'[235] He cannot change his laws or his promises; he

* * * * *

231 The contrast here is between the Vulgate wording *Nam et si* For even if' and
the more emphatic *Sed et si* 'But even if' of the *Psalterium iuxta Hebraeos* PL 28
(1890) 1206A.

232 Cf John 12:31.

233 Cf John 16:33.

234 A conflation of such phrases as Exod 3:15 ('this is my name for ever') with 2
Cor 9:9 ('his righteousness endures for ever'); on the immutability of God's
promises compare *In psalmum 85* 95–6 above.

235 Exod 3:14

is truthful, and everywhere he wishes to be found righteous in his words, when there is judgment.[236] And he picked out his sheep before he laid the foundations of the world, that they might be 'holy and spotless in his sight, in love.'[237] And as Paul again says elsewhere: 'Those whom he foreknew, he also foreordained; those whom he foreordained, he also called; those whom he called, he also justified; those whom he justified, he also magnified.'[238] As this is revealed to the bride through the spirit of her spouse, she says with faith: 'If God is for us, who is against us? It is God who justifies; who is there that will condemn? Who will separate us from the love of Christ? I am persuaded that neither death, nor life, nor angels, nor principalities, nor powers, nor things present, nor things to come, nor strength, nor height, nor depth, nor any other creature shall be able to separate us from the love of God which is in Christ Jesus our Lord.'[239] And this is to say: 'I will not fear evil, since you are with me.' The only evil that is truly to be feared is divorce from Christ. There is a marriage; he has declared himself a bridegroom, he has taken me as his bride, I have come into his hands,[240] and the marriage cannot be dissolved, since he who joined the bond cannot change.

As a modest bride will be completely dependent on her husband, so a flock of sheep will be completely dependent on the care of its shepherd. Thus the faithful flock says to its shepherd, 'Your rod and your staff, they have comforted me.' At first sight this sentence seems rather silly; green pastures give rest to the weary, and clear waters refresh the fatigued, but what comfort is bestowed by rod and staff? Yet they do bestow comfort, and in the greatest measure, against the raids made by demons plotting to divert the flock from the paths of righteousness. I am aware that some of the ancients[241] understand by 'rod' the Lord's rebuke, since on occasion he inflicts sufferings in order to correct his church and call it back to him, and by 'staff' a harsher punishment, for as Solomon says: 'He who spares

* * * * *

236 The passage is a loose paraphrase of Ps 50:6/51:4 and Rom 3:4. In technical language, a person who is 'found righteous' is 'justified,' the translation adopted for the passage from Romans below, which refers to human beings rather than to God.
237 Eph 1:4
238 Cf Rom 8:29–30.
239 Rom 8:31, 33–4, 35, 38–9
240 A quasi-technical phrase denoting the submission of the wife to her husband's jurisdiction
241 Erasmus has in mind Pseudo-Jerome *Breviarium in psalmos* PL 26 (1845) 885, Augustine *Enarratio in psalmum* 22 PL 36 182, and Origen *Commentarius in psalmos* PG 12 1262.

the rod hates his son; but he who in truth loves him instructs him with vehemence.'[242] Paul repeats this view in writing to the Hebrews: 'Whom the Lord loves, he punishes. He reproves each son whom he receives.'[243] The same occurs in Ecclesiasticus: 'Bend the neck of thy son in his youth, and strike his sides while he is yet an infant.'[244] To conclude, Paul also uses a rod to threaten the Corinthians.[245] Then there are those who interpret the rod as that of the church, with which it threatens the wrongdoer, while the staff is that which it uses to give succour to the penitent.[246] Both of these are pious sentiments, but not, I think, particularly well suited to this passage, which says, not 'my rod and my staff,' but 'your rod and your staff.' It is more appropriate to remain within the pastoral imagery, and take 'rod' and 'staff' as the same thing, which is not uncommon in the Bible; or if there is a difference, we could take the rod as the grace which guides the faithful by precepts and prevents them from wandering from the paths of righteousness, while the staff would be used by the shepherd to keep off wolves and robbers. But the actual flock of sheep has no rod or staff of its own, just as the apostles too were without them;[247] all its trust is in the guidance and protection of its shepherd, who says: 'Do not be anxious for what you shall eat, or how you shall clothe yourselves, but only seek the kingdom of God, and all these things will be given to you,' and 'Do not fear those who kill the body, but cannot kill the soul,' and 'Take no thought for what you will say or how you will speak,' and 'Vengeance is mine, and I will repay,' 'Who rejects you, rejects me.'[248] This rod, this staff of Jesus our shepherd are the feeble flock's comfort against the terrors of every evil. There is indeed a rod which deflects from the straight path, and there is a staff which is broken and pierces those who lean on it;[249] but this is not the way of the rod which belongs to the groom guiding his bride or of the staff which he uses to protect her. In Paul's words, the enemy has 'weapons of fire,'[250] and only Christ can divert these with his staff; is

* * * * *

242 Prov 13:24
243 Heb 12:6
244 Ecclus / Sir 30:12
245 1 Cor 4:21
246 This is the interpretation of Arnobius the Younger *Commentarium in psalmum* 22 PL 53 354D.
247 Matt 10:10
248 The quotations are from, respectively, Matt 6:25 and Luke 12:31, Matt 10:28, Luke 21:14, Rom 12:19 and Heb 10:30 (alluding to Deut 32:35), Luke 10:16.
249 Cf Isa 36:6.
250 Eph 6:16

not this great comfort in the course of the soldier's journey? How tenderly, dearly beloved, our Lord Jesus loved his bride; he neglected nothing which could give her protection, refreshment, and comfort.

The benefits that we have mentioned are enormous, but his unbounded love and inexhaustible kindness were not content to stop here. What more could be added? He added even in this life a sort of ovation,[251] a kind of prelude or introduction to the everlasting triumph. What is this, you ask? Let us listen to the bride herself as she relates her joys. 'You have prepared in my sight a table against those who afflict me' she says. Here is another wonderful comfort. Not content with his constant presence with his bride in faith and spirit, as he had promised,[252] he further prepared for her a victory banquet, in which he gives her his own body for life-giving food, and he offered her a cup of his own blood from which she might drink as often as she wished, so that in this new and unheard-of way also he might be with his sheep, in bodily form and in visible sacraments.[253] Now let the Jews vaunt their manna! This, in truth, is the bread which comes down from heaven,[254] bringing life and immortality to all who consume it worthily; this is the cup which brings the drunkenness of spiritual joys. The delights of this feast are not recognized by those who are not governed by the heavenly shepherd; only the sheep are nourished by the flesh and inebriated by the blood of the spotless lamb, who offered himself for their salvation, and whose most holy blood they drink. But this table which gives honour to its sons, this royal banquet, is prepared against those who ceaselessly trouble the flock of Christ. Why is this table set *against* those who are not admitted to it? Because they are dogs, and what is holy is not given to dogs;[255] but it is shown to them, so that they may watch and waste away as they see the delights, the riches, the triumph, the happiness, and the concord

* * * * *

251 Erasmus is using 'ovation' here in the technical sense of a lesser form of triumph.

252 Matt 28:20

253 Erasmus here diverges from the interpretation of Pseudo-Jerome (*Breviarium in psalmos* PL 26 [1845] 885), who interprets the table as Scripture, and to some extent from that of Origen (*Commentarius in psalmos* PG 12 1262), who refers it to the heavenly banquet (the latter sense will appear more fully in the third section of the commentary, 196–7 below) and chooses instead the more usual interpretation, exemplified in Arnobius the Younger (*Commentarium in psalmum 22* PL 53 354D–355A), who identifies the table with the Eucharist.

254 John 6:59/58, 33. The whole passage, verses 26–59/58, gives the context, with a sustained allusion to the manna of Exod 16:14–36.

255 Matt 7:6

enjoyed by those who cling faithfully to Christ their Lord. For what could exalt a human being more than by sharing in the Lord's body and blood to become one with Christ, in the same way that bodily food and drink are converted into the substance of the eater and drinker – although here it is rather the case that those who eat and drink are changed into what they consume. And they become one not only with Christ their head, but since they share in the same meal and are animated by the same spirit they become one among themselves. Similarly, just as all the members constitute one body, so the head and the body in a sense constitute one individual. And since the Father, Son, and Holy Spirit are one, there results an inexpressible unity, so that God is all things in everything.[256] The church's enemies look on at this triumphal banquet, some mocking, some envious, some unbelieving; but meanwhile the sheep are filled, made joyful, strengthened, and intoxicated by the heavenly food. Angels revere the sight, and to the sheep it brings happiness and salvation, but to impious spirits it is an object of fear and terror, for nothing makes them tremble more than the spiritual exultation of those who sing as with one voice the praises of the Lamb,[257] who has broken their tyranny and snatched his sheep from the hands of the wolves.

So now let the world go on its way, swollen as it is with deceitful honours, drunk with crazy pleasures. As for those who despise empty benefits which will shortly exist no longer, and yearn with their whole hearts for the benefits of heaven, let the world pity them and think them abject and miserable. Such is the honour given by the Lord to those whom the world regards as worms, and with such joys he cheers those who the world thinks are not even alive: as the text says, 'For thy sake we are killed all day long; we have been counted as sheep for the slaughter.'[258] These are the spiritual joys that 'the ear of man has not heard, the eye of man has not seen, nor have they gone up into the heart of man' – for they are the delights of angels and not of men – yet even in this life God 'has prepared them for those who love him,'[259] who have passed beyond the nature of men and have become worthy to join the company of angels and of the divine nature. This is the hundredfold that the Lord promised his own in this world,[260] and it is a pledge of life everlasting, which will happen in the world to come.

* * * * *

256 Cf 1 Cor 15:28.
257 Cf Rev 5:12–13, 15:3.
258 Ps 43/44:22, Rom 8:36
259 1 Cor 2:9
260 Cf Matt 19:29.

Now let the Jews – ravenous, panting with thirst, miserable, ragged, and parched as they are – let them boast of their table, which they consider holy if it is untouched by pig meat or by eels; let them adore their shew-bread which might not be touched except by priests[261] – despite the fact that when they lost their priesthood they lost their shewbread with it. Let them boast of their sacrifices of dumb animals – which they also lost at the destruction of the temple, since only there were they allowed to perform sacrifice. Let them vaunt their table free of leaven, when in their hearts they have the 'leaven of malice.'[262] What do those unhappy people eat, what do they drink? They nibble at the bad-tasting, bitter husk of the barley-ear, but they do not touch the inner kernel;[263] they refuse to touch pig meat in the fleshly sense, but in the spirit they are nourished by the food given to pigs, bran and pea-pods.[264] And let the pagans compare their tables with the tables of the church. What did they eat at them? The flesh of beasts sacrificed to demonic beings. What did they drink? The wine from which they made libations to demons, who were present like guests at the feast, but not in the splendour that the poets imagine;[265] rather they reaped the benefits of their worshippers' madness and fed to their destruction. What are their hymns? They sing of Jupiter almighty – adulterer, sister's husband, lover of boys. Drunken worshippers sing hymns to the Egyptian bull or the snake Aesculapius or the buffoon Bacchus.[266] Dearly beloved, we would be seated at

* * * * *

261 1 Sam 21:4–6, Matt 12:3–4, Mark 2:25–6, Luke 6:3–4
262 1 Cor 5:8
263 This image is used several times by patristic writers on allegory to express the concept of an inner truth hidden in an unpromising exterior. Erasmus uses it also in the *Enchiridion* CWE 66 35. See Charles Béné, *Érasme et saint Augustin* (Geneva 1969) 268.
264 An allusion to the story of the prodigal son; Luke 15:16
265 Erasmus may have in mind such phrases as Horace's *noctes cenaeque deum* 'O nights and banquets of the gods!' (*Satires* 2.6.65), used to describe the highest pleasure imaginable.
266 The unrestrained love affairs of Jupiter or Zeus, including those with the married woman Alcmene and the boy Ganymede, and his marriage to his sister Juno or Hera (probably referred to here, though *incestus* may carry a wider connotation) were of course an embarrassment to many long before they were seized on by Christian writers. The Egyptian bull is Apis, worshipped in the form of a living bull in Egypt (see Herodotus 3.27–9, Pliny *Naturalis historia* 8.184–6, Augustine *De civitate Dei* 18.5 PL 41 563–4). Aesculapius, god of healing, was commonly shown accompanied by a snake and sometimes identified with it. Bacchus, or Dionysus, was the god of ecstasy and intoxication, hence 'buffoon.'

such evil and deadly tables even now had not our shepherd the Lord Jesus in his mercy taken us away from the table and the cup of demons and brought us to this most excellent feast, this heavenly banquet, where our heavenly Father presides with his Son, giving us everything. At this table the members of Christ are seated, around it stand the angels with deep joy and fearful trembling, and in inexpressible unison of heavenly and earthly beings that most pure Lamb is celebrated, who by his death redeemed his fellow banqueters and with his living body and blood gives them sustenance and gladness.

This inexpressible happiness of the church is signified by the word 'oil' in the text of the prophet: 'You have anointed my head with oil.' (The preposition 'in' derives from the Hebrew idiom and is unnecessary in Latin.)[267] This oil is the hidden 'oil of gladness' with which God had anointed above all his fellows him who is 'fairer in form than the children of men.'[268] The followers of Epicurus also have their perfumes, with which they anoint themselves before they drink their fill to the point of madness. But the other is the oil of the Spirit, which alone makes the minds of men truly joyful; those who are anointed with this preparation are a sweet savour to God in every place, the odour which brings life to those who obey Christ their shepherd, but death to those who are lost – that is, to the swine.[269] For those who investigate natural phenomena tell us that ointments are a deadly poison to pigs,[270] and demons desire to cross over into pigs, as animals closely related to them.[271] But marjoram ointment is not so deadly to pigs as are the torments caused to evil spirits by the concord and spiritual rejoicing of the faithful in Christ. This feast was seen with prophetic eyes by the man who exclaims in wonder: 'Behold how good and how pleasant it is for brethren to dwell together in unity. It is like the ointment on the head which runs down upon the beard, the beard of Aaron, which goes down to the hem of his garments.'[272] As the most important part of the outer man is the head, so the chief part of the inner man is the spirit. This is a spiritual banquet, a spiritual oil, and it is the spirit of man that it cheers. And the head of the

* * * * *

267 The Vulgate reads 'Impinguasti in oleo caput meum,' as does the main version of Felice da Prato *Psalterium* 14 recto, but the latter gives the marginal alternative 'impinguasti oleo.' The variants occur because the Hebrew preposition used here to denote the instrument is also very often used to mean 'in.'
268 Ps 44:8, 3/45:7, 2
269 Based on 2 Cor 2:14–16
270 Specifically, oil scented with marjoram; cf *Adagia* I iv 38
271 See Matt 8:30–2, Mark 5:12–13, Luke 8:32–3.
272 Ps 132/133:2

church is Christ, in whom 'abides in bodily form the whole fullness of divinity.'[273] 'From his fullness' all the members of the church 'receive grace for
grace.'[274] And so the ointment has run down from the head of Christ onto
those who are in truth brothers, united by the same spirit[275] and dwelling
together with the same opinions, the same mind, in the banquet chamber of
the church. It flows first into the beard – whose beard? The beard of Aaron,
the high priest. In bygone days kings and priests were anointed with holy
oil, and Christ was both king and priest, king in winning the kingdom
for God his father, priest in sacrificing himself for the world's salvation.
From him the unguent flows into the beard, into the apostles and the martyrs, who were strong in the power of the spirit (bearded, one might say)
and were not afraid to die for the Lord's flock. From there the fragrance
of Christ was spread throughout the whole world, and the sweet savour of
the gospel reached the furthest of the nations, dealing death to the swine,
giving life to those who believe. This, of course, was the costly ointment
which the woman in the Gospel poured from its broken jar over Jesus' head,
and in John's account over his feet also, 'and it filled the whole house'[276]
– the house being the church. From those strongest of men the ointment
flowed down to the hem of Jesus' garment, that is, to the least member of
the church, down to the young girls who run up, attracted by the sweet
smell of spiritual unguents, as the bride herself prophesies in the Song of
Solomon: 'Your name is as oil poured out; the young girls love you.'[277] Who
are these young girls? Clearly they are supported in great numbers by the
church's king Solomon, who with his spirit protects and feeds them until
they grow up and attain appropriate strength of mind.[278] For no one, however young or infantile, is kept from this table, if only he is grafted onto
the body of Christ, which is the church.[279] (It is not absurd to call the same
thing 'body' and 'garment,' for the relationship between body and soul is
the same as that between garment and body; within the body is the soul,
within the garment the body. The outermost part of the body is the skin,
of the garment the hem).[280]

* * * * *

273 Col 2:9
274 John 1:16
275 In Latin, *eodem conglutinati spiritu*; on *conglutinare*, see n39 above.
276 Matt 26:7, John 12:3
277 Song of Sol 1:2–3
278 Perhaps a distant reminiscence of Eph 4:13
279 Cf Rom 11:17–24.
280 There is a similar comparison in *De puero Iesu* CWE 29 69–70; the simpler and
      more obvious image of the body as a garment is found at Job 10:11.

In past times, the body and blood of the Lord were given to babies reborn in baptism, and this usage, practised by the church for so long, was a
commendable one. It was given also to neophytes, and today it is withheld
from none who desires it, however humble, insignificant, poor, or unimportant; on the one condition that the ointment has flowed down to him from
the head of our own Aaron, he is welcomed to this banquet. But those who
are not anointed with this oil must not come near the Lord's table, lest they
eat and drink judgment to themselves, not discerning the body and blood
of the Lord.[281]

The method of preparation of the holy oil is explained by Moses with
great reverence,[282] and his actions were a type expressing spiritual realities.
No one can prepare this oil except God, who alone bestows his Holy Spirit,
and any human being who wishes to make it commits an offence worthy
of death. This was what the man Simon attempted in seeking to obtain the
gifts of the Spirit with money, but he heard the reply: 'Thy money perish
with thee.'[283] It is a pity that Simon's example has been surpassed by so
many; what in him was a crime is now a custom. But what are the functions
of correctly prepared oil? It invests kings, it consecrates priests, and it sanctifies all the vessels of the temple.[284] And the honour of these titles flows
down from Christ, the head, to the members of Christ. All those who have
become one with him are kings; in this world they hold sway over wayward desires and triumph over Satan through Christ, while in the world
to come those who here have suffered with him and for him will reign together with him. And they are priests, if they continue to come to this table
to offer the sacrifice of praise, and daily to sacrifice themselves to God, a
living victim, acceptable and reasonable.[285] For although only a priest may
consecrate the body and blood of the Lord, the offering is made in common
by all the faithful.

There is testimony to this kingship and priesthood in Revelation,
where the church givers thanks to its shepherd: 'You have redeemed us
by your blood out of every tribe and tongue and people and nation, and
have made us a kingdom and priests to our God, and we shall reign on
earth.' St Peter is in agreement when he directs Christ's sheep with these
words: 'But you are a chosen race, a royal priesthood, a holy nation, God's

* * * * *

281 1 Cor 11:29
282 Exod 30:22–5
283 Acts 8:18–23
284 See 1 Sam 10:1, Exod 29:1–7, 40:9–11.
285 Cf Rom 12:1; the phrase is also used in the canon of the Roman mass.

own people.'[286] As for the vessels, there is abundant testimony in Paul, himself called a chosen vessel.[287] In his epistle to the Romans he mentions 'vessels of mercy, which he has prepared beforehand for glory, so that he might make known the riches of his glory.'[288] Again, in the epistle to Timothy, he makes a distinction between vessels prepared for honour and those prepared for dishonour; for both even now 'are found in the great house' (which in the wider sense of the word is the visible church) so that it may include all those reborn by washing.[289] In this house are Paul, a vessel of gold or rather of jewels, and Cyprian,[290] a vessel of silver, and Sabellius and Arius,[291] vessels of clay. Even such vases God can dispose of to his glory. It is true that something composed naturally of gold cannot become wooden, and something made of clay cannot become silver – or the contrary. However, in the house of the church, a vessel that has deteriorated from its proper purity can 'purge itself from these' so that it becomes 'a vessel for noble use, consecrated and useful to the master of the house, ready for any good work.'[292]

Consequently, none are admitted to this heavenly table unless they are kings, priests, and vessels consecrated to the Lord by the oil of the Spirit. If sin reigns in a person's mortal body, if he is a slave to vices and wayward desires, he ought not to approach this table. What does he risk if he does so? He risks being pushed away and cast into the outer darkness.[293] He who has not yet sacrificed to God the members of his flesh, which war against the spirit,[294] ought not to take his place at this table. What danger would attend him? What happened to Uzziah might happen to him: Uzziah was struck by the hand of the Lord; he was a king but not a priest, and yet he dared to go to the altar to offer sacrifice.[295] Thus anyone who has not yet learned to 'possess his vessel in sanctification and honour,' but is still

* * * * *

286 Rev 5:9–10, 1 Pet 2:9
287 Acts 9:15
288 Rom 9:23
289 2 Tim 2:20–1; the passage that follows draws extensively on the imagery used by Paul.
290 St Cyprian of Carthage (d 258) is evidently taken as representative of the church Fathers in general, valuable but of a lower grade than the writers of canonical Scripture.
291 On Arius and Sabellius see *In psalmum 85* 70 nn302 and 303 above.
292 2 Tim 2:21
293 Matt 8:12, 25:30
294 1 Pet 2:11, Rom 7:21–3
295 2 Chron 26:16–20

stained with desires and lusts, 'like the gentiles,'[296] should withdraw from this table, lest the wood of his vessel take fire or the clay be shattered. If in days gone by it was not permissible to use unsanctified vessels in the Lord's temple, vessels to receive water, or blood, or incense, or suchlike,[297] then how essential is purity of heart and body for those who receive Christ himself! And so the person who has not yet been anointed with holy oil, the oil of gladness and of exultation,[298] must not join this banquet but must meanwhile seek another oil with which to cleanse himself and become worthy to be anointed with the first. There is an oil mixed with wine for healing wounds, there is the oil of forgiveness that is used for anointing the sick.[299]

The pagans look at this table, more than royal and overflowing with heavenly joys, and perish of starvation. The Jews look at it and are torn apart with envy, because they were called first and refused the invitation, so making a place for strangers.[300] Those they thought of as dogs have now been adopted as sons and feed on the bread of heaven at the king's table, while they who considered themselves sons are demoted to the rank of dogs.[301] The synagogue has an annual feast in commemoration of the passover, but since it clings to the letter it has no oil; it eats lamb with bitter herbs.[302] But the church, being full of joys and anointed with the oil of spiritual grace, has a daily celebration of the passover with a spiritual feast, in commemoration 'of the Lord's death until he comes.'[303] And this is not celebrated with funeral dirges, as the Jews mourn their leader Moses,[304] but rather the church keeps her members mindful of the Lord's death 'with psalms and hymns and spiritual songs'; anointed with

* * * * *

296 1 Thess 4:4–5
297 Exod 40:9–13
298 Ps 44:8/45:7; cf 164 above.
299 The Samaritan treated the injured traveller's wounds with oil and wine at Luke 10:34; the sick are anointed with oil at James 5:14. If he is thinking of contemporary practice, Erasmus may have the sacrament of extreme unction in mind; alternatively, sickness may be a metaphor for sin, and the oil simply signify forgiveness and absolution.
300 Cf Matt 22:1–14, Luke 14:16–24.
301 Cf Matt 15:26–7, Mark 7:27–8.
302 Exod 12:3, 8
303 1 Cor 11:26
304 The first edition has here a marginal reference to Deuteronomy 34, which describes the death of Moses and the mourning for him; it is clear from the passage, however, that this mourning took place immediately after his death and not as a repeated commemoration.

the oil of heavenly grace, she 'sings to God in her heart.'[305] It is this feast
to which we are called by St Paul when he says: 'Christ our passover is
sacrificed for us, therefore let us keep the feast, not with the old leaven or
with the leaven of malice and wickedness, but with the unleavened bread
of sincerity and truth.'[306] For this is not a funeral feast, but a triumphal
banquet, celebrated with hymns and songs, as it says in Psalm 41: 'with
the voice of exultation and praise, the sound of the banqueter.'[307] For this
reason it is called 'eucharist,' which means 'thanksgiving.' In it we hear
the song of Moses: 'Let us sing to the Lord, for he is magnified glori-
ously,'[308] and there is also a reference in Revelation: 'Great and marvellous are your works, Lord God,' and again in another passage they sing
to the victorious Lamb: 'You were slain, and by your blood you have ran-
somed us for God out of every tribe and tongue and people and nation,
and have made us a kingdom and priests to our God, and we shall reign
on earth.'[309] As I have said, the synagogue hears these exultant voices of
the church singing in concert and is torn apart with envy; the world hears
and wastes away; those of other tribes hear and shout, 'Woe unto us'; devils hear and tremble. Meanwhile the bride of Christ is supreme, having
overcome all her persecutions, rejoicing in her true priesthood, and sacrificing without cease the living and immortal Lamb. You see, my friends,
how much material the treatment of this mystery offers, and I should like
to remain longer in contemplation of this feast; but I must finish the psalm,
and some other suitable place will be found for these things, if the Lord
so wills.

To proceed, then, to the exposition of what remains. It is in accordance
with scriptural usage on occasion to give the name of 'mercy' to generosity freely bestowed. So the church is giving thanks to its shepherd, so that
he may think it worthy of being refreshed with such feasts until the end
of the world, that is, until the second coming: 'Do this' he says 'in remembrance of me until I come.'[310] The psalm continues: 'And your mercy shall
follow [*subsequetur*] me all the days of my life.' The sentiment is clearer in
St Jerome's version: 'But thy goodness also shall follow [*subsequetur*] me
all the days of my life' (although the Greek has καταδιώξει, 'will pursue'

* * * * *

305 Col 3:16
306 1 Cor 5:7–8
307 Ps 41:5/42:4
308 Exod 15:1
309 Rev 15:13, 5:9–10
310 Cf 1 Cor 11:24–6.

[*persequetur*], that is, it will not abandon me until the end. By 'my life' he means this life on earth, a point made by the article in Greek, τῆς ζωῆς. Consequently translators often render the article by the demonstrative pronoun, writing 'this world' for '[the] world,' and it would not be impossible to translate here 'all the days of this life.'[311] The Jews in their misfortune await their Messiah in vain; he has already come, in accordance with the pronouncements of the prophets, and he will not abandon his bride until he comes again, not this time as redeemer but as judge of the living and the dead.[312] Those who fear judgment should take care that they receive it among the living.

There still remain the last words describing this greatly blessed state. And what are they? 'And that I may dwell in the house of the Lord through the length of days.' The bride of Christ has no lasting home here,[313] but meanwhile pitches camp and signs with longing for that celestial home not made with hands which is in the heavens.[314] In that place all are fed with the body and blood of Christ, yet not in the riddling form of sacraments, but present and made plain in manifest form.[315] No troubles interrupt the hymns sung at that feast; angels and devout men and women will raise their voices together in complete harmony, and without ceasing will praise him who lives for ever. The days of man are brief,[316] and the whole of the time the church remains on earth, even if it extends to thirty thousand years,[317] is a single moment compared with eternity and with that day which knows

* * * * *

311 The version of Jerome's *Psalterium iuxta Hebraeos* (PL 28 [1890] 1206A) couples 'goodness' (*benignitas*) and 'mercy' (*misericordia*). Unlike Greek, Latin has no definite article, so that *mundus* might represent in English 'the world,' 'a world,' or 'world.'

312 2 Tim 4:1, although the words were and are probably better known from the Nicene and Apostles' Creeds

313 The argument is taken from Pseudo-Jerome's treatment of this line in *Breviarium in psalmos* PL 26 (1845) 886A.

314 Cf 2 Cor 5:1. The use of the word 'celestial' when the quotation itself contains 'which is in the heavens' suggests hasty composition.

315 A reminiscence of 1 Cor 13:12

316 Job 14:5

317 A somewhat literal interpretation of Ps 89/90:4 ('a thousand years in thy sight are but as yesterday when it is past') resulted in a widespread acceptance of an equivalence of 'God's day' to a thousand human years, so the figure here would equal a month to God. But other calculations made earthly existence last for only six of God's days, and it is possible that Erasmus is simply using a random figure to indicate a very long time.

no close,[318] that is, with perpetuity. In that place will be perfect rest, perfect happiness, and the 'equal feast'[319] of which a taste suffices to inspire the bride of Christ and to convince her that here she desires nothing else from her spouse than to be more closely joined to him and to live for ever in the house of the Lord.

I have now taken advantage of your kindness in order to expound the psalm, as far as my talents will allow, in two senses. But I see you are not yet sated with this banquet, and so I shall now briefly explain the moral sense.[320] I have already covered a lot of this ground in passing, but I shall go over it again, and if I have omitted any useful information I shall discuss it, making as it were gleanings from the vineyard.[321] And now I ask you, dear friends, to listen with renewed and eager attention to this new way of expounding the psalm. Let each of you consider that this psalm is relevant only to himself; let each of you ask himself whether he is really a sheep belonging to Christ, whether he can sing this psalm not only with the voice of his tongue but with that of his heart.[322] The melody will only be pleasing to God if one's feelings are in tune with one's voice and if one's mind is not looking for something other than that expressed in the psalm. If anyone finds himself in a position where his life and his wishes clash with the psalm, he should pray to the Lord that by his grace he too may become a sheep and with complete harmony may say, 'The Lord is my shepherd, and I shall lack nothing.' For no one can truthfully say 'I shall lack nothing' unless he has committed himself with complete faith to Christ's rule and pastoral care. So if someone sings outwardly with his lips, 'The Lord pastures me, and I shall lack nothing,' while inwardly his heart is singing another song, 'My wealth, or my noble birth, or my rank, or my intelligence, or my learning will pasture me,' then the tunes will not harmonize. The soldier says, 'The horse carries me, the king feeds me';[323]

* * * * *

318 A reminiscence of a phrase in the *Exultet*, the proclamation at the opening of the liturgy of the Easter Vigil: 'the morning star, which knows no setting' (*occasum*, as in the text of Erasmus); cf n193 above.

319 Prov 15:15

320 Erasmus now begins the tropological exposition of the psalm, moving from the church to the moral life of the individual.

321 *Racematio*, a rare word used in classical sources only in one passage of Tertullian. The metaphor of the vineyard owes something to the parables at Matt 20:1–6 and at Matt 21:33–41, Mark 12.1–9, Luke 20.9–16.

322 Compare Arnobius the Younger *Commentarium in psalmum* 22 PL 53 354C.

323 Cf Horace *Epistles* 1.17.20.

one man will rely on his strength, another on his youth, and a third will put his trust in the favour of princes. Whatever a person chooses in which to repose his trust, he sings this psalm to it: 'You will pasture me, and I shall lack nothing.' But his iniquity deceives him. In this world no one has ever been so fortunate that he could truthfully say 'I shall lack nothing' – but it was truthfully said that they lack nothing who fear the Lord. And it was truthfully said, 'The rich have been in want and suffered hunger, but those who seek the Lord shall not have less of any good thing.'[324]

Now perhaps at this point someone may reflect: 'How can this that I hear be true? Didn't the blessed Job lack much? Wasn't he in great need? Wasn't he bereft of his children, deprived of his home and possessions, and didn't he finally lose his physical health, his body covered with sores?[325] Didn't Lazarus lack much, lying on the rich man's threshold and dying of disease and hunger?[326] I suppose those people lacked nothing who in Paul's words wandered "in sheepskins and goatskins, being afflicted and tormented."[327] Or Paul himself, who says that he had passed his time in toil and hardship, in hunger and thirst, fasting often, cold and naked.[328] Did he lack nothing when, as he writes to Timothy, he had no one to take his part at the first hearing, but was abandoned by everyone?[329] When he was in the grip of poverty and grew used to leather for a bed, did he lack nothing?'[330] Beyond a doubt all those mentioned were sheep, who had Christ as their shepherd. The psalm cannot lie, but this objection is too obvious to be gainsaid.

Consequently we must solve this problem by a correct understanding of the psalm's meaning. First of all, it is one thing *to be absent* [*abesse*], another *to be lacking* [*deesse*], just as it is one thing *not to have* [*carere*], another *to need* [*egere*]; and again *to need* is different from *to be deficient in* [*opus habere*]. Those things that we do not have are *absent*, those that we need are *lacking*. Things we *do not have* include things we do not wish to have; in this way those who are not hermaphrodites do not have the characteristics of both sexes, and none of us has antlers. We are so far from needing these things that we do not want to have them.[331] Similarly, a good man

* * * * *

324 Ps 33:10–11 / 34:9–10
325 Job 1–2
326 Luke 16:19–21
327 Heb 11:37
328 2 Cor 11:27
329 2 Tim 4:16
330 Probably a reference to Paul's stay with tentmakers; Acts 18:3
331 The technical philological discussion is lightened with an example perhaps inspired by the logical fallacy known as *ceratina*, 'the horns fallacy,' quoted or

is *deficient* in many things that he does not *need*. We are deficient in those things that would be useful to us if we possessed them but whose absence does not result in want and discomfort. Thus many people are deficient in physical strength, or quickness of intelligence, or other qualities of this type, which the truly devout man would put to good use if he had them. But those things are said to be *lacking* which lessen human happiness, and for this reason the psalm that we have just quoted says, 'He shall not have less of any good thing.' There is *less* where there is not sufficient for the highest happiness. Much, or rather all, of the things prayed for by those belonging to the world is lacking. They ask for an endless number of things, and yet the more they obtain, the further they are from what they are seeking. Everyone by nature seeks happiness.[332] But the prayer of good sheep is simple and asks one thing only, that they may attain eternal life, and that through Christ. Furthermore, although their physical nature desires food and clothing, the spirit wishes for nothing that does not lead to eternal life, and to all their prayers is added the condition 'if God knows that this will help towards salvation.' And the sheep is convinced that whatever affliction may occur is sent by God, since it knows that what is unpleasant to nature is often useful for the health of the spirit. Perhaps Lazarus would have been corrupted by wealth; as it was, his poverty brought him to Abraham's bosom. Considered in this light, the sheep of Christ lack nothing, for all things work together for their good.[333]

The Greek here has ὑστερώσει, which means rather 'will not attain what is sought.'[334] Thus the martyr in the midst of his torments, and at the point of death, can say with truth: 'The Lord is my shepherd, I shall lack nothing.' Can he suppose that he lacks anything when he is passing from exile here to perpetual joys? 'Seek much, lack much,' and in the same poet's words,

* * * * *

referred to in many ancient sources (for example Aulus Gellius 18.2.9): 'What you have not lost, you have; you have not lost horns; therefore you have horns.' The joke about hermaphrodites may also originate outside Erasmus: for instance, W. Pantin *The English Church in the Fourteenth Century* (Cambridge 1955) 165 refers to a Dominican who interpreted the decree *Omnis utriusque sexus* of the Fourth Lateran Council (1215) enforcing annual confession to parish clergy as applying only to hermaphrodites; he become known in the curia as 'Father Richard of both sexes.'

332 Cf Thomas Aquinas *Summa contra gentiles* 2.55.13: 'Man naturally desires happiness.'

333 Luke 16:19–23, Rom 8:28

334 The Septuagint reading is actually ὑστερήσει, in accordance with the normal form of the verb.

'with the growing pile of wealth follows worry'[335] – but the fault is not in
the objects, rather in our reaction to them. However, it is in general true
to say that those who put their whole trust in Christ their shepherd and
who remain in his paths do not go without those things required by our
bodily needs, especially since nature is content with only a little, and moderation with less.[336] But greediness is never satisfied. In days gone by, what
lack was felt by the prophets and the sons of prophets? They lived in exile,
they wandered in the wilderness, and yet none of them died of hunger or
thirst. What lack was felt by John the Baptist in the wilderness? His clothing
was provided by camel's hair, his sustenance by wild honey and locusts –
whether these were the topmost shoots of plants, or a kind of animal which
certain races are said to dry in the sun and use for food.[337] What lack was
felt by the apostles when they left all their possessions, or held in common such resources as they might have, and preached the gospel without
charge?[338] Finally, what lack is felt today by those who undertake a more
than extreme poverty, not allowing themselves so much as to touch any
money?[339] Surely we see that the promise of the gospel is true – surely,
they abandon one mother and receive in return a hundred, they leave one
sister and one home and receive a hundred sisters and homes.[340] Surely
such people too can say with truth, 'The rich have been in want and suffered hunger, but we who seek the Lord do not have less of (or, in other
readings, are not deprived of, or deserted by) any good thing.'[341]

At this point I can hear voices raising clamorous objections: 'Many of
that type are not seeking the Lord, but pandering to their own bellies.' Such

* * * * *

335 Horace *Odes* 3.16.42, 17
336 'Nature is content with little' was proverbial. See Cicero *Tusculan Disputations*
5.34.97 and Boethius *Consolation of Philosophy* 2 prosa 5.16; cf *Ecclesiastes* LB V
817C / ASD V-4 160:522 and *In psalmum 33* 339 below.
337 Matt 3:4, Mark 1.6. The ordinary meaning of the Greek word ἀκρίδες is 'locusts'
or 'cicadas,' referring to insects, but there was a common view that the tips
or shoots (ἄκραι) of young plants were intended instead; see Isidore of Pelu-
sium *Epistles* 1.132 PG 78.270. In his *Paraphrasis in Marcum* CWE 49 17 Erasmus
appears to incline to the view that the locusts were insects.
338 Alluding to the symbolic interpretation of 'leaving their nets' in Matt 4:20,
Mark 1:18, Luke 5:11; cf 136–7 above. For common property, see Acts 2:44–5,
4:32; for preaching without charge, Matt 10:8.
339 A reference to the mendicant orders. Elsewhere Erasmus himself is to the fore
among the 'voices raising clamorous objections' (below) to their way of life,
which he castigates for hypocrisy in *Moria* CWE 27 132–3, for example. But see
the Colloquy Πτωχοπλούσιοι CWE 39 468–98, with n4 (483–4).
340 Matt 19:29
341 Ps 33:10–11/34:9–10

voices, if their allegations are correct, act for the Lord; but if so many are provided with a livelihood by their deceitful appearance, how much less will be the need of those who seek the Lord in truth and from their hearts? Still, if it does happen that the devout lack such requirements, their shepherd sees to it that their needs are not real needs, but rather abundance. What is lost when God does not give what our desires demand, if he gives us things a hundred times better? Those who desire nothing except what is pleasing to the Lord invariably have what they desire; here is the source of all Christian riches. The three children were delivered from the furnace by the Lord, but St Paul died by the sword.[342] To the blessed Job he restored twofold all his possessions, but Lazarus died in abject poverty.[343] The one did not possess too much, since his heart was not attached to wealth; the other lacked nothing, since after a finite term of poverty he found eternal rest. So however hard pressed you are by domestic wants, even if you can scarcely maintain your wife and children, do not be afraid to say: 'The Lord is my shepherd; I shall lack nothing.' The Lord is making trial of your patience, and either he will look favourably on you when he has done so, or he will compensate for your poverty with good of far greater worth.

On the other hand, those who are lacking in faith, hope, and charity, who lack modesty, decency, and innocence; these are the people truly in need, even if their possessions are more than those of a thousand Croesuses.[344] But those who possess these qualities are overflowing with riches, even if they live in the direst poverty. Such a sheep was St Paul: he recalls his want, his poverty, and his afflictions but makes plain the greatness of the riches hidden under the appearance of misfortune, saying: 'As unknown, and yet known; as dying, and behold we live; as sorrowful, yet always rejoicing; as poor, yet making many rich; as having nothing, and yet possessing everything.'[345] What lack could be felt by those to whom he had previously written: 'All things are yours, and you are Christ's'?[346] They lacked nothing precisely because they belonged to Christ, and for those who belong to Christ, Christ in turn belongs to them. Whoever possesses him possesses the fount of all good things, while those who are not satisfied with the things which lead to true happiness truly experience lack. Yet Christ will not allow those whom he has once taken into his charge to lack

* * * * *

342 Dan 3:19–23, 91–4/19–28; Eusebius *Ecclesiastical History* 2.25 PG 20 207B–C
343 Job 42:10; Luke 16:22
344 *Adagia* I vi 74, referring to the proverbially rich king of Lydia
345 2 Cor 6:9–10
346 1 Cor 3:22–3

anything; on the contrary, he supplies in abundance everything that leads
to eternal life – but he alone knows what it is that he gives us. Something
is said to be lacking when its absence tortures us with longing: Paul said,
'I desire to be dissolved and to be with Christ';[347] and when Nero took his
own life with his sword he was not deprived of life but obtained what he
desired.[348] On the other hand, those whose shepherd is the devil lack everything – even those things they possess.[349] The avaricious man has as great a
lack of what he owns as of what he does not.[350] 'The things you have,' says
the proverb, 'you lack less than the things you don't' – but it should be 'lack
more.'[351] He wants the things he doesn't have if he thinks he has a chance
of getting them; but the things he does have he desires the more intemper-
ately the more he has of them, and the worry of retaining what he owns is
a worse torture for him than that of acquiring what he does not yet have.
If one cannot use what one has in one's grasp, one does not have it, unless
of course we are to suppose that the serpent which kept the golden fleece
in the myth actually owned what it guarded.[352] Hunger for possession fits
the part of the poor man rather than the rich; but to be in need of what you
have is certainly an extreme sort of need! A man becomes a praetor and
then thinks himself hard done by unless he becomes consul; the ex-consul
tries to become dictator; having become dictator, he tries to become king;
and having obtained a crown he looks around for a second, then a third,
a fourth, a fifth, until he can become world emperor. Even then he is not
satisfied, but looks around for other worlds to rule.[353] In the same way another cannot amass sufficient benefices, adding bishopric to bishopric, abbey
to abbey; even this whole conglomerate does not satisfy him, but he tries
to obtain a cardinal's hat, and then the papacy. But surely at this point you

* * * * *

347 Phil 1:23
348 The emperor Nero, having been declared a public enemy by the senate, com-
     mitted suicide in AD 68.
349 Cf Matt 13:12, 25:29, Mark 4:25, Luke 8:18, 19:26.
350 Proverbial; see Publilius Syrus 684, Otto 225. Erasmus' source was probably
     Jerome Ep 53.10 PL 22 549.
351 Perhaps a vernacular proverb; I have not been able to trace it.
352 The golden fleece sought by Jason and the Argonauts was guarded by a ser-
     pent or dragon; see for instance Ovid *Metamorphoses* 7.149–56.
353 This *cursus honorum*, going far beyond a normal political career, is based on
     Plutarch *Moralia* 470B–C (*De tranquillitate animi* 10) but ends with a favourite
     allusion to Alexander, for whom proverbially 'one world was not enough'
     (Juvenal *Satires* 10.168; cf *In psalmum* 1 CWE 63 13, and a different version at
     Apophthegmata IV 58 LB IV 201D–E).

might hear someone say: 'I lack nothing?' Far from it. Earthly domination is
sought after eagerly, power is extended even as far as the angels and souls
separated from bodies.[354]

I have said all this, my dear friends, not in order to lay charges against
secular or ecclesiastical authority, but to demonstrate the insatiable ambition of humankind. Thus the heart of the avaricious man never says, 'It
is enough'; the heart of the vindictive man never says, 'It is enough'; the
heart of the man addicted to pleasure never says, 'It is enough.'[355] Only the
little sheep of Christ says: 'I shall lack nothing.' So when some acquaintance of yours or some fleshly impulse puts before you such pagan words
as 'Unless you seek out high office, you will be nothing but plain John,
you will be despised, trampled underfoot, and utterly rejected by everyone.'[356] 'How should I canvass for office, by bribery and simony?' 'However you may.' These days scarcely any other method is possible; 'simony'
long since ceased to be a word in current use.[357] Again, when your urges
towards avarice say to you, 'Increase your property, you don't want to go
short in your old age or let your children go short,' you say, 'How shall I
increase it?' 'Oh, by fair means if possible – otherwise any way you can,
so long as you *do* increase it.'[358] To this and other such advice the sheep of
Christ must faithfully reply: 'The Lord is my shepherd, I shall lack nothing.' When the flesh says, 'You give more to the poor than your means will
allow; your wife is fertile, your household is constantly increasing, your
profits are getting less and prices are going up,' then the spirit must reply:
'The Lord is my shepherd, nothing shall I lack.' But regrettably we often
hear among Christians sentiments even more pagan than these. The magistrate or judge says, 'I have purchased this office at vast expense: if I am
to stick to impartial justice, my fortune will soon revert to scrip and staff.'
The merchant says, 'If I don't cheat and deceive and perjure myself, I shall
scarcely get back my investment.' The craftsman says, 'If I don't filch a bit
of the material I've been lent, my craft won't give me enough to live on.'

* * * * *

354 A hit at papal indulgences, which claimed to be able to shorten the time spent
by souls in purgatory. Such claims could be explicit and extreme; A. Renaudet
Préréforme et humanisme à Paris (Paris 1916) 21 n2 cites a preacher in 1482 stating that 'the souls in purgatory are under the pope's jurisdiction, and if he
wished he could empty purgatory completely.' Cf *In psalmum 85* 84 above.

355 Cf Prov 30:17, where it is fire that never says, 'It is enough.'

356 A vernacular proverb that survives in French

357 An ironic reference to current practice; Pope Alexander VI (1492–1503), for
instance, was widely held to have won his election through bribery.

358 Horace *Epistles* 1.1.66: 'si possis recte, si non, quocumque modo rem.'

In short, the flesh tells us, 'You will be nothing if you jealously guard your innocence; "dare something worthy of imprisonment and tiny Gyaros, if you wish to be something."'[359] Words of this sort never cause the sheep of Christ to stray from what is right or from God's teachings: the sheep has always on its heart's lips: 'The Lord pastures me, I shall lack nothing.' Let the world admire its own in their happiness, surrounded with children, lucky in their beautiful daughters, well provided with lands and money, rich owners of chests stuffed with gold, themselves lofty with honours; for me he is happy enough for whom the Lord is as God,[360] that is, the man who trusts in him.[361] All those who trust in the Lord are happy, and whoever is joined to him already possesses all things with him. To his sheep he is honour, glory, righteousness, wisdom, riches, life, and utterly certain bliss.

Consequently, if we want to accept the rule of the good shepherd, let us be good sheep and look to no other apart from our shepherd Jesus. Let us be sheep in innocence, simplicity, and goodness, not in stupidity. For in fact this beast does not threaten others with its horns like cattle, nor tear flesh with its teeth like wolves, nor kick with its hooves like horses, nor inspire terror with its voice like lions, nor catch creatures with its claws like cats, nor have poison like vipers – in fact it is so harmless that even when it is provoked it makes no counter-attack. It is mute at the hands of the shearers[362] and even when it is slaughtered it does not cry out as pigs do. It has but a single sound to ask help from its shepherd and to call the flock together. Yet although it is such a gentle animal, no other creature offers from its own resources a greater variety of uses. The sheep clothes us with its wool, supplies us with skins for our protection, and produces milk, which is nutritious as food and effective as medicine. There is no other part of its body that is not suitable for human nourishment; even its excrement, quite apart from its use as a fertilizer, is said to be both helpful and valuable when preparing cheeses.[363] Those who are truly Christ's sheep are the same; they are useful to both friends and enemies, and they are incapable of hurting anyone. They are not carnivores, they do not live by what they can snatch, but they are content with the food given them by

* * * * *

359 Juvenal *Satires* 1.73–4. Gyaros is a waterless Aegean island that has often been used as a prison settlement.
360 Cf Pss 32/33:12, 143/144:15.
361 Ps 2:13/12
362 Cf Isa 53:7.
363 Presumably as an alternative for rennet

their shepherd, whose voice they follow as he leads them out and brings them back. The first mother of the human race heard the voice of a thief, not of the shepherd; then Adam heard his wife's voice, and by eating the fatal food he brought death both to himself and to all his posterity. The serpent, a crafty animal, utterly unlike the flock of sheep, offered something sweet and delightful. But his promises were empty: 'You shall not die, and you shall be like gods.'[364] This was not the voice of the good shepherd but of a deceiver and a thief; it was not food that he offered but deadly poison. And so Eve was led astray, despoiled of her sheep-like simplicity, and expelled from those most blessed pastures, because she had not remained close to God, the best of shepherds, but listened to the voice of a brigand.

The devil has not now ceased to do in various ways what he then did through the serpent; he offers things that seem pleasant and makes empty promises. Yet the sheep of Christ does not listen to his voice, but placing its entire trust in Jesus its Lord it says: 'The Lord is my shepherd, and I shall lack nothing. Neither death nor life will tear me away from him,[365] but I shall constantly remain by his side in the place of pasture where he has put me' – or 'made me lie down.' I was straying like a sheep that was lost;[366] he brought me back to the fold on his shoulders.[367] I was stained, and he washed me with his blood; I was sick and he healed me, feeble and he strengthened me. He gave me faith and hope of heavenly joys. He breathed 'love' into me, 'which many waters could not extinguish,'[368] and through all this he placed me in the unity of the church, in the company of all the saints. Before this I endured a harsh slavery, I was fed on the pods given to swine, and I was not allowed to sate myself even on these;[369] then finally he gave himself to me, so that I might have rest in this happiest of companies, in these pastures. Outside the church, my brethren, there is no true peace, no true rest, no quietness of mind.[370]

At this point someone will ask 'How can I know if I am within the unity of the church?' I shall give you a clear indication. As long as you remain in charity with God and your neighbour, you remain in the company of the church. As long as you feel within you the pledge of the Spirit, in

* * * * *

364 Gen 3:4–5
365 Rom 8:38
366 Cf Ps 118/119:176.
367 A reference to the parable at Luke 15:5
368 Song of Sol 8:7
369 Again a reference to a parable; cf Luke 15:16.
370 Cf 144 and 146–7 above.

which you cry 'Abba, Father,'[371] you can be sure that you are not lacking in true charity. You cannot be removed from this happy society by any created being, not by the princes of this world, not by the pope, not by death or life or Satan, unless you yourself wish it.[372] Only God has this power, and he does not wish to do what is in his power; indeed, he is not even able to renege on his promises,[373] and he has promised that he will never abandon those who have fixed their hope in him. Still, the outward fellowship of the Catholic church must not be rejected by the devout, even if its ministers openly abuse their power. They are the representatives of the church, and to avoid public unrest this must not be despised. The Lord will remove such men when he himself sees fit; the part of a Christian is to be at peace with all, in so far as he is able.

Again, someone may ask: 'If the Lord feeds us and places us in the pastures of the church, what is the bishop doing when he leads us into the church through baptism? If he does not pasture us why does he have a shepherd's crook? Why is he called a shepherd?' There is one prince among shepherds, Jesus our Lord, who in truth governs his church, which he alone knows in certainty and which he feeds with the life-giving nourishment of his word; but there are things that he performs through his servants, who in some measure fulfil his role. It is the priest who reads and interprets Scripture to you, but the Lord who opens your heart. The priest sprinkles you with water, anoints you with oil, adds salt, gives you a white garment and leads you to the inner parts of the temple, but it is the Lord who forgives your sins, the Lord who pours his spirit upon you.[374] You should honour the man who fulfils his office and administers the sacraments, but adore him who renders the sacraments efficacious; to him indeed is due all glory. Even though he who administers the sacraments may be a hireling, 'a thief and a robber,'[375] the sheep do not go without their shepherd, who lavishes his grace upon them even when he uses evil men to dispense his mysteries. This should give comfort to the sheep, so that if they see bishops or priests openly indulging in wicked behaviour they will not suppose that such men

* * * * *

371 Cf Rom 8:15, Gal 4:6 (modelled on Mark 14:36).
372 This remarkably subjective view of church membership is a corollary of Erasmus' efforts to preserve dialogue between Catholic tradition and the moderate exponents of reform.
373 Compare 154 n208, and In psalmum 85 86 above.
374 Cf the colloquy Convivium Religiosum CWE 39 196; on the 'white garment,' see Militis et Cartusiani n11 CWE 39 338.
375 John 10:1

have shut off the way to the flock's salvation. Priests have been entrusted with the management of functions not their own. If they fulfil this task properly, they will receive ample reward from the highest of shepherds; but if not, Christ still lives and has not ceased to care for his bride. If their teaching is good but their lives evil, then do what they say and not what they do. If their lives are suspect but their teaching sound, give their lives the benefit of the doubt. If they openly lead immoral lives and teach wicked things, you should fly from them as you would from wolves. But fly from them in such a way that you tolerate them, not kill them; shun them only so far as you may without leaving the fellowship of the church on account of human vices. If those in charge play the part of wolves, it is the part of sheep to bleat after their true shepherd; he will take vengeance on thieves and robbers, and he will not desert his flock. There was a time when the Lord's flock lived under Annases and Caiaphases,[376] under idolatrous emperors, but this did not prevent the members from continuing as sheep.

However, the psalm is relevant not only to sheep but to shepherds; as they take the part of Christ, so far as human resources allow they should follow the example of the greatest shepherd, attracting all they can to the pastures of the church, leading back with fatherly care those who have strayed, feeding the sheep with the health-giving food supplied by the teaching of the Gospels, leading the weary with friendly encouragement to the waters of refreshment, instructing those already on the way by setting an example of religious behaviour and by supplying constant counsel, until they can gather all their strength and with their whole heart turn to the Lord. In this they should look to nothing but the glory of the highest shepherd and the safety of the Lord's flock, following the exhortation of him who when he had thrice professed his love of the Lord received from him the charge of his sheep – to feed them,[377] not to oppress them with his might. 'Feed the flock of God that is among you, overseeing them not by constraint but willingly as God would have you, not for shameful gain but eagerly, not as domineering over those in your charge but being examples to the flock.'[378] Here someone may say, 'Then must I taken on this laborious task for nothing?' No, indeed. 'So what is the reward?' 'When the chief Shepherd is manifested, you will obtain the unfading crown of glory.'[379] These men then must go before their sheep and lead them in the paths of

*****

376 The Jewish high priest and his father-in-law in John 18:13–24, cf Matt 57–66
377 John 21:15–17
378 1 Pet 5:2–3
379 1 Pet 5:4

righteousness, constantly urging, advising, and encouraging them, so that they are courageous and well prepared against the ambushes and assaults of the devil. They must guide their sheep with the rod of their teaching and support them with the staff of comfort, until they attain to freedom and cheerfulness of spirit and can be counted worthy to be transported from the spiritual joys of a good conscience to the eternal banquets of those who dwell in heaven.

Moreover, the higher the place a man has attained among shepherds, the closer he ought to approximate to the image of the highest Shepherd of all. That chief shepherd washed his disciples' feet, and told them as he did so that his act was to be an example they should imitate.[380] But when did he offer his own feet for anyone to kiss? Mary Magdalen's action was a mystery, not an example.[381] Indeed, it would not have been astonishing if Christ had offered his feet for his followers to kiss, since he allowed them to adore him; he was God, after all. But Peter did not allow Cornelius to fall at his feet.[382] The man who does this spontaneously may act from motives of religion or of love – but what can be the motives of the man who demands it? Love may kiss even the hem of a garment, and when the hem of Christ's garment was touched it gave healing,[383] as did aprons sanctified by contact with the apostles.[384] But in these days, when to demand miracles constitutes lack of faith, even if simple people's pious instincts make them offer such honours, they ought to be refused for the sake of Christian modesty. Julius Caesar provoked much resentment by offering his foot to be kissed by a man of senatorial rank approaching him; his behaviour seemed not that of a Caesar, but of a Procrustes.[385] But he who is in truth the greatest king and the supreme high priest,[386] even when it was Judas who came to kiss

* * * * *

380 John 13:5–15
381 Luke 7:38
382 Acts 10:25–6
383 Matt 9:18–22, Mark 5:25–34, Luke 8:43–8; Matt 14:36, Mark 6:56
384 Acts 19:12
385 This anecdote does not seem to be traceable in classical sources, although the tradition recorded in, for instance, Suetonius *Lives of the Caesars*: Julius 1.78 is quite close: when a senatorial delegation came to offer him honours, Caesar did not bother to stand up. Procrustes was a mythical brigand who disposed of his victims by placing them on a bed and stretching them or lopping pieces off them so that they would fit the measurements exactly.
386 The word used is *pontifex*, which properly refers both to the priesthood held by Julius Caesar and to the papacy, although the Vulgate uses it also for the Jewish high priest.

him did not stick out his foot but offered his face.[387] However, I think I
had better put an end to these comparisons, lest I seem to be indulging in
recriminations rather than offering advice. Let the shepherd extend his foot
to the sheep in outward appearance if circumstance or custom demand it,
so long as inwardly they are close to his heart; let him ride about on fine
horses, carried high above the crowd, surrounded like a king by courtiers,
and let him lead his armed forces in outward appearance, so long as in his
soul there is fatherly care, complete modesty, and love befitting the vicar of
Christ.[388]

I come back now to the sheep, which have been led to pasture. Every
Christian should behave in Christ's pasture in such a way that day by day
he grows and is strengthened. There are many sacraments in the church,
some which start people on their way, some which carry them further, and
some which make them perfect. Then there is the many-sided teaching im-
parted to beginners, to those more advanced, and to those who are made
complete. Those receiving instruction are taught the elements, while those
already born anew are given more advanced material. Our Lord speaks
about this double form of teaching in the Gospel according to Matthew:
'Go and make disciples of all nations' – instructing them in the catechism,
'baptizing them in the name of the Father and of the Son and of the Holy
Spirit, teaching them to observe all that I have commanded you' – leading
them to the paths of righteousness.[389] He promises a complete teaching in
St John's Gospel: 'I have yet many things to say to you, but you cannot
bear them now. But when the spirit of truth comes, he will teach you all
the truth.'[390] St Paul, too, had the 'milk' of teaching, which sustained children, and he had the wisdom which he spoke among the perfect.[391] And
although not everything is equally suitable or profitable for everyone, the
fertile pastures of Scripture are full of things to give nourishment to infants in Christ, to supply growth to those who are maturing, and to bring
adults to 'the fullness of the measure of Jesus Christ';[392] and there are many
things to heal the sick and to strengthen the weary. How is it then that we

* * * * *

387 Matt 26:48–9, Mark 14:45, Luke 22:47
388 In the 'outward appearance' of this description Erasmus probably has in mind
      Julius II, whose triumphal entry into Bologna at the head of his army he recalls
      in Ep 1756, in *Annotationes in Acta apostolorum* LB VI 455, and in *Apologia ad
      blasphemias Stunicae* LB IX 361A.
389 Matt 28:19–20
390 John 16:12–13
391 1 Cor 3:2, 2:6
392 Eph 4:13

see so many Christians who partake of all the church's sacraments, who frequently come to the Lord's table, who daily feed on the word of God, daily run through, recite, and chant Holy Scripture – especially among priests and monks – and who still become no better filled out but remain lean and skinny, idle, and listless, though it is a well-fed, joyful, and eager form that the Lord loves. Sometimes the fault lies with hired shepherds who neglect the flock and feed themselves. All they do for the flock is to make music[393] for them. They do not give them the food of teaching, or if they do teach anything it is human rather than divine, gratifying to the ears rather than imparting health to the soul: it is their own food they offer, not that of Jesus Christ. And in part the listeners themselves are to blame, since often they are not really sheep, not chewing the cud when they have taken their food. How is this so? They hear the law of the Lord, but they do not meditate on it.[394] Only clean animals chew the cud,[395] but anyone who is dominated by love of money or other external concerns is an unclean beast, and the word of God, the soul's only food, here falls on useless ground and does not bear fruit.[396]

When shepherds see that a sheep is not chewing the cud, they realize that it is sick and apply medicines. Now if one takes stock of the seriousness of ambition as an illness of the soul, and the seriousness of avarice, and of devotion to pleasure, it will not seem remarkable that those under the sway of such forces are unable to chew over the food of the gospel. And what constitutes chewing the cud? Animals that ruminate are incapable of biting, because they have teeth only in their lower jaw. When they take food in their mouths, they use these teeth to mash the food against the gum of the upper jaw, and in this state the food goes into their upper stomach; then when they have leisure they bring it back into their mouths and slowly chew it over before they send it down to the stomach. They do this usually after being watered, when lying down.[397] The Pharisees, then, were not sheep; whatever food they were given by the Lord they tore at

* * * * *

393 Erasmus here uses the rare word *cantillo*, apparently confined to Apuleius among classical writers.

394 Pss 1:2, 118/119:47, 70; cf *In psalmum* 1 CWE 63 30. On the meditation/rumination parallel see D. Baker-Smith 'Erasmus as Reader of the Psalms' ERSY 20 (2000) 11–16.

395 A reference to Jewish dietary laws (for example, Lev 11:3), here as often understood by Erasmus in an allegorical sense

396 Cf Matt 13:4–6, Mark 4:4–7, Luke 8:5–7.

397 This observation may derive from Aristotle *Historia animalium* 9.50 632b and/or Pliny, *Naturalis historia* 11.61.

with their teeth, using it to slander him. But Christ's sheep have for palate their understanding, which they use in simplicity to take in health-giving doctrine; they mash it somewhat with serious consideration, turning it over in their minds; then they commit it to their upper stomach, that is, their memory. Then, refreshed by drinking from the spirit, they retire from the hurly-burly of worldly cares, and lying down in the pastures of the Lord they recall to the understanding those things which they have stored in their memory and chew them over again with more careful consideration. Then finally they direct it to their stomach, so that from there it may be absorbed into the whole body and become the substance of the mind. Our stomach is our emotional disposition;[398] if we love what we have learned and believe it, we have sent food to our stomach. And if we have begun to practise through acts of charity what we have received, then by vigour and activity we show that the food has become the substance of the spirit, bodily agility being evidence of a good digestion, which is accompanied by a good appearance. Every animal has its own natural functions, and if we see that these are performed swiftly and correctly we recognize that the animal is in good health. Now the special function of charity is to injure no one and to do good to all. Do you wish me then to show you how to tell whether you have become more active in the service of the Lord? If you have grown quicker to perform what piety demands, more courageous in bearing injuries, stronger in faith, more ardent in love; if the flesh is less important and the spirit is stronger and rules in you, then give thanks to your Shepherd and pray that he may bring to perfection the work he has begun in you.[399] The fruits of the spirit show that the soul is well fed.[400]

What I have here described as digestion, the first psalm calls meditation. The law of God is the food of the soul, and 'blessed is he who meditates on this' and practises it, not simply as he pleases, but 'day and night,'[401] which clearly corresponds with Paul's admonition 'Let us not grow weary in well-doing.'[402] What are the effects of meditation? It brings forth fruits that are pleasing to God and will never perish. For the psalm continues

* * * * *

398 Latin *affectus*; Erasmus indicates that the necessary end of the process is an emotional, not an intellectual, apprehension of the truths of religion, a central point in his whole approach. Compare for instance *Ratio verae theologiae* LB V 83F–84A; see also *In psalmum 1* CWE 63 44; *In psalmum 85* 47 above; *In psalmum 33* 368 below.

399 The Latin is a reminiscence of 2 Cor 8:6.

400 Cf Gal 5:22.

401 Ps 1:1–2; cf *In psalmum 1* CWE 63 30–1, *In psalmum 38* LB V 444F.

402 Gal 6:9

without a pause: 'And he shall be like a tree planted by the streams of water, that yields its fruit in its season; and its leaf shall not wither.'[403]

This passage is relevant even to those who hold the law in their mouths but have not digested it and teach the people things which they themselves neither perform nor have any love for. But eventually they must learn what they teach; one who is cold himself will scarcely kindle enthusiasm in others. Consequently, no one can be effective in feeding the Lord's flock unless he is himself fed by the Lord. As far as the church's sacraments are concerned, those who receive them worthily are not injured by the wickedness of those who administer; but it is extremely rare for a person to be brought round to a good disposition by the teaching of someone wicked. I do not deny, however, that even this is possible. There is no more efficacious food for souls than spiritual learning, which we should at no time fail to acquire. Indeed, this is our daily bread,[404] and unless our minds are constantly being refreshed with it, they grow thin, then they become weak and inactive, and finally they die. The first concern of the true shepherd, which he must always be aware of, is that the sheep should lack nothing. He should not offer them food from lips that are cold and unmoved but from a heart burning with love: fire kindles fire.[405] Similarly the sheep who are about to receive the health-giving word should make ready the stomach of their mind, so that they may be empty and eager to take what they are given. Only those who 'hunger and thirst after righteousness'[406] obtain fulfilment from these pastures, just as food is no use to the body when the stomach revolts at its consumption. Shepherds cure such a revulsion by placing a rock of salt in the field, so that the sheep may lick it and be cured of the nausea which afflicts their stomachs.[407] So those who feel a lack of enthusiasm should lick the rock which is Christ, and from him extract by prayers an appetite for the wisdom of the gospel. There are those who partake of the sacraments, not from true feeling but as it were out of habit, insufficiently concerned about the spirit. And yet the flesh of the sacraments profits noth-

* * * * *

403 Ps 1:3
404 Cf Matt 6:11.
405 Cf *Adagia* III iii 48.
406 Matt 5:6
407 Similar practices are mentioned by Aristotle (*Historia animalium* 8.10 596a) and Pliny (*Naturalis historia* 24.3). The closest parallels, which mention salt specifically as a cure for nausea, are Palladius 12.13.3 and Columella 7.3.20; Erasmus points out that the salt would be a block or 'rock' (*petra*), to clarify the parallel with Christ (from 1 Cor 10:4).

ing: 'It is the spirit which gives life.'[408] There are those who remain stuck at the outer layers of Scripture in the manner of the Jews, without ruminating on the mystical wisdom hidden within. There are those who recite a great string of psalms every day, but with the tongue only, not with the spirit. Hence it is that such vast numbers exhibit such weariness of soul, such lack of warming charity, such weakness and lack of resources that at the least temptation they fall, and one tiny word is sufficient to bring them to every extreme of vengefulness. In my opinion there is no other deficiency so great as this among those who live an enclosed life, especially among nuns.[409] I approve of sacred songs, and I commend readings from Scripture, in which they occupy a large proportion of their daytime and a certain part of the night – especially if at the same time they 'sing with their spirit and their mind.'[410] With these occupations the mind is kept from the many evils that leisure tends to engender in human beings. But more effective is the living voice of the shepherd, giving instruction, bestowing rebukes, imploring, spurring on, affording consolation, inflicting terror. In former days nuns would spend their time constantly in church, where they would hear the bishop preaching, and from among them proceeded great numbers admired even by men and strong to the point of martyrdom. But now, alas, almost all our nuns are such that whatever constancy they have is due to iron bars; and she who would leave were it possible has already left. The chief cause of this weakness is that they seldom receive the opportunity to hear the word of the Lord. Those set over them are very often silent, more adept in pleasures than in study, or if they do have any teaching to impart it is uninspiring and inappropriate. Priests who are banished to the supervision of nuns are usually those who because of their sluggish minds and slowness of wit are useless to the world or burdensome to their confrères. For this reason neither those parents who throw their daughters into this type of life nor the civic authorities should allow their concern to slumber.

* * * * *

408 Cf John 6:64/63.
409 While Erasmus' attacks on most aspects of monasticism are of course frequent, he is often particularly severe on its institution among women: see the paired colloquies *Virgo* μισόγαμος and *Virgo poenitens* CWE 39 279–301, 302–5; also the *Life of Jerome* CWE 61 31. His criticisms in this regard are in line with those of the Protestant Reformers: see Steven Ozment *When Fathers Ruled: Family Life in Reformation Europe* (Cambridge, MA 1983) 15–25.
410 1 Cor 14:15

Sheep that desire to demonstrate to their shepherd that they are well fed do not show him the food in their mouths; they make it clear that they are well fed by the good condition of their fleece, the shape of their body, and the swiftness of their movements. In the same way, those who learn off the Holy Scriptures, who recite and chant them, are not for that reason suddenly well nourished, but when they are strong to endure injury, eager in performing religious obligations, and friendly and cheerful of spirit, then you may deduce that they have been properly fed. There are those, as I have said, who can bear only what is pleasing, whose ears itch for delights, and who take to themselves the sort of masters who amuse them with pleasures rather than healing them with truth, however bitter-tasting. But sheep in good health are especially fond of willow leaves,[411] because they are bitter, and they prefer salty grazing to sweet. So those who are not yet purged of fleshly desires and who feel nausea in the face of those that are heavenly should ask their shepherd that he may deign to lead them to the waters of refreshment where they may drink more copious draughts of the spirit, the fiery force of which dries up the phlegm in the stomach,[412] and that he may make them turn completely to God, when in their previous lukewarm state they divided themselves between the world and Christ, limping with both legs, as it were,[413] since no one can serve two masters.[414] In Revelation, too, Christ threatens the lukewarm and declares he will spew them out unless they grow hot.[415] Indeed, there is no group of people more unfortunate than this, and perhaps none more incurable. This lukewarm state arises from the phlegm of the emotions becoming infected, which causes fever in the mind, so that we find no pleasure and no means of growth in spiritual learning. Let us then hurry to the waters of refreshment, so that we may grow warm with love. It may be objected that this is ridiculous, since cold water as a rule refreshes those who are too hot; it does not fire the lukewarm. Beloved, the figure is not ridiculous if we interpret it appropriately. This is water

* * * * *

411 On the complex Christian symbolism of willow leaves, see H. Rahner *Greek Myths and Christian Mystery* (London 1983; German original 1963) 286–327. Here they indicate sensual restraint and spiritual vitality.

412 A reference to the influential medical theory of the four humours (blood, phlegm, yellow and black bile); an undue preponderance of one of these in the body would give rise to disease. Phlegm or mucus was believed to be the coldest of the humours. See E.D. Phillips *Greek medicine* (London 1973) 48–52.

413 Cf *Adagia* III iii 56: *Aliud stans, aliud sedens* 'One thing on his feet and another sitting down.'

414 Matt 6:24, Luke 16:13

415 Rev 3:16

which heats by cooling. How is this? It cools the heat of desires, which 'rebel in tumult against the spirit,'[416] and when these are cooled the human mind grows warm towards those things that are of the spirit.

This is made clear by the prophet when he says: 'He has turned my soul.' For Paul divides the human soul into three parts: the flesh, which tends towards earthly things, the spirit, which strives towards heavenly things, and the soul in the middle, which moves this way and that.[417] Our natural emotions belong to this last part: concern for personal safety, tenderness towards one's wife, dutiful affection towards our parents and children, and regard for neighbours and friends. These we have in common with the pagans, and to some extent even with brute beasts. If these feelings are attached to the spirit, so that those whom we love we love only in Christ and if the need were to arise we would prefer to abandon them rather than depart from the love of Christ, they turn the soul towards the spirit. But if in order to gratify such feelings we depart from God's commandments, the soul is turning to the flesh. So in order that the whole man's spirit be aglow, our shepherd must turn the soul to himself. When this has happened, the soul becomes quick and eager, and those things that previously were hateful become delightful. Then when our soul has been refreshed in these waters, has received the heat of the spirit, and has turned away from the pleasures and conveniences of this world, our shepherd will lead it along the paths of righteousness, so that it may make its way in rapture by way of the forty mystical mansions[418] to a land flowing with milk and honey.[419] These mansions are the steps of the virtues, which the psalm mentions as being fifteen in number, leading up to the heavenly temple, which is the house of the Lord.[420]

* * * * *

416 Cf 1 Pet 2:11.

417 Cf 1 Thess. 5:23, with Erasmus' paraphrase LB VII 1026C, and Screech 101–3.

418 Literally the resting places or 'mansions' on the journey of the Israelites from Egypt to the promised land which are listed in Numbers 33; spiritually they are often taken to represent the individual's progress in the Christian life. See *In psalmum 33* 282 and n36 below and Screech 60; following Screech, I have translated *alacriter* as 'in rapture' – it seems clear from Erasmus' use of the word in contexts referring to ecstasy (see n458 below) that this is the meaning he intends.

419 Exod 3:36

420 Not one psalm, but the fifteen (119/120–133/134) which are headed *cantica graduum* (AV 'songs of degrees') and which according to Cassiodorus (*Expositio in psalmum 119* PL 70 901C, probably deriving from Jewish sources) correspond to the fifteen steps in the Temple at Jerusalem. It is likely that they were pilgrimage hymns and so extend the idea of a spiritual journey.

The word 'way' [*via*] occurs very frequently in biblical texts, some-times standing for a particular kind of life, as in Acts 9: 'men of this way,' and Acts 19: 'about the way of the Lord.'[421] The word 'path' [*semita*] is less common. Both words can be used in a good or a bad sense, especially since in verse or writings resembling verse it is the custom in Scripture to re-peat the same sentiment using different words. But it is less common for 'path' to be used in a bad sense; I will pass over examples, for brevity's sake. What we call 'way' is ὁδός in the Septuagint, and 'path' is τρίβος. Legal writers, too, make a distinction between 'road' [or 'way,' *via*], 'track' [*iter*], and 'bridle-path' [*actus*];[422] of these, the widest is the road, which must be wide enough for vehicles to turn in it, and the bridle-path is next in width. A track may even be a pedestrian route, but it must be possible to drive [*agere*] mules or horses along a bridle-path. A road accommodates wagons also; often it is paved and public, like those in the city which divide up neighbourhoods or which separate buildings from the city walls, and also those outside the city like the Appian Way and the Sacred Way.[423] A public road is called λεωφόρος [people-carrier] by the Greeks, since an estate may be liable to provide a road for some one or other individual, not for the people.[424]

A path [*semita*] seems to be so called as being half a track [*semi iter*], both because it is narrower and because it is not public property. Here I do not need to remind you of the famous Pythagorean catchphrase 'Do not travel by the way of the people.'[425] Who are those who go by this route, which 'carries people'? Consider how the masses lead their lives, and you will see the answer to your question. They love, they hate, they bring law-suits, they make war, they indulge their whims and fancies, they canvass for office, they consort with prostitutes, they commit adultery, they use fraud, deception, theft, usury, embezzlement, and perjury to increase their prop-erty. Some of them creep along, some walk, some are borne in carriages,

* * * * *

421 Acts 9:2, 19:23
422 For instance, *Digest* 8.3.1; but Erasmus' discussion relies more heavily on Varro *De lingua latina* 5.35.
423 The Sacred Way was not outside Rome, but ran from the Forum to the Capitol, as is clear from Varro 5.47; a surprising slip.
424 Erasmus is referring to *servitutes*, still current in Roman law, which are liabil-ities incurred on an estate, such as the provision of roads or aqueducts (see *Digest* 8.3.1).
425 Cf *Adagia* III v 27; there is a discussion of most of the precepts believed to be Pythagorean at at *Adagia* I i 2.

on litters and on curule chairs,[426] some ride on camels, elephants, mules, horses, and ponies; but all alike are driven by their own desires and so travel by the way of the people. This is the broad way which most people tread to their death. From this way, beloved, our shepherd leads us apart when he proclaims: 'I am the way, the truth, and the life'[427] and 'Enter by the narrow gate; for the gate is wide and the way is broad that leads to destruction, and those who enter by it are many; how narrow is the gate and how confined the way that leads to life, and those who find it are few.'[428]

This way which is narrow and known to few is often called a path in the Scriptures. But the wicked, too, have their paths, which the wisdom of Solomon warns us against: 'My son, do not walk with them; hold back your foot from their paths ... Such are the paths of all who are greedy; they take away the lives of their possessors.'[429] Thus those who are slaves to ambition, lust, and wanton living have their own paths and their own snares; this especially applies to hypocrites, who are deceived by their own paths and snares and who also use them to lure others to their doom. It was these whom the Lord singled out in his words 'Beware of false prophets.'[430] But our shepherd does not lead us through random paths but through the paths of righteousness. For Christians there are many paths but only one righteousness, while the Jews have as many righteousnesses as they have works. Our righteousness is Christ, who through faith justifies everyone who comes to him.[431]

It would not be out of place, in my view, to interpret this passage as referring to the different estates of life. One might say that the laity, married people, soldiers, and courtiers walk by the way of righteousness if they

* * * * *

426 The privilege of sitting in a particular kind of chair was a perquisite of the higher ('curule') magistracies of ancient Rome.
427 John 14:6
428 Matt 7:13–14
429 Prov 1:15, 19
430 Matt 7:15
431 Cf n194 above. Erasmus refers to the doctrine of justification by faith that is so conspicuous in the Pauline Epistles; though emphasized by some of the 'pre-reformers,' it had acquired new importance in light of the debate initiated by Luther. Erasmus' intention here is irenical, but as is clear from the earlier passage (152–3 above) he understands the formula in synergist terms: the initial gift of righteousness unfolds in good works through the cooperation of the human will with grace. This position is quite distinct from the concept of righteousness as something earned through merit, an attitude that Erasmus engages with two paragraphs below.

live upright lives each in his own manner, while those who have professed
perpetual chastity and contempt for the things of the world walk by the
paths of righteousness provided that they remain true to their profession.
And yet it is not a style of life but rather a pious disposition which commends one to God, and among those who claim to follow the strictest rule
of life there are, sadly, far too many who go by the way of the people. Consequently it is more appropriate to say that all those who live their lives
according to God's commandments, whatever may be their particular style
of living, advance by the paths of righteousness. If someone strays off in
any direction in which greedy desires beckon, there the road will offer him
a very broad expanse to wander in. But where he does not draw back, first
of all from God's commandments, and also from those human commandments which conduce to godly behaviour, there the path is narrow and has
no space for him to leave it. In this manner married people who preserve
an honourable marriage innocent of infidelity walk in the paths of righteousness; merchants who commit no fraud, sailors, cart-drivers, soldiers,
and courtiers who do nothing contrary to God's command all walk in the
paths of righteousness.

But even in the middle of the ascent of virtue there often lurks the
fatal evil of pride, and for this reason the prophet has added 'for his name's
sake,' with these words excluding any human merit and illuminating the
goodness of Christ. I know that some people are shocked if they hear talk
of 'excluding merit,' but these words are used more than six hundred times
by St Augustine, and by many other orthodox writers.[432] If indeed we can
speak of any human merit, it is so tiny that we may as well treat it as
nothing – and certainly we cannot claim it as our own, since even this merit
results from God's generosity. These words, then, are in the same spirit as a
verse of the Thirtieth Psalm: 'For you are my strength and my refuge, and
for your name's sake you will lead me and feed me.'[433] And so, my dear
friends, if one of you should feel himself increasing in spiritual strength,
less burdened by the flesh, and more eagerly soaring to the things above,
he should take care lest he claim for his own what he has freely received
and so not only fail to benefit from the gift but also lose what he already
has. He should say to his shepherd, 'Not to me, O Lord, not to me, but to
your name give glory,' and again, 'In God I will make my strength.'[434] In

* * * * *

432 Most relevantly, Augustine on this very phrase, *Enarratio in psalmum* 22 PL 36
    182
433 Ps 30:4/31:3
434 Cf Pss 113B/115:1, 59:14/60:12.

this way you will escape pride, and also the Lord in his goodness will so increase his generosity towards you that you may confidently say even this: 'For even if I walk in the midst of the shadow of death, I will not fear evil, since you are with me.'

Here too the change of person has its point. Previously the bride was rejoicing in her good fortune; now in the face of danger she looks round and sees that she possesses nothing of her own that can inspire such confidence, so she turns to her shepherd and says, 'Since you are with me.' Paul, too, when he runs through what God has accomplished through him, adds, 'Yet not I, but the grace of God that was with me.'[435] My dearest friends, let us too learn to speak in this way, if we have done something upright or holy. Let us not say, 'I have overcome that temptation' but 'The Lord's mercy has set me free from that temptation.' Not 'I made him adopt better ways of thinking' but 'The grace of God was pleased to use me, his unworthy servant, to convert him to better ways of thinking.' The sheep of Christ should not indulge in those boastful words which we now hear from those who demand to be considered Christ's true sheep, such as 'Anyone in this city who has been preserved from the plague of heresy owes it to my words' and 'Thanks to my sermons, these people have become much better than they were before' and 'I have sown spiritual seed in you: yield up your fleshly harvest' and 'We are the pillars of the church, which will collapse if we do not sustain it on our shoulders.' These are the words of Pharisees, obscuring the glory of Christ our shepherd; and we hear them from the mouths of those who clothe themselves in the fleece of simple sheep. Let us rather be true sheep of Jesus Christ; let us accept no credit beyond that of simple service for the good actions we have performed, but let us give all the glory to the Lord, who does all things for his name's sake. Let us allow him to triumph in us, so that one day we may triumph with him. Let our trust in him make us strong and courageous. If we wish to stand firm, let us stand on the rock of Christ – if we try to rely on our own weakness, we shall fall immediately.

Further, let us not speak to men like this: 'The grace of God was with me,' or 'I owe my qualities to God's grace'; let us say to Christ himself: 'I shall not fear evil, since you are with me.' The words we address to men we speak with our lips, and frequently they are rather different from what we feel in our hearts; but the words we address to God are true and come from the heart, for then we are speaking to him 'who sees our heart and

* * * * *

435 1 Cor 15:10

inmost being.'[436] Moreover, in biblical idiom the Lord is said to 'be with' those on whom he looks with favour. A thief or robber whose robbery turns out successfully, or an adulterer who gets the women he desires, or a man possessed by anger who inflicts vengeance on someone he hates, could not then say with truth, 'Today the Lord was with me.'

The Septuagint translation 'in the middle of the shadow of death' is rendered by Jerome 'in the valley of the shadow of death.'[437] By the shadow of death is meant that utter darkness which exists in hell, or – figuratively – in the souls of the wicked who do not know God, or at least do not fear him. The words include all the things that normally strike people with terror, such as bereavement, exile, poverty, disgrace, physical pain, death, hell, the devil. What is there to be feared by one who does not fear hell? And yet many things frighten our human nature that in truth are not evil, and many attract it that should properly be dreaded. The true evils are those which make us evil, and this cannot be done by poverty or exile, illness, or death.[438] Now the whole sum of evils [mala] is appropriately styled in Hebrew 'evil' [malum], just as in the Gospel it is said that the Lamb 'takes away the sin of the world'[439] – that is, the whole body of sin. The Greek of the Septuagint, κακά, is quite compatible with this sense, since by not adding an article it shows that we should understand not these or those evils, but the whole species of evils.

What is it that gives so much confidence to a mere sheep and prevents it fearing either death or hell? 'Since your rod and staff themselves will comfort me.' This is Jerome's reading from the Hebrew, which also joins this verse to the preceding one. I know that some people interpret the rod as that of brotherly reproof,[440] in accordance with the lines 'The righteous man will reprove me in his mercy, and will reproach me.'[441] The staff is then the healing offered by penance. One who strays is struck, not killed, by the rod, and when he no longer pleases himself, to avoid despair he is given the support of the staff of penance, which promises peace to him who has fallen. While I agree that all this is the church's power, and that

* * * * *

436 Rev 2:23; compare also Wisd 1:6.
437 The Vulgate rendering 'in the middle,' based on a faulty reading in the Septuagint, is corrected as 'in the valley' in the *Psalterium iuxta Hebraeos* PL 28 (1890) 1206A.
438 The formulation is Stoic, though not of course incompatible with Christianity.
439 John 1:29
440 Arnobius the Younger PL 53 354D *Commentarium in psalmum 22* refers the rod to the discipline of the church.
441 Ps 140/141:5

the interpretation is a pious one, in expounding the Scriptures I prefer a simple, unforced, and consistent interpretation. This psalm is in its entirety one of consolation, and there is no admixture of harshness. These words in fact relate to what was said a little earlier: 'Since you are with me,' that is, since you have helped me. And how did you help? With rod and staff, or to put it at its simplest, by your direction, which ensures that even what is evil turns to good for me. Perhaps the rod is that with which you guide us, which will not let us stray from the paths of righteousness, and the staff is that which supports the weary on the way. Or the rod may be the commandments and the staff the consolation that sustains the soul with the hope of heavenly rewards. And nothing prevents us from taking the rod as Holy Scripture, which shines before us in all our actions and tells us what to shun and what to seek, thus guiding us along the paths of righteousness, as it is said: 'Your word is a lamp to my feet, and a light to my path.'[442] Then the staff is the hope of rewards to come, which supports the minds of the faithful and prevents them giving way in the face of afflictions, so many of which lie before those who walk in the paths of righteousness. For 'the hope of a prize lessens the whip's force,'[443] and 'the hope of the righteous ends in gladness,' in Solomon's words.[444]

The psalmist does not say that he is actually walking in darkness and the shadow of death, but rather by making a hypothetical supposition he allows a hyperbole. A similar passage is 'If I ascend to heaven, you are there.'[445] In the same way here: if I were to walk through hell, with you as companion I should fear nothing. Why should anyone fear the darkness, if he has the light of the world with him? Why should he dread death, if he is joined to the fount of life? 'The hope of good gives strength, the hope of good also makes the mind resolute.'[446] To a great extent hope is supplied by

* * * * *

442 Ps 118/119:105
443 This dictum, attributed to a 'sage' in the *Concio de puero Iesu* CWE 29 67, appears also in the *Expositio super Apocalypsim* 'Vox Domini praeparantis cervos' erroneously attributed to Aquinas; the ultimate source is unclear. The whip might suggest a Greek proverb referring to contests at Sparta in which boys competed in endurance under flagellation; see Xenophon *Constitution of the Lacedaemonians* 2.9 and Tertullian *Ad martyres* 4.7 PL 1 (1844) 626.
444 Prov 10:28
445 Ps 138/139:8
446 This line forms a Latin hexameter; with a following pentameter it appears not infrequently in medieval and Renaissance authors; Walther 30180, 34005. At *Adagia* IV iv 63 Erasmus wrongly attributes the couplet to Ovid; the model is in fact Ovid *Heroides* 11.61.

the waters of refreshment. Holy Scripture indeed bestows much comfort, promising immortality to those who follow in Christ's footsteps and travel by the path of righteousness – yet here we see the kindness and munificence of our shepherd, who gives us another fine solace. 'You will prepare' says the psalm, or 'you have prepared in my sight a table against those who afflict me' or 'in the sight of my persecutors.' (In the writings of the prophets it does not make much difference whether the future or the past tense of verbs is used.)

Just as generals, in order to encourage their soldiers to fight with greater enthusiasm, used to give them largesse or a banquet in excess of the payment hoped for, so here the shepherd, having promised everlasting life to his sheep, meanwhile gives them here and now a sort of pledge, a taste, as it were, of that eternal banquet.[447] Much toil is involved in the journey through the paths of righteousness, but there is prepared the table of a calm, quiet, and cheerful conscience, for as Solomon says 'A mind without cares is like a perpetual feast.'[448] The practice of piety, which is Martha's part,[449] involves bodily toil, but toil is destroyed by the companion of deeds well done, the joyfulness of a spiritual mind. Joy is also mentioned among the fruits of the spirit;[450] no one will take this joy away from us,[451] but it will be made complete in the world to come. How many times St Paul refers to this joy! 'For the kingdom of God,' he says, 'is not food and drink, but righteousness and peace and joy in the Holy Spirit.'[452] And when he is facing many dangers and many ills, what does he write to the Corinthians? 'I am filled with solace, with overflowing joy, in every affliction.'[453] Whence comes this cheerfulness in the midst of that whole train of evils he speaks of here? Clearly, he was seated at that table which the Lord has prepared for his soldiers, he was anointed with the 'oil of spiritual happiness,'[454] and he had grown drunk from the Lord's cup of fine wine.[455] Those who think that religious devotion is something doleful and unpleas-

* * * * *

447 A favourite parallel, found also in *De puero Iesu* CWE 29 67 and *In psalmum 38* LB V 465F
448 Prov 15:5
449 Cf Luke 10:38–42.
450 Gal 5:22. Erasmus uses very similar words in Allen Ep 2260:183, to Peter Gillis, written in January 1530.
451 John 16:22
452 Rom 14:17
453 2 Cor 7:4
454 Cf Ps 44:8/45:7.
455 *praeclaro calice*, a reference to the Vulgate text of this verse

ant are wide of the mark. Such indeed is the religion of the Pharisees, but true piety offers far more comfort than irksomeness. When the mind of a devout person has been refreshed with these spiritual delights, he does not begrudge their tables to the Epicureans and the followers of Apicius,[456] he does not long for Sicilian tables,[457] for he has banquets a hundred times more magnificent than these. He has perfumes, not of the kind that flatter our noses with a trivial and fleeting little pleasure, but those which buoy up the soul with continual joy; he has the cup of wine that truly cheers the heart of man, that causes a holy and sober drunkenness.[458] For he has the new wine which once made the apostles seem drunk – to those who had not tasted the delights of this table.[459]

The table is prepared in the face of those who persecute Christ's sheep; it refreshes the pious and gives pain to the wicked. The good cheer which the faithful possess is something secret, it is true, and yet it appears most plainly in their speech and shines out in their faces. And so it happens that when the wicked hurl abuse at the pious, and the pious are not disturbed but return blessings for curses,[460] the wicked grow more enraged than if these had been insults, particularly those who are incorrigible. But others, observing the constant calm and cheerful aspect of the pious amidst all these insults and tortures, realize that the spirit of God is at work in them and are themselves converted to a pious life. For this reason the table is prepared for those who cling with complete trust to Christ their shepherd in the sight of the wicked, so that as the sheep begin here their enjoyment of the delights of heaven, those who are lost begin to feel here the tortures of hell, their final destination. Tyrants have devoted their entire mental resources to seducing the faithful from Christ by inhuman punishments; but when they perceive that all their power, their bluster, and their threats are despised and that the martyrs continue with a serene expression in the midst of torture and fire and the most cruel butchery, their own mental suffering is greater than the martyrs' physical torment. They may be moved to repentance by these examples, but since they were earlier blinded by ill will and did not wish to see what they saw, they are forced to repent too

* * * * *

456 M. Gavius Apicius was a notorious gourmet, a contemporary of Tiberius (Tacitus *Annals* 4.1), whose name became proverbial for the type, as for instance in Seneca *Consolatio ad Helviam* 10.
457 *Adagia* II ii 68
458 On this topos, see Screech 73–4.
459 Acts 2:13
460 Cf 1 Pet 3:9.

late, and to sing uselessly that miserable song: 'Are not these they whom we once held in derision ...?'[461]

Let us suppose for the moment that there is no resurrection, and that the soul does not survive the death of the body. Who is there who would not prefer to live under the rule of such a shepherd, to be nourished in such pastures and refreshed by such waters, to enjoy such safety, and recline at such a rich table, than under the devil's tyranny to keep following through right and wrong the world's false goods, which torture him who hunts them with yearning and rend him who has them to pieces with worry about keeping them, desire for increasing them, and fear of losing them, but which cannot offer the soul true repose?[462] Then what if we now turn our eyes to eternity, and compare the fates of the pious and the wicked? 'And your goodness,' says the psalmist, 'refreshes me not only here, but will complete what it has begun. You who gave a token will grant the fulfilment of your promise, that I may partake in this feast with my joy made complete, all the days of my life. Though now I dwell in this bodily tent as a stranger, the guest of a few short days,[463] then I shall be received into the heavenly Jerusalem, which is our own native land, and I shall dwell in the house of the Lord throughout the length of days, where my happiness will be everlasting, secure, and complete, and all ills will have been completely wiped out.'[464]

I shall now let you go, if I may first briefly go over the whole psalm continuously. The first requirement of salvation is that we should be sheep – that is to say, simple and tractable – and that we should recognize our shepherd, Jesus, and permit ourselves to be pastured by him. Then, we must let him lead us into the pastures of the church, where the forgiveness of sins gives the soul peace and rest, and soon we are led by a more abundant knowledge of the Scriptures and greater gifts of the Spirit to the waters which refresh our spirits and add strength to our faith and love. From here we progress to the precepts of a life more perfectly in conformity with the gospel; we are strengthened in this and our spiritual resources are increased, so that we are even prepared for martyrdom, because we trust in the care of our shepherd. On this there follows Mary's best part, which will

* * * * *

461 Wisd 5:3
462 The argument appears also in the *Enchiridion* CWE 66 60, and in *De puero Iesu* CWE 29 68.
463 Cf Wisd 5:14 with Heb 11:13.
464 Pseudo-Jerome *Breviarium in psalmos* PL 26 (1845) 886 gives a similar exegesis of this verse.

never be taken away;[465] that is, a rapture of the spirit, when through usage those things which at first were bitter grow sweet. This is a taste of eternal felicity.[466]

The same progression is acknowledged by the church. The bishop leads the catechumen away from the herd of goats by teaching him the creed. He is brought to the forecourts of the church; through baptism he is taken to pasture; he is received into the communion of the sacraments with the sheep, and as he makes progress in living a holy life he is nourished at the waters of refreshment, until he belongs entirely to the spirit and loves nothing but God, or at least nothing that he does not love for God's sake. When he has shown the church that this is his state, he is led to those offices which require an upright and dependable man. Of his own will he makes profession of virginity. He gives his possessions to the poor. He becomes a deacon; he takes on the burden of the episcopate. He walks in the narrow way, and is not made proud by his honours or corrupted by his rank but gives all glory to the Lord Jesus, in whose person he stands. In this way he does not exult in material prosperity, nor is he cast down by adversity. He relies on the protection of the Lord, whose leadership he follows in all things, and so he is fearless in the face of every assault by the forces of evil. His temptations he turns into consolation, and as on a staff he supports his soul on the hope of things to come. From his services in the world outside, with all their attendant irksomeness, he retires to the chamber of a good conscience, where he is refreshed by spiritual banquets and made happy by spiritual oil, and being made drunk with a small taste of heavenly joys he easily rejects anything that leads him away from Christ. Then he grows tired of all that he sees, and sighs, longing for a closer union with the Lord, for the ceaseless enjoyment of his presence face to face. Into this presence may that best of shepherds, our Lord Jesus Christ, see fit to bring us; to whom with the Father and the Holy Spirit be glory for ever. Amen.

* * * * *

465 Luke 10:42, also cited famously in *Moria* CWE 27 152
466 A recurrent reference in Erasmus; as well as the *Moria* cited above, compare *De contemptu mundi* CWE 66 167, *De puero Iesu* CWE 29 69, *Paraphrasis in epistolam ad Romanos* CWE 42 48, and *In psalmum 38* LB V 465C. See Screech 173–9.

A MOST USEFUL DISCUSSION CONCERNING PROPOSALS FOR WAR AGAINST THE TURKS, INCLUDING AN EXPOSITION OF PSALM 28

Utilissima consultatio de bello Turcis inferendo, et obiter enarratus psalmus 28

translated and annotated by
MICHAEL J. HEATH

Sultan Suleiman abandoned his siege of Vienna on the night of 14/15 October 1529, having failed to force the gateway to the Hapsburg Empire. Christendom had in fact survived its sternest test at the hands of the Muslim invader; the Ottoman Turks were never again to come so close to breaking into western Europe. Naturally, Erasmus and his contemporaries could not foresee this and knew little of the disturbances to the east that prevented Suleiman from pressing home or renewing the attack; for the next few months, dire prophecies and nervous uncertainty abounded in the West.[1] In this atmosphere of fearful anticipation Johann Rinck, a lawyer of Cologne, asked Erasmus to speak his mind on the principle of war against the infidel.[2] Erasmus responded with the *Utilissima consultatio de bello Turcis inferendo*, dated 17 March 1530 and published by Froben's press at Basel; it begins with an exposition of Psalm 28 (29 in English versions) and was therefore subsequently included, slightly incongruously, among Erasmus' psalm commentaries. In fact, scriptural exegesis plays a minor role in what amounts to a political memorandum on a subject of pressing importance.

In his *Enarratio primi psalmi*,[3] contemporary with the 'political' *Adagia* of 1515 and the *Institutio principis christiani*, Erasmus expounded the psalm 'above all according to the tropological sense,' drawing out the moral meaning and applying the divine message to contemporary Christendom; he returns here to the same mode of exegesis, naturally enough, in what may be considered a prologue to his detailed examination of the Turkish question. Psalm 28 had received little attention from the patristic and medieval commentators on whom Erasmus drew for philological and exegetical inspiration in his earlier writings on the psalms; the most extensive commentary had been that of Richard of St Victor,[4] who applied the psalm to the very different topic of the monastic novitiate. Erasmus reads this exceptionally enigmatic text as a hymn to God's omnipotence (and thus, obliquely, as a proclamation of human impotence) and as an exhortation to the faithful to give him the honour due to his majesty. In this reading, the Turks figure as the latest in a series of divine warnings to those who have gone astray. From the plagues of Exodus, the threats in Leviticus and Deuteronomy, the sufferings of the Homeric Greeks and Trojans, and the prophecies of the Apocalypse to the recent outbreaks of syphilis, sweating-sickness, and bloody revolution, Erasmus catalogues the woes that have chastised

* * * * *

1 See for example Ep 2399 and Williams *Radical Reformation* 189.
2 Rinck's letter has not survived.
3 CWE 63 6–63
4 PL 196 285–322

the faithless but also hints that the remedy lies within the first two lines of the psalm. The prospects for military success are gloomy against those whom Erasmus, along with many contemporaries, regarded as the voice or the scourge of God;[5] urgently needed is reconciliation with God, whose anger against his people must be appeased by sacrifice, by a thorough reform of the institutions and morals of Christendom. Erasmus' exegesis of the psalm makes it clear that the message of this treatise is consistent with his long-standing diagnosis of the ills of his era.

But if *De bello Turcico* reflects exactly the familiar ethical principles and political thought of Erasmus, it also marks a development in his more specific political opinions, whose evolution James D. Tracy terminates, too abruptly, in about 1516.[6] Detailed examination of the Turkish problem leads to Erasmus' most precise response to the question of 'holy war,' which had figured episodically in his earlier discussions of just and legitimate war.[7] So precise and practical and up-to-date is Erasmus' piece that it has even been suggested that it was prepared for the Diet of Augsburg,[8] though one must wonder whether Erasmus' even-handed distribution of the blame for Christendom's plight would have appealed to the partisan delegates there. His lucid analysis of the historical, political, strategic, and economic factors that complicated the question made uncomfortable reading for those accustomed to the simplicities of crusading rhetoric.

De bello Turcico bears the marks of rapid composition. A letter to Bonifacius Amerbach early in 1530[9] asks for Luther's book on the Turkish war, *Vom Kriege widder die Türcken*, 'as soon as possible,' although internal evidence suggests that it did not arrive in time to be used in the present work. But Erasmus' repetition in *De bello Turcico* of themes, examples, and even

* * * * *

5 See C.A. Patrides '"The Bloody and Cruell Turk": The Background of a Renaissance Commonplace' *Studies in the Renaissance* 10 (1963) 126–35 and J.W. Bohnstedt *The Infidel Scourge of God: The Turkish Menace as Seen by German Pamphleteers of the Reformation Era* (Philadelphia 1968).

6 *Politics* 8 and 113. The distinction between 'thought' and 'opinions' is nonetheless a useful one; Tracy attributes Erasmus' political opinions largely to his experience of specific local conditions in the Netherlands. Here, similarly, he is dealing with political realities rather than humanist abstractions.

7 For example in the adage *Dulce bellum inexpertis* (IV i 1 LB II 966–8), the *Institutio principis christiani* 11 CWE 27 287, and *Querela pacis* CWE 27 314; see also Ep 858:85–165 on evangelizing the Turks.

8 George Faludy *Erasmus of Rotterdam* (London 1970) 238

9 Ep 2279; Allen's conjectural date of March 1530 is based on the date of *De bello Turcico*.

whole sentences used in recent letters,[10] and the quotation of marginally relevant authors on whom he had recently been working, like St Cyprian and Berengarius of Tours,[11] suggest a need to use material ready to hand. This is particularly true of Erasmus' lengthy account of the Turks' astonishing rise to power from obscure beginnings, about which he had previously written nothing. He transcribes more or less word for word a treatise, based on the Byzantine annalists, by his friend Giambattista Egnazio, from whom he had received a copy on publication fourteen years earlier.[12] Egnazio's treatise provided solid evidence of the Turks' intrinsic unworthiness and thus suited Erasmus' contention that their present pre-eminence could have been achieved only with special divine permission. Pursuing this rigorous dialectic, Erasmus ignores the contemporary vogue for travellers' tales and shows little interest in the religion, morals, and customs of the Turks.[13] In some ways his treatise recalls the older genre of the crusading oration, and his reference to the two fifteenth-century masters of the form, Aeneas Sylvius (Pope Pius II) and Cardinal Joannes Bessarion, reinforce this impression; many clichés of the genre find a place here, but not always in their original context.[14] One duty of the orator was to impress on his audience the justice and necessity of fighting the Turks because of their maltreatment of their Christian subjects, and thus Erasmus dusted off his copy of Vives' *De Europae dissidiis et bello Turcico* (1526);[15] we cannot be sure that he had read Vives' more recent publication on the topic, *De conditione vitae christianorum sub Turca* (1529).

But Erasmus' purpose was not to persuade his readers that they must instantly rush to arms against the infidel, as emperors, princes, popes, and preachers had urged through the centuries. He recognized, of course, the

* * * * *

10 For example Epp 2134:223–7, 2209:185–9, 2223:11–15, and 2249:24, all on the 'plagues' besetting Christendom

11 See nn63 and 155 below.

12 See Ep 588 and M.J. Heath 'Erasmus and War against the Turks' in *Acta conventus neo-Latini Turonensis* ed J.-C. Margolin (Paris 1980) 991–9 and 'Erasmus and the Infidel' ERSY 16 (1996) 19–33; these papers explore a number of the themes sketched here.

13 The growing interest in Oriental exotica is documented in R. Schwoebel's *Shadow of the Crescent* and in the bibliographical work of C. Göllner *Turcica: die europäischen Türkendrucke des XVI Jahrhunderts* 2 vols (Bucharest 1961–8).

14 See for example nn57, 114, 165, 168, and 173 below. The conventions of the genre are outlined in my *Crusading Commonplaces* (CC); for the background see Housley *Later Crusades* 376–420. Erasmus mocks such orations in the prefatory epistle to the *Moria* CWE 27 84.

15 See Ep 1847 and n236 below.

urgency of the situation, given the Turks' apparently unstoppable advance through the Balkans and across the Hungarian plain to the very gates of Vienna; but *De bello Turcico* is above all a contribution to Reformation polemic. Erasmus devotes most of the work to an examination of the twelve-year-old controversy over Luther's views on resistance to the Turk,[16] given crucial importance both by the Turk's recent conquests (Syria, Egypt, Rhodes, Belgrade, Hungary) and by the acceptance and exaggeration of Luther's views by other dissenters such as the pacific Anabaptists. Erasmus had probably been prompted to ask Amerbach for Luther's *Vom Kriege widder die Türcken*, published on 23 April 1529, by reading a grimly humorous dialogue by Joannes Cochlaeus, *Dialogus de bello contra Turcas, in antilogias Lutheri* (June 1529). The author poses as the orator of King Ferdinand, brother to Emperor Charles v and claimant to the Hungarian throne. Cochlaeus contrasts Luther's early views on the crusade ('spoken' by Luther in person) with the words of *Vom Kriege*, put in the mouth of 'Palinodus' (that is, 'Recanter'), the later incarnation of Luther.[17] Cochlaeus' work was the most recent and most comprehensive in a series of attacks on Luther's position made both by theologians, such as Clichtove, Bernard of Luxembourg, and Eck, and by humanists such as Vives and More.[18]

Luther first entered the fray in 1518, when elucidating his Ninety-five Theses in the *Resolutiones disputationum*. Drawing on Isaiah 10, he argues that the scourges of God should not be resisted, since the Almighty sends them to incite humankind to reform; to resist is to fight the consequences and the punishment of our sins, rather than the sins themselves. The only way to overcome a scourge such as the Turks is to follow the path of repentance.[19] His arguments were condemned, along with many others, in the papal bull *Exsurge Domine* (15 June 1520); Luther replied that experience had shown that such resistance was in any case futile, both on the battlefield and on the drawing-board: 'So many meetings, so many debates, so many plans: and yet, by God's command, we have seen all our aspirations

* * * * *

16 See K.M. Setton 'Lutheranism and the Turkish Peril' *Balkan Studies* 3 (1962) 133–68 and Heath cc 13–21 and notes.

17 In Ep 2338 Erasmus describes Luther's revised views as a *palinodia*, which may well indicate that he knew of them through Cochlaeus' book. On Cochlaeus, with whom Erasmus frequently corresponded, see CEBR I 321–2.

18 Clichtove *De bello et pace opusculum* (Paris 1523) 28–9, Bernard of Luxembourg *Catalogus haereticorum* (Paris 1524) 87, Eck *Enchiridion* 21 (sig H iv–v); on the humanists, see R.P. Adams *The Better Part of Valor* (Seattle 1962), for example 274–6 on More's *Dialogue concerning Tyndale*.

19 *Works* 31 91

come to nothing, until we have become a laughing-stock to the Turks, who say: "They're attacking us with bulls and pardons."'[20] When the Sorbonne condemned the original proposition, once more, as false if not heretical,[21] Luther replied in a way echoed (perhaps unwittingly) by Erasmus at the end of *De bello Turcico*. In his *Confutatio determinationis doctorum Parrhisiensium*, Luther argued that the way to win over the Turks was not by arms but by acts of charity coupled with wholesome preaching: '"Preach the gospel to every creature" [Mark 16:15]: are not the Turks God's creatures?' If Christians wish to fight, cries Luther, let them fight the invisible enemy in their midst with the sword of the spirit. 'To speak my mind openly, I should as unwillingly take up the sword against the Turk as against my Christian brother.'[22] Such assertions gave strength to other 'accursed voices,' as Erasmus calls them, such as the Anabaptists, who claimed that it was better to live under the Turk than under pope or emperor.[23] Erasmus had no time for such extremism, though the notoriously unproductive crusading plans of the pontiffs and the fabled nonchalance of the Christian princes did occasionally lead him to question their motives himself.[24]

Luther's supposed unwillingness to countenance a campaign against the Turks had produced a decade of censure and condemnation from theologians and humanists when, in 1529, he apparently underwent a change of heart. But *Vom Kriege widder die Türcken* is less a recantation than a redefinition of his position, brought about by the crisis on the eastern border of Christendom. Luther is as adamant as ever that the clergy must not be involved in warfare; the Christian must fight by means of prayer, repentance, and reform, so that the Turk, God's scourge, will be forced to stand alone, 'without the devil's help and without God's hand.'[25] But Luther makes it clear that the emperor has the right to lead an army against the Turk to protect those of his subjects who have been physically harmed by the invader. Luther thus allows a defensive war (on much the same terms as Erasmus in his 'pacific' writings), but advises that if dissension at home prevents an adequate resistance being made, it would be better to concede some territory than to suffer another disaster like that of Mohács three years before.

* * * * *

20 *Assertio omnium articulorum … per bullam Leonis x novissimam damnatorum* article 34 (Wittenberg 1520) sig g iv recto / WA 7 140
21 Erasmus quotes the censure; see 234 and n134 below.
22 *Confutatio* (1523) 214–17
23 See 257 and n234 below.
24 See n262 below.
25 *Works* 46 170

He also complains of Christians' inadequate knowledge of the Turks, some of whose virtues show Christians in a poor light, and of their religion, which is in some respects no worse than that professed by the pope. Luther did his best to remedy this ignorance with his 1530 edition of the work of Georgius de Hungaria, his 1542 German translation of a book on Islam by Ricoldus de Montecrucis, and his apparent blessing and preface for Biblian-der's 1543 edition of the Qu'ran, the first printed Latin translation;[26] unlike Erasmus, Luther was interested in the character of Christendom's potential conqueror.

But the conclusion of *Vom Kriege* is strikingly similar to that of Eras-mus in *De bello Turcico*: 'I would not urge or bid anyone to fight against the Turk unless the first method, mentioned above, that men had first repented and been reconciled to God, etc, had been followed. If anyone wants to go to war in another way, let him take his chances.'[27] This is not the only point of agreement. Erasmus found it hard to refute many of Luther's propo-sitions largely because he agreed with him, for example over the futil-ity of crusade-collections, the dangerous and increasing absolutism of the princes, and the advisability of making territorial concessions. Most impor-tantly, he had as little confidence as Luther in the victory of an unreformed Christendom.

Erasmus probably knew of Luther's redefined position through Coch-laeus' *Dialogus*, published two months after *Vom Kriege widder die Türcken* and evidently designed to enlist support for King Ferdinand in his forth-coming campaign to rescue Hungary and protect Vienna. Cochlaeus had lit-tle difficulty in demonstrating some inconsistency and illogicality in Luther's pronouncements on war against the Turks, the situation having evolved so rapidly in a dozen years; in any case, Luther made no claim to be a sys-tematic thinker in the secular domain. Unabashed, he published in Septem-ber 1529 *Eine Heer-predigt widder den Türcken*,[28] addressed to the army about to defend Vienna, an exhortatory pamphlet based on a famous interpreta-tion of Daniel 7, which apparently prophesied the imminent destruction of

* * * * *

26 On Georgius, see n236 below; Ricoldus (a thirteenth-century Dominican mis-sionary) wrote his *Contra sectam Muhumeticam* as a handbook for fellow mis-sionaries; the *praemonitio* of Bibliander's edition, published at Basel, is at-tributed to both Luther and Melanchthon in different printings: *Machumetis Sarracenorum principis eiusque successorum vitae ac doctrina, ipseque Alcoran* sig a 2.

27 *Works* 46 184

28 WA 30-2 160–97; it was first printed anonymously at Wittenberg; it seems un-likely that this 'military sermon' was actually delivered *viva voce*.

the Turks. But once more Luther stressed that this was to be a campaign against the Turks, and not a crusade, with all its implications of clerical involvement and evangelization by force. It is unlikely that Erasmus knew this work, though he was well aware, and duly sceptical, of the role played by such prophecies in bellicose propaganda.[29]

This, briefly, is the controversy to which Erasmus contributed *De bello Turcico*. In an age when a revival of the old crusading spirit seemed to many the only answer to the Turkish menace, it is one of the least enthusiastic endorsements imaginable of the warlike proposals emanating from curia and chancelleries alike. To say that without thorough spiritual and moral reformation Christendom has no prospect of winning a war against the Turks is tantamount to arguing against it; if reform will lead to the withdrawal of God's scourge, a military campaign will then be superfluous, and Christians may rely on the omnipotent power evoked by the psalm. Erasmus could have expected as much obloquy as Luther had attracted for a decade. But in fact the reception of *De bello Turcico* was muted, either because Erasmus' influence was on the wane, as he reflects rather bitterly towards the end of the piece, or because the controversy itself cooled with the withdrawal of the Turks. The original Froben edition was reprinted a number of times in or just after 1530, by C. Wechel at Paris, H. Vietor at Vienna, anonymously at Cologne, in two settings by Michaël Hillen at Antwerp, twice more in 1547 (Basel and Cologne), and in a partial German version not long after the first publication.[30] But the *fortuna* of the treatise makes a short tale; Erasmus was informed by a correspondent that Mercurino Gattinara was reading *De bello Turcico* shortly before he died,[31] and in 1531 he defended himself against the charge of inconsistency laid by Alberto Pio by pointing out that he had given advice on the conduct of war both in the *Institutio principis christiani* and in *De bello Turcico*.[32] Yet Erasmus makes no subsequent reference to the work in his extant writings, and it seems to have fallen into oblivion as the circumstances that produced it faded from memory. At

* * * * *

29 See 244 and n176 below.
30 It also appears, of course, in tome v of the *Opera* of 1540 and 1703–6, and was one of the works republished by J. Maire at Leiden in 1643. See F. van der Haeghen *Bibliotheca Erasmiana: Répertoire des oeuvres d'Erasme* (Ghent 1893) and ASD v-3 27–8, which also lists modern translations into Spanish and French. Extracts from an earlier version of my translation appeared in *The Erasmus Reader* ed E. Rummel (Toronto 1990) 315–33; that version is here thoroughly revised.
31 See Ep 2336 from Cornelius Scepper (28 June 1530).
32 *Apologia adversus rhapsodias Alberti Pii* LB IX 1193B

the end of the sixteenth century, the French moralist Jean-Aimes de Cha-
vigny reviewed a hundred years of the crusade debate but, when he came
to Erasmus, quoted the longish passage on 'holy war' from the adage *Dulce
bellum inexpertis* rather than *De bello Turcico*.[33] It could be argued that the
adage does contain the essence of Erasmus' thought on the topic, but *De bello
Turcico*, probably Erasmus' most detailed examination of any political question, deserves to be better known, if only as evidence of his extraordinary
versatility.

The text translated here is that established by A.G. Weiler in ASD V-3
31–82. Erasmus never revised the treatise, and the only variants are printing
errors in the subsequent editions. The translation is preceded by a 'working
version' of Psalm 28, representing the Latin text used by Erasmus together
with a fairly literal English version.

MJH

* * * * *

33 *Discours parenetique sur les choses turques* (Lyon 1606) 84–8; on *Dulce bellum inexpertis* see n7 above.

PSALM 28

1 Adferte Domino, filii Dei, adferte Domino filios arietum.

2 Adferte Domino gloriam et honorem, adferte Domino gloriam nominis eius. Adorate Dominum in atrio sancto eius.

3 Vox Domini super aquas; Deus maiestatis intonuit; Dominus super aquas multas.

4 Vox Domini in virtute; vox Domini in magnificentia.

5 Vox Domini confringentis cedros, et confringet Dominus cedros Libani.

6 Et comminuet eas tanquam vitulum Libani, et dilectus quemadmodum filius unicornium.

7 Vox Domini intercidentis flammam igneam.

8 Vox Domini concutientis desertum, et commovebit Dominus desertum Cades.

9 Vox Domini praeparantis cervos, et revelabit condensa.

10 Dominus diluvium inhabitare facit, et sedebit Dominus rex in aeternum.

11 Dominus virtutem dabit populo suo; Dominus benedicet populo suo in pace.

1 Bring to the Lord, you sons of God, bring to the Lord the sons of rams.

2 Bring to the Lord glory and honour, bring to the Lord the glory due to his name. Worship the Lord in his holy temple.

3 The voice of the Lord echoes over the waters; the God of glory has thundered; the Lord is upon many waters.

4 The voice of the Lord is power; the voice of the Lord is majesty.

5 The voice of the Lord breaks the cedars in pieces, and the Lord shall break the cedars of Lebanon.

6 He shall smash them like a calf of Lebanon, and be beloved like the son of the unicorns.

7 The voice of the Lord divides the flames of fire.

8 The voice of the Lord shakes the wilderness, and the Lord shall shake the wilderness of Kadesh.

9 The voice of the Lord makes the hinds calve, and will open up the thickets.

10 The Lord dwells above the flood and will take his seat as king for ever.

11 The Lord will give strength to his people; the Lord will bless his people in peace.

A MOST USEFUL DISCUSSION CONCERNING PROPOSALS FOR WAR AGAINST THE TURKS, INCLUDING AN EXPOSITION OF PSALM 28

DESIDERIUS ERASMUS OF ROTTERDAM TO MASTER JOHANN RINCK, A MOST DISTINGUISHED MAN AND AN EMINENT LAWYER, GREETING[1]
Distinguished sir, since it appeared to me that I should never match your letter in scholarship, elegance, or kindliness, I have made up my mind to surpass you in the abundance, or should I say the flood, of my words by as much as you surpassed me in all other respects.

We can all see what kind of web the monarchs are weaving: a great many are engrossed in collecting the sinews of war,[2] some in mustering generals and armaments; but hardly any do I see considering how to change life for the better, which is the most vital of their functions and concerns everyone in equal measure. Again, I am constantly amazed by the numbness that has gripped the hearts of the Christian people. Although we are admonished by so many afflictions from on high, more numerous than those the Egyptians suffered and harsher than those described in the Apocalypse of St John,[3] yet we are worse than the Phrygians,[4] and are no whit changed for the better by the severity of the Lord, as he challenges us time and again to produce better fruit. On the contrary, like wretched slaves hardened against the lash, we squander the deity's indulgence towards our persistent sinfulness and emerge still more rebellious against the compassion that sends these passing ills to urge us to reform our lives. We have become so inured to wars, banditry, riots, party strife, looting, pestilence, famine, and shortage that they are no longer considered misfortunes.

* * * * *

1 The dedicatory letter is Ep 2285; on Rinck, see CEBR III 161–2.
2 That is, money; Cicero *Philippica* 5.2.5
3 See Exod 8–13 and Rev 15–16.
4 The Trojans, proverbial for their obstinacy; cf *Adagia* I i 28: *Sero sapiunt Phryges* (with a contemporary aside) and I viii 36: *Phryx plagis emendatur.*

God has acted like a faithful physician, always trying some new treatment; he sent among us an unprecedented and incurable form of leprosy, commonly known as the French pox (for no good reason, since it is rife in every land), striking humanity with a truly dreadful scourge.[5] So far from this horrible disease teaching us chastity and sobriety, we have actually turned it into a joke: it has apparently reached the point where, among your courtiers, who suppose themselves such fine and witty fellows, anyone not infected with the disease is considered a boor and a bumpkin.[6] How else can I describe this than as farting at the Lord, and, as the saying goes, giving him the finger[7] as he seeks to correct us?

There followed an intractable dispute over doctrine, and it was far from straightforward; it was indisputably given a foothold,[8] in no small degree, by the devious behaviour of those whose good sense should have tempered[9] the people's folly. But those who are the target of criticism give no thought to mending their ways, and their critics set no example of improvement in their lives. And we are not far short of turning this latest appalling disaster for Christendom into a funny story or a joke.

Of all the punishments that God threatens in Leviticus 26 and Deuteronomy 28 against those who break his commandments, is there a single one that has not been visited upon us? For how many years now have

* * * * *

5 Syphilis, supposedly introduced to Europe by Columbus's returning sailors, spread rapidly in the wake of the French army returning from Naples in 1495; the French called it 'mal de Naples,' though, as Erasmus said in the colloquy *Diversoria* (CWE 39 372), it was common to all nations. As a sign of modern degeneracy, it figures frequently in Erasmus' correspondence (for example Ep 1593), along with the sweating-sickness (see n22 below) and in the *Colloquia* (for example Ἄγαμος γάμος *sive coniugium impar* and *Adolescentis et scorti*). On the background, and modern doubts about the introduction and spread of the disease, see J. Arrizabalaga, J. Henderson, and R. French *The Great Pox: The French Disease in Renaissance Europe* (New Haven 1997).

6 Erasmus often used syphilis as a symbol of corruption in high places, for example in the colloquies *Militis et Carthusiani* (CWE 39 334–5) and Ἱππεὺς ἄνιππος, *sive Ementita nobilitas* (CWE 40 884) and in *Julius exclusus* (CWE 27 171).

7 These deliberately shocking expressions are found in *Adagia* I vii 76: *Oppedere* and II iv 68: *Medium digitum ostendere*, literally 'to brandish the middle finger,' described by Erasmus as a gesture of supreme contempt.

8 Literally 'a handle'; cf *Adagia* I iv 4: *Ansam quaerere*.

9 *sale condiri*: cf Mark 9:50, Luke 14:34, and Col 4:6 on the 'salt' (wit, good sense) of the gospel; probably a reference to the princes who supported Luther for political reasons.

we witnessed all the horrors of war? 'What shore is not stained with our blood?'[10] How often have we felt the Turkish sword, avenging our transgressions against the covenant we made with God? What kind of plague have we not suffered, in country and town alike, so that flight has meant merely exchanging one danger for another? How often have we known 'the staff of our bread to be cut short'? How many, in every land, 'eat their ration of bread and are not satisfied'?[11] Recently in Italy, that most fertile of regions, how many have starved to death?[12] It may be that so far no one has 'eaten the flesh of their sons and their daughters,'[13] but is it not true that we all live by devouring one another? The nobles plunder, the farmer sells his produce at four times its value, merchants impose huge price rises, and craftsmen charge as much as they please for their services.[14] Everyone cheats his neighbour by some sort of fraud and trickery. We see stately churches ruined, images destroyed, priests expelled: did not God lately send 'beasts of the field,'[15] laying waste all about them, when those marauding bands of peasants were unleashed against us?[16]

Nor have we escaped the curse mentioned in Deuteronomy: 'They marry wives and another sleeps with them.' It is now nothing new for us 'to sow where another shall reap, to plant a vine from which we shall not drink, to have foreigners rule over us.'[17] Does it not seem therefore that God, having in vain applied all possible remedies, as it were, now speaks to us through the prophet: 'Where can you still be struck, if you will be disloyal still?'?[18] This is not the voice of cruelty but of supreme mercy. In the same way the physician, full of fatherly concern for his patient, is heartsick to see all his skill powerless against some crippling disease; yet charity, which, as Paul says, 'hopes for all things,'[19] does not allow him to abandon the sick

* * * * *

10 Horace *Odes* 2.1.36
11 Cf Lev 26:26 and Ezek 4:16.
12 In the winter of 1528–9; see Epp 2109 and 2115.
13 Lev 26:29 and Deut 28:53
14 Frequent complaints in Erasmus' letters at this time; for references, see Allen Ep 2192:118n.
15 Lev 26:22
16 In the Peasants' Revolt of 1524–5, condemned in the adage *Ut fici oculis incumbunt*: 'As warts grow on the eyes' (II viii 65 CWE 34 75) as 'anarchy' infinitely worse than the misgovernment of princes; cf Ep 1606:20–33. In Ep 1633:18 Erasmus guesses that 100,000 peasants have been slain, but in Ep 1686:18 suggests that harsh measures have been necessary to 'cure the disease.'
17 Cf Deut 28:30 and 38–44.
18 Isa 1:5
19 1 Cor 13:7

man as a pitiful, hopeless case. 'While there's life, there's hope,'[20] he says, and racks his brains to discover some unfamiliar yet effective treatment.

Similarly the Lord, most merciful and most eager for humankind's salvation, uses unheard-of remedies to persuade us to reform our lives. He has let loose a disease, as unknown to all the doctors as it is incurable, which brings horrifying torment to men, women, and even girls in the full flower of their youth and beauty; they become temporarily insane, whirling their heads and arms around in monstrous fashion.[21] No small number, in different countries, have been possessed by this new species of frenzy or delirium. Recently he has unleashed a new kind of pestilence, a deadly sweating-sickness,[22] which arose in Britain but with incredible speed has spread the length and breadth of the world, bringing death to many and the utmost terror to everyone, for several reasons: it is new, and thus leaves the doctors powerless; it carries off its victims within a few hours; it returns without warning to those it has left; and the progress of its dangerous infection is swift and widespread.

One should acknowledge that evil is sent by a merciful Father to heal us through terror rather than to hurl us to destruction. What is this but the voice of the Lord crying: 'Repent, for the kingdom of heaven is at hand'?[23] In the Psalms, the Lord declares in a tone of weariness: 'For forty years I was close to this generation, and I said: "They are a people whose hearts are ever astray."'[24] We outdo the Hebrews both in the number of years and in the depth of our afflictions; how I hope that we do not also outstrip them in the hardness of our hearts, always turning towards the worse and resisting the skill and care of the physician! For at present the prophetic voice does not cease to cry: 'If you hear his voice today, do not harden your

* * * * *

20 *Adagia* II iv 12; Erasmus combines this adage with the same Pauline quotation in the colloquy *Inquisitio de fide* CWE 39 422 to express his hope for a reconciliation between the church and Luther.

21 Presumably St Vitus' Dance (chorea), which, as well as causing the uncontrollable spasms described, occurs most commonly in the 5–15 age group, predominantly among girls

22 Erasmus had a dangerous bout of the 'English sweat' in 1511: see Ep 226:5n. The disease had recently broken out in Germany for the first time, after being largely confined to Britain since its appearance in 1485. See also Allen Ep 2209:106–98, for an extensive discussion of the disease, and D.F.S. Thomson and H.C. Porter *Erasmus and Cambridge* (Toronto 1963) 78–80.

23 Matt 3:2

24 Ps 94/95:10; Erasmus uses a variant found in some early Latin psalters: the usual reading is 'I was indignant with.'

hearts.'[25] Calamities of this kind, which constantly beset us, are nothing but messages from the Lord, calling us back to him. For just as the Lord promises joy to those who observe the Law, so he threatens sorrow only to those who spurn the Law. But the reason why he sends these calamities follows in the same chapter: 'They shall indeed accept punishment for their sins, because they rejected my judgments and scorned my laws. Yet I have not entirely rejected them or so scorned them that they were destroyed and my covenant with them broken.'[26]

Let us therefore acknowledge that these scourges are messages from God, who desires not to destroy but to heal us, as Psalm 28 teaches: 'The voice of the Lord echoes over the waters' (that is, over the peoples, tossing to and fro on an ever-changing sea of passions and doctrines), 'the God of glory has thundered, the Lord is upon many waters, the voice of the Lord is power, the voice of the Lord is majesty; the voice of the Lord breaks the cedars in pieces, the voice of the Lord divides the flames of fire, the voice of the Lord shakes the wilderness, the voice of the Lord makes the hinds calve.'[27]

Happy are those in whom the omnipotent voice of the Lord does all these things, and it does them, of course, in all who do not stop up their ears. If only the voice of the Lord would[28] thunder in power, and through its healing terror move our hearts to repentance! If only it would thunder in majesty, and make all human haughtiness abase itself to him in perfect obedience. If only it would thunder upon the waters of our hearts, where charity has grown cold:[29] whenever we have departed from the one thing that is good, we have flowed away like water, tossed by human passions and whirled about with every wind of doctrine.[30] If only the voice of the Lord would gather the waters in one place, and the dry land of faith appear before us which, warmed by the sun of charity, will bring forth virtues of all kinds.[31] If only the voice of the Lord would break in pieces the cedars within us, and not mere cedars of the forest, but the cedars of Lebanon![32]

* * * * *

25 Ps 94:8/95:7–8
26 Lev 26:43–4
27 Ps 28/29:3–9
28 'would not' in the original edition, obviously an error
29 Cf Matt 24:12.
30 Cf Eph 4:14.
31 This sentence is inspired by Gen 1:9–25.
32 In the Old Testament (for example Ezekiel 31 and Daniel 4) the cedars of Lebanon symbolize earthly might, loftiness, and wide expansion, as they were the glory of the vegetable kingdom in Palestine.

The world has its cedars, but they are coloured purple;[33] the church has its cedars, but coloured white[34] ('Lebanon' in Hebrew means 'radiant whiteness').[35] These have in our day grown tall with ambition and fierce pride; they do indeed appear lofty in the world's eyes, wafting over humanity the pleasant perfume of a distinguished name and achieving a sort of immortality – but before God they lie on the ground exuding an unpleasant stench. If only the voice of the Lord would break these cedars, and in their place plant fruitful olives that will bring light to the house of God.[36] No one can break these cedars except that fatted calf,[37] sacrificed to the Father for our sake, the only one of all who is flawlessly white, the son of the rhinoceros,[38] that is, of the Jewish race which, heedless of the spirit, turned the letter of the Law like a single horn against Christ. But if he is born in us through faith, he will be the son, glorious and beloved, of twin-horned creatures, since we shall turn both horns, not against him, but against the desires of the flesh.

If only the voice of the Lord would divide in us the flames of fire with which the whole Christian world has been burning for so many years now: the flames of jealousy, hatred, ambition, and avarice, those passions by which we are completely won over to the things of this world. The fire has taken hold and spread to the whole of humanity: the flames reign in triumph. Only the voice of the Lord can divide the flames, so that the greater part of their heat shall be offered to God, the remainder to our neighbour, and nothing at all given to anger, lust, and ambition.

May it come to pass that the Lord will shake our wilderness, desolate, wild, and teeming with dangerous creatures. For it cannot be cleansed

* * * * *

33 The colour of nobility and magistracy in the Roman world
34 *dealbatus*, literally 'whitened,' a reminiscence of the phrase used by Christ to describe hypocrites in Matt 23:27; see also *Adagia* III vi 23: *Paries dealbatus*.
35 *candor*. Apparently the name relates to the snow on the mountains; cf Jer 18:14.
36 Cf Exod 27:20 on the oil to light the Tabernacle. Erasmus is making his familiar complaint concerning the worldliness of contemporary prelates; see for example *Moria* CWE 27 137–9, a passage including the (disregarded) symbolism of their white and purple vestments.
37 Cf Luke 15:23, the parable of the prodigal son, evoked by the reference in the Latin version of the psalm to the 'calf of Lebanon' (Vulg Ps 28:6). In his commentary on Luke, St Ambrose compares the sacrifice of the fatted calf to that of Christ; see *Expositio evangelii secundum Lucam* 7.232 (on 15:23) PL 15 (1845) 1761. Erasmus takes this up in his own Paraphrase (LB VII 409–10).
38 Ps 28/29:6. There is uncertainty over the animal named in the Hebrew, interpreted variously as a 'single-horned' creature (hence Erasmus' 'rhinoceros' and the 'unicorn' in AV) and as an ox or buffalo.

unless it be shaken by the voice of the Lord: hunters have horns with which to flush wild creatures from their lairs. The boar is an evil beast, but avarice is worse. The bear is an evil beast, but lust is worse. The lion is an evil beast, but cruelty is worse. The viper is an evil beast, but envy is worse. If the Lord will consent to shake with his voice all the thickets of our wilderness, through true repentance and confession it will be transformed: out of barrenness will come fertility; out of darkness, light; out of impenetrable jungle, a broad path, and instead of dangerous beasts it will produce for us harts with winged feet who thirst, not for the things of this world that slip away with the world, but for a well of water springing up into eternal life.[39] In that day the depths of the forests shall be opened up for us and, when the base desires that fight against the spirit have been scattered and our disputes over doctrine cut off, there shall rise from the wilderness a temple dedicated to the Lord in which, with hearts united and with one voice, all people shall proclaim the glory of their redeemer.[40]

If all this does not come to pass, the fault lies, not with the Lord, but with us, who stop up our ears like asps, pressing one ear to the ground and covering the other with our tails,[41] deaf to the voice of the Lord and to the wisdom of his song. Because we love the earth, we cannot hear the voice of heaven; because we pervert the Scriptures to serve the flesh, even if the voice reaches us we render it useless to ourselves.

But how can our ears be opened? For this too is a gift of God. He must be appeased with a sacrifice, that he may give us ears to hear, and for this reason he cries: 'Bring to the Lord, you sons of God, bring to the Lord the sons of rams, bring to the Lord glory and honour, bring to the Lord the glory due to his name; worship the Lord in his holy temple.'[42] Now, the sons of God by profession are all who have been reborn through the mystery of baptism, but the voice here is addressing in particular those who have succeeded to the role of the apostles, and it is to them that the prophet says: 'If you are truly the sons of God, bring to the Lord what he thirsts after, what he loves and cries out for.' What are we to bring? The sons of rams. You yourselves must be the rams, the right and proper leaders of the Lord's flock, emulating the prince of shepherds, Jesus, who was assuredly

* * * * *

39 Erasmus conflates Ps 41:2–3/42:1–2 with John 4:14.
40 Cf *In psalmum 33* 322 below.
41 An adaptation of Ps 57:5–6/58:4–5. The asp was supposed to resist the wiles of the snake-charmer in this peculiar fashion: see T.H. White *The Book of Beasts* (London 1954) 173.
42 Ps 28/29:1–2

the miraculous ram that Abraham saw caught in the thicket;[43] he sacrificed himself to the Father, and you too must sacrifice to the Lord those parts of you that are on earth, so that by your teaching and your pious example you may offer up lambs manly in spirit,[44] and the sons of rams. But be sure that you bring them, not to yourselves, but to the Lord, to whom the flock belongs. The Pharisees used to travel over land and sea to bring in converts;[45] in truth, they offered them, not to the Lord, but to themselves. The Christian domain must be extended only in such a way that we may offer, not dogs or swine,[46] but the sons of rams, and we must not convert them to our own glory or profit, but rather, like faithful servants, we must offer them to the Lord. If not, he will exclaim: 'You have multiplied the nation, but not increased the joy.'[47] Therefore, you sons of God, bring to the Lord, time and time again, the sons of rams, seeking not your own, but the things which are Jesus Christ's.[48]

The psalm has not yet touched on the source of almost all the people's woes. The words apply not only to the principal servants of the church, but also to secular princes. The people usually take their cue from the princes,[49] although sometimes, too, the people obtain their deserts when the Lord allows the hypocrite to reign.[50] No hypocrite, indeed, is more dangerous to the church than the wolf who claims to be a shepherd[51] or the tyrant who claims to be a king; all hypocrisy is of course hateful to the truth of Christ but, as none is more damaging than this, so none is more hateful to God. Therefore, you sons of God, cherish the glory of God and consider your

* * * * *

43 Gen 22:13; on the symbolic role of the ram see also *In psalmum 22* 135 above and *In psalmum 33* 306 below.

44 The customary Hebrew sacrifice was of an unblemished male lamb, *masculus sine maculo*; hence Erasmus' *agnus spiritu masculus* here. See Exod 12:5, Lev 1:3 and 10, and Lev 22:19.

45 Cf Matt 23:15. In his annotation on this verse (*Et facitis eum filium gehennae duplo quam vos* LB VI 120), Erasmus refers to 'the new example of those who make Christians by force of arms,' perhaps with the excesses of missionaries in the Americas in mind; but this also fits in with his views on reconciling the Turks to Christ, 265 below.

46 A reference to the proverbs quoted in 2 Pet 2:22, mocking relapsed Christians. LB reads *carnes* 'flesh' instead of *canes* 'dogs,' suggesting a reference to vain sacrifices, described for example in Isa 66:3.

47 Isa 9:3

48 Cf Phil 2:21.

49 Cf *Institutio principis christiani* 1 CWE 27 219.

50 A reminiscence of Job 34:30; cf the colloquy *Convivium religiosum* CWE 39 184.

51 Cf *Adagia* I iv 10: *Ovem lupo commisisti.*

own whatever is his. If God accomplishes something through you, do not turn it to your own profit or glory, but 'bring to the Lord the glory and honour.' This is not all: 'Bring him the glory due to his name.' He delights in offerings, but he wishes his name to be honoured through them, the name besmirched by the godless conduct of Christians and reviled among the heathen. 'Worship the Lord': not wealth, or power, or all the world's pomp, but the Lord. Whatever is dearer to us than God we worship instead of God. Where? Not only in churches built by men's hands, which are open to godly and ungodly alike, but 'in his holy temple,' that is, in a pure and holy conscience. For in the end the only true worshippers are those who worship the Lord in the spirit.[52] There are many, in every land, who worship a wooden cross with a kiss, who fall down before an image of Christ, who prostrate themselves at the Lord's Supper, who bend the knee at the name of Jesus,[53] but there are not so many who worship him in his temple, built by the Holy Spirit. If monarchs, pontiffs, and the other great men of the state do so, the Lord will pour his grace abundantly upon the people; this is the meaning of the prophetic words: 'The Lord dwells above the flood' and, remaining always with us, 'will take his seat as king for ever.'[54] Blessed are those whom this king rules, for he will not desert his people for eternity; under his protection the people, however weak and helpless, will have nothing to fear. 'The Lord himself will give strength to his people' and, though the whole world curse them, threatening war and bloodshed, yet 'the Lord will bless his people in peace,' a peace that the world cannot give, nor the world take away, unless the people themselves cast it aside.[55]

Therefore let us not turn a deaf ear to the Lord when he calls so often; he is now calling to us once more through the not unexpected truculence of the Turks,[56] and it merely makes our deafness the more unpardonable that we have been alerted so often but have failed to waken to the danger. How often has this race of barbarians, their very origin obscure, inflicted defeat on the Christian people? What cruelty have they not visited upon us? How many cities, how many islands, how many provinces have they

* * * * *

52 Cf John 4:23–4.
53 Cf Phil 2:10. Erasmus recommends such outward displays of piety for young children only, for example in *De civilitate* 3 CWE 25 279–80.
54 Cf Ps 28/29:10.
55 Cf Ps 28/29:11; the formal exposition of the psalm ends here.
56 A play on *Turcarum truculentia*

not wrested from Christendom? Have they not reduced our religion from a broad empire to a narrow strip? Indeed these opening moves seem to suggest that, unless we are shielded by God's right hand, in a few years the remainder of the Christian world is likely to succumb to them.

If all this happened by chance, Christian sympathy would still make the whole body of Christendom grieve for one of its members in distress. But since at present it is incontrovertible that the Turks have not won an immense empire by their own virtue, and that ours has been dashed to pieces as a punishment to us, all who rejoice in the name of Christian must not only groan with pity but must also give succour to their brother nations in their distress; besides the fact that through our religious fellowship these woes must be considered common to us all, there is a danger that they will become common to us all in reality. 'It becomes your business when your neighbour's wall is on fire';[57] in fact, it becomes the whole city's business whenever a single house catches fire. We must therefore give them succour, but in two different ways, if we are truly anxious to be rid of the danger. We must make all necessary preparations for such an arduous war, but first we must make the preparations without which military might will be in vain. We have frequently taken the field against the Turks, but so far with little success; either because we have not abandoned the things that anger God and cause him to send the Turks against us, just as he sent frogs, lice, and locusts upon the Egyptians long ago,[58] or because we have placed our hopes of victory in our own strength, or perhaps because we have not done Christ's work but have fought the Turks in a Turkish frame of mind.

The situation therefore demands that I should say something about preparations of both kinds, if it can first be demonstrated that the Turks have grown so great, not through their own piety or their own valour, but because of our foolish indolence. For at first the name of the Turks was so inglorious[59] that it is scarcely to be found in any ancient writer, except that Pliny, in book 6 chapter 7, mentions, between the Thussagetae and the Arimphaei who dwell near the Rhiphaean mountains, the

* * * * *

57 Horace *Epistles* 1.18.84 (*Adagia* III vi 71), a tag cited in many contemporary crusading orations; see Heath cc 41–2.

58 Exodus 8–10

59 Contemporary investigations of the Turks' pedigree were very often intended to demonstrate their unfitness to rule; on this point, and for a commentary on much that follows here, see Heath 'Renaissance Scholars.'

'Turcae' who at that time lived there, in rocky valleys bordering on the deserts.[60] Pomponius Mela, too, merely mentions their name,[61] such was the obscurity of the tribe from which it is probable that this race sprang,[62] which has now extended the bounds of its encompassing cruelty through so many spacious and opulent regions. Cyprian also mentions their name in his book *On Double Martyrdom*,[63] as if they were already in his time sworn enemies of the imperial name. There are some scholars who think that when Ptolemy refers to the 'Tusci' in the Asian part of Sarmatia, we should read 'Turci' or 'Turcae';[64] what other writer, they ask, ever placed the Tuscans in Asia?

But there can be no argument about their name in later years: as many authorities testify, these specimens of humanity, whose inhumanity has for long centuries afflicted and worn down Christendom, burst out from the shores of the Caspian Sea into Persia and Asia Minor over seven hundred years ago.[65] They had no single leader, but roved about in scattered bands and laid waste whole provinces by brigandage rather than

* * * * *

60 *Naturalis historia* 6.7.19; Erasmus quotes Pliny almost word for word on these tribes of Northern Scythia.

61 *De chorographia* 1.19.116, manifestly Pliny's source

62 Erasmus' caution is commendable; the Turks came originally from much further east than Scythia.

63 *Liber ad Fortunatum de duplici martyrio*, added by Erasmus to Cyprian's *Opera* in his new edition of January 1530 (Basel: Froben); the passage in question (27), on the penalties for desertion from the imperial army to 'the Turk,' appears on page 520. It was suspected in the sixteenth century that this treatise was Erasmus' own work: see the edition by J. Pamelius (Antwerp 1568) 581 and PL 4 (1844) 897 note (*Turcam*).

64 *Geographica* 5.9; in the second map of Asia, the 'Tusci' are placed between the Caspian Sea and the Sea of Azov. Erasmus published the Greek text in 1533. Willibald Pirckheimer was probably working on a commentary on Ptolemy, whose text he had published in Latin translation in 1525, when he died in December 1530 (see Ep 2760); the emendation was certainly made by Joannes Cuspinianus (1473–1529), though it only appeared posthumously in the 1540 Strasbourg edition of his *De Caesaribus* (page 638).

65 On contemporary controversies over the timing and location of the Turks' first incursions, see Heath 'Renaissance Scholars' 463–7. The following account of Turkish history, until the time of Selim, is a close paraphrase of an essay by Giambattista Egnazio, 'De origine Turcarum,' placed at the end of the roll-call of Byzantine emperors in book 2 of Egnazio's *De Caesaribus libri* III (Venice: Aldus 1516) sig Fg, 4 verso–8 recto; Egnazio sent Erasmus a copy in 1517 (Ep 588). See also Epp 2249 and 2302, letters to Egnazio in 1530 dealing with numerous themes of the *De bello Turcico*.

war.[66] Then, well versed in these arts, they found a man to hire them in Machumet,[67] prince of the Saracens, or, as the saying goes, a lid to fit their saucepan.[68] After repeated victories under his leadership, the hired slaves begin to covet power; they attack the Saracens, rout Machumet in battle and butcher him. Note the foundations of Turkish rule. The supreme power was transferred to Trangolipix Mucaletus, previously the Turks' commander. He called in another party of Turks and sent his nephew Cucumetius to invade Arabia, while a second nephew, Asanus, was to attack the province of Media and confront the Romans there. Although neither nephew was successful, he sent his brother Aleimus against the Romans again, and when this expedition proved not completely unsuccessful, Trangolipix soon afterwards seized his chance against the Romans and ravaged and partly conquered the whole of Asia up to the Black Sea.[69]

However, the Turks' progress was more than once brusquely interrupted by the virtue of the French,[70] until the emergence of Othoman[71] (according to some calculations, the present ruler Solyman[72] is the tenth of his line), a man of humble origins, from peasant stock – but a talented

* * * * *

66 Erasmus contrasts *latrocinium* and *bellum,* a distinction often made by Latin orators (for example Livy 29.6.2, Cicero *In Catilinam* 1.10.27) and developed in a famous chapter of St Augustine's *De civitate Dei* (4.4).

67 Mahmud of Ghazni (971–1030), founder of an empire stretching from Isfahan to Lahore

68 *Adagia* I x 72

69 In fact it was Mahmud's son Masud who was overthrown at the battle of Dandanqan by the founders of the Seljuk Turkish state, the brothers Chagri and Tughril Beg (the latter transcribed by Egnazio, following his Byzantine sources Zonaras and Cedrenus, as 'Tangrolipix'). In 1071 Chagri's son Alp Arslan (= Asanus) routed the armies of the Byzantine empire at Manzikert in Armenia. 'Cucumetius' is presumably a corruption of Qutalmish, cousin of Tughril, and 'Aleimus' is no doubt Tughril's half-brother Ibrahim Inal. These transcriptions are also found in the Byzantine sources. On all this, see C.E. Bosworth *The Ghaznavids* (Edinburgh 1963), especially chapter 9 and the genealogical tables, and C. Cahen *Pre-Ottoman Turkey: A General Survey of the Material and Spiritual Culture and History c 1071–1330* trans J. Jones-Williams (London 1968).

70 A reference to the Crusades

71 Osman I (d 1326) destroyed the last remnants of the Seljuk empire and gave his name to the new dynasty.

72 Suleiman II, the Magnificent (ruled 1520–66); confusingly he is sometimes referred to as Suleiman I (as in CEBR III 298–300). The number of Ottoman sultans was much discussed at the time, since certain prophecies predicted the fall of the dynasty after a particular number of rulers (anything from seven to fifteen); see Heath 'Renaissance Scholars' 469–70.

cut-throat. He took advantage of internal quarrels to seize control of the Turkish forces, no more lenient with his own people than with adversaries. He came to power in about 1300, and within twenty-eight years considerably extended the tyrannical rule of the Turks, conquering most of Bithynia and storming a good many towns on the Black Sea. He was succeeded by his son Orchan who, helped by discord among the Greeks, took Prusia from them;[73] he was the first to cross into Europe, summoned by Cantacuzenus, who was engaged in a struggle with the Paleologi.[74] At the same time he increased his power by murdering a relative: he had married the daughter of Caraman[75] and, by doing away with his father-in-law's son, he seized the greater part of his domains. Having ruled for twenty-two years, he passed the state to his son Ammurat[76] who, at the instigation of Paleologus, transported twelve thousand Turks to Europe and campaigned quite successfully against the Bulgars and the prince of the Peloponnese.[77] He began then to covet the riches of Europe and, while

* * * * *

73 Orkhan (ruled 1326–62) took the Byzantine town of Bursa in the first year of his reign and made it his capital.

74 A party of Turks crossed into the Balkans in 1345 to aid the future Byzantine emperor John VI Cantacuzenus against John V Paleologus, whom he ousted in the following year; on this and subsequent relations between Christendom and the Turk, see the narrative histories of P.H. Coles *The Ottoman Impact on Europe* (London 1968), D.M. Nicol *The Last Centuries of Byzantium 1261–1453* (London 1972), S.J. Shaw *Empire of the Gazis: The Rise and Decline of the Ottoman Empire (1280–1808)* (Cambridge 1976) and K.M. Setton *The Papacy and the Levant (1204–1571)* 4 vols (Philadelphia 1976–84); for a Turkish perspective see H. Inalcik *The Ottoman Empire: The Classical Age 1300–1600* (London 1973). A useful work on the confused chronology and topography of these events is D.E. Pitcher *An Historical Geography of the Ottoman Empire from Earliest Times to the End of the Sixteenth Century* (Leiden 1972). On the crusading theme the essential work, with a rich bibliography, is Housley *The Later Crusades* especially chapters 2–4 and 13–14.

75 Karaman, a Turkish emirate in southern Asia Minor, was ruled by a powerful dynasty, the Karaman-Oghlu, who were in constant conflict with the Ottomans. Their state was not finally absorbed by the latter until late in the fifteenth century. This marriage seems apocryphal (Orkhan married John VI's daughter Theodora in 1346, though he did have previous wives), but in 1387 Murad I did defeat his son-in-law the Karaman emir Ala al-Din (*Encyclopedia of Islam* [Leiden 1960] IV 623).

76 Murad I (1362–89), the first Ottoman to take the title Sultan

77 The Bulgarian strongholds of Sofia and Nis fell to Murad's troops in 1385–6; the Peloponnese (Morea), ruled by Byzantine and Latin governors, was raided but not conquered during Murad's reign. Perhaps the sources confuse Manuel

pretending to take vengeance on the emperor's enemies as he had done
before, crossed the Hellespont with Genoese ships supplied for the purpose,
attacking Abydos and seizing Gallipoli[78] as well as other cities. Next he invaded Serbia and Bulgaria, captured Adrianople[79] and, on meeting the enemies' forces, routed them with colossal slaughter; Lazarus, prince of Serbia,
was killed, but soon afterwards one of his servants assassinated Ammurat
himself.[80]

He left two sons, but Pazait treacherously murdered his brother Solyman;[81] next, having killed the prince of the Bulgars,[82] he laid claim to the
greatest part of his domains. Fired by these successes, he laid waste Bosnia,
Croatia, and the furthermost regions of Illyria; for eight years he block-
aded Constantinople and would have taken it with ease had not an army of
French and Hungarians recalled him from his task; Pazait met and crushed
the enemy at Nicopolis[83] and returned to the interrupted siege, pressing the
city hard for two years. He seemed unlikely to give it up, had not the news
arrived that Tamberlane, prince of the Scythians, had invaded the Turks'
territory with a massive army. Pazait met him at Mount Stella on the fron-
tier between Galatia and Bithynia, but the omens were against him, since

* * * * *

Cantacuzenus, Despot in the Morea (1349–80), with Manuel II Paleologus,
whose stronghold in Thessalonica was taken after a lengthy siege in 1387.

78 The strategically vital port of Gallipoli was first taken (c 1354) by Orkhan's
son Suleiman at the head of a band of Turkish mercenaries and settlers, helped
by Genoese ships – according to their Venetian rivals. It was recaptured by the
crusader Amadeo of Savoy in 1366, but ceded definitively to the Ottomans by
Emperor Andronikos IV in 1377. Abydos, though on the route from Anatolia
to Gallipoli, is on the opposite shore of the Dardanelles (Hellespont).

79 Adrianople, the chief city of Thrace, was taken by the Turks c 1366 and subsequently became the new capital of the Ottoman state (Edirne).

80 At the first battle of Kosovo in 1389; according to some accounts, the assassin
was Lazar's son-in-law.

81 Bayezid II (1389–1402) inaugurated an Ottoman tradition by having his rival
strangled (see Inalcik [n74 above] 59–64); Turkish historians call his brother
Yakub.

82 The circumstances of the death of the Bulgarian Tsar Jan Sisman are unclear;
his capital Trnovo was taken in 1393 by Bayezid's son Suleiman, but some accounts say that he was only captured and executed two years later. The strong
Bosnian kingdom began to disintegrate after the death of the able Tvrtko I in
1391.

83 The 'crusade' of Nicopolis occurred in 1396. The Christian army was led by
Sigismund of Hungary, with a French contingent under Jean, count of Nevers,
and Marshal Boucicaut; the dismal story is told by Froissart. Bayezid then
resumed the blockade of Constantinople begun in 1394.

200,000 Turks are reported to have perished in that battle. Pazait was captured, bound in a cage with golden chains, and is said to have been carried about in it, wherever Tamberlane went, until his dying day.[84] All this happened in about 1397.

One of Pazait's surviving sons, Machomet, treacherously disposed of his brother Orchan and ruled the Turkish state alone. Having recovered the territory seized by Tamberlane, he plundered the Bulgars and Wallachians and established his court at Adrianople.[85] Machomet was succeeded by his son Ammurat. He attacked the prince of Mysia, put out his two sons' eyes, and then married their sister;[86] these auspicious beginnings encouraged him to raid the Wallachians, Hungarians, and Germans and then, turning towards Epirus, he took Croja and snatched Thessalonica from the Venetians.[87] Defeated in a great battle by the Hungarians, however, he sought and obtained from them a ten-year truce;[88] but this was broken, at the instigation of Pope Eugenius, and the Hungarians attacked Ammurat again, but it was a signal disaster for our cause. For in one battle, fought at Varna, perished Ladislaus king of Poland and Cardinal Julian, and in a second, at Basila, a number of Hungarian magnates were slain and the common

* * * * *

84 Bayezid was captured by Timur Lenk's Mongol army at the battle of Djibukabad near Ankara in 1402, and died, possibly by his own hand, in humiliating captivity in 1403.

85 Mehmed I (ruled 1413–21) emerged victorious from a prolonged power struggle among the sons of Bayezid, though his brother Suleiman is also considered to have ruled as sultan in Rumelia (European Turkey) from about 1402 until his death in 1411. The other participants were Musa, Isa, and Mustafa; the Orkhan mentioned by Erasmus and his sources is unknown. Mircea of Wallachia (1386–1418) supported a pretender to Mehmed's throne and suffered punitive expeditions in 1416–17.

86 Mysia is glossed by Erasmus' source, Egnazio, as Serbia; the reference is to George Brankovic, despot of Serbia, whose daughter Mara was married in 1435 to Murad II (ruled 1421–51; CEBR II 469–70). The atrocity against George's sons, held hostage by Murad and accused of treachery, took place in 1439.

87 The Albanian citadel of Kroya was captured in 1415; it was retaken by the Albanians in 1443 and became the centre of the heroic resistance led by George Castriot (Scanderbeg) until 1478. The Venetian post at Thessalonica, having changed hands several times, was finally taken by the Turks in 1430. During this period Turkish raiders penetrated as far as Carniola, which probably explains the 'Germans' here.

88 In the winter of 1443–4 the Hungarian hero János Hunyadi advanced deep into Turkish-held Balkan territory, took Sofia, and inflicted several defeats on Turkish armies, with the aid of Ladislas king of Hungary and Poland (CEBR II 470).

soldiers slaughtered to a man.[89] The ambition and the disagreements of the Christian commanders combined to hand the Turk the victory.[90] Soon a quarrel between brothers handed him the Peloponnese;[91] at last, while reclaiming Epirus, which had revolted, and vainly besieging Croja, he died, some say of a broken heart. He had ruled for thirty-four years.[92]

He was succeeded by his son Machomet, whose insatiable appetite for conquest overshadowed the tyranny of all his ancestors.[93] He overthrew the two Christian empires of Constantinople and Trebizond,[94] he captured twelve kingdoms from the Christians and took two hundred cities.[95] Among them was the island of Chalcis, and Scodra, formerly Venetian possessions; he stormed the Black Sea city of Capha[96] and assailed the island of Rhodes, though without success.[97] Having stormed Hydruntum, he made war on

* * * * *

89 The battle of Varna, 1444, and the second battle of Kosovo, 1448. The breaking of the truce, usually attributed to the papal legate Giuliano Cesarini rather than to Pope Eugenius IV, and the defeat at Varna were still the subject of controversy; they provided an example of disastrous clerical involvement in war for the Reformers (cf Luther's *Vom Kriege* [*Works* 46 167], attacked by Cochlaeus *Dialogus* 23 and 27–8), while jurists moralized on the sanctity of contracts made even with an infidel; for references, see my edition of René de Lucinge *De La Naissance, duree et chute des estats* (Geneva 1984) 91 n8 and Housley *Later Crusades* 470.

90 This reflection on ambition and dissension on the Christian side is not found in Egnazio, and is the only instance of Erasmus departing significantly from his source. The theme of dissension among Christians, which reappears several times below, is a commonplace of crusade oratory; see Heath cc 41–3 and 97.

91 Demetrius Paleologus and his brother Thomas, joint Despots in the Morea from 1448 and notorious for their quarrels; the Turks finally conquered the Peloponnese in 1460.

92 Murad died in February 1451, having ruled for less than thirty years; on Kroya and the Albanian revolt, see n87 above.

93 Mehmed II, the Conqueror (1451–81; CEBR II 422–3); particularly informative on this and the next two reigns is Schwoebel *Shadow of the Crescent.*

94 Constantinople fell to the Turks on 29 May 1453 and Trebizond, the last Greek 'empire,' ruled by David Comnenius, in 1461.

95 These figures are an approximation cited by many commentators; perhaps the original source is a Venetian ambassador to Mehmed, quoted by Philippe de Commynes (*Memoires* ed J. Calmette [Paris 1925] II 338).

96 Chalcis, chief city of Euboea (Negroponte) fell in 1470, Skodra (Iskenderiye) in Albania in 1479, and Kaffa, a Genoese colony on the Black Sea, in 1475.

97 Rhodes was the seat of the Knights Hospitaller, whose heroic resistance under Pierre d'Aubusson in 1480 relieved an almost unbroken run of Christian defeats at the hands of Mehmed.

Italy, and for three years wrought havoc there;[98] such was the panic everywhere that Pope Sixtus, in utter despair, left his apostolic city and prepared to flee to France.[99] Soon afterwards, while planning a terrible war against his elder son, he died, in the year 1481. There followed a murderous contest for the throne between the brothers, but the elder, Zizim, was beaten and Pazait took control.[100] He made war on the Egyptian sultan several times, but without success, and in the end the Turks were compelled to make a treaty with the enemy.[101] Thereupon, in the year 1492, he attacked the inhabitants of the Ceraunian mountains[102] and imposed the Turkish yoke on peoples who until that day had always lived in freedom. In the seventh year after this, having assembled a fleet, he took Methon, Naupactus, and Dyrrachium[103] from the Venetians. Again, the Turks most cruelly laid waste the region around Forum Julium.[104] Pazait's son Selim ousted his father and seized power.[105] This Selim or, as others have it, Zelim, was followed by Solyman,[106] a worthy successor to his forebears.

Observe, indeed, how profitable their impiety has been to them, as long as we have neglected the duties of true piety. We fight endlessly among ourselves over some useless plot of ground in what are worse than civil wars,

* * * * *

98 The Turks occupied Otranto for thirteen months in 1480–1, but withdrew on the death of Mehmed; see n121 below.

99 After the fall of Otranto, Sixtus IV (1471–84) contemplated transferring his seat to Avignon as a precaution: see D.M. Vaughan *Europe and the Turk: A Pattern of Alliances (1350–1700)* (Liverpool 1954) 83.

100 Zizim, the famous Prince Djem (in fact Mehmed's third son; CEBR I 393–4), was proclaimed sultan at Bursa, but the second son, Bayezid II (1481–1512; CEBR I 103–4), had the support of the janissaries at Istanbul, where he was raised to the throne. The eldest son, Mustafa, had been strangled by his father's order for adultery.

101 In 1491; the sultan of Egypt, Kait Bey, had been supporting Djem's continuing revolt. On the comparatively diplomatic reign of Bayezid, see S.N. Fisher *The Foreign Relations of Turkey 1481–1512* (Urbana 1948); on this treaty, 41–2.

102 In Epirus

103 Modon, Lepanto, and Durazzo (Durrës) on the Dalmatian coast, taken between 1499 and 1501

104 The Friuli district of Venezia; Forum Julium is the modern Cividale del Friuli. Frequent raids between 1469 and 1499 even reached as far as Vicenza.

105 Selim I (1512–20; CEBR III 237–8), the Grim, deposed his father with the aid of the janissaries, and shortly afterwards had him murdered; he also disposed of two elder brothers. Egnazio's account, published in 1516 before Selim's triumphs in the East, ends here.

106 Suleiman II (1520–66), known in the West as 'the Magnificent' and to his own people as *Kanuni* 'the Lawgiver.' See also n72 above.

Suleiman the Magnificent
Silver-point drawing by Albrecht Dürer, dated 1526
Museé Bonnat, Bayonne

and meanwhile the Turks have extended their rule, or rather their reign of terror, far and wide.[107] To the north, it stretches to the Black Sea, to the east it is bounded by the Euphrates, and to the south by Ethiopia; for within the last few years the Turk has conquered the whole of Egypt and Syria together with Phoenicia and Palestinian Judaea.[108] In the west it reaches to the Ionian Sea and, if you turn from there to the north, it extends to the Danube; in fact, it has now leaped far beyond that barrier and reached the river Borysthenes.[109] Consider, if you will, how broad, rich, and various are the lands enclosed within this compass. The whole of Asia Minor, containing no less than twelve nations; the whole of Thrace, including Constantinople, called Byzantium by the ancients, once the seat of Christian emperors and now the seat of the Turks; in Europe the two parts of Mysia[110] as far as the Danube, a great part of Dacia,[111] all Macedonia, all Greece, with all the islands of the Aegean Sea, both the Sporades and the Cyclades: all these suffer the ruthless bondage of Turkish rule. Venice still, at the moment, clings on to those two most noble of Mediterranean islands, Crete, now commonly called Candia, and Cyprus,[112] but only, I understand, by paying tribute for them.

I have given but a fleeting glimpse,[113] as it were, of these places; if anyone were to look more closely, how many once wealthy kingdoms, how many famous cities would he find, not so much enslaved as extinct? What now[114] is the once prosperous Peloponnese? What now is the renowned

* * * * *

107 Erasmus often evokes the Turks' pleasure at seeing Christians fight one another, for example in *Adagia* IV i 1: *Dulce bellum inexpertis* LB II 961F and *Querela pacis* CWE 27 310 and 319. Similarly, Erasmus suggests (again to Johann Rinck) that this spectacle brings Christianity itself into disrepute among unbelievers (*Precatio pro pace Ecclesiae* CWE 69 113), a point often made in discussions on the conversion of the Turks: see Heath CC 95–8.
108 All conquered in Selim's great expedition of 1516–17
109 The Dnieper
110 The Roman provinces of Upper and Lower Moesia, covering parts of modern Bulgaria and Serbia
111 Another Roman province, covering roughly modern Rumania
112 Cyprus was to fall to the Turks in 1571, the city of Candia in 1669, and the last Venetian outpost on Crete in 1715.
113 Cf *Adagia* III i 49: *Per transennam inspicere*, literally 'to see through a lattice,' a cover preventing closer inspection of the goods.
114 There follows a 'lament for Greece,' a variant on the hackneyed *Ubi sunt* (Where are they now... ?) theme and a commonplace of crusading oratory from Pius II and Bessarion onwards; see Schwoebel *Shadow of the Crescent* 147–75 and Heath CC 26–32; among the practitioners of the genre were Janus

market-place of all the world, Corinth? What is Attica, once known for its elegance as the Greece of Greece? Where now is that cradle of wit and nurse of all the best learning, Athens? One is shown a hamlet so obscure that its very name is in doubt. Where is Lacedemon, which alone bred true warriors? Why should I go on to recall something whose memory is so fresh that the details remain fixed in the eyes, ears, and senses of us all, the capture of Rhodes?[115] What need to recall the countless bloody raids into Hungary and the death of Louis, king of Hungary?[116] Or indeed, in this very year, the savage rape of all Hungary, the expulsion of King Ferdinand, the extraordinarily ferocious attack on Vienna, and the devastation of Lower Austria, perpetrated with unbelievable inhumanity?[117] I have outlined the general position in passing; what if one were to examine each event in detail? How terrifying our defeats would appear, how frequent the Turks' victories, how great our loss and sorrow! Indeed, we might perhaps all be subject to the Turk already, had it not been for that obscure man called Sophy,[118] who curbed to some extent the Turks' insatiable appetite for conquest, had not the fortunes of war gone against them with the Egyptian sultan, and had not revolts at home, among themselves, somewhat delayed their cruel onslaught against us.

Why, then, are they so successful? Inquire into the origins of the race, and you will find a combination of profound obscurity and utter barbarity.

* * * * *

Lascaris and Marcus Musurus, Greek exiles known to Erasmus. For a bibliography of the similar tradition in vernacular Balkan literature, see D. Obolensky *The Byzantine Commonwealth* (London 1971) 413–14.

115 Cf n97 above. Rhodes, citadel of the Knights Hospitaller, fell in December 1522 after a siege of six months whose progress was followed with breathless interest throughout Christendom; see Ep 1362:80–2, where Vives gives news of the island's fall.

116 At Mohács on 29 August 1526; see n187 below.

117 On the events of 1529, see the introductory note 202 above and n230 below.

118 Erasmus here calls the Sophy, the ruler of Persia, *terrae filius*, 'a son of the earth' (*Adagia* I viii 86) because he seemed to have sprung from nowhere to open a 'second front' against the Turk: rumour had it that his invasion of Turkey, in alliance with the more mythical Prester John, had caused Suleiman to raise the siege of Vienna; see Heath CC 61–2. The career of the dynamic Shah Ismail, who ruled in Persia 1500–23, gave encouragement to Christian strategists, and intermittent but bloody warfare between the Shiite Persians and the Sunnite Turks continued throughout the sixteenth century, deflecting the Turkish offensive from Christendom more than once; see for example Epp 3007 and 3119 on the war of 1535–6.

The foundation of their power? a mercenary soldier and the murder of a prince, their sworn lord, by the most unspeakable treachery. Examine their rise to power, and you will find an empire won by brutality and extended by banditry; you will find deadly marriages; you will find brother sinfully slain by brother, fathers driven from power by their sons, treachery alongside perfect cruelty – to say nothing for the moment of their religion and way of life. They rule because God is angered: they fight us without God, they have Mahomet as their champion, and we have Christ – and yet it is obvious how far they have spread their tyranny, while we, stripped of so much power, ejected from much of Europe, are in danger of losing everything. Who is unaware that this race of Turks now has open access to us by land? For now that the Turk holds both Upper and Lower Mysia,[119] the regions bordering on Thrace, up to the river Danube, the way along the river towards us is not difficult and lies open. In the same vicinity he holds the Dalmatians and Illyrians in subjection, not to mention Pannonia,[120] which he has so often attacked. By sea, of course, he threatens all Italy, but especially Sicily and the kingdom of Naples, from Epirus. He still holds Hydruntum,[121] the furthermost town of Italy, and is said to have occupied Brundusium at one time. Now he has opened up against Austria, and only God knows how she is to escape. And where, all this time, has the warlike spirit of the Germans been slumbering?

Can we attribute the Turks' success to their piety? Of course not! To their valour? They are a race debilitated by debauchery[122] and fearsome only as brigands. What, then, is the answer? They owe their victories to our sins; we have fought against them but, as the results plainly show, in the face of our God's anger. For we assail the Turks with the self-same eagerness with which they invade the lands of others. We are inspired by the craving for

* * * * *

119 Cf n110 above.
120 Pannonia was a Roman province centred on the great Hungarian plain south of the Danube, including parts of the modern Croatia, Bosnia, and Serbia.
121 Erasmus is misinformed. The Turks occupied Otranto only in 1480–1 (Schwoebel *Shadow of the Crescent* 131–4), but they did construct fortifications much admired and imitated by Christian engineers. Some Turks left behind took service with the duke of Calabria and performed prodigies of valour for him against Sixtus IV; see my edition of René de Lucinge *De La Naissance, duree et chute des estats* (Geneva 1984) 48 and n17. The Turkish fleet frequently raided Brindisi (Brundusium) at this time.
122 On this stereotypical portrait of the Asiatic, and its connection with the theory that the Turks were the scourges of God, see Heath cc 65–8.

power, we covet riches; to put it bluntly, we fight the Turks like Turks.[123] Moreover the chronicle of these events shows clearly enough that it was always our quarrels, our ambition, our inherent faithlessness that brought about the worst of these disasters. The unrelenting feud between Palaeologus and Cantacuzenus opened the door to the Turks in Europe. The sworn treaty broken at the instigation of Eugenius flung us into a fatal battle. Faith must surely be kept, even with an enemy.[124] Another thing that caused us considerable trouble was the death by poison of Pazait's brother Zizim: captured in battle by the Rhodiots, he later fell into the hands of Pope Alexander VI; when King Charles of France claimed him, he was handed over but given poison first, so that he died before reaching Milan, if rumour is to be believed.[125] If we had gone to war with the Turks in the proper way, in harmony among ourselves, with hearts that were pure beneath the banners of Christ, relying on his aid alone, Christendom would never have been reduced to its present straits. But I shall say more of this in the proper place.

Before that I must briefly take issue with two sets of opponents: those who, wrongly, are fired up for war on the Turks, and those who, also wrongly, argue against making war on the Turk.[126] Both groups seem to me to be equally mistaken, though for very different reasons. For although not every campaign against the Turks is legitimate and holy, there are cases when failure to oppose the Turk amounts to nothing less than the betrayal of Christendom to its most implacable foes and the abandonment of our brethren already enslaved beneath their foul yoke.

But when the ignorant mob hear the name of the Turks, they immediately fly into a rage and clamour for blood, calling them dogs and enemies of the Christian name; it does not occur to them that, first of all,

* * * * *

123 A frequent motif in Erasmus' pacific writing; cf *Institutio principis christiani* CWE 27 287, *Querela pacis* CWE 27 310, and *Adagia* IV i 1: *Dulce bellum inexpertis* LB II 966E.

124 Cf Cicero *De officiis* 3.29.107. On this principle, increasingly recognized as a cornerstone of international law, and its application to the Turks, see Heath CC 21–2 and notes.

125 In fact Djem, beaten in the power struggle with his brother Bayezid (see n100 above), fled to Rhodes in 1482 to seek the aid of the Christian princes. After a long imprisonment in France and Rome, during which he was used as a diplomatic pawn, he died in 1495, probably by poison, while on his way to Naples with the French. See Fisher (n101 above) 27–50.

126 The positions represented by advocates of the Crusade and by Luther; see the introductory note 204–8 above.

they are human beings and, what is more, half-Christian;[127] they never stop
to consider whether the *casus belli* is legitimate, and secondly whether it
is practical to take up arms and provoke an enemy who will strike back
with redoubled fury. They do not reflect that the church has no more dangerous foes than sinners in high places, especially those in holy orders,
and, finally, they do not realize that from time to time God, displeased
by our sinfulness, makes use of savage barbarians to reform us. Sometimes examples of Turkish cruelty are depicted for us, but in truth this
ought to remind us how reluctant we should be to make war on anyone
at all, for such amusements are common to all the wars in which, for
so many years now, Christian has impiously fought Christian. We curse
their cruelty in these pictures, but greater asperity was used at Asperen,
not by Turks, but by our own countrymen, many of them even friends.[128]
The memory of that calamity is too fresh; there is no need for me to re-
open the wound. Therefore, if the subjects of these pictures truly shock
us, we must curb our own impetuosity, which so easily leads us head-
long into war. For what a Christian does to a fellow Christian is more
cruel, even if the deeds themselves are much the same. What a hideous
spectacle it would be if paintings of all the things perpetrated by Christians against Christians in the last forty years were to be laid before men's
eyes! So much for those who simply scream: 'War on the Turks! War on the
Turks!'

Now let me deal with those who err in a very different way; their mistaken argument is perhaps more plausible, but no less dangerous. For there
are those who think that the right to make war is denied totally to Christians.[129] I find this view too absurd to require refutation, although there
has been no lack of people willing to contrive similar accusations against
me, because in my writings I am lavish in my praise of peace and fierce

* * * * *

127 Cf *Adagia* IV i 1: *Dulce bellum inexpertis* LB II 967D and 243 and 258–9 below.
    Contemporary polemicists often asserted that the Turks were better Christians
    than their opponents; see M.J. Heath 'Islamic Themes in Religious Polemic'
    Bibliothèque d'Humanisme et Renaissance 50 (1988) 289–315.
128 The sack of Asperen took place in July 1517; see Tracy *Politics* 85 and 97–
    9. The atrocities committed by the Black Band in the service of the Duke of
    Gelderland made a lasting impression on Erasmus, who often refers to the
    insurgents as 'worse than Turks'; see for example Epp 643 and 1001. I have
    retained the play on *asperiora ... Aspera*, though the English is less vigorous
    than it should be.
129 This extreme position was adopted most notably by the pacific Anabaptists;
    see Williams *Radical Reformation*, especially 225–32.

in my detestation of war.[130] But honest men reading my works will recognize, without any prompting from me, the manifest impertinence of such knavery.[131] I teach that war must never be undertaken unless, after everything else has been tried, it cannot be avoided, because war is by its very nature such a plague that, even if undertaken by the most just of princes in the most just of causes,[132] the wickedness of both officers and men means that it almost always does more harm than good. St Bernard goes further in calling 'malicious' the militia of this world; he calls soldiering 'worldly' whenever ambition, anger or the hope of booty call us to arms; anyone who falls in such a war, he says, is dead for all eternity, while he who kills and conquers lives on – as a murderer.[133] Now I come to those who agree with Luther's contention, in which he claims that those who make war on the Turks are rebelling against God, who punishes our sins through them. The theologians of Paris have censured his opinion in the following brief sentence: 'This proposition, applied universally, is false, nor does it conform to Holy Writ.'[134] They attack it as false, not heretical, and they do not condemn it outright, but deny that it is universally true, meaning, unless I

* * * * *

130 In particular the *Querela pacis* (1517) and the adage *Dulce bellum inexpertis* (1515); see the edition of the latter by Y. Rémy and R. Dunil-Marquebreucq (Brussels 1953) for a full list of Erasmus' pacific writings.

131 Erasmus had defended himself against such charges in the *Apologia contra Stunicam* of 1522 LB IX 370D, citing the final chapter of the *Institutio principis christiani* CWE 27 282–8, in which he laid down rules for the conduct of war. The next sentence here quotes this chapter verbatim (282). On the Sorbonne's attacks on Erasmus' supposed pacifism, see J.K. Farge *Orthodoxy and Reform in Early Reformation France: The Faculty of Theology of Paris 1500–1543* (Leiden 1985) 186.

132 On the 'just war,' a concept stretching back into antiquity but given shape by St Augustine and rules by Aquinas, see J.A. Fernandez 'Erasmus on the Just War' *Journal of the History of Ideas* 34 (1973) 209–26, E. Rummel *Erasmus' Annotations on the New Testament* (Toronto 1986) 163–7, and Tracy *Politics* 64–6.

133 *De laude novae militiae ad milites Templi liber* 2 PL 182 923; he plays on *militia/malitia*. See also 250 and n207 below. Erasmus uses the same example in *Adagia* IV i 1: *Dulce bellum inexpertis* LB II 964E and *Institutio principis christiani* CWE 27 284.

134 Erasmus quotes literally the *Determinatio ... super doctrina Lutheriana* issued by the Sorbonne on 15 April 1521 (Parisiis: in officina Ascensiana sig b 6 verso); see Farge (n131 above) 165–9. Luther had developed the theme of non-resistance to the scourges of God in the fifth article of his *Resolutiones disputationum* of 1518 (*Works* 31 89–91); this same proposition was condemned as erroneous (but not heretical) in Leo X's bull *Exsurge Domine*, dated 15 June 1520. On the controversy, see the introductory note 205–8 above.

am mistaken, that sometimes war against the Turks is justifiable, and sometimes not, depending on the circumstances. As far as Scripture is concerned, it is beyond dispute that long ago the Hebrews, at God's bidding, fought a bloody war with the Allophyli[135] and, again, Moses himself, helped by the sons of Levi, executed 23,000 of his own people because of the molten calf.[136] But here someone will raise the question as to whether this right was transferred to Christians,[137] especially since the Hebrews almost never went to war without specific orders from the godhead. If one removes entirely the Christian's right to make war, however, one must by the same token remove the magistrate's right to punish offenders. For war is nothing more than the punishment of the many by the many if their crimes cannot be dealt with in any other way. Now although the Gospel allowed the adulterous woman to go,[138] nowhere does it remove the magistrate's legitimate rights, even if it does not anywhere openly approve them. Besides, Paul seems to approve of the sword which is carried to punish the wicked and reward the virtuous.[139] Someone may quibble over this, saying that Paul was discussing a pagan magistracy, which he wanted Christians to obey on the grounds that if they seemed to be undermining authority and good order in the state the gospel would be brought into disrepute; it can be answered that since there is no other way of keeping peace in a Christian state either, there is a need for secular magistrates who will deter criminals by fear of punishment if they will not observe laws and customs. If we grant the magistrate this power, we must also grant monarchs the right to make war.

I am also utterly convinced, however, that everything else must be tried in preference to war breaking out between Christians; nor must it be undertaken for any reason, no matter how serious or just the cause, unless all possible remedies have been exhausted and it cannot be avoided. For if the craving for power, or ambition, or a private grudge, or a desire for revenge has inspired the war, then it is plainly not a war, but mere

* * * * *

135 The Philistines: 1 Sam 7:10–13
136 Exod 32:26–8; the Septuagint, followed by English versions, says that only 3,000 were slain.
137 As Erasmus had done in *Institutio principis christiani* CWE 27 286–7 and *Querela pacis* CWE 27 305; his answers there were distinctly more negative. But the Philistines and other enemies of the Israelites were often presented as prototypes of the Turks in crusading oratory; see Heath CC 16–17.
138 John 8:3–11
139 See Rom 13:4; this text was much exploited by crusading orators, including St Bernard and Pope Pius II; Heath CC 20.

brigandage.[140] Moreover, while it is the special responsibility of Christian princes to carry on war, yet they must not resort to this most dangerous of expedients without the consent of their citizens and of the whole nation. Finally, if absolute necessity dictates that a war must inevitably be fought, Christian clemency demands that every effort be made to involve as few as possible in the war and to finish it as quickly as possible, with the least possible bloodshed.[141] On this account, Theodosius was admired – and admired by that most admirable of men, Ambrose – because he abstained from participation in the sacraments on the grounds that his victory had been stained with the blood of the enemies he had slaughtered.[142] Note that the Romans usually determined the splendour of statues and triumphs according to the number of enemies slain!

Now Ambrose, who extolled this action of Theodosius, does not approve of war, however necessary or just, unless it is fought in a spirit of piety, with all hopes of victory placed in God, and no other aim but the peace of the state.[143] When we ask how the Christian commonwealth can survive if there is no one to protect it with laws and with force, there are always some who reply with another question: how did the Christian commonwealth survive, and grow, at a time when it had no secular magistrates, no arms, no artillery? Well, although it was fitting that the church should arise initially from such foundations, there is no necessity for things to remain permanently the same. It grew through a series of miracles, which are not to be looked for now.[144] In any case, even then the peace of the church was to some extent safeguarded by the pagan magistrates, for no individual was permitted to kill a Christian.[145]

* * * * *

140 Cf n66 above.
141 Erasmus echoes the opening section of his chapter on war in the *Institutio principis christiani* CWE 27 282.
142 The slaughter took place at Thessalonica in 390. Ambrose wrote to the emperor imposing penance upon him (Ep 51 PL 16 [1880] 1209–14) and praised Theodosius' willing submission in the funeral oration *De obitu Theodosii* 34 (ibidem 1459). Erasmus tells the story more fully in Allen Ep 1855:120–75.
143 These principles are enunciated for example in Ambrose's *De officiis* 1.29 PL 16 (1880) 68–70 and Sermon 62 *De bellico tumultu* PL 17 (1879) 754–5. Nonetheless, Ambrose could be invoked by proponents of the crusade like Aeneas Sylvius, Pope Pius II (Ep 131 in *Opera* 681); see also Heath CC 13.
144 Perhaps a reference to the long-standing controversy over why miracles were apparently much more frequent in the early church; cf *Julius exclusus* CWE 27 171 and n26.
145 A reference to the fact that even under the Roman persecution, accused Christians were given the benefit of due legal process; see for example the cele-

As for Luther's argument, I would add that if it is not lawful to resist the Turks, because God is punishing the misdeeds of his people through them, then it cannot be permissible to call in a doctor during illness, on the grounds that God also sends diseases to cleanse his people. He also uses the wiles of Satan to the same end, and yet we are commanded to resist them.[146] It is therefore lawful also to fight off the Turks, unless God sends a clear sign to prohibit it. If we are incited to war, however, not by concern for the peace of Christendom but by a craving for more power, a lust for riches, or any similar reason, if we go into battle relying on our own strength rather than on God's aid, or fight without principles, it is clear that the war will be fought in the face of God's anger. I would go further: if God inflicts the Turks upon us so often to urge us to reform our lives, and yet we take up arms without amending the things that have provoked God to inflict these cruel barbarians upon us, then all the omens will be against us in the war. This has been the case, very obviously, up to now; I fear that in the future we shall see much worse, unless we turn with our whole hearts towards the Lord and offer him the sacrifice that the psalm suggests to us.

But some people maintain that it is lawful for Christians to wage war against Christians but not against the Turks, because Paul says that it is not his business to judge outsiders, having enough to do to judge those within the community.[147] The Turks are outsiders and have nothing to do with the church; if it is lawful for us to kill the Turks, why did not the church long ago arm herself against the gentiles who cruelly persecuted those who confessed the name of Christ? But Augustine refused to allow it, even at a time when our numbers and our wealth were greater than theirs; in fact, he interceded on behalf of some who had murdered Christians and asked the emperor not to execute them; he gives no other reason than that the glory of the martyrs would be sullied by such a course.[148] We read that idolatrous emperors vented their merciless fury upon the lives and property of Christians, but never do we read that the Christians took up arms in self-defence

* * * * *

brated exchange between the emperor Trajan and Pliny the Younger (*Epistles* 10.96–7) and Tertullian *Apologia* 2–3 PL 1 (1879) 317–32.

146 Cf Eph 6:11 and 1 Pet 5:9.

147 1 Cor 5:12

148 Ep 139.2 PL 33 535–6, on punishing the Donatists; cf Ep 100 (ibidem 366–7). In the *Declarationes ad censuras Lutetiae vulgatas* of 1532 (LB X 906E–907B tit 23 prop 2) Erasmus uses the same episode to defend his own views on the punishment of heretics: it is better to take up arms against the Turks, who have attacked and oppressed Christians physically, than against heretics, though in both cases the best course of all would be persuasion by words.

or to exact revenge. They sought refuge in flight, the one relief that God granted them. Some writers, however, including Tertullian, think that flight was not merely a concession but was permitted at that time as part of a divine plan, since there were as yet few to proclaim the gospel teaching, and their flight would thus spread the gospel more widely.[149] Now that it has spread throughout the world, flight would be a kind of denial.

If we are not allowed to flee, still less are we allowed to rush to arms. But the mass of Christians wrongly believes that anyone is allowed to kill a Turk, as one would a mad dog, for no better reason than that he is a Turk.[150] If this were true, then anyone would be allowed to kill a Jew, but anyone who ventured to do that would not escape punishment under civil law. The Christian magistrate will punish Jews who break the laws of the state, to which they are subject; but they are not put to death because of their religion, since Christianity is spread by persuasion, not force; it is sown like seed, not pushed down people's throats. This right, by which Jews are punished in the same way as Christians, was also exercised, long ago, by pagan rulers against their Christian subjects, and the Turks would now enjoy the same right if, God forbid, we were living under the laws of the Turkish empire. Therefore any who believe that they will fly straight up to heaven if they happen to fall in battle against the Turks are sadly deluding themselves;[151] you will reach heaven only if your conscience is pure, even if, for Christ's sake, you offer your life when the tyrant summons you to worship idols.[152]

What is more, such was the clemency of the church's leaders in days gone by that they were reluctant to see even relapsed Jews punished with death. This is evident from the fourth chapter of the distinction *On Consecration*, 'A great many Jews...'[153] For King Sisemand had discovered that many Jews who, renouncing their former impiety, had professed the Chris-

* * * * *

149 *De fuga in persecutione* 6 PL 2 (1844) 108–10, based on Matt 10:23
150 Cf *De vidua christiana* CWE 66 234.
151 Erasmus frequently attacks this belief, which could be deduced from many papal pronouncements on the crusade from Urban II onwards: see Heath cc 87–9 on its history and its place in Reformation controversy. Erasmus denounces the granting of plenary indulgences to soldiers in any war in *Julius exclusus* CWE 27 174 and *Querela pacis* CWE 27 320.
152 A reference to the early Christian martyrs, who were offered the chance to renounce their faith by worshipping the emperor's statue and the images of the Roman gods; see n145 above.
153 Gratian *Decretum* pars 3 *De consecratione* d 4 c 94; Erasmus quotes the canonist almost word for word. Sisemand was Visigothic ruler of Spain 631–6.

tian faith had not only relapsed into their old blasphemy but were also practising detestable Jewish rites and had circumcised their children and slaves; he asked the church's leaders how he should punish a crime of such magnitude. The reply, in a decree of the tenth Council of Toledo, was that such Jews must be rebuked by papal authority and summoned to return to the practice of true Christianity; any who refused to conform voluntarily would be coerced by sacerdotal punishments: the children to be removed from their parents' society, the slaves to be set free in view of the physical injury they had suffered.[154] It is already clear that priests have no right to kill anyone. But nowadays blasphemy against Christ and the Virgin Mother, even without any relapse, is punished with a death worse than mere execution, and anyone lapsing into heretical error is consigned to the flames, even without the additional charge of blasphemy. On the other hand Berengarius, who repeated his abominable errors, was not only not executed, but was not even stripped of his position as archdeacon.[155] A Christian who has turned back to paganism is also burned. But it would be more just to burn the Jew who as an adult has learned his catechism and voluntarily confessed Christ than someone who was baptized as an unschooled infant.

My purpose here is not to reprove the (perhaps necessary) severity that is customary now, but to show that the more the Church's original piety was alive in her, the more she shrank from wars and executions. St Ambrose approves of the emperor's beating back the barbarian raids into Italy, but he only approves so long as warfare is accompanied by faith and the love of religion, and even then, he says, this is not the way of gospel perfection.[156] You see how carefully, how hesitatingly, he gave his approval to war. To remove the power of the sword from secular princes and magistrates entirely, however, is quite simply to undermine the whole foundation of the state and to expose the lives and property of the citizens to the violence of criminals; but, equally, there can be no valid precedent for priests becoming involved in the business of war, to say nothing of fighting in

* * * * *

154 Decree 59 of the Council usually numbered Toledo IV, held in 633; see C.J. Hefele and Dom H. Leclercq *Histoire des Conciles* III-1 (Paris 1909) 266–77.
155 Berengarius of Tours (c 999–1088), though several times relapsing into heretical views on the Eucharist, suffered no more than brief imprisonment. Erasmus was at this moment editing a work by Berengarius' opponent Alger, *De veritate corporis et sanguinis Dominici in Eucharistia*; see Ep 2284.
156 Cf *Expositio evangelii secundum Lucam* 10.53 PL 15 (1887) 1909. In his *Annotationes in Lucam*, Erasmus makes the same use of Ambrose in a long disquisition on war relating to Luke 22:36; see Anne Reeve *Erasmus' Annotations on the New Testament: The Gospels* (London 1986) 209–13.

person. Their fight is for God, and they must not become involved in secular strife. War is such a soulless business that it could almost be called
pagan; if it is right for priests to make war, it would be equally right for
them to play the executioner. These days, when papal regulations forbid a
priest to practise medicine,[157] on what grounds is he allowed to make war,
since a doctor's energies and skill go to saving life, and a warrior's to taking it? But the analogy of curing sickness does not entirely fit the present
case, for the use of drugs does not entail loss or injury to anyone, whereas
anyone using war to cure his injuries only does so by contriving the death
of others. If war is begun in an unjust cause or conducted in an improper
way, it is no more acceptable than someone trying to ward off illness by
witchcraft.

Another point requiring discussion here is whether somebody who is
aware of his sin, and acknowledges that his illness is sent by an angry God,
is allowed to ward off the illness with all permitted remedies while still remaining disposed to commit the same sins as before. For he appears to be
clearly resisting the will of God. Now although it may be allowed that the
first law of nature allows everyone to look after their health if there is any
hope of an improvement, yet, even if looking after their health does not
constitute a new charge, it is clear that they sin most grievously in rejecting
God's mercy, which urges them to reform their lives. They plunge themselves into the gravest danger: not only may the illness not be eased, but
even worse troubles may befall. For it is the height of impiety to think that
the doctor's art can cure illness without God's blessing. We are in a similar
position if, while acknowledging that the Turkish invasions are sent to persuade us to reform our lives and to live in mutual harmony, we nonetheless persist in our sinfulness and believe that we can ward off disaster, in
the face of God's anger, by our own efforts. If we challenge the Turks after
breaking sworn oaths and treaties,[158] we are like an invalid seeking help
from a sorcerer, not a doctor. Thus the best advice to the invalid would
be that he should first make his peace with God, acknowledge that God's
hand is lighter on him than he deserves, and beg for the Lord's mercy while
agreeing to mend his ways. Similarly, the soundest advice for our Christian princes now would be to persuade them that before rushing into battle

* * * * *

157 It was possible for a priest to obtain a licence from the pope to practise
    medicine provided that he did not accept remuneration for his services; see
    R. Cooper *Rabelais et l'Italie* (Geneva 1991) 239 n9.
158 Cf n89 above and the chapter on spurious treaties in *Institutio principis chris-
    tiani* 8 CWE 27 275–6.

they should eradicate all the things that offend God and cause him to send the Turks so often against us. Otherwise, if we promise ourselves victory by our own efforts, we merely delude ourselves and provoke the deity to ever more anger against us, since in truth we are resisting God, not fighting the Turks.

But there is no need for me to list all the things that turn God from us; let everyone examine their own conscience and they will find enough there. God has again 'made all things prisoner to sin, that he may show them all mercy.'[159] We all have our different faults, and some sin more obviously than others, but we all need the mercy of God. Yet the principal and most glaring faults are the most cunningly disguised. What are they? How I wish that what I am about to say, reluctantly and with a heavy heart, concerned fewer of us, or none at all! How terribly far the shepherds of the church have fallen below their archetype![160] How completely the worst of cankers, ambition and avarice, have corrupted us! Then again, for how many years have we seen foreign princes striving against one another with implacable hatred? The Greeks and Trojans waged war over Helen for ten years. How much longer has the 'Helen' of Milan been fought over?[161] What misfortunes has Italy not suffered? What troubles has France not endured? Even the victorious lands weep. It is better not to touch on the mystery of the war we have fought for so many years with the Gelderlanders,[162] a most sensitive point with us; and, without listing every last case, what province is there now where the common people are not poor and miserably afflicted by an incredible shortage of every commodity? Where now is to be found any vestige of true faith, of Christian charity, of peace and harmony? What age ever saw fraud, violence, rapine, and imposture practised so freely?

* * * * *

159 A conflation of Rom 11:32 and Gal 3:22
160 Christ; cf for example John 10:14, Heb 13:20
161 This clarifies the allusion to 'foreign' princes a little earlier; the French claim to the duchy of Milan was a major issue in the series of wars between Hapsburg and Valois, mostly fought in Italy, from 1494 until 1559. On Helen of Troy as a proverbial source of discord, cf *Adagia* I iii 69: *Haec Helena*; Erasmus uses the adage in a similar context in *Institutio principis christiani* 9 CWE 27 277 and in Ep 2713 (applied to Hungary). In a crusading oration of 1459, Pius II had asked how long Christians should be prepared to fight for the Holy Land if the Greeks fought for ten years over Helen (*Opera* 907).
162 See Tracy *Politics* chapter 4 'The Mystery of Our War with Guelders' (71–107); Karel van Egmond, duke of Gelderland, had waged intermittent war against the house of Hapsburg since 1492, with French support, and Erasmus regarded these campaigns in his native land as a particularly painful example of 'civil war' between Christians; cf 233 and n128 above on the sack of Asperen.

And yet all the while, like true Christians, we hate the Turks! If we really want to heave the Turks from our necks, we must first expel from our hearts a more loathsome race of Turks,[163] avarice, ambition, the craving for power, self-satisfaction, impiety, extravagance, the love of pleasure, deceitfulness, anger, hatred, envy; having slaughtered these with the sword of the spirit,[164] let us rediscover a truly Christian spirit and then, if required, march against the flesh-and-blood Turks under the banners of Christ and, with him as our champion, defeat them. For God promised this in Leviticus, but only to those who keep his law: 'You shall put your enemies to flight, and they shall fall in battle before you; five of you shall rout a hundred, and a hundred of you ten thousand.'[165]

However, this triumph will be most acceptable to Christ if, instead of slaughtering the Turks, we manage to join them to us in a fellowship of worship and faith. He delights in such victories, he who rejoices in the name of Saviour, who kills that he may give life and wounds that he may heal.[166] Destroy a Turk to make a Christian, fell an infidel to raise up a true believer: such killing is a work of piety fully acceptable to God. Let it therefore be our only goal, our principal preoccupation, to extend the kingdom of Christ rather than our own. Otherwise, to slaughter Turks is simply to increase the kingdom of the dead.[167] To possess what the Turk possesses, to rule those he rules and to look no further will make us prouder and still more covetous, but it will not make us happier, and there will be a danger that we shall degenerate into Turks instead of bringing them into Christ's fold.[168]

Anyone who contemplates, beside Syria and Palestine, all the kingdoms of Greece, all the provinces of Asia Minor, where the apostles once

* * * * *

163 Erasmus uses the expression *hi Turcae* ('these Turks') to describe the sins of Christendom in a similar context in the adage *Sileni Alcibiadis* (III iii 1; CWE 34 275); Luther pursues a similar line in his *Confutatio* 216.

164 Cf Eph 6:17.

165 Lev 26:7–8; Cochlaeus (*Dialogus* 75 recto) uses this text to encourage Ferdinand in his war against the Turks, as does the pilgrim Barthélemy de Salignac to encourage Francis I in *Itinerarii terrae sanctae descriptio* (Paris 1525) 59 recto.

166 Cf Deut 32:39.

167 *Orco litare*, literally 'to sacrifice to the Lower World.' Erasmus uses the expression in the same context in Ep 858:121.

168 An echo of John 10:16, a prophecy frequently invoked to foretell the conversion of the Turks (Heath CC 50). Erasmus here summarizes a passage on converting the Turks in Ep 858:85–165; see also 407–11. These passages apparently convinced Luther that Erasmus agreed with him; see Allen Ep 2285:127–8n.

preached the gospel, which are now virtually abandoned to the tyrannical rule of the barbarians, cannot fail to grieve with all his heart and pray that the name of Christ, which now seems confined within such narrow bounds, will be recognized, praised, and worshipped throughout the whole world, as the psalm says: that all the nations, in different tongues but with a single voice, and in a single temple (that is, in the unity of the church) shall sing glory to their redeemer.[169] For St Paul shows us good hope that one day the stubborn Jewish race will be gathered into the fold, and with us will acknowledge the one true shepherd, Jesus.[170] There is yet more reason to hope this of the Turks and other barbarian nations, none of whom, I hear, worships idols; on the contrary, they are halfway to Christianity.[171] If so few disciples were able to pass the whole world beneath Christ's yoke,[172] equipped with no weapons other than their confidence in God's promises and the sword of the Spirit, why should not we do the same, with Christ's aid, since besides our Christian princes we have so many doctors of theology, so many outstanding prelates, so many cardinals, so many to proclaim the perfection of the gospel? The Lord's arm is not short,[173] unless we are deprived of his grace. The outcome of the whole undertaking depends on a nod[174] from him who said: 'Without me you can do nothing.'[175] Under his protection, one man may rout a thousand; if he is estranged from us, then however large the army, however meticulous the preparations, all will be in vain. But provided that our all our hopes are first anchored in him, nothing need prevent us from considering the methods suggested by human counsel, which must be applied in such a way that nonetheless we still depend entirely on the protection of eternal God; we cannot hope to enjoy his favour if in theory we fight on his behalf but in reality wage war against his will.

* * * * *

169 Cf Ps 28/29:9.

170 Romans 11. Erasmus' actual words are another reminiscence of John 10:16; see n168 above.

171 See n127 above.

172 Cf Matt 11:29–30.

173 Isa 59:1. Cf Pius II's crusading oration in 1459: 'The Lord's arm is not short, but his mercy has been placed out of reach because of our sins' (*Opera* 909; see also 684). But Luther used the same text to show that a military campaign was not necessary (*Confutatio* 214–15).

174 A common image in antiquity, which Erasmus sometimes uses ironically to indicate aristocratic arrogance; see Tracy *Politics* 68. But he had also used it of God in his paraphrase on the Third Psalm (CWE 63 154 and n1).

175 John 15:5

Now, to discover whether the war is begun with God's consent and whether it will end in success, there is no need to turn to the prophets,[176] or to consult an oracle, as David did after the ephod had been brought to him,[177] or to seek a triple sign, as Gideon did.[178] Jews and Gentiles may demand miracles, but the faithful do not. Still less must we follow the Gentiles and employ augurs and soothsayers. No oracle is more trustworthy than the Holy Scriptures, no augury more certain than the sure knowledge that the enterprise is just. If your sword is drawn from the sheath out of concern for peace in the world, or compassion for your persecuted brethren, or devotion to your religion; if all your hope of victory lies in God's protection; if your eye is fixed steadfastly upon the glory of Christ and the service of the Christian flock, consider that your question has been answered by God from the mercy seat:[179] 'Go forward: you shall be victorious.' But if the Holy Scriptures seem to protest against your intent, consider that an angel has announced that you must not act. If cruelty, or the desire to extend your domains, or a passion for plunder calls you to arms, be warned that no flight of birds could be more ill-omened.[180] For even if things appear to go well for a time, for those who begin a war under such auspices this is not success but a treacherous lure leading them on to ever greater disaster. Because of our wickedness and humanity's lack of trust in God, it often happens that all the signs point to certain victory, though in fact heaven is preparing some dreadful calamity. In the same way, in Homer a 'baneful dream' was sent down that incited the Greeks to war by promising victory – and led them to total defeat.[181] Similarly, we read in the Holy Scriptures that a lying spirit from the Lord, in the mouths of all the prophets, promised a glorious victory to Ahab king of Israel, when in fact the Lord was planning his destruction. For he was mortally wounded at the opening of the first battle, paying the penalty for ignoring Micaiah. He listened to the four hundred prophets, all induced to lie by the spirit, and spurned Micaiah, who alone spoke the

* * * * *

176 Prophecy and prognostication played a large role in contemporary crusading propaganda; see Heath cc 45–59.
177 1 Sam 30:7–8
178 Judg 6:17–21 and 37–40
179 Cf Exod 25:17 and 22, Num 7:89.
180 A reference to a Roman method of divination: cf *Adagia* II vii 20: *Meliores nancisci aves,* literally 'To meet with better birds,' where Erasmus also attacks bogus predictions.
181 *Iliad* 2.6 and 8; Erasmus quotes 'baneful dream' in Greek.

truth.[182] I reckon that our monarchs too should beware of such prophets. For instance, there are some who promise victories using rings and divination, while others use undershirts and lucky swords, and still others ventriloquy and the stars;[183] there are also those who base their promise of success on human strategy and human soldiery.[184] We have, they declare, this many soldiers, and that many cannon; we shall attack here and here, and outwit the enemy like this and like that; God with us or no, victory is ours! Another lot cry from the pulpit: 'Go forth and win the day; the Lord delivers the enemy into your hands, you shall harry them with your iron horns until you destroy them all utterly.'[185] They thunder out these mighty speeches (sometimes merely for cash) and imperil the people, at no danger to themselves: they stay at home, far from the flying weapons, and look to their kitchens[186] and their bellies. It is notorious that such preachers have often

* * * * *

182 See 1 Kings 22 and 2 Chronicles 18. Luther uses this episode in a similar context: casting himself as Micaiah, he compares the legates and commissaries from Rome, recruiting for the crusade, with the prophets of Baal, and warns the people: 'Go out and fight the Turks, resisting the scourge of God, and you shall die just as Ahab died' (*Assertio omnium articulorum* WA 7 141).

183 An assortment of contemporary methods of divination. *Dactylomantia* (divination by rings) is described by Henricus Cornelius Agrippa von Nettesheim in *De occulta philosophia* I 47 (1531; repr Leiden 1992) 174–5. In Ep 396:73–9 Erasmus complains of the veneration accorded to saints' clothing, including *indusia* (undershirts), while their writings are ignored; cf the colloquy *Peregrinatio religionis ergo* CWE 40 642–3. He condemns the 'nonsense' of lucky swords in *Adagia* I x 97: *Equum habet Sejanum* and in the *Moria* CWE 27 129. Ventriloquists were supposed to be possessed of a prophetic spirit; see L. Ricchieri *Antiquae lectiones* (Paris 1517) v 10 and Rabelais *Le Quart Livre* chapter 58. Erasmus condemns judicial astrology as vain and seditious in two *Adagia*, II iii 78 and II vii 20, and casts doubt on it, in the context of the Turks, in the *Panegyricus* CWE 27 11.

184 On this topic, see Heath CC 60–80. One such plan had been circulated by Leo x to the Christian princes in 1515–17; cf Ep 335:170–5 and, on Leo's frustrated efforts generally, Housley *Later Crusades* 125–6 and 416–17, and Tracy *Politics* 109–111.

185 Based on 1 Kings 22:11–12 and 15. On the methods of popular preachers advocating the crusade, see Schwoebel *Shadow of the Crescent* 40–2. In Ep 2256:19–21 (16 Jan 1530) Erasmus describes a recent preaching campaign of this sort in Brabant – to which 'nobody contributes a penny.'

186 Cf *Adagia* v i 1: *Tu in legione, ego in culina* 'You're in the army, I'm in the kitchen,' a tag from Plautus' *Miles gloriosus*. On churchmen as 'firebrands of war,' cf *Institutio principis christiani* 11 CWE 27 286 and especially *Querela pacis* (CWE 27 307–9); see also n217 below.

in the past been the harbingers of war; I hope that there are none of them
about now!

At this point I shall perhaps appear to some to have undertaken to
argue *against* a Turkish war. Not at all: my purpose, rather, is to help us
to wage war on them successfully and to win truly splendid triumphs for
Christ. For merely to clamour for war against the Turks, calling them inhuman monsters, enemies of the church, a race defiled by every sort of crime
and villainy, is simply to betray the ignorant mob to the enemy. In recent
times, for instance when we have been hearing of Hungarian defeats, and
most recently of the tragic death of Louis and the sad fate of Queen Mary,[187]
and now of Hungary's throne seized and Austria cruelly laid waste, I have
often been surprised to see other nations, and even Germany herself, completely unconcerned, as though all this were no concern of ours. We tighten
our fists, and spend on pleasures and trifles what we are reluctant to spend
on the defence of Christendom.

I am not unaware of the excuses many people make for this attitude.
This charade, they say, has been played out[188] too often by the Roman pontiffs, and the outcome has always been farcical: either nothing has been
done or the situation has deteriorated. The money collected, they say, has
stuck fast in the hands of popes, cardinals, monks, generals, and princes; the
common soldiers are licensed to take plunder in lieu of their pay. We have
heard so often of crusading expeditions, of recovering the Holy Land; we
have seen so often the red cross emblazoned with the triple crown, and the
red chest beside it;[189] we have heard so often the sainted sermons promising
the earth; we have heard so often of doughty deeds and boundless hopes –
and the only thing to triumph has been money. Therefore, since the proverb
warns that it is quite shameful to trip over the same stone twice,[190] how can
we, who have been misled thirty times over, believe any more promises,

* * * * *

187 Louis II of Hungary (CEBR II 352–3) was drowned in a swamp while fleeing
     from the disastrous field of Mohács (29 August 1526); his young bride Mary
     was forced to take refuge in Moravia under the protection of her brothers,
     Emperor Charles V and Ferdinand. In 1529 Erasmus had dedicated to her the
     De vidua christiana, which includes a eulogy of the late king (CWE 66 186; see
     also the introductory note 178–9).
188 Erasmus adapts appropriately the tag *Acta est fabula* 'the play is over'; cf *Querela
     pacis* CWE 27 320. The arguments paraphrased here are essentially those of
     Luther.
189 The triple crown was the papal emblem. Indulgences were carried in the chest;
     cf Ep 2205:79–81.
190 *Adagia* I v 8: *Iterum eundem lapidem offendere*

however splendid, when we have been blatantly fooled so often? This very question has almost led the public to reject indulgences altogether.[191] We came to realize, they say, that it was just business. From time to time the label was changed: one minute it was the Turkish campaign; the next the pope was struggling with a war; then it was the jubilee, which became a double jubilee – to double the profits (under Alexander, there was even a triple jubilee,[192] perhaps because he was disappointed with sales). Then again, even more than plenary power was on offer, and purgatory was in danger of losing all its inmates.[193] Another time, there was the building of St Peter's in the Vatican.[194] On other occasions, St James of Compostela was in need,[195] the Holy Spirit, the giver of all things, was begging for aid, the monks of Mount Sinai needed help,[196] and finally those owing restitution to the church were offered a very generous deal and the chance to make amends for their thefts, even for property taken from looted churches.[197] Why go on? There was no limit and no end to these arrangements.

The princes used to hive off part of the money to obtain a papal brief for themselves; deans and officials took a share, as did commissaries and

* * * * *

191 Cf the passage on Leo x's campaign 248–9 and the letter cited in n185 above. Even Cochlaeus, in defending crusade indulgences, was obliged to go back to 1456 for an example of their success (*Dialogus* 51).

192 In 1500, under Alexander vi. Celebrations of the holy year or Jubilee, originally arranged in 1300 by Boniface viii to occur every hundred years, became more and more frequent, being reduced to an interval of twenty-five years by Paul ii in 1470; cf Ep 1211:173–4 and n26 and M. Creighton *History of the Papacy* (London 1901) vi 71–2.

193 Sixtus iv's bull of 1476 (H.J.D. Denzinger *Enchiridion symbolorum* [Barcelona 1955] 269–70) represents the first authentic application of an indulgence to the souls in purgatory. A plenary indulgence offers full remission of the canonical penance due for sins committed.

194 St Peter's was begun by Julius ii in 1506; Luther's Ninety-five Theses were directly provoked in 1517 by an indulgence granted by Leo x to all who contributed to this cause.

195 The cult of St James was in decline, and the shrine at Compostela had fallen into disrepair; see the colloquy *Peregrinatio religionis ergo* CWE 40 623–4. On the general popularity of St James as an object of pilgrimage, see Epp 1202:247–50 and 1697:70–2.

196 See Epp 594:7–12 and 1132:25–35, on a monk from St Catherine's on Mount Sinai authorized by Leo x to collect money in Germany.

197 Cf passages satirizing personal absolution of this kind, granted to former soldiers, in the colloquies *Militaria* CWE 39 60 and *Funus* CWE 40 773. A more direct condemnation of the practice is found in Erasmus' book on confession, *Exomologesis* LB V 165A.

confessors. Some were given a share to make them talk, others, to buy their silence. Not the least part disappeared among the agents (criminals, as such people usually are) and the hawkers of documents. All these little games were played quite openly, time and again, and the dull-witted folk of Germany, and the even duller French, knew what was happening but put up with it. When the sea had flooded western Flanders, and the whole region presented a pitiful sight, the most liberal indulgences were very soon prepared. The cause, and to some extent the influence, of the late pope Adrian, touched everyone deeply. More than enough was collected to help those in distress. Legates were sent to inspect the area and to report on the best ways to repair the damage; the disaster was portrayed in paintings. There is no need for me to recall where the money disappeared to, but certainly none of it was put to the use for which it had been collected.[198] These and many other objections are raised nowadays whenever we suggest that everyone should assist the rulers against the Turks' cruelty, and I only wish I could clearly show that all these claims are without foundation.

In the past, this cause has been enthusiastically taken up by a number of popes and, surprisingly, by none other than Bernard, who was both a monk and a saint.[199] Bessarion and Pius II[200] did their utmost. The idea has generated several orders of crusaders;[201] the most plentiful provisions have been set aside and high ranking posts invented. What the result has been is clear from the record. Leo X[202] devoted all his efforts to it, and sent into every Christian province his cardinal-legates, who were no lightweights

* * * * *

198 On this scandal of 1515–16 in Erasmus' homeland, see the references in ASD V-3 67. On the devastation wrought by contemporary floods in the Netherlands, see S. Schama *The Embarrassment of Riches: An Interpretation of Dutch Culture in the Golden Age* (London 1987) 34–41 and n46.

199 St Bernard of Clairvaux preached the Second Crusade in 1146–7, and wrote a panegyric of the new militant Order of the Templars, to which Erasmus referred earlier (n133 above), pointing out that Bernard had little time for ordinary soldiers: hence the 'surprise' here.

200 The two most celebrated fifteenth-century advocates of a new crusade; see Schwoebel *Shadow of the Crescent* 157–60 and 57–81 respectively. For their crusading speeches, reprinted at intervals throughout the sixteenth century, see Pius II *Opera* 678–89 and 872–932 and Bessarion *Orationes contra Turcas* in PG 161 641–76.

201 The most famous being the Templars, founded c 1119 for the defence of Christian pilgrims in the Holy Land and dissolved in 1314, and the Knights Hospitaller of St John, recently defeated on Rhodes (n115 above) and re-established by Charles V on Malta in 1530.

202 See n184 above.

but men of the greatest learning; but nowhere were the envoys heard with much enthusiasm, even though Luther had not yet written against papal indulgences and had not yet published his thesis that to wage war against the Turks is simply to resist God, who sends them to scourge us.[203]

It seemed advisable to say all this, and indeed the situation demands it: we must not think it enough to scream abuse at these 'Turkish brutes' but must conceive a plan that will enable us, if eventually it comes to war, to fight the Turks with more success than hitherto and recall men's minds, perhaps understandably distracted, to their Christian duty. Today the force of evil besets us more closely, and we have princes who are both outstanding in their exercise of power and distinguished by their zeal for the faith: the emperor Charles, his brother King Ferdinand, and the most Christian King of France, Francis, their ally at last – if only it had been sooner.[204] And in this enterprise the illustrious king of England, Henry, will not be found wanting, to prove his piety and uphold his title: for he has won the right to be called Defender of the Catholic Faith.[205] Let us pray, and let us also hope, that the Lord Jesus, in his compassion for us, will inspire his vicar Clement VII with a resolve worthy of himself and will strengthen and foster the resolution that he is rumoured – and all good Christians believe it – to have adopted.

I have already described in sufficient detail the ways in which we may ensure a successful outcome to this war, namely that, first of all, we appease the Lord's anger, that our intentions be pure and honourable, that all our trust be in Christ, that we fight beneath his standard, that he triumph in us, and that we obey the commands of our God and march against the enemy as though his eye were always upon us. For if the theft committed by one man, Achan, brought defeat to the whole nation of Israel,[206] what can we hope for if we are encumbered with the sins of all our sinful soldiers? Their mercenary outlook incites them to every outrage, as they set out for war intent on plunder and return to plunder more, sometimes more ruthless towards their own folk than towards the enemy, carting their whores with them,

* * * * *

203 See n134 above.
204 The Peace of Cambrai in 1529 had brought a (temporary) halt to the Hapsburg-Valois wars; cf n161 above. *Rex christianissimus* was the courtesy title of the kings of France.
205 Henry VIII was awarded the title by Leo X in 1521 after publishing his book against Luther. Cochlaeus boasts (*Dialogus* 48 recto) that the emperor and his brother bear equally auspicious titles.
206 See Joshua 7.

drunkenly dicing in camp, swearing, quarrelling, brawling. Does anything attract them to war except the freedom to transgress and the expectation of plunder? If we wish for God as our shield, and yet cannot be the kind of soldiers St Bernard describes (he is not sure whether to call them monks or soldiers, such was their uprightness of character, such their fortitude in battle),[207] at least let our consciences be clear, and let us not provoke the Lord, beneath his very banners, by our wickedness. In producing such soldiers, a heavy responsibility lies with their commanders, and still more with their monarchs: if they are driven by cupidity and the attractions of ever-increasing power rather than by the welfare of the state (although, in my opinion, this is hardly to be suspected of our present rulers), then all our efforts, however strenuous, will end in failure. Again, if the pope – heaven forbid – should reason as follows: 'I shall extend my sovereignty, the first-fruits will grow from the new churches,[208] I shall consolidate my power, I shall set my cardinals and my liegemen to govern cities and provinces, and by means of this war I shall rule the monarchs themselves' – then I am afraid that such a campaign would do great damage to Christendom. But it is up to us to prevent all this; it is within our power to equip our minds for the battle, and the Lord will grant us a happy outcome.

Now, if some idiot laughs and calls all this nonsense, let him be quite sure that he will not have to laugh on the other side of his face.[209] I would not mind being accused of talking rubbish had not our campaigns against the Turks so often been unsuccessful. And can we complain that our efforts are unsuccessful, since until now we have been doing Satan's work, though in the name of Christ, and making war in the face of God's anger? The Lord cries out through Isaiah, he cries to us every day; the words were written for us: 'Put away the evil of your deeds, out of my sight; cease to do evil and learn to do good ... Come, and let us argue it out.'[210]

He promises priceless rewards, he threatens appalling punishments, yet we are deaf to both promises and threats. We ignore his goodness, we

* * * * *

207 In *De laude novae militiae ad milites Templi liber* 3–4 (PL 182 924–7); see also nn133 and 199 above.

208 Annates, originally revenues from vacant benefices, had first been claimed for the papal treasury by John XXII in 1319 and had now become a more or less fixed tax on new appointments. Luther claimed, in *An den Christlichen Adel (To the Christian Nobility)* (1520) that they had been instituted originally as the clergy's contribution to crusade funds (*Works* 44 144).

209 Literally 'to laugh the Sardonian [bitter] laugh'; cf *Adagia* III v 1: *Risus Sardonius*.

210 An adaptation of Isa 1:16–18

disdain his threats, and we grumble at his punishments. We whine about wars, though we bring war upon ourselves. We complain when peace is gone, though we squander the tranquil hours of peace on riotous living, and even in peacetime there is no peace among us. The enemy has laid down his arms, but internal rivalries boil up, quarrels, disputes, and riots; even though no one falls in battle, many perish in drunken brawls. We complain that the earth does not respond to our prayers, even though we respond so rarely to God's commands; we murmur against God because the fields are barren, even though we produce nothing for God but leaves, thistles, and tares.[211] We are surprised when rain falls constantly from the sky, even though our own hearts are so dry that hardly anyone sheds a single tear for his sins. We complain about shortages and high prices as if we did not ourselves create, first shortages, then high prices, no matter how abundant the crop, through greed, avarice, and the arts of the monopolist.[212] We are upset because less grows than usual, even though the things that do grow are not distributed to those who need them. To sum up, we complain of so many evils, and yet we give no thanks for God's goodness; we complain of evils as though our own evil lives entitled us to something good. We bemoan the ill luck of our age, even though amid so much misfortune we find opportunities to be evil, and even though some people, not without cause, proclaim that the end of the world is at hand,[213] yet we go on, not only making marriages, lawful and unlawful, as in the days of Noah,[214] but also banqueting, lobbying for honours, scrambling for office, building tall, straining to seize power, tying one estate to another, one city to another, one realm to another, like so many pieces of string.[215] Let us therefore hearken to the Lord's voice and to his commands, and he will hear the people's voice as they cry to him. If we have done what he commanded, and he has not done what he promised, let us go to him, let us dispute with him; he who seeks only to be merciful will not reject such arguments.

It remains for me to say something about winning back the hearts of humankind. My own opinion is that the people will be rather more

* * * * *

211 Allusions to Christ's parables in Matthew 13 and 21

212 Cf the chapter on economics in *Institutio principis christiani* 4 CWE 27 260–2.

213 This was a theme of Luther's *Vom Kriege* of 1529; see *Works* 46 18 n3, 181 and 200.

214 The unbridled behaviour that led to the Flood (Genesis 6) is recalled in the Gospels as Christ prophesies the end of the world: Matt 24:37–8, Luke 17:26–7. The allusion is explained more fully at the end of the colloquy *Cyclops* CWE 40 869–70.

215 *Adagia* I viii 59

enthusiastic about this war if they see it undertaken, in a spirit of true harmony, by their supreme and lawful monarchs. The first place must go to
the emperor Charles, with his lieutenants, the second to the Most Christian King,[216] the third to King Ferdinand, who is most nearly threatened by
those barbarians, and after them the other princes. For, to tell the truth, it
is not seemly for cardinals, bishops, abbots, and priests to conduct affairs
of this sort, as it is not consistent with Holy Writ or with the statutes of the
church; finally, it has never yet been successful.[217] For (and I don't know
why) Mars is always less favourable to men who are pledged to more holy
business, and the soldier always obeys a secular captain more willingly
than a priestly one. Moreover, many stratagems used in war are dictated
by necessity rather than honour, to meet particular circumstances, and are
better left to men less concerned with the teaching of gospel perfection.
War is a business governed by necessity rather than nobility, even though
at one time almost all titles of nobility seem to have sprung from it; count,
duke, baron, marshal, and landgrave: these were apparently an authoriza-
tion or a reward for risking one's life to preserve peace in the state. But all
such titles and offices, even if you add 'king,' are far beneath the dignity
of those who are the successors of Christ, although they too in their turn
owe honour and obedience to princes who measure up to their duties. Fair-
minded princes, who barely acknowledge the pope himself when it suits
them, will pardon a man who speaks the truth. God alone judges the worth
of our lives; for the rest, as far as the political order is concerned, there is
no bishop so humble that he does not surpass any monarch by virtue of his
high calling. Ambrose was bishop of a single city, yet he ruled Theodosius,
an emperor worthy of the name and ruler of a broad empire.[218]

    We read that Christ never made war but rather gave us a heavenly phi-
losophy, showed us the path to immortal life, counselled sinners, rebuked
unbelievers, encouraged the faint-hearted, supported the weak, strove to

* * * * *

216 Francis I: cf n204 above. In October 1529 Francis I did indeed offer to march as
    Charles' lieutenant to assist in the relief of Vienna; A.J.G. Le Glay *Négociations
    diplomatiques entre la France et l'Autriche* (Paris 1845) II 714.
217 Erasmus often deplores the involvement of the clergy in war. Cf n186 above
    and see *Adagia* II v 1: *Spartam nactus es, hanc orna* CWE 33 240–2 and III iii 1:
    Sileni Alcibiadis CWE 34 275. The classic case is his satire *Julius exclusus* CWE
    27 168–97. Cochlaeus (*Dialogus* 23–8) vigorously defends 'the usefulness of
    priests against the Turks' in four chapters, attacking Luther's strictures and
    demonstrating how churchmen have been involved in successful crusades in
    the past; see also Luther's *Vom Kriege* in *Works* 46 167–9.
218 See n142 above; Ambrose was bishop of Milan AD 373–397.

win a multitude for his Father, by his goodness bound the worthy and the unworthy to him, and cured all manner of sickness. These are truly exalted and kingly acts; by comparison, all the military duties of aristocracy are plebeian and even servile. I am not taking from princes the honour due to them, which Paul too grants them;[219] I am suggesting an order of precedence. And yet it happens (and I don't know how) that many churchmen neglect their more honourable role and busy themselves with lower things, even though no one who possesses jewels and gold is so stupid as to despise them and find more joy in lead and iron. How badly the words go together: cardinal-commander, bishop-general, abbot-lieutenant, priest-sergeant; they are like a statue that is half gems and half mud, or a centaur, a mixture of man and horse.

I would not argue that every one of them should be deprived of his possessions in an armed uprising, but if the Lord were to inspire the servants of his church to lay aside – voluntarily – their worldly wealth, I believe that Christianity would be none the worse for it and that they themselves would gain not a little more respect and peace of mind. It would be only fair to leave them sufficient income to ensure them an honourable, decent, and even dignified standard of living. The probity of their lives and the excellence of their holy teaching would add to their influence. In only one situation would they become involved with princes: if ever the latter, through inexperience, anger, or ambition, were inclining towards tyranny, they would guide them to the proper path by wholesome and fatherly admonition. But in truth those who occupy the next place to Christ should be unsullied by these more mundane duties. In Britain both churchmen and rich revenues are held in high esteem. Yet in that country no bishop or abbot possesses a scrap of land outside the church, no fortresses, no cannon, no armed retainers. None of them mints his own coins, with the single exception of the archbishops of Canterbury, and that only as a mark of respect: the death of St Thomas of Acre procured them this honour. The archbishop is never involved in any warlike business, but takes care of his churches.[220]

* * * * *

219 For example in Rom 13:1–7 and Titus 3:1
220 This eulogy doubtless arises from Erasmus' warm feelings for William Warham; see Dominic Baker-Smith ' "Inglorious glory": 1513 and the Humanist Attack on Chivalry' in *Chivalry in the Renaissance* ed S. Anglo (Woodbridge 1990) 133–6. According to Rogers Ruding *Annals of the Coinage of Great Britain* (London 1840) II 180–2, the privileges of the archiepiscopal mint at Canterbury, revoked in the tenth century, were restored by Richard I in 1189, nineteen years after the murder of St Thomas Becket (coins struck by Warham were known to Ruding). The title *Acrensis* (of Acre) was inscribed on a lead

However, I fear that one may wish, rather than hope, to see others follow this pattern; and it is useless to attempt reform by violence.

To sum up, the people will be less suspicious if they see their lawful sovereigns conduct the business in a spirit of harmony, and if most of the funds are entrusted to the leading states so that it is ready for use whenever the need arises. If all suspicion is to be avoided, the campaign must not be made an excuse for undermining the freedoms and the laws of the states, or of the Christian kings and princes. As far as possible the immunity of the churches must be preserved so that, while we make ill-starred plans to ensure peace on the Turkish front, we do not harass all Christendom with civil war and, while destroying the Turks' tyranny, bring a new tyranny, worse than the Turks', upon ourselves.

Now, although no war, and this one especially, the most serious of all, can be fought completely without money, the demands made must be moderate, to allow the poor to survive. Let the princes bear in mind the wars, betrothals, coronations, foreign tours, direct and indirect taxes, monopolies, changes in the value of money, and countless other factors that have impoverished the people and exhausted the state coffers over many years, and how much hardship is still being caused by the shortage of essentials and by poverty. If you want something, you must pay four times the true price.[221] But does not everyone know that hunger and thirst lead to revolt? Moses found that out long ago.[222] And still we see almost the whole burden falling on the peasants and the poorest classes.

I can already hear some people yelling: 'Let those rich, ignorant, pleasure-besotted abbots be plundered! And those bishops, who squander their princely fortunes! And those canons, burdened with benefices, yet living as they please!' Revolutionary words! Why not yell, at the same time: 'Let all the rich men be plundered! And the officers of state and the aristocrats!'? For some of these too hoard their riches or, worse, fritter them away. But not all bishops are the same, and there have to be bishops, just as there have to be officers of state. What is more, the precedent of plundering the bad ones opens the door to indiscriminate plundering. It is fairer to protect the good by sparing the bad than to inflict injustice on them while justly punishing the wicked. Not to mention the fact that a tendency to suspect

* * * * *

tablet in Canterbury; cf the colloquy *Peregrinatio religionis ergo* CWE 40 642. On continental episcopal mints and their role in debasing the coinage in Erasmus' time, see CWE 1 317–18 and 327–8.
221 Cf n212 above.
222 See Exodus 16.

the worst often misleads the people, and that intolerable wickedness can be punished by lawful means; moreover, there will be fewer bad ones overall if good men are chosen. Finally, it will make little difference if money is snatched from these squanderers only to be squandered still more recklessly. The envy of soldiers and people towards the wealth and ease of the clergy is an old sore; if the princes were to pander to it now they would merely be adding fuel to the flames.[223] 'The war,' they say, 'is being fought for Christianity; it is right that they should pay the most.' What is this I hear? The princes and people have no connection with Christianity? Do not princes take up their office on the specific understanding that they will safeguard the peace of Christendom? If they do so, are they doing more than fulfilling the oath they swore? And when the people take arms, is it not merely a duty they cannot shirk without committing the most serious offence? 'We are fighting,' they say, 'for a crowd of idlers.' No, you are fighting for yourselves, when you go to war for your wives and children, 'for hearth and home,'[224] as the saying goes, for your churches and your priests. The latter are not idlers; they have a special role, which is to pray, teach, give consolation and counsel, and perform the sacred rites; they beg God to forgive the sins of the people and obtain victory for your arms by their prayers. We may justly call them idlers if Moses was idle when, throughout the Hebrews' battle against the Amalekites, he did no more than pray to God. But the battle was won more by his prayers than by their arms.[225] The eyes keep watch for the whole body, the hands labour for the whole body, the stomach digests for the whole body; each member, working for the whole body, also works for itself.[226] I am suggesting here that, if the clergy cannot be entirely exempted, their contribution should be a moderate one, although it is not unfair that those who possess fiefs should pay in due proportion, and that those who wish to share the spoils share the toils.[227]

* * * * *

223 *Adagia* I ii 9: *Oleum camino addere*
224 An adage not in the *Adagia* but very common in Latin oratory, for example Sallust *Catiline* 52.3 and 59.5 and Cicero *In Catilinam* 4.11.24
225 See Exod 17:8–13, a text cited in crusading orations to define the church's necessary role; cf Heath cc 17–18. Cochlaeus (*Dialogus* 14 verso) and Eck (*Enchiridion* H 5 recto) exploit it against Luther.
226 Erasmus often uses the commonplace image of the state as a body; see for example *Institutio principis christiani* 1 CWE 27 233–4 and 237. Cf 1 Cor 12:12–26 on the church as the mystical body of Christ.
227 *honoris/oneris* (honour/burden), a favourite pun of Erasmus; cf *Moria* CWE 27 138.

There is a way to find sufficient finance for the war, without over-burdening the people, if the princes will cut down on unnecessary expenditure, and if they do, they will see how much extra revenue remains in their coffers. Could anyone reckon up exactly how much they waste on parades, presents, banquets, elaborate embassies, games, and gambling? If they think it holy and pious to fight the Turks, what alms could they offer more pleasing to God than to increase their revenues by thrift[228] and to divert their money from useless pageantry to works of piety? What I say about princes must also be applied to anyone who is rich. It will be doubly pleasing to God if what is spent on this holy work has been diverted from unholy works. In this way, no one will be poorer for contributing, and all will be richer by the extra deposit of virtue.

The people's suspicions would also be diminished if decisions, once made, were carried forward more quickly. Until now, the money has been collected at top speed but the task completed at dead slow, if not full stop.

It remains to reply briefly to those who maintain that this war has nothing to do with the Christian religion but that it is merely a struggle for the throne of Hungary between two princes; the Turk – when asked – has given assistance to one of them but only supports him because he dreads his mighty neighbour, whose realm seems to grow every day and who, in addition, has a brother whose power is awesome even to the Christian princes.[229] It would have been wiser, they say, to share the kingdom with John,[230] or even to abandon it to him entirely, than to stir up so powerful and so bloodthirsty a nation against Christendom.[231] Sometimes it is better to seek an expedient course than to stand on one's rights; sometimes the greatest profit is to be made from giving up one's rights.[232] To tell the

* * * * *

228 An allusion to the Ciceronian maxim *magnum vectigal parsimonia* (thrift is a great source of revenue) which lies at the heart of Erasmus' chapter on royal bookkeeping in the *Institutio principis christiani* 4 CWE 27 262 and n12

229 Erasmus himself suggests in Ep 2211 (to More) that Suleiman's invasion of 1529 was inspired by dread of King Ferdinand and his brother Charles v and raises the suggestion of partition that follows here.

230 John Zápolyai, *voivode* (ruler) of Transylvania (CEBR III 241–3), arrived too late to help King Louis at Mohács (n187 above), and after that disaster offered his services to Suleiman, with whose aid he was installed as ruler in Buda. Ferdinand was elected king of Hungary by another faction, however, and a bitter struggle ensued, continuing even beyond Zapolyai's death in 1540; see Housley *Later Crusades* 129–34.

231 Luther suggested this expedient in the *Vom Kriege* of 1529 (*Works* 46 201–2); Cochlaeus calls it a 'counsel of despair' (*Dialogus* 67 verso).

232 Cf *Institutio principis christiani* 11 CWE 27 284–5.

truth, I myself would have advised surrender had I been asked my advice in earnest; but I have no doubt that Ferdinand, a ruler endowed with
singular wisdom and piety, has good enough reason for the course he has
chosen. It is not my place to comment on matters about which too little is
known. But let the others answer this: do they think it right that in future
the Turks should decide who is, or is not, to be a king? Soon, bishops will
be appointed to suit them! And again, what if God, seeing their cruelty
carried to such extremes, has sent us this chance of putting a stop, at last,
to their insatiable lust for conquest? And if we do not move, do we really
think that they will remain passive, when they have never ceased to extend
the bounds of their realm?

It is already no secret that the emperor's great power, increased but recently when he crushed the French,[233] renders him suspect to some princes,
especially as they know well that the pleasures of power often know no restraint; but such fears are easily allayed by the greater power of gentleness
and humanity in our most excellent emperor. Nevertheless, other accursed
voices are to be heard, claiming that it is easier to be a Christian under
Turkish rule than under the Christian princes or the Roman pontiff.[234] If
such people speak from the heart, either they have no idea at all what it
means to live under Turkish rule, or else they are themselves Turks at heart
and are weary of the Christian faith. Seeing that the Scythians and the Ic-
thyophagi found the Roman empire's yoke insufferable, shall we choose to
place our necks beneath the Turkish yoke?[235] Let them exaggerate to their
heart's content the severity, rapacity, and violence of certain princes: what

* * * * *

233 At Pavia in 1525 and Landriano in 1529; the peace of Cambrai (1529) had just
put an end to the latest outbreak of Hapsburg-Valois rivalry.

234 Some Anabaptists openly proclaimed this: see Williams *Radical Reformation*
186 and 225 and S. Cramer and F. Pijper eds *Bibliotheca Reformatoria Neer-
landica* (The Hague 1903–14) V 646, 648 and VII 344; also Vives *De conditione
vitae christianorum sub Turca* (1529) A 2–3 / *Opera omnia* V 449. But Luther's opponents also attributed this view to him because he had praised the sultan's
character and some Turkish institutions; Cochlaeus *Dialogus* 6, 8 and 61–2, and
Eck *Enchiridion* A 2 recto, who says: 'The Lutherans prefer to have that dog the
Turk as their master rather than their most noble and magnificent emperor.'
In a moment of exasperation, Erasmus expressed a similar wish himself (Ep
1433:14–15).

235 The sense is that even the worst of barbarians, the proverbially uncivilized
Scythians (cf *Adagia* IV ix 85, which describes the Turks as modern Scythians) and the primitive Ichthyophagi (Fish-eaters; see Pliny *Naturalis historia*
6.25 and 32), preferred their liberty to the glorious civilization represented
by Rome.

comparison can there be with the Turks' savagery? What man is there with a little spirit left who would not rather meet his end in battle than endure humiliating slavery under those barbarians? The Jews are in a better case among us than the Christians among the Turks, who treat them less like humans than like packhorses.[236] They kill off the children and old folk, and round up the young men and girls who are fit for labour (and for lust); they collect them and then disperse them all over the land. Should the Christians somehow get together and acquire some property, the Turks will seize it and disperse them to new masters. Should anyone dare to mutter against their law, he is horribly tortured and executed. Should anyone deny the name of Christ, he may end up as a pasha. Anyone choosing to serve in such harsh and humiliating servitude must be a most wretched slave even in his heart of hearts.[237]

But what shall I say about their system of government? Where is the rule of law among them? Whatever pleases the tyrant, that is the law.[238] Where is the power of a parliament? What room is there for philosophy? For schools of theology? For holy sermons? For true religion? Their sect is a mixture of Judaism, Christianity, paganism, and the Arian heresy.[239] They

* * * * *

236 The humiliating enslavement of Christians by the Ottomans was a common-place of crusading oratory (Heath CC 33–7), and the information here was widely available. Erasmus had probably read Vives' *De Europae dissidiis* (1526; see Allen Ep 1847:34–6) and perhaps his *De conditione vitae christianorum sub Turca* of 1529, which contains many of Erasmus' points and was in part a re-ply to the Anabaptists (see n234); More also treated the subject in his *Dialogue Concerning Tyndale* (1528) and returned to it in the *Dialogue of Comfort Against Tribulation* (1534). In 1530 appeared five new editions of the most influential treatise on life in the Ottoman empire, by the former slave George of Hungary, *De moribus, conditionibus et nequitia Turcorum* (c 1480), one of which had an introduction by Luther; see J.A.B. Palmer 'Fr Georgius de Hungaria, OP' *Bulletin of the John Rylands Library* 34 (1951) 44–68 and Schwoebel *Shadow of the Crescent* 208–9.

237 *Mancipii capillos in corde gestet oportet*, literally 'he must wear a slave's haircut in his heart,' an image explained in *Adagia* II iii 28: *Servilis capillus*

238 Erasmus adapts slightly (substituting 'tyrant' for 'prince') a famous maxim of Ulpian, incorporated in the *Digest* of Justinian 1.4.1; cf *Panegyricus* and *Institutio principis christiani* 6 CWE 27 43 and 264.

239 Hostility and ignorance characterize most Christian responses to Islam at this time; cf N. Daniel *Islam and the West: the Making of an Image* (Edinburgh 1960). Available accounts of Muslim doctrine, such as Nicolas of Cusa's *Cribratio Alcorani*, concentrated on the possibility of converting the Turks: see Schwoebel *Shadow of the Crescent* 220–5. Later sixteenth-century travellers did reveal the existence of intellectual culture, including 'schools of theology' and

acknowledge Christ – as just one of the prophets.[240] The Jews do the same, but teach that he was merely human, which is more detestable than the doctrine of the Arians, who recognized Christ as a god, and even a great god, but denied that he was the true God and God by nature, because they held that no creature is God by nature.[241] What! do the Turks prefer that pestilent and wicked man Machumet to Christ, at whose name every knee bows, in heaven, on earth, and in the depths of the earth?[242] Who would not prefer to live in the remotest desert, among lynxes, wolves, leopards, and serpents, than among such people, where every day are to be heard hateful blasphemies against Christ, which it is the greatest impiety to laugh at, though to keep silent is a torment worse than death; to contradict them means certain but lingering death.[243] Let all such ideas be absent from the thoughts of all who love Christ! If fate decrees that some should have the great misfortune to fall beneath the inhuman Turkish yoke, let the limit of their submission be outwardly to serve the barbarians but inwardly to keep Christ in their hearts. Then indeed, like the Israelites who served Pharaoh by making mud bricks,[244] let them cry to the Lord; let them imitate the blessed Lot who, living among the Sodomites, was daily tormented by seeing and hearing the abominable sins of the city;[245] let them imitate the Hebrews, sitting and weeping by the waters of Babylon because they could not sing the Lord's song on Zion;[246] let them do what is allowed, and sing praises to the Lord in their hearts.[247] Let them imitate Daniel,[248] and by fasting and constant prayer beseech the Lord to hear and to free his people from miserable exile.

Again, there are some who consider that the Turk is too strong to be overthrown by an attack, even if the whole of Christendom were to pool its

* * * * *

philosophy: see C.D. Rouillard *The Turk in French History, Thought and Literature (1520–1660)* (Paris no date) especially 315–17.

240 Cf Ep 2643:14.
241 See *In psalmum 85* 70 and n302 above.
242 Cf Phil 2:10.
243 *Mors, nec ea simplex*: the expression in Latin implies torture; cf Livy 40.24.8. In fact, as travellers and Reformers were to point out, the Ottomans exercised a degree of religious toleration in their domains as a matter of policy; cf Heath 'Islamic themes' (n127 above) 297–300.
244 See Exod 1:14.
245 Genesis 19; and see 2 Pet 2:8.
246 See Ps 136/137.
247 Eph 5:19
248 See Daniel 9.

resources of men and money;[249] it would be a battle against a hydra[250] with innumerable heads, not just seven. Even if they were to be crushed in ten battles, they would not lack soldiers to continue the struggle. In addition, it is all too easy to wage war as they do, burning, butchering, destroying, and then retreating; a tiny band of desperate men can wreak total havoc. But this is not the way Christians fight. Therefore, they say, this war cannot be decided by one or two battles, and if it must go on for several years to ensure success, it will consume all the treasure of Christendom and devour all our best generals. And if the price of our victory is so many orphans, widows, and tears, what if victory should fall to the enemy? But, they continue, let us assume that everything falls out as quickly and successfully as we would wish, let us imagine that our armies have seized all the Turk's possessions everywhere: where shall we find garrisons to guard so much territory? Unless perhaps you think we should exterminate all the peoples living there? If we spare the conquered, they will surely plot rebellion, and even if we have crushed every vestige of humanity there, will the neighbours remain quiet? for the Turk has some allies. Shall we therefore allot a garrison to each region, and appoint a governor, until the people are accustomed to our rule? To whom shall we entrust these posts? To cowards and felons? Things will go from bad to worse. To the brave and energetic? We shall deprive ourselves of the leaders we need, and our strength will drain away.

To these arguments I think I must reply that I too do not welcome war against the Turks unless absolute necessity drives us to it. And I admit that victory is scarcely to be expected unless the Lord stands by us; if we have striven to obtain his favour, though we be but a hundred against ten thousand,[251] victory is ours. But it will be futile to promise ourselves this unless a complete and conspicuous reformation of life takes place throughout Christendom. There are so many Christians whom a harsh fate condemns

* * * * *

249 Cf Luther's argument 256 and n231 above. One of the tasks of crusading orators was to persuade their audience that the Turks' reputation for invincibility was a myth; Heath cc 62–70. The ensuing development, on the impracticality of a military solution, seems to be Erasmus' own, reflecting his consistent opposition to all wars of conquest.

250 A reference to Hercules' battle with the hydra of Lerna 'which some say had a hundred heads, some eight, of which one was immortal'; *Adagia* I x 9 *Hydram secas* CWE 32 238

251 Cf Lev 26:8, one of the Lord's promises preceding the threats enumerated by Erasmus earlier (213). In this way he returns to his opening theme, the necessary regeneration of Christendom, and prepares the way for the conclusion.

to suffer the Turkish yoke, and there are probably a good many Turks who are weary of their barbaric tyranny; these last would willingly embrace our faith if they saw a more humane system in the offing;[252] but if it merely means changing one kind of slavery for another, it is easier to bear the one we know.

Furthermore, some people complain that a few Christian princes impose an unbearable yoke on their people, and add something to the burden every day, so that they seem for some time to have been building their own Turkish tyranny; the allegation is not entirely groundless, though I could wish that it were completely without foundation. If you compare the present with the state of things seventy years ago,[253] as our forefathers describe it, it is unbelievable how much the freedom of the people, the status of the towns, the authority of parliaments, and respect for the church's hierarchy have all declined; conversely, how much the power of princes – and their demands – has grown and, in a word, how much more applicable is that too-famous maxim, 'what pleases the prince, that is the law.'[254] Even if our predecessors do not mention these things, the change is abundantly clear from reading annals and documents that are not particularly old. I am not blaming the princes: perhaps our obstinacy deserves to be repressed with a heavier hand. The complaint is more serious when directed at the princes of the church, especially those who manage the Roman pontiff's affairs. If one compares their deeds with those of their predecessors set out in the annals and papal decrees, one discovers an immense difference. If the Lord would consent to inspire them with concerns more exalted than money, honours, and worldly pleasure, many who now shrink from them as from tyrants and bandits would willingly submit to the fathers once more. To remove this suspicion from their minds, it is necessary that these prelates distance themselves from any form of luxury, ambition, avarice, and tyranny.

It is an old complaint that the number of cardinals has much increased;[255] if the supreme pontiff could provide them with ambitions worthy of Christ along with their red hats, the church would indeed have

* * * * *

252 Cf n168 above.
253 This commentary on the growth of absolutism may include a more specific comment on the decline of civil liberties in Erasmus' homeland since the reign of Charles the Bold (1467–77); cf Tracy *Politics* 35–40.
254 See n238 above.
255 Cf Erasmus' complaints about this in Ep 2375:46–54 (1 Sept 1530). In the *Julius exclusus* he presents one such increase as a political manoeuvre (CWE 27 181), whereas Luther in 1520 (*An den christlichen Adel*) protests against the extravagance and uselessness of cardinals, of whom thirty-one had been newly

cause for celebration. For they were called cardinals because, by the sanctity of their lives, the holiness of their learning, and the ardour of their Christian piety, they should be, above all others, the supports[256] on which the house of God is built. Their rank should indeed be owed to outstanding virtue, and their status gives them considerable powers of persuasion so long as wholesome Christianity plays its part. It is to be hoped that there are some such among them, and it may well be that the Lord, moved by the people's prayers, will make them all like this, but in these turbulent times it is as well to offer some redress for grievances. People grumble about the high cost of the title; although elsewhere in the world there are plenty of wealthy bishops, archbishops, and abbots, they complain that everything the cardinals own comes under the pope's jurisdiction; that it takes three or four bishoprics and abbeys, and a host of other livings, to sustain the dignity of one cardinal; that they consort with kings and to some extent wish to be considered superior to kings, which is why some of them strive to rival kings in their flamboyance, and indeed to surpass them. Some critics fear that, from such beginnings, if their ambition overwhelms their piety, they will go on from being the allies of kings to become kings themselves, and eventually the masters of kings. If someone replies: 'What harm is there in such honour being paid to the church?' the critics will at once retort: 'Enough, you perfect fools! The Christian world has enough lords and potentates, even before the ranks of the princes are doubled; fathers are needed, the Christian flock lacks fathers, everywhere there is a dearth of fathers.' Already the more impudent tongues are not afraid to wag against their way of life, contrary to the teaching of Holy Writ, which forbids the people to curse their rulers.[257] Here, although we may stop their mouths on other points, refuting some and putting a more favourable interpretation on others, they can say: 'We are giving away no secrets; these are no vague or ambiguous charges. What all the world knows cannot be hidden; they themselves parade their luxury and pomp before us. Among them we see the authors of schisms;[258] we see some stripped of their office, others

* * * * *

created by Leo x in July 1517, bringing a reported 300,000 ducats to the papal treasury (*Works* 44 141–2).
256 *Cardines* in Latin means 'hinges' or 'supports.'
257 Exod 22:28
258 Probably a reference to the 'schismatic council' at Pisa in 1511, discussed at length in the *Julius exclusus*; see cwe 27 178–85. 'Julius' also describes his exile while a cardinal; ibidem 171–2.

beggared by fines, many thrown into prison, some banished, a few, even, executed!'[259]

Arguments can be found to counter this sort of malicious talk, but nonetheless we should find the people far more willing both to contribute money and to lend a hand if the princes of the church were to apply a Christian moderation to the conduct of their office. In fact, let us all, from highest to lowest, and including everyone in between, ensure that we remove from our hearts and from our lives everything that is hateful in God's sight. For if in Isaiah he turned his face from the offerings of those whose hands were full of blood,[260] there is all the more reason for him to turn from these wars of ours if we march off more laden with sins than with arms. All of this implies that if we make war on the Turks while God is angry, we can expect nothing but woe, defeat, misery, and confusion. But if we are to take the necessary steps and reform our lives to win back God's mercy, the princes must take the lead; it is scarcely to be expected that there will be no one wicked among the people, however desirable that may be. But it does not matter quite so much what the common soldiers are like if the monarchs and generals agree to do what is right. We must all join together and with constant prayers and entreaties beseech the Lord to consent to make this possible.

Now there are some who suspect that the princes are being very devious here; under the pretext of a Turkish war, they will plunder the towns, countryside, and people, overthrow the rule of law, suppress the liberties of the state, remove the authority of parliaments, destroy respect for the church's hierarchy; a tiny clique will govern as the mood takes them, and, in the Turkish fashion, force of arms, and not the rules of honour, will hold sway. Thus it will happen, they say, that just as Octavius, Lepidus, and Antony joined forces to suppress the liberties of the Roman people,[261] so, after a few trumped-up disturbances, pope, emperor, and Turk will make a treaty and betray Christendom.[262] I believe that these impious and

* * * * *

259 Perhaps an allusion to the plight of Cardinal Wolsey, who fell from power in October 1529. Early in 1530 Erasmus reported rumours that the cardinal, virtually a prisoner, might well face execution (Ep 2253:22–6).

260 Cf Isa 1:15.

261 The short-lived triumvirate that avenged the murder of Julius Caesar and instituted a reign of terror from 43 BC

262 Cf Ep 891:31–3, an earlier version of this conspiracy theory from Erasmus himself; see Tracy *Politics* 113–15. Tracy identifies 'collusion among the princes' as one of Erasmus' stock themes (6–7, 38 and n144, 103–4). On 'trumped-up

treasonous suspicions must be utterly rejected and condemned. To my mind, far better things are promised by Clement's goodness, the emperor's piety, King Ferdinand's integrity, the Most Christian King's humanity, and the loyalty of the German princes. The idea of the universal monarchy, which certain princes are supposed to covet,[263] frightens some. 'Even if,' they say, 'we capture all the Turk's possessions, look at the map and you will see how little this is beside the rest of the world; when can we hope for an end of war? The same ambition defeated Alexander, and he failed in his design; it cost the Romans dear, and they never achieved what they pursued with such persistence.' Monarchy is in fact the best thing, given a prince in God's image, but such is human frailty that the safest solution lies in a number of medium-sized powers allied to one another by the bonds of Christianity.

Others fear that the commodities that come to us from Turkish lands will cost more than they do now. They cite the example of sugar, which now costs four times more and is adulterated into the bargain; they feel that there is a danger that the same will happen to all the rest. But, again, I have no doubt that the emperor's sense of justice will take care of this. For it is unfair that all should bear the cost and few take the profit.[264]

Someone will press me here, and say: 'Why such a long speech? Tell us plainly, do you think we should go to war or not?' If the Lord had spoken to me, I should readily speak out; as it is, it is easy to say what I should like to see done – what will actually happen is a different matter. But although I cannot predict the outcome and know too few details about the enterprise, I am supplying material to enable our wise monarchs to debate the matter more perspicaciously. I am not arguing against war, but I am doing

*　*　*　*　*

disturbances,' cf *Adagia* IV i 1: *Dulce bellum inexpertis* LB II 968B in the context of the Turkish war and, more generally, *Institutio principis christiani* 11 CWE 27 284 and *Querela pacis* CWE 27 305–6.

263　Presumably a reference to the ambitions attributed to Charles V. On Erasmus' scorn for the concept, see *Institutio principis christiani* CWE 27 285 and n16 (CWE 28 533).

264　After Selim's conquests in 1516 (see 229 above), Europe lost sugar supplies from Syria; the Turks had little use for sugar and did not encourage the trade. Sugar then became virtually a Spanish monopoly (hence the reference here to Emperor Charles V, who was also king of Spain), being produced principally in Sicily, the Canary Isles, and the new Spanish colonies of the Caribbean. Sugar was so lucrative that it was shipped from the New World in convoy with treasure and pearls, and sugar ships had been attacked in the 1520s by French and English freebooters. See N. Deerr *The History of Sugar* (London 1949) I 76–80, 123 and 147.

my utmost to show how it may be begun and conducted with success. For since we are setting in train the most dangerous of all enterprises, it must either result in total disaster for Christendom or bring complete success. 'What?' you may say, 'must we therefore endure, without striking back, all the ills that Turkish cruelty has inflicted on us for centuries, the ills that afflict us now and threaten us in the future?' It is hard, I know, but it is better to endure any hardship, if it be God's will, than to invite utter ruin.[265]

The best solution of all would be to conquer the Turks' empire in the same way that the apostles conquered all the nations of earth for their emperor, Christ;[266] the best alternative is to conduct an armed campaign in such a way that they will be glad to be defeated. It will be particularly useful if they see that Christianity is not mere words and observe in us hearts and minds worthy of the gospel, and secondly, if worthy evangelists[267] are sent in to reap the harvest, men who will pursue the things that are Christ's, and not their own.[268] Thirdly, if some cannot so quickly be persuaded, let them continue for a time to live under their own law, until gradually they come to agree with us.[269] Long ago, Christian emperors used this method to abolish paganism by degrees.[270] At first they allowed the pagans to live on equal terms with the Christians, in such a way that neither interfered with the other. Then they deprived the idolaters' temples of their privileges. Finally, after forbidding the sacrifice of victims in public, they abolished completely the worship of idols. In this way our religion grew gradually stronger, paganism was stamped out, and the signs of Christ's triumph filled the world.

I thought it worthwhile, distinguished sir, to send you these thoughts, which arise out of my studies, even though they do not make a good match with

* * * * *

265 panolethria; Adagia I x 27
266 A long-standing ideal of Erasmus; cf Institutio principis christiani 11 CWE 27 287 and Querela pacis CWE 27 314, Adagia IV i 1: Dulce bellum inexpertis LB II 966D–E, and the exposition of Psalm 33 326–7 below. Luther suggested the same, on the authority of Paul in Galatians 6:10 (Confutatio 214).
267 Not to be confused with scholastic theologians, though Folly seems to suggest that these might bore the Turks into submission; Moria CWE 27 129.
268 Cf Matt 9:37–8 and Phil 2:21.
269 On the contemporary debate over enforced conversion, see Heath CC 89–99. Erasmus' liberal view is, for once, echoed by Cochlaeus (Dialogus 13–15).
270 This method was used by the emperor Theodosius between 385 and 392; see Ambrose's commendation in De obitu Theodosii 4 PL 16 (1880) 1449 and n9. On Ambrose and Theodosius, see 236 and 252 above.

the subject of war; my aim is to inspire you to propose something better based on the wisdom of the law, in which you have won such high esteem. I beg you urgently to do so. You will thereby uphold the reputation of the Rinck family, whose chief merit, it is agreed by all, is that it has always devoted itself to serving the state to the best of its ability, and continues to do so. May the Lord Jesus preserve you and those dearest to you, my incomparable friend.

From Freiburg, 17 March in the year of our Lord 1530

AN EXPOSITION OF PSALM 33

Enarratio psalmi 33

translated and annotated by

EMILY KEARNS

The *Enarratio psalmi 33* was written in the winter of 1530–1, following what Erasmus describes as a period of apathy and 'writer's block' subsequent to his illness of the preceding summer.[1] It was composed as a gift for Konrad von Thüngen, prince-bishop of Würzburg, a man active in the religious politics of the day and a patron of scholars.[2] The choice of psalm was not Konrad's, nor was it left to Erasmus; the suggestion came from a mysterious 'other' or 'others,'[3] most likely someone close to Konrad and perhaps a mutual connection such as Daniel Stiebar (Epp 2069, 2079, 2128, 2322) or Augustinus Marius (Epp 2303, 2314, 2321, 2361).[4] Erasmus was not happy with the choice. 'Although the Holy Spirit's words nowhere fall short of wonderful fruitfulness' he complains to Sadoleto in March 1531, shortly after the work's completion, 'still, in comparing [the psalms] few seem to me more barren than this one.'[5] He professes displeasure with the result, not perhaps entirely insincerely; in particular, he blames his usual fault of overhasty composition, too deep-seated a habit to overcome, and as in several of the psalm commentaries there are indeed signs of haste and carelessness.

Once the work had been commissioned, we can imagine that Erasmus turned to his patristic predecessors. His justified doubts on the authenticity of the *Breviarium in psalmos* then attributed to Jerome did not normally prevent him from drawing quite heavily on it,[6] but in this case only a brief outline sketch of a commentary on Psalm 33 is preserved; consequently Augustine is the main source among Latin authors, though no doubt Cassiodorus and Arnobius were also quarried.[7] His other important source was the commentary of Basil,[8] to which he refers at least as often as to Augustine. Occasionally, in fact, he does little more than paraphrase one or the other author, taking a set of typological examples from Augustine (283) or a *Parabolae*-type comparison from Basil (335). In other cases, the introduction of particular subject matter may be inspired by its appearance at that point in the commentary of one of his models: the excursus on the tongue (348–51),

* * * * *

1 Allen Ep 2442:3–14
2 On Konrad (c 1466–1540) see CEBR III 321–2.
3 Allen Ep 2442:13, 2443:13–14
4 On Stiebar and Marius see CEBR III 287–8 and II 391–2 respectively.
5 Allen Ep 2443:14–16
6 See introductory note to *In psalmum 85* 6 n19 above.
7 Augustine *Enarratio in psalmum 33* PL 36 300–22 / CCL 38 273–99; Cassiodorus *Expositio in psalmum 33* PL 70 232–41 / CCL 97 293–304; Arnobius the Younger *Commentarium in psalmum 33* PL 53 368–9
8 *Homilia in psalmum 33* PG 29 349–85

for instance, though a favourite Erasmian subject, parallels a similar section in Basil. Elsewhere, however, he takes issue with his predecessors. Augustine's explanation of *ferebatur in manibus suis* in the text of 1 Samuel is far-fetched and inattentive to the Hebrew and Greek texts (291–2 and n97). Basil may show admirable piety when he writes on 'I will bless the Lord at all times,' but his exegesis is still unrealistic and inadequate (315 and n229).

But while Erasmus thus signals his differences with authors he is happy to cite and for whom he feels an overall respect, it seems that conversely he drew some material from predecessors he prefers not to acknowledge. In rejecting Basil's view that it is possible to pray literally 'always,' he adopts a commonsense, verbally based explanation ('always' = 'very often') which is strikingly similar, even in phrasing, to that given by the fourteenth-century biblical scholar Nicholas of Lyra, elsewhere the target of his scorn.[9] Nicholas was criticized mainly for his lack of philological method, but it is clear that an equally significant offence was his overemphasis on the *sensus litteralis* of Scripture and neglect of what Erasmus saw as the more important allegorical senses, faults he consistently associates with the Jewish exegetical tradition on which Nicholas in fact drew. In addition, Chomarat has found other traces of Jewish exegesis in the text.[10] However, Erasmus is unlikely to have delved very far into this unsympathetic terrain: his source in at least one of these instances is the work of Felix Pratensis,[11] which was clearly one of his tools in all the later psalm commentaries and is frequently what is intended by a reference to 'Hebrew experts.' Here, his reluctance to acknowledge his source by name may simply be due to stylistic considerations; the psalm commentaries are heavily imitative of patristic models, and to introduce too many contemporary references would risk striking a jarring note.

In substance, the work is closely akin to most of the other psalm commentaries. Peter Bietenholz has argued that it contains some of Erasmus' most detailed exposition of his views on the providential workings of history and the relationship between literal and allegorical truth.[12] It is certainly in this material, found chiefly in the first section, that the work's main interest lies. Erasmus is able to concentrate so heavily on the theoretical side not because of the psalm itself, but because of its heading:

* * * * *

9 See 316 and n242 and 358 n446 below. On the use made by Erasmus and other biblical humanists of Nicholas of Lyra, see CWE 63 Introduction xxv, xlviii.
10 See 289 n87 and 345 n395 below, with Chomarat *Grammaire et rhétorique* 669.
11 See CWE 63 Introduction xxii.
12 Bietenholz *History and Biography* 13–50, especially 23–6

'A psalm of David when he changed his face before Abimelech, and he dismissed him, and he went away.' This demands an explanation, and in devoting a relatively large proportion of his work to an examination of the events referred to in 1 Samuel (Vulgate 1 Kings) 21 and the discrepancies between that account, the psalm heading, and a third allusion in Mark 2:26, Erasmus is following the lead of his predecessors. The work is nonetheless top-heavy, as its author was aware. But even when he embarks on the exegesis of the psalm itself, he treats the first few verses in much more detail than the rest, and the work gives the impression of hurrying rather desperately to a close which will remain within some sort of bounds.

After the first edition, published by Froben in March 1531, the *Enarratio* was reprinted only in the collected editions: Basel 1540, Leiden 1703–6, Amsterdam 1969– . This translation is based on the Amsterdam text (v-3 92–160, itself established from the first edition), corrected where necessary.

E K

1 Psalmus David quum mutavit vultum suum coram Abimelech, et dimisit eum, et abiit.

2 Benedicam dominum omni tempore; semper laus eius in ore meo.

3 In domino laudabitur anima mea, audiant mansueti et laetentur.

4 Magnificate dominum mecum et exaltemus nomen eius in idipsum.

5 Exquisivi dominum et exaudivit me, et ex omnibus angustiis meis eripuit me.

6 Accedite ad eum et illuminamini, et facies vestrae non confundentur.

7 Hic pauper clamavit et dominus exaudivit eum, et ex omnibus tribulationibus liberavit eum.

8 Immittet angelus domini in circuitu timentium eum et eripiet eos.

9 Gustate et videte quam suavis est dominus; beatus vir qui sperat in eo.

10 Timete dominum, omnes sancti eius, quoniam non est inopia timentibus eum.

11 Divites eguerunt et esurierunt, inquirentes autem dominum non minuentur omni bono.

12 Venite filii, audite me, timorem domini docebo vos.

13 Quis est homo qui vult vitam, qui diligit videre dies bonos?

14 Prohibe linguam tuam a malo, et labia tua ne loquantur dolum.

15 Declina a malo et fac bonum: inquire pacem et persequere eam.

16 Oculi domini super iustos et aures eius in preces eorum.

17 Vultus autem domini super facientes mala, ut perdat de terra memoriam eorum.

18 Clamaverunt iusti, et dominus exaudivit eos, et ex omnibus afflictionibus eripuit eos.

19 Prope est dominus his qui tribulato sunt corde, et humiles spiritu salvabit.

20 Multae tribulationes iustorum, sed de omnibus his liberabit eos Dominus.

21 Custodit dominus omnia ossa eorum, unum ex his non contereretur.

22 Mors peccatorum pessima, et qui oderunt iustum delinquent.

23 Redimit dominus animas servorum suorum, et non delinquent omnes qui confidunt in eo.

1 A psalm of David when he changed his face before Abimelech, and he dismissed him, and he went away.

2 I will bless the Lord at all times: his praise always in my mouth.

3 My soul shall be praised in the Lord: let the gentle hear and be glad.

4 Magnify the Lord with me, and let us exalt his name in itself.

5 I sought out the Lord, and he heard me, and he rescued me from all my troubles.

6 Approach him and be enlightened, and your faces shall not be confounded.

7 This poor man cried out, and the Lord heard him, and delivered him from all his tribulations.

8 The angel of the Lord will send into the camp of those who fear him, and will rescue them.

9 Taste and see how sweet is the Lord; happy is the man who hopes in him.

10 Fear the Lord, all his saints, since those who fear him have no lack.

11 The rich were in need and hungry, but those who seek the Lord will not lose any good thing.

12 Come, you sons, listen to me, I will teach you the fear of the Lord.

13 Who is there that wishes for life, who desires to see good days?

14 Keep your tongue from evil, and let not your lips speak deceit.

15 Turn from evil and do good: seek out peace and pursue it.

16 The eyes of the Lord are upon the righteous, and his ears are towards their prayers.

17 But the face of the Lord is upon those who do evil, to cut off their memory from the earth.

18 The righteous cried out, and the Lord heard them, and rescued them from all their afflictions.

19 The Lord is near to those whose heart is troubled, and he will save the humble in spirit.

20 Many are the tribulations of the righteous, but the Lord will deliver them from all of these.

21 The Lord guards all their bones: not one of them shall be broken.

22 The death of sinners is terrible, and those who hate the righteous man will fail.

23 The Lord redeems the souls of his servants, and none who trusts in him will fail.

TO THE MOST DISTINGUISHED PRELATE AND ILLUSTRIOUS PRINCE
KONRAD, BISHOP OF WÜRZBURG, DUKE OF FRANCONIA,
DESIDERIUS ERASMUS SENDS GREETINGS[1]

I consider it a mark of the highest felicity, most distinguished bishop, that
so great a prince should stoop to receive my humble self, a man of the
lowest rank, among your dependants, and even – such is your generosity – among your friends, and that you should wish this to be known by
signs which are far from ordinary. However, the fact that I had attracted
the favour of a man of outstanding power and influence in both lay and
ecclesiastical spheres, whose pre-eminence is assured by his ancient pedigree, did not give me so much pleasure as the hope I felt that the tem-
pest which currently afflicts the Christian religion might grow calm, since
I saw that Scripture and true piety were dear to the great princes in charge
of the church's affairs. But I should quite rightly be thought ungrateful
if through my own negligence I allowed so desirable a privilege – which,
prompted by a chance occurrence rather than requested by myself, you offered with such affection in your exceptional kindness – to lapse. For with
long silence, or as the Greeks more elegantly put it, 'lack of speech,'[2] mutual good will grows cold, then gradually dies; but it draws nourishment
and strength from correspondence and from small exchanges passing this
way and that.

But in order not to detain your most reverend highness with a futile
letter containing nothing but the ordinary courtesy of a greeting, I have
added a recent small work of mine, a psalm which I have expounded, so
that it may serve not only to remind you of your dependant, but can also
be stored like a gift and drawn from at will, when it may bring you some
pleasure if you are burdened with cares or be of some use when you turn
your attention from outward affairs to spiritual matters – if, that is, there is
anything at all in it that can be of benefit to such a patron. Certainly, I hope
that through you it may bring no little benefit to others. I am sure, best of
shepherds, that whatever inspires or increases piety in the Lord's flock, by
whatever means, you count as your own gain, and I pray that the supreme
prince of shepherds may preserve you as long as possible to care for and
protect that flock.

It was a custom among the ancients for dependants and freedmen to
express their gratitude to their patrons by sending them a small gift from

* * * * *

1 The dedicatory letter is Ep 2428.
2 Ἀπροσηγορία ruins many friendships' is an anonymous quotation in Aristotle
  Nicomachean Ethics 8.5 1157b.

time to time.[3] So please think of this as a little new year's present from a humble client, of meagre fortune but devout heart.

Freiburg im Breisgau, 21 February 1531

* * * * *

3 Erasmus has described himself as Konrad's *cliens* (translated as 'dependant') and now makes explicit the comparison with the Roman relationship of *cliens* and *patronus*, in which a relatively rich and powerful patron gave protection and sometimes financial support to a client in exchange for various services.

AN EXPOSITION OF PSALM 33

There is an immense difference, dearest brothers, between diamond and glass, yet the difference between body and soul is much greater, and by far the greatest distinction is that between divine and human. My reason for choosing to begin thus is the hope that your eyes and ears may become worthy of the performance which, if Christ so grants, I wish to produce for you today. This way in due course you will gain from it both much pleasure and immeasurable profit. Those who frequent amphitheatres to watch gladiatorial combats or actors dancing out a comedy or tragedy bring eyes and ears well matched to such entertainers and leave the theatre worse than they went in. If any among you should possess such eyes and such ears, you ought to pray to the Lord that he will give you in his mercy the eyes of a pure heart to see the things of the spirit and pure ears with which to perceive the secrets of heavenly wisdom. Neither the circumstances of birth nor the physician's art can bestow such eyes or such ears; only he in whose spirit we are born afresh and who makes new the whole man can implant such eyes in our souls and give such ears to our spirit. So, dear brothers, you should continually join together in beseeching his kindness that what our weakness causes us to lack he may lavish on us from his abundant goodness. Otherwise, if you look with human eyes at what is brought before you, I fear that it will seem nothing out of the ordinary, but material just such as one reads in plenty in secular histories also.

But, not to trespass further on your patience, I bring before you Psalm 33. Before we come to the exposition of the psalm, we must carefully investigate its superscription, for if this did not give us the circumstances, who could have guessed them from the actual psalm? The superscription is this: 'A psalm of David when he changed his face before Abimelech, and he dismissed him, and he went away.' The story is found in the first book of Kings, chapter 21,[1] and it will not be out of place to remind you of it in brief so that you will be able to follow the rest more easily. David's great successes had brought the envy of Saul upon him in great measure, and through Jonathan's information he had come to realize just how implacable was the anger of this king, who was absolutely determined to do away with the hated David by any means possible. He saw no hope of safety except in hiding and flight, and he went to Nob in the area of Gilead, one of the priestly cities, where at that time Abimelech, also known as Achis, the great-grandson of Eli, was priest. David fled to him for refuge, alone and unarmed; he trusted no one, and no one could safely give assistance to David or take him in, so terrible is the thunderbolt wielded by the anger of a king, especially when the king is foolish and insane like Saul. 'Like the roaring of a lion,' says the wise son of David 'so is the anger of a king.'[2] And again: 'Heavy is a rock, and sand weighs much, but the anger of a fool weighs more than either.'[3] Anger knows no mercy. It was with such a king – foolish, proud, envious, and maddened all at once – that this David of ours had to deal. The priest Abimelech was astonished that David had come without companions and asked him what had happened. David removed all suspicion from the priest's mind with his reply, saying that the king had commanded him to transact some secret business and wanted no one else to know it: to this end he had told his servants to stay in fixed places until he had accomplished his instructions. This prevented the priest asking any further questions, since he knew that it is unsafe to pry into the secrets of princes. But David was beset by another hazard, that of hunger, and impelled by this he asked if there was any bread to hand, or anything else to put an end to his hunger. His hunger must have been terrible for him to make no distinction between types of food, and it was not safe to ask others for food, in case his identity became known in this way. Abimelech said that he had no bread except the sacred loaves, which no one might touch except the priests; but wanting to help someone in difficulties, he asked

* * * * *

1 The reference to 1 Kings in the text follows the Vulgate title; however most English Bibles apart from the Catholic Douai-Reims version (1582–1609) follow Hebrew precedent in calling it 1 Samuel, the title used in the notes below (in this case the reference is to 1 Sam 21). As Erasmus observes, the proper names can vary in different versions and the translation here retains those used by Erasmus in order to accommodate his remarks at 294 below.
2 Prov 19:12
3 Prov 27:3

whether David's attendants had kept themselves pure from sexual intercourse. Again David concealed the fact that he was alone, and answered
that this was now the third day that his attendants had kept themselves
free from sexual contact, adding that nonetheless something which needs
purification through pure vessels is not itself pure;[4] this is in accordance
with the saying of St Paul, 'To the pure all things are pure.'[5] The priest's
humanity emboldened him to relax somewhat the rigour of the Law, but
David, being of the spirit, teaches that the Law has been set aside whenever a person's safety is imperilled, whether he is pure or impure from
sexual contact. For a human body is holier than any number of holy loaves,
and our Lord in the Gospel approved this deed of David's, using it as
an example to defend himself and his disciples against the slanders of the
Jews.[6]

David refreshed himself and put on the sword of Goliath, with which
he had killed that man[7] – for the sword was preserved, wrapped in cloth
behind the ephod,[8] as something holy, a reminder of a most glorious deed.
He had explained why he had come unaccompanied, but the priest might
wonder why this great warrior had come completely unarmed. He antici-
pated this inquiry, saying that the king's business was so urgent that he had
had no opportunity to arm himself. The priest showed a certain amount of
humanity, but it cost him dear. For when Saul found out from Doeg the
Edomite that Abimelech had given food and weapons to David and had
consulted the Lord on his behalf, he summoned the priests to him and had
them killed; and not content with this, he massacred the whole city of Nob,

* * * * *

4 The text of 1 Sam 21:5, which Erasmus is paraphrasing here, is problematic, and the variant readings may conceal a corruption. Most modern versions agree in essentials with NEB, which concludes the verse 'how much
  more will they [the young men's bodies] be holy today?' But alternatively
  the original sense may have been that since (as usual in war) the weapons
  of the supposed young men were consecrated, they would render even
  common bread holy. Something of this is reflected in the versions used
  by Erasmus: 'and this journey is profane [or, polluted], hence it will be
  sanctified today because of my equipment' (Septuagint); 'further, this journey is polluted, but even so it will be sanctified today in the vessels'
  (Vulgate: 'porro via haec polluta est, sed et ipsa hodie sanctificabitur in
  vasis').
5 Titus 1:15
6 Mark 2:25–6
7 Cf 1 Sam 17:51.
8 A sacred vestment (Exod 28:6–12, 39:2–5); a linen version is worn by Samuel
  (1 Sam 2:18) and David (2 Sam 6:14).

sparing neither infants at the breast, nor the mothers who gave them suck, nor oxen, nor asses.[9] This ruthless cruelty towards the innocent gives an indication of the extent of Saul's hatred of David. Abimelech made a convincing excuse, but anger knows no discrimination, and madness has no ears.

When David found there Doeg the Edomite, who looked after Saul's mules, he thought it unsafe to stay there and fled to Achis the king of Gath, hoping that among a foreign people he would be unknown and escape notice. But at once he was hindered by the fame acquired for him by his courage. He was recognized by Achis' servants, who said, 'Is not this David, the king of the land? Is not this the man for whom the women sang in the marketplace "Saul has killed his thousands, and David his tens of thousands"?' This was the song that had been the chief stimulus of Saul's anger against David, but however much envy the words provoked, they went deeper into David's heart. The servants hated him, it seems, as one who was once an enemy, and they envied the victor his achievement in laying low Goliath, the strongest man of his race; perhaps, too, when they recognized the sword it sharpened their memory of that glorious deed. As for the phrase 'king of the land,' that was relevant not only to Saul but to Achis, king of Gath. What could David expect but death? So he had recourse to a last trick. When the king's attendants brought him to Achis, he 'changed his face,' pretending to be mad and suddenly collapsing in the arms of those who led him, leaning on the doorposts while spittle ran down his beard.[10] Achis, appalled by this horrible sight, asked his servants in anger, 'When you saw a lunatic, why did you bring him for the king to see? Such unlucky sights are not fit for the eyes of a monarch. Do we have no madmen ourselves, that you confront my sight with this show as a novelty?' Thus the king's servants received poor thanks for their pains, and were told to send David away, so that he might not enter the royal palace in his madness. A man was saved by his apparent insanity, when his deserving actions had put his life in danger.

So far I know you think that you have not heard anything important. That is not surprising, since I have shown you only the shell of the nut, you have tasted only the husk of the grain, and I have been showing you, till now, a closed Silenus.[11] If the Lord will deign to be present

* * * * *

9 This part of the story is told in 1 Sam 22:9–19.
10 On Erasmus' interpretation of this episode, see the extended treatment in Screech 223–40.
11 This favourite Erasmian image, particularly useful in expounding figurative interpretations of the Scriptures, is treated most fully in *Adagia* III iii 1. See CWE 63 Introduction xl.

with us, then as we crack open the nut, as we grind fine flour, as we open
the Silenus, your minds will be delighted with spiritual dainties and fed
with health-giving food, and will be astonished in the contemplation of divine wisdom. For the rest, the bare narration of historical fact, there are
many similar stories told in secular history. Ulysses, for instance, feigned
madness in an attempt to be left at home,[12] and Junius Brutus escaped
danger by pretending to be stupid.[13] Those who have committed a crime
often take refuge in such devices, when no other chink is open for their
escape.[14] But no Christian ought to think that there is nothing here but
the simple story of what happened. What happened did not happen accidentally but through God's particular dispensation. 'Particular,' I say, because nothing either among humans or among angels comes about except
by God's choice, but not everything comes about in such a way as to give us
a sketch of higher things. If we open the Silenus, we shall see that in that
human David there is hidden another, more sublime, David, and in Saul
another and more dangerous tyrant. If we open our eyes of faith, in that
famished refugee, exposed to so many dangers, who 'changed his face,' we
shall see him who is truly called the king of heaven and earth, our Lord
Jesus Christ, while in Saul – envious, arrogant, frenzied, and thirsting for
the blood of the innocent – we shall see the perpetual enemy of the human race, the prince of darkness, the lord of this world, in Paul's words,[15]
who was first chosen by God and then, because of his pride, was cast away
from the face of the Lord, as was Saul. It was he who as soon as the world
was created was driven by envy to bring humankind to ruin, and who
spared no device in his attempt to destroy Christ, who was to overthrow
his tyranny.

I have opened the doors, but before we can enter this holy of holies
we must bow our heads; otherwise, if we carry them high, we shall injure ourselves. The doorway is low, but within is revealed the greatness of
what is heavenly. For our sake Christ changed his face even in the Scriptures;[16] let us for his sake change our mouths and our eyes, so that in the
words of this same psalm we may taste and see how sweet the Lord is.

* * * * *

12 To avoid the expedition against Troy; Hyginus *Fabulae* 95, Apollodorus *Epit-
ome* 3.7
13 Livy 1.56
14 Cf *Adagia* III ii 75: *Reperire rimam* 'To find a chink.'
15 Cf Eph 6:12; also John 12:31, 14:30, 16:11.
16 There is a play on *ostium* ('doorway,' literally 'mouth') and *os suum* ('his face'),
perhaps with a reference to John 10:9; cf also Matt 7:13–14, Luke 13:23–4.

The wisdom of the flesh puffs up,[17] and a narrow and low entrance does not admit those who are swollen. So if there is any among you who thinks himself wise – this is Paul's advice – let him become a fool to the world with Christ his king, so that he may be truly wise.[18] Those who are swollen with the philosophy of Aristotle, Averroes, or Plato generally despise the mystical allegories of the Bible; some even laugh at them and take them for fantasies. What remains for such men then but by the same token to reject the authority of Christ and the apostles? We read that Moses put up a bronze serpent in the desert.[19] That is history, I admit, and completely true. But is it nothing else but history? It might be credible if our Lord himself had not explained the figure when he said in the Gospel: 'As the serpent was lifted up in the wilderness, so must the son of man be lifted up.'[20] The prophet Jonah was swallowed by a whale and on the third day spewed out again alive.[21] This is not a fiction: what is told really happened. But is there nothing else it represents to us? We could believe that nothing further is concealed if Christ had not stooped to open the mystery, saying, 'A sign will not be given to them except the sign of Jonah the prophet: as Jonah was in the belly of the whale three days and three nights, so the Son of Man will be in the heart of the earth.'[22] Do you see what power and holiness is enclosed within that Silenus? We read that manna came down from heaven for the Israelites in the desert.[23] It is impious not to believe that the story is true; it is equally impious to believe that it shows nothing more exalted. Our Lord himself both relates the event and shows the allegory when he says that the fathers of the Jews did not eat the true manna – that is, the bread that comes from heaven – but only a representation of that bread.[24] For the true manna was Christ, and the manna that came down in the desert for the Hebrews was a type of Christ. The one manna nourished the body for a little while, the other gives eternal life to both body and soul.

In Jerusalem there was a magnificently constructed and very holy temple. Everyone knows that, but not everyone is aware of the temple's

* * * * *

17 1 Cor 8:1
18 1 Cor 3:18
19 Num 21:8–9
20 John 3:14
21 Jon 1:17–2:10
22 Matt 12:39–40
23 Exod 16:13–36
24 John 6:31

meaning. Yet Christ told us the meaning when he said: 'Destroy this temple, and in three days I will rebuild it.'[25] God does not live in buildings made with hands: rather the whole fullness of divinity in bodily fashion inhabits the true temple, Christ.[26] Do you see how lofty the mystery concealed in that Silenus is, how it demands adoration even from the angels?

It would be a lengthy business to deal with each individual example. When the Lord says to the Jews, 'If you believed Moses, you would believe me, for it was of me that he wrote,'[27] he is saying that the whole of the Old Testament is a prophecy of Christ. And when he speaks of 'the Law and the prophets, down to John,'[28] he makes it clear that the one who was prefigured in the types of the Law and the oracles of the prophets has now come. Shadows yield to the truth; in vain you expect the fulfilment of promises when the thing promised has come before your eyes. Again, when he says, 'Look at the Scriptures, in which you believe you have life,'[29] he is teaching us that the whole of Scripture has a mystical meaning. The Scribes and Pharisees whom he addresses with these words knew the Law and the prophets by heart, but in order to find true life in them, they are told to examine the hidden content. Lastly, in Luke, walking with the two disciples he opened the Scriptures to them, beginning with Moses and all the prophets.[30] What is the meaning of 'opened'? It means he showed them the allegory hidden in the history. What of 'beginning with Moses'? This means 'from the figures of the Pentateuch.' There is a difference between a figure and a prophecy: a figure is a silent person, or an action, that speaks, while a prophecy is words that speak. Both are predictions, though they speak in different ways. During a period of political disturbance at Gabii, Sextus Tarquinius sent a messenger to his father Tarquin the Proud, to ask his advice on what action he should take in these circumstances. His father gave no reply but took the messenger into the garden behind his house, as though for a stroll, and there he cut off the topmost heads of the poppies with the staff he was holding. After this he sent the man away without an answer. The messenger returned from his mission and said that he

* * * * *

25 John 2:19
26 Cf Col 2:9.
27 John 5:46
28 Matt 11:13, Luke 16:16
29 John 5:39
30 Luke 24:27, 32; Erasmus picks up the word 'opened' in verse 32 because it fits with 'opening the Silenus' (278 and n11 above) and opening doors (279 above)

had not been given a reply. Tarquinius asked whether any action had been performed, and the messenger, along with other events, told him about the decapitation of the poppy-heads. He related how and what he had seen, but did not understand the secret; Tarquinius understood that he should remove the heads of the leading men.[31]

This is what the Apostle means when he writes to the Hebrews 'At many times and in many ways God once spoke to our fathers in the prophets.'[32] He spoke through the creation of the world. Everything that we see in this most beautiful of theatres has its own voice, and all speak of the creator's power, wisdom, and goodness. In the words of the psalm, 'The heavens declare the glory of God, and the firmament shows forth the work of his hands: there is neither speech nor language, of which their words are not heard.'[33] So it is not simply that they speak, but that they say something sublime, something worthy above all things of being heard. Is it not something great to know the nature of God, which cannot be seen? The wonderful creation of these things speaks to us of that nature. Is it not a splendid thing to grasp God's eternal virtue and divinity? This too God has revealed to men. He has done this by speaking through the works that he created, as Paul says in his letter to the Romans.[34] But not content with this, he has spoken to us through the precepts of the Law, he has spoken through figures, he has spoken through the prophets,[35] he has spoken through histories with a hidden meaning. The departure from Egypt, the crossing of the Red Sea, the progress through the desert, the 'mansions,' the tent, the pillars of fire and of cloud, the rock from which flowed water, the brazen serpent raised on a stake, the manna dropping down from heaven, the land flowing with milk and honey – these, and all the rest, have their own voice, and speak to us a heavenly wisdom.[36] Again, the passover, the burnt offerings, and countless other rituals speak to us of Christ, provided only

* * * * *

31 The story is in Livy 1.54.6.
32 Heb 1:1
33 Ps 18/19 2, 4. This is a literal translation of the Vulgate text; NEB has 'and this without speech or language or sound of any voice.'
34 Rom 1:20
35 This phrase is from the Nicene Creed.
36 The events during the passage of the Israelites from Egypt to the promised land described in Exodus have traditionally been interpreted (from the Gospels onward, as Erasmus mentions above) as referring typologically to the salvation of the world through Christ's sacrifice. The 'mansions' are the resting-places on the journey, equivalent to stages of spiritual progress; see *In psalmum* 22 189 and n419 above.

that we are not deaf. The Stoics were deaf, claiming that the world was not created.[37] The Epicureans were deaf, claiming that God does not direct it. Anaxagoras was deaf, denying that God exists.[38] And today the Jews are deaf, refusing to understand the Law in a spiritual sense and still fantasizing about their Messiah, waiting for the restoration of the Temple and the performance of their sacrifices. Yet John the Baptist showed that such figures are a representation of Christ, when he said: 'Behold the lamb of God, behold him who takes away the sin of the world.'[39] What else was he saying but this: 'You celebrate the passover with the old observances, sacrificing a lamb without blemish, the blood of which once freed you from the angel of destruction. But this is the true lamb – not of Moses, but of God – who alone will cleanse the world of every sin by his own blood.' The most blessed Paul agrees with this: 'Christ our passover is sacrificed. Throw out the old leaven, that you may be a new piece of dough; let us feast in the unleavened bread of sincerity and truth.'[40]

In many other places Paul is good enough to open for us the mystery of the spirit.[41] Moses struck the rock, and water flowed forth.[42] The Jew sees nothing here but the letter. What of Paul? 'They drank from the spiritual rock which accompanied them; and the rock was Christ.'[43] Who would dare to frame an interpretation along these lines if we did not have so sure an authority? Of manna he says: 'They all ate a spiritual food.'[44] But not everyone has eaten manna: it came down only for a certain time. And none among the Jews is saved who has not eaten of that spiritual manna which is

* * * * *

37 Although most Stoics believed in a history of repeated world-cycles, creation was actually an important part of Stoic physical theory; see D.E. Hahm *The Origins of Stoic Cosmology* (Columbus, OH 1977) 57–90. Erasmus' statement would be more true of Aristotle (for example *Physics* 8.1 251b–253a).

38 Anaxagoras was accused of impiety, but on the grounds of his teaching that the sun and moon were not divine, obviously not a position Erasmus would have quarrelled with. The central tenet of his philosophy was that the universe is directed by Mind, which does not sound like an atheistic view, despite Socrates' disappointment with it (Plato *Phaedo* 97B–99). Can Erasmus be thinking of Diagoras of Melos, surnamed the 'godless' or 'atheist' (see n158 below)?

39 John 1:29

40 1 Cor 5:7–8, with the order of clauses changed

41 The following examples are all given in the corresponding place in Augustine's *Enarratio in psalmum 33* 1.3 PL 36 302.

42 Exod 17:6–7

43 1 Cor 10:4

44 1 Cor 10:3

the doctrine of Christ from heaven, learned through faith. Likewise the following: 'They were all under the cloud, and all under Moses were baptized in the cloud and in the sea.'[45] According to the letter this is false, but in an allegorical sense it is entirely true. And what does he say about the sons of Abraham, the one born of a handmaid, the other of a free woman? 'These,' he says, 'are the two testaments.'[46] Again, he shows us a second Abraham, the father of all believers, and another circumcision, the circumcision of the heart, and other sacrifices of sheep: 'Put to death those parts of you that are on earth.'[47] And all through the Epistle to the Hebrews what else does he do but make the whole of the Law spiritual for us, as he writes of a new priest 'after the order of Melchizedek?'[48] In his letter to the Corinthians, he mentions a few events of the Old Testament, and then in order to avoid verbosity in relating individual examples he summarizes them, saying: 'But all these things happened to them in figures, yet they are written for our sakes, in whose time the end of the ages has come.'[49] If 'all things happened to them in figures,' then we must believe that there is nothing in Scripture that is without a spiritual mystery.

In addition, I could cite Peter, the chief of the apostles, who expounds the Flood and the ark in terms of baptism and faith, through which we are received into the church and attain eternal salvation.[50] Again, in Acts, while the Jews understand David's words 'You will not leave my soul in hell, nor suffer your holy one to see corruption' in a simple sense, it is he who dares to affirm that they do not stop short at the literal application to King David, but are a prophecy of Christ, whose soul came back from hell and re-entered his buried body.[51] After this Christ dies no longer, and death has no more dominion over him.[52]

I decided to drive this home with numerous examples, both in order to remedy the error of those who read biblical accounts with little more religious spirit than if they were reading Herodotus or Livy, and also to encourage belief and attentiveness in those who are convinced that Christ lies hidden in all the Scriptures that have come to us through the

* * * * *

45 1 Cor 10:1–2
46 Gal 4:24
47 Col 3:5; literally 'your members,' identified by Paul as the bodily appetites
48 Heb 5–6; the 'new priest' is Christ.
49 Cf 1 Cor 10:11, with a reminiscence of 1 Cor 9:10.
50 1 Pet 3:20–1
51 Acts 2:25–32, quoting Ps 15/16:10
52 Cf Rom 6:9.

Holy Spirit. 'The letter kills,' says Paul, 'the spirit gives life.'[53] The letter does not always kill, but there are occasions when it kills completely, and there are occasions when it is of little or no advantage, when it does not give life unless you come to Christ. The Jew is circumcised and is killed by the letter. The Apostle proclaims: 'If you are circumcised, Christ will profit you nothing.'[54] Those who read of the bronze serpent set up on a stake and of how those who looked on it were cured of snakebite commit no sin in believing the narrative. But what is the advantage? If they believe the result came about through natural causes, there is none. If they credit it to God's power, they gain some benefit, but they are not set free from their sins unless they look on the crucified Christ. In the end, there is life where there is Christ. This principle will be useful to you not only here, but whenever you hear a passage of Scripture read or read it yourselves.

Now, if we may, let us return to the drama which the Holy Spirit has placed before our eyes. It is no novelty in allegorical writings for David to take on the role of Christ; I have discussed this phenomenon at length elsewhere.[55] So our David, strong of hand,[56] to whom his heavenly Father entrusted the kingdom of the church, and whom he anointed with the oil of gladness above all his comrades[57] (whether you adduce Moses or the patriarchs, or the prophets, or him who was higher than the prophets, John the Baptist) – our David, during his efforts to free his chosen ones from the tyranny of the devil, experienced each and every kind of evil wiles. First he had to endure the most devious temptations in the wilderness,[58] in the same way as Saul had begun the assault on David, putting him in danger on the pretext of kinship, not so that he might conquer, but so that he might die.[59] As Saul had his slaves to put his raging cruelty into action, so with the devil: what devices did he not use against Christ through the Scribes and Pharisees, through the impious Jews, taking them as his instruments? He began by sowing secret envy in their hearts, which soon broke out into adverse criticism: 'This man is not from God: he does not keep the sabbath,'

* * * * *

53 2 Cor 3:6
54 Gal 5:2
55 See *In psalmum* 22 125–6, 133–4 above; see also CWE 63 Introduction xxv–xxvii, *In psalmum* 2 78–80. The passage that follows treats the gospel narrative in terms of the story of David and Saul.
56 On 'strong of hand' see *In psalmum* 85 14 n11 above.
57 Cf Heb 1:9, quoting Ps 44:8/45:7.
58 Matt 4:1–11, Mark 1:12–13, Luke 4:1–13
59 1 Sam 18:12–25

'We know that Christ remains for ever,' and 'If this man were a prophet, he would know what sort of woman this is who touches him,' and 'He is a wine-bibber, he dines with tax-collectors and with sinners.'[60] This un- treated wound developed into open abuse: 'You are a Samaritan, you have an evil spirit'; 'He casts out devils through the help of Beelzebub.'[61] From abuse they moved on to stones and to casting him from a high point.[62] Eventually an evil spirit of the Lord[63] attacked first the Scribes, the Phar- isees, and the priests, next the elders and the princes, and finally the whole people, so that with one voice they all shouted out 'Take him away, take him away, crucify him.'[64] Yet on countless occasions that sweetest of musi- cians had played all his tunes, had sounded all the chords of his heavenly music, to take the madness from the minds of the Jews, or at least to lessen it;[65] sometimes he would gently call them to salvation, sometimes exhort them to repent, sometimes promise them everlasting happiness, sometimes refute them with passages from Scripture, and sometimes rebuke them and threaten them with woe if they did not mend their ways. Yet he made no impact, and Saul's anger grew ever worse. He became envious of David's achievements. He was stung by the words of the song 'Saul has slain his thousand, and David his ten thousand';[66] and he was stung by the chil- dren's words 'Blessed is he who comes in the name of the Lord, the king of Israel, Hosanna in the highest.'[67] Often, when the people saw Christ's miracles, they would glorify God, saying, 'A great prophet has risen up among us, and the Lord has visited his people.'[68] This song about Christ spread through the whole of Judaea and also through the neighbouring countries. There was no comparable song about the Phar- isees, because they did nothing comparable. Consequently, they were an- imated by the spirit of Saul, and refused to listen to the words of the wise enchanter,[69] but with Saul they said, 'What is left for him but the

* * * * *

60 Respectively, John 9:16, John 12:34, Luke 7:39, Matt 1:19
61 John 8:48, Luke 11:15
62 John 8:59 and 10:31, Luke 4:29
63 Cf 1 Sam 16:14, referring to the affliction of Saul.
64 John 19:14
65 An allusion to Christ as David, who played the lyre for Saul to cause the 'evil spirit from the Lord' to depart from him (1 Sam 16:14–23). Compare *In psalmum 38* LB V 418D, 420B.
66 1 Sam 18:7–8, also 1 Sam 21:11, 29:5
67 Matt 21:9, Mark 11:10, John 12:13
68 Luke 7:16
69 Ps 57:6/58:5

kingdom, when he has reduced us?'[70] What can be done with an illness which grows worse when medicines are applied to it? What can be done with a wound which is intensified by soothing lotions? He cast out devils, he cleansed lepers, opened the eyes of the blind, made cripples whole, healed the sick, brought the dead to life; he taught, he fed, he encouraged, he promised. The more good he did for them, the more he provoked their hatred towards their benefactor: 'I have shown many good works to you,' he said, 'for which of them do you cast stones at me?'[71] Saul hurled at David the accusation that he was an enemy, and that he was plotting to obtain the throne. What did the Pharisees accuse Christ of? They said that he spurned the Law, that he misled the people, that he uttered blasphemies.

For so many years, then, the devil had exercised his savagery towards the devout, from Abel onwards – or rather, he exercised his savagery on Christ through the members of Christ, working through his own instruments, until the time when Christ himself came and changed his face in front of Achis, although also in front of Abimelech he had changed his voice, concealing his flight and pretending to form an embassy, doing one thing and seeming to do another. In David this seems to be deception, although he had an excuse; in Christ there is nothing akin to falsehood. Everything that happens, happens through the divine plan. There are things which the Lord concealed, things which he pretended, and things which he spoke in a way he knew could not at that time be understood. But there was none of these things that did not lead to our good, and the motive was not pointless deception but tenderness, which humbles itself to accord with our weakness. He was given food by a priest, but the food was sacred loaves, thus forming a prelude to the abandonment of ceremonies and legalisms; and he was given arms by a priest, so that he might use the Law itself to convict those who are quick to claim that they follow the Law but interpret it wrongly. This is the sword that he drew against the Pharisees, puffed up as they were with their false knowledge of the Law; he dealt them a fatal wound with the very object he had received from them.[72] 'Whose son is the Christ?' – he asks for a sword, and they give him one, saying, 'David's.' Our David is now armed; how does he deal the death blow? He says, 'Then how does David, speaking in the spirit, call him Lord, saying "The Lord spoke to my lord; sit on my right hand"'? Struck by this

* * * * *

70 Cf 1 Sam 18:8.
71 John 10:32
72 As David killed Goliath with the latter's sword, 1 Sam 17:51; 277 above

sword they fell silent, because they did not realize that according to the body Christ was known as David's son but according to his divine nature as David's Lord.[73] Again, when the Pharisees spoke ill of him because his disciples plucked ears of wheat as they went through a wheat field on the sabbath, the Lord found his sword from our own passage: 'Have you not read what David did, when he was in need and hungry, how he ate the bread of the Presence, which it was not lawful for any but the priests to eat?'[74] And what was the Pharisees' reply? They did not hear the word but grew silent, wounded by their own sword. They did not dare to deny a deed related in books which even they credited with sacred authority, and they did not dare to condemn the deed, to avoid diminishing the greatness of David's name, their chief boast. But now hear the fatal blow: 'The sabbath is made for man, not man for the sabbath; so the Son of Man is lord even over the sabbath.'[75] Every time we read in the gospel 'And they were not able to reply to him,'[76] our own David drew his sword against proud Goliath. When he was asked which was the greatest commandment in the Law, he asked, 'What do you say it is?' The Pharisee replied, 'That you love the Lord your God with all your heart, all your soul, and all your strength, and your neighbour as yourself.' Abimelech offered him a sword, and with it he aimed at the Pharisee's neck: 'Do this, and you will live.'[77] For the Pharisee was full of hatred, envy, self-importance, and greed; he put his trust in fasting, in wordy prayers, in the width of prayer-shawls, in washing of hands and vessels, ignoring the true purpose of all those things.

Achimelech (some manuscripts give the name in this form) means 'my brother is the king.'[78] The Law is in a sense composed of two parts, the letter or the flesh, and the mystical sense or the soul. These two senses are like brothers; they love to be together and do not wish to be separated. But the Jews tried to pull them apart, using the letter to fight against the spirit. In the same way, Ishmael and Isaac were brothers,[79] but Ishmael was the elder, because according to Paul what comes first is not the spiritual, but that pertain-

* * * * *

73 Matt 22:42–6, Mark 12:35–7, Luke 20:41–4
74 Cf Matt 12:3–4, Mark 2:25.
75 Mark 12:27–8
76 Luke 14:6, a similar episode
77 This is a conflation of two episodes: the sympathetic presentation of a scribe in Mark 12:28–34 (less close is the variant at Matt 22:34–9) and a less sympathetic portrayal of a lawyer's questioning at Luke 10:25–8.
78 So Jerome *De nominibus Hebraicis* PL 23 (1845) 812
79 See 284 n46 above.

ing to the soul,[80] and milk comes before solid food.[81] So Christ, the leader in spiritual teaching, received the sword from his brother with which to cut the throats of proud rabbinic scholars, whose arrogance comes from trust in the letter; yet the letter, if it is torn from their hands and if the spirit is added to it, becomes the living and active word of God, reaching further than any two-edged sword, penetrating as far as the division of soul and spirit, of sinews and of marrow, the discerner of thoughts and of the intention of the heart.[82] For this reason Paul does not give his approval to speaking in tongues, unless a prophet – that is, a spiritual interpreter – is present.[83] Now see the distinction between these two brothers. 'If the whole church were to come together and all were to speak in tongues, and unbelievers or outsiders came in, would they not say you were out of your minds?' Such is the brother born from the handmaid. 'But if they all prophesy,' he says, 'and an unbeliever or outsider enters, he is convicted by all and called to account by all. For the secret parts of his heart are made open, and so falling on his face he will adore God, declaring that God is truly in your midst.'[84]

Abimelech, further, is hungry. He has nothing but a few loaves, which can feed only a small number of people, whereas Christ is the rich head of a household who offers both new and old supplies from his treasure-house,[85] and calls the whole human race to his sumptuous feast – even the weak, the blind, and the lame,[86] not only the Jews, as though they were privileged initiates. Among the Jews so much veneration attached to those loaves that they would rather see a layman die from hunger than give him any part of the sacred loaves. Even today the Jews deny that David ate the loaves, since that is not actually related in the account, which says only that Abimelech gave David the sanctified bread.[87] They believe that David

* * * * *

80 1 Cor 15:46, contrasting *spiritale* 'to do with the spirit,' with *animale* 'to do with the soul or mind'; thus here Erasmus effectively identifies the 'soul' or animating principle (*anima*) with the 'flesh.' Elsewhere (eg 1 Thess 5:23) Paul uses a tripartite division of the human person into body, soul, and spirit, and this too may be used by Erasmus; on his use of 'soul' generally see Screech 96–112.
81 Cf 1 Cor 3:1–2.
82 Heb 4:12
83 1 Cor 14:27–8
84 1 Cor 14:23–5
85 Matt 13:52
86 Probably an allusion to Luke 14:21
87 Erasmus' source for this statement is unknown. On the surface, it may suggest that he had indirect access to contemporary rabbinical exegesis, but equally it is very much the sort of thing he might have guessed for that tradition.

committed both adultery and murder, but not that when his life was in peril
he ate the sacred loaves. Naturally, these are the same people who, although
they rescue an ox which has fallen into a pit, sabbath though it may be,
still accuse the Lord of a terrible crime because he cured human beings
on the sabbath, not with medicines but with words.[88] Moreover, those who
were prevented by their religion from entering the praetorium, so that they
could be pure to eat the passover meal, were not prevented by religion from
leading a holy, innocent, and well-deserving man to the cross. We read that
Abimelech gave the bread, but where do we read that David refused it?
And if he was hungry when he took it, why did he not eat it? He abstained
because of the religious prohibition. Then why did he ask for it? Why did
he plead the purity of the vessels, and the journey? I ask you, what could
be more hair-splitting than these childish refrains? Such are the sophistries
to which the Jews' rabbis sell themselves – would that there were none like
them among Christians! If they press the letter so far, David took only one
sanctified loaf – but in the Gospels of Matthew, Mark, and Luke we read
that he took the bread of the Presence, that he ate it and gave it to his
companions.[89]

It does not make very much difference to the mystical sense whether
the priest's name is Achimelech or Abimelech, as the Greek reads, so long
as we agree that just as John the Baptist presents a typological figure of
setting aside the Law, so Abimelech represents the Mosaic law understood
in a gross sense. Abimelech in Hebrew means 'my father the king.'[90] This
of course is the voice of the Jewish people, constantly boasting that their
father is God and king. The psalmists take over this vaunting of God as
father when they say, 'I have said, you are all gods and children of the
Highest.'[91] It is a king's privilege to give laws, and they boast of this too,
claiming that it was God who gave them this privilege. But they do not
understand the end – that is, that Christ is the perfection of the Law for
salvation to every believer.[92] Consequently, without Christ the Law is death,
or rather there is no Law, because, as Paul says, the Law is spiritual.[93]

* * * * *

88 Cf Matt 12:11, Luke 13:15.
89 There is indeed a discrepancy between the account of 1 Sam 21:6 and those
    given in Matt 12:3–4, Mark 2:25, Luke 6:3–4.
90 Cf Augustine *Enarratio in psalmum* 33 1.4 PL 36 302.
91 Ps 81/82:6
92 Rom 1:16
93 Rom 7:14

You see how lacking in sweetness the Law is if one pays such attention to it: how much trouble it has given us in this passage alone! The Book of Kings gives the priest's name as Achimelech or, the reading I prefer, Abimelech, while Mark has Abiathar instead.[94] (Matthew and Luke do not give the priest's name.) Again, the Book of Kings calls the king of Gath Achis, while the heading of the psalm has Abimelech, although it is certain that the psalm is referring to the same episode, there being no reference elsewhere to David's 'changing his face' in front of any king, being dismissed, and going away. Then there are great discrepancies between the translators of the Septuagint and Jerome's reading. The Septuagint's version is as follows: 'And he changed his face in front of him, and dissembled on that day, and drummed on the city gate, and his spittle flowed down onto his beard, and he was carried in his arms and fell down at the city gates.'[95] Jerome translates as follows: 'And he changed his face in front of Achis, and collapsed into their hands, and struck at the doors of the gate ...' and so on. Again, observe how much Augustine differs from both versions. This is his reading: 'He dissembled [affectabat] and drummed at the doors of the city, and was carried on his own hands, and he fell down at the doors of the gate, and spittle ran down over his beard.'[96] The word given in the Greek version as προσεποιήσατο was perhaps translated by someone as affectabat: for if one dissembles, one 'affects' to see what is not there. But St Augustine's explanation of this passage is that affectabat means that he felt affection for the human race. This interpretation is completely true in its application to Christ, but that is not the sense implied in the words of the passage, and I cannot recall affectare used by any author for affectum esse [be (well) disposed towards]. Certainly προσποιεῖσθαι can only refer to a pretence.

The words given by Jerome as 'and he collapsed into their hands' are read by the Septuagint as καὶ παρεφέρετο ἐν ταῖς χερσὶν αὐτοῦ [and he was carried in his hands/arms], 'and he was carried in his own hands.' This too is ambiguous. The pronoun may or may not be reflexive, referring either to David or to Achis the king, so that he would be held by force in the king's hands like one raving - translated by Jerome as 'to collapse.' St Augustine takes it as David carrying himself in his own arms, and this too

* * * * *

94 1 Sam 21:1, Mark 2:26. I reproduce Erasmus' versions, following the Vulgate and its variants. Most English Bibles give the first name as Ahimelech.
95 Erasmus gives a fair translation of the Septuagint, except that the order has been changed: the 'spittle' clause should come last.
96 *Enarratio in psalmum 33* 1.2 and 9 PL 36 301, 306

has a certain sense. Being unable to support their bodies on their feet, mad-men do in fact support themselves on their hands as they slip over in this direction and that, just as drunkards stagger about and sometimes fall to the ground. But I am not convinced that these words apply to Christ as he held the consecrated bread in his hands and said to his disciples 'this is my body.'[97] This has no relation to the Hebrew original, as Jerome gives it, and the word used by the Septuagint will not permit this sense either. Παραφέρεσθαι means, not to be carried in any manner, but to be carried with force and violence to a place it were better not to go. Again, for Jerome's 'he struck at the doors of the gate,' the Greek version has ἐτυμπάνιζεν, that is, he hit the doors making a great noise. But whether this has any allegorical connection with the body of Christ, which when stretched out on the cross gave out a wondrous noise, I leave for others to consider.[98] Furthermore, the Greek twice has 'the doors of the city,' while Jerome never mentions the city, but has only once 'the doors of the gate.' A reference to the doors of the royal palace seems more reasonable, for just afterwards come the words 'let him not enter my home'[99] – unless we suppose that the king's house was just next to the city gate. That is not impossible, since the castles of rulers usually include one of the city gates, and in Jewish society lawsuits were heard at the gates of the city – a function proper to the king. Support for this supposition is given by the fact that when Absalom was plotting for the crown he would come to the gate in the morning and scrutinize the cases.[100] Again, there are the words of the psalm: 'He will not be confounded when he speaks at the gate with his enemies.'[101] Similarly, as we are told by who-ever it was who contaminated St Jerome's commentary on the psalms – an unforgivable sacrilege, committed I suspect with the aid of material from the Jewish commentaries[102] – David was recognized at the city gate by the

* * * * *

97 Matt 26:26. This is the interpretation of Augustine *Enarratio in psalmum* 33 1.10 PL 36 306 and of Pseudo-Jerome *Breviarium in psalmos* PL 26 (1845) 919.

98 Again, the interpretation of Augustine (*Enarratio in psalmum* 33 1.9, 2.2 PL 36 306, 308) and of Pseudo-Jerome (*Breviarium in psalmos* PL 26 [1845] 919), who compare Christ's body on the cross to the stretched animal skin on a drum. See also F.P. Pickering *Literature and Art in the Middle Ages* (London 1970) 285–307 for the harp or lyre in this context.

99 Most texts of the Vulgate in fact read 'Shall this man enter my home?' while the Septuagint gives 'This man shall not enter ...'

100 2 Sam 15:2–6

101 Ps 126/127:5

102 For Erasmus' views on the *Breviarium in psalmos* see the introductory note to *In psalmum* 85 6 n19 above.

king's servants and, fearing to be killed by them, took refuge in the palace. From all this it seems that although there are discrepancies in the words of the different versions – the Septuagint, Jerome's translation, and the old recension used by Augustine – there is agreement in the basic sense, even though at first glance it appears that there is disagreement here too.

Now we come to another obstacle to delay our progress. The Book of Kings says that David came on his own to Abimelech, while according to the gospel he and his servants ate the sacred loaves. Again, how could they eat *loaves*, when Abimelech gave only one loaf? Some writers explain the first problem by taking the words to mean not literally 'alone,' but 'without his normal retinue'; one who normally travels with fifty servants might be said to come alone if he arrives with only two. It is also possible that David actually gave some of the loaves to his servants who were hidden away somewhere so that he might not be recognized by anyone else. But even if we suppose that David was completely alone, it does not seem to me that the truth of the gospel is in danger, for the question at issue there is what is permissible, not how many people ate the sacred loaves. The priest assumed that David had servants somewhere with him and that he wanted to share the sacred loaves with them. He agreed to this, and gave the loaves. As far as the priest's permission is concerned, then, the servants too ate the loaves. Now nothing in Scripture implies that Abimelech was at fault in this action, so that whether it was David's servants or David alone who ate, we have an equally good example with which to confute the attacks of the Jews. All the same, the servants are mentioned because David was a prophet, considered equal in dignity to a priest. So the Pharisees could have objected, 'How can you compare your disciples with David, who was not completely a layman, as they are?' Obviously they could be compared with David's servants, who were ordinary people – 'when they were starving they were allowed to do what the Law clearly prohibited; will you find fault with my disciples for doing what the Law permits, apart from your objection about the sabbath?'

The problem of 'loaf' or 'loaves' is easily solved. In the Book of Kings, 'bread' [*panis*] means not one loaf of bread, but bread in general, as distinct from other foodstuffs; in the gospel it means a loaf of bread.[103] If, for instance, someone were to say 'For three days now I've eaten nothing but bread [*panem*],' he would be speaking the truth even if he had eaten ten loaves [*panes*] in that time, provided he had not eaten any other kind of food.

* * * * *

103 The word translated above as 'loaf' is the word for 'bread'; Latin expresses 'a loaf of bread' simply as 'a bread.'

The difficulty of the names is apparently more troublesome to explain. Mark gives the name Abiathar, Kings that of Abimelech, but there is also a third name, Achias, in the fourteenth chapter of that same book. Lest we be in any doubt about this last, there is added the name of his father, uncle, grandfather, and great-grandfather: Achias was the son of Achitob, brother of Ichabod, and son of Phineas, who was the son of Eli the priest.[104] Then there is a great difference between the names Abimelech and Achis, which cannot be smoothed over by saying that the similarity of the words gave rise to error. But 'Achias' and 'Achis' are very similar, although one is a priest, one a king. In the parts of the Books of Kings that follow, we read that David took refuge with Achis king of Gath, and fought against Saul under his command.[105] It seems inexplicable that he should have wished to be an ally of the man whom shortly before he had feared so greatly, and so the Jews say that this man was the son of the earlier Achis. He was known as Maoch, not Achis; because his father had rejected David, he abandoned the use of his father's name, and took that of his mother, who was called Macha.[106]

When verbal discrepancies of this sort, or different versions of events, occur in secular authors, however eminent – as frequently they do – we can ascribe them to forgetfulness, ignorance, or some other chance factor. Sometimes, among conflicting narratives, none represents the truth – not surprisingly, when even on the points where they are most in agreement they do not always tell the truth. But when something of this sort seems to be the case in Scripture, any suspicion of forgetfulness or error must be far from the minds of Christians. Livy, Thucydides, Herodotus, Plutarch, and all the rest were learned, eloquent, and careful, but being only human they were sometimes mistaken and can mislead. But the heavenly Spirit whose inspiration gave birth to the Holy Scriptures cannot falter and knows nothing of deceit. If some apparent difficulty occurs to inhibit our understanding, we shall rely on this principle as basic, and when we have made sure that noth-

* * * * *

104 1 Sam 14:3. As Erasmus makes clearer below (297) both Pseudo-Jerome *Breviarium in psalmos* PL 26 (1845) 919 and Basil *Homilia in psalmum* 33 PG 29 349–52 consider that Abimelech and Achis/Achias are the same person.

105 1 Sam 21:10–15, 27:1–28:2

106 The Vulgate reads 'ad Achis filium Mahoc' (1 Sam 27:2) translating Hebrew 'Achis son of Maoch/Mahoc,' but because in Latin Hebrew names are indeclinable, the phrase could also be taken to mean 'Mahoc son of Achis.' But this of course is unlikely to be a Jewish interpretation.

ing is due to the carelessness of copyists, we shall conclude that the verbal differences stimulate our curiosity, and the apparent absurdity is signalling to us to examine a hidden mystery.[107] If we cannot find the mystery, we should recognize that we are slow of wit or unworthy and not blame Scripture; we should try to acquire more learning and repeatedly ask the Lord to open the hidden treasure for us.

In the case of this episode, we see that different names are used, and we agree that this is not due to copyists' errors. We must be sure, then, that this change conceals a mystery. First, it is not in dispute that the priest had two names: in chapter 21 he is called Abimelech, while in chapter 14 of the same book he is Achias (or Aias, as others write it). What then is to prevent him from having three names, since there are some biblical examples of this practice? Some explain the difficulty in another way. Kings calls Abimelech simply 'priest,' while Mark describes Abiathar the chief priest,[108] and these people take the second man to be son of the first. It could then be that the son was chief priest at the time, and that the deeds were those of both men acting in concert. It is not accidental, either, that Matthew and Luke suppress the priest's name, while Mark supplies it but gives a name different from that used in the Book of Kings. 'Priest' is a title that expresses authority, and authority is the important point here. Perhaps if the priest's name had been given it would have lessened the priest's authority in the eyes of some and given an opportunity for denigration. Finally, it is quite likely that the name of Abiathar was both better known and more acceptable to the Jews, since he was the only priest to escape the slaughter and join the circle around David, sharing every danger with him. In chapter 22 we are told that the man who joined David was the son of Abimelech;[109] whether he was also the Abiathar whom Mark calls the high priest is not quite clear, but it is not inherently implausible. Mark then clothed the deed with priestly authority and added the title 'high priest' so that the Jews could not say, 'What does it matter to us what this man or that man did?'

* * * * *

107 This idea is given classic expression by Origen in his *Explanatio in evangelium secundum Ioannem* 13.60 PG 14 521B–C, and is used by Augustine in his commentary on this psalm, specifically in connection with the changes in proper names (*Enarratio in psalmum 33* 1.7 PL 36 305). Erasmus repeats the idea several times in his psalm commentaries, for example *In psalmum 4* CWE 63 239, where he extends it to the providential presence of textual variants.

108 1 Sam 21:1, Mark 2:26

109 1 Sam 22:20

Now, what is the meaning of the name Abimelech? 'The kingdom is
my father's.'[110] Here we have a type of the Jew who asserts the rule of
the letter and tries to drag all people away from the freedom of the spirit
to the slavery of the letter. What does Abiathar mean? 'My father is the
dew.'[111] Here is a people that embraces the spirit of the Law; for them dew
from heaven refreshes the minds of believers with new sustenance. Abimelech is killed: the letter with its rituals is put aside. Abiathar is received
into David's retinue. Where now is the temple of the Jews? Where is their
priesthood, their sacred rites? All has been destroyed, only Abiathar was
saved, who through faith attached himself to David strong of hand.[112] It
was from the letter that Christ received bread and a sword, but he broke
the bread and blessed it, so that it might become spiritual food; he drew the
sword against the proud, refuting them with the evidence of Scripture and
even cutting the throat of the tempter himself. Read the Gospel, and you
will find that when Satan tried to trap Christ by quoting Scripture, Christ
gave no reply except from the Scriptures. 'It is written, you shall not tempt
the Lord your God.' 'It is written, man cannot live by bread alone.' 'It is
written, you shall worship the Lord your God and serve him alone.'[113]

But since a full treatment of this mystery is not particularly germane
to our subject, I will not detain your pious attention any longer but hurry
on to matters especially relevant to our theme. In Kings we have Achis, in
the psalm's heading Abimelech. This divergence does not come about from
an error, but from a mystery. It would not be absurd if we were to believe the opinion of learned and devout men that this king of Gath had two
names, but the early writers on Scripture, including St Basil,[114] have explained the difficulty with a good deal of probability. They think that Achis
was the king's own name, while Abimelech was a sort of extra name shared
by many others. In the same way in Roman society Julius was the individual name of Gaius Caesar, but afterwards the title Caesar came down to all
his successors, and the name Augustus also came to be shared by all. Similarly the names Claudius, Nero, Vespasian, Pius, and Antoninus were common to many individuals. In Egypt also we come across many Pharaohs and

* * * * *

110 Pseudo-Jerome *Breviarium in psalmos* PL 26 (1845) 919, Augustine *Enarratio in
psalmum 33* 1.4 PL 36 302
111 Cf Jerome *De nominibus Hebraicis* PL 23 (1845) 812.
112 On this Davidic formula see *In psalmum 85* 14 n11 above.
113 Matt 4:7, 4, and 10 respectively
114 *Homilia in psalmum 33* PG 29 349–52, the source of much of the detail that
follows

Ptolemies. When Abraham was in Egypt he found the king was Pharaoh, and then Joseph was in Pharaoh's power. Again, three generations later, in the time of Moses, Pharaoh was in power. Then much later Solomon married the daughter of Pharaoh, as we read in 3 Kings chapter 3.[115] In the same way most of the kings of Gath were called Abimelech, although the proper name of this one was Achis. In Genesis 20 we find an Abimelech king of Arare at the time of Abraham.[116] In chapter 26 Abimelech is referred to as king of the same people when Isaac travelled there after his father's death.[117] All the same, as far as I know, we nowhere read that this Achis, king of Gath, was called Abimelech, except in the writings of the early scholars,[118] who thought that the psalm's heading was more appropriate to David in Gath, where he feigned madness, although they admit that it relates to both events. David changed his face in front of two men, Abimelech the priest when he hid his fear and put forward the urgent business of the king, and also Achis when he hid his sanity and behaved outwardly like a madman. This too is to change one's face, just as one who 'feigns hope in his face, buries grief deep in his heart'[119] is obviously changing his face. Furthermore, we read of our Lord that 'his face was going to Jerusalem.'[120] He changed his face when he seemed like a gardener to Mary Magdalen, and when he seemed like a fellow traveller to the disciples on the road to Emmaus.[121]

We have then the reason for the difference in name; it remains to search into the mystery. What is the meaning of 'Abimelech'? 'My father is the king.' And of Achis? 'How is it?'[122] So Abimelech is a name belonging to one who boasts of his noble birth, Achis to one moved by surprise and lack of trust. Now if the Lord has opened your eyes and your ears, here of course you see the doubting people of the synagogue, never ceasing to boast that their father is God, that while other races worship idols, they alone know the one God. You hear them claiming, 'We are the sons of

* * * * *

115 1 Kings 3:1
116 Arare is Erasmus' version, Gerar or Gerara that of the Septuagint and Vulgate texts.
117 Gen 26:1
118 Basil *Homilia in psalmum 33* PG 29 349–52 and Pseudo-Jerome *Breviarium in psalmos* PL 26 (1845) 919
119 Virgil *Aeneid* 1.209
120 Cf Luke 9:53.
121 John 20:15, Luke 24:13–35
122 So Pseudo-Jerome *Breviarium in psalmos* PL 26 (1845) 919 and Augustine *Enarratio in psalmum 33* 1.4 PL 36 302

Abraham, we have never been in servitude to any.'[123] But it is all untrue.
No one knows God the Father who does not know his Son,[124] and those who
deny God by their actions are shameless to claim that they worship him.
For that reason Christ says to them 'Your father is the devil.'[125] And it is
ridiculous for them to boast that they are the sons of Abraham, when they
refuse to imitate Abraham's faith. Lastly, they are lying in claiming never
to have been in servitude to anyone, when they were slaves of the letter, of
every vice, of the devil. I think you now realize the identity of Abimelech,
in front of whom our David changed his face. But this same Abimelech becomes Achis,[126] when on hearing Christ's heavenly teaching and on seeing
his miracles he asks in amazement, casting doubt and suspicion on them,
'How is it?' The man of flesh does not see those things which are valuable
spiritually,[127] and never ceases to say, 'How is it?' Thus Nicodemus asked,
'How can a man be born again, when he is old?'[128] But the same words
can also be the words of one who wishes to learn. So that most holy Virgin
asked the angel, 'How will this be?' and the apostles said, 'Lord, explain
the parable to us.'[129] The Pharisees frequently approached the Lord, apparently in this way, but in order to set a trap for him, not because they were
eager to learn. 'Is it permitted to give tribute to Caesar, or not? Which is
the great commandment in the law? What good thing must I do to gain
eternal life? How did he get his learning? How can he say that his father
is God, when he is the son of the carpenter and Mary, and his brothers are
among us? How can this man be the Christ, when he says that he will die?
How does he perform miracles, when he is a sinner who violates the sabbath? How can he be called the Messiah, when he is from Nazareth, and
we were promised a Christ from Bethlehem?'[130] Abimelech and Achis are
still alive in the Jews of our own day, whom we hear asking, 'How can
the law have been abolished, when God promised us an everlasting testament? How could Christ have been born from a virgin? How can you believe that he was the Messiah, when he did not free his people? How can
one who was crucified, dead, and buried have been God? How could he

* * * * *

123 Cf John 8:33.
124 Cf John 14:6, Matt 11:27.
125 John 8:44
126 This refers back to the supposed meaning of the two names, n122 above.
127 Cf 1 Cor 2:14.
128 John 3:4
129 Luke 1:34, Matt 13:36
130 The questions are based respectively on Matt 22:17, Matt 22:36, Matt 19:16,
     John 7:15, Matt 13:54–6, John 12:34, John 9:16, John 7:41–2.

come to life again when he had been dead?' Unhappy people of Gath! You bury the grace of the gospel and are buried under the weight of a terrible slavery, not only an outward slavery – for that is a trivial disaster – but an enslavement of the mind. Would that the Lord might sometime consent to give them a new heart, so that instead of being people of Gath (a name they do not want, though rejoicing in the reality) they might become Jews, which they love to be called, when nothing could be further from the truth. 'Jew' is the name of one who makes acknowledgement;[131] but what has that to do with those people, who deny Christ with their lips, their hearts, and their deeds? Indeed they not only deny him but assail with blasphemies that name which is to be trembled at and adored even by the angelic powers. It was to this people, full of empty boasts (in accordance with the name Abimelech) and unbelieving (as with the word Achis) that our own David came. For it was in vain that he had sent so many prophets to them, whom they had savagely put to death.[132] What was he to do? He came himself, but he changed his face – not in front of the Father, for the Word remained God with God in that glory which he had before the world was born.[133] He changed his face in front of Achis, taking on the form of a slave, and appeared in the guise of a man.[134] He hid that face which is the splendour of his glory, and took on a human body and came as though masked, in a play. I hope my words will not cause distress; this way was the best for those he came to heal. How could they have endured that glorious visage most like the Father's, when they could not look on the face of Moses after it had received some light from his meeting with God?[135] Moses covered his face with a veil, Christ veiled his divine nature in a mortal body. What could be a greater change of face than for the Word to be made flesh,[136] for the one who is from eternity in the Father's bosom,[137] creator, preserver, and controller of all things, to become an infant crying in the bosom of his mother? He knew hunger, thirst, weariness, grief, and tears; far more, he was taken prisoner, bound, condemned, flogged, scourged, spat upon; was crucified instead of a criminal among criminals and at the end he died

* * * * *

131 Thus Jerome *De nominibus Hebraicis* PL 23 (1845) 853
132 Cf Matt 21:33–40, Luke 20:9–16.
133 Cf John 17:5.
134 Cf Phil 2:7.
135 Exod 34:29–35. Erasmus tacitly corrects the Vulgate, which makes Moses' face 'horned' rather than 'shining.'
136 Cf John 1:14.
137 John 1:18

and was buried. Could not then the angels, whose only delight is to look upon the face of God's son in heaven, truly have said: 'Alas, how he was, how changed from him ...'[138] – from him who with his countenance gives blessed felicity to all the heavenly spirits, compared with whose light the sun is absolute darkness, with whose beauty whatever this world finds delightful is hideous?

It should not affront your piety if when dealing with things that are unspeakable I speak haltingly, in the only way I can, using human words. David pretended to be mad, but in Christ there was no pretence. He hid for a while his divine nature, he did not abandon it; he put on human nature, he did not feign it. In only one circumstance could it seem that there was a pretence: that he took on the role of a guilty person, when it was he who makes all people righteous. But this was not deceit, since head and body are identical. In this sense Christ was in a way a sinner, in that he took onto himself the sins of his own body. Otherwise the words he recited on the cross – 'the words of my sins are far from my salvation'[139] – would not be appropriate to him. If it is true that one who takes another's debt upon himself becomes a debtor, then he who transfers the sins of all mankind to himself becomes in a sense a sinner: for if he is punished on their behalf, he would seem to take on the sins. This David of ours, with his face so changed, was seen by the holy man Isaiah, not with his bodily eyes but with the eyes of prophecy, when he said: 'He has no form or comeliness, and we saw him, and there was no beauty, and we desired him. He was despised, and the last of men, a man of sorrows, acquainted with weakness. His face was as though hidden and despised, and hence we did not esteem him. But he bore our sicknesses, and carried our sorrow; and we thought of him as one afflicted, stricken by God, and humbled.'[140] Up to this point he has drawn a picture of a guilty and condemned man. But what follows? 'But he was wounded for our iniquities, and bruised for our sins. The chastisement of our peace was upon him, and by his stripes we are healed. All we like sheep have gone astray, we have turned every one to his own way, and the Lord has laid on him the iniquity of us all.'[141] Now had he not utterly changed his face when he says in the mystical psalm 'I

* * * * *

138 Virgil *Aeneid* 2.274
139 Ps 21:2/22:1 (cf Matt 27:46, Mark 15:34). The Jerusalem Bible has 'How far from saving me, the words I groan.'
140 Isa 53:2–4
141 Isa 53:5–6

am a worm and no man, scorned by men and rejected by the people'?[142]
You see, my dearest friends, the greatness of the mysteries which are hidden in the Silenus of history. David's action was not great, and yet the sight
that the event represents to us is a marvel even to the angels.

We have done well now to leave David and come to Christ. We have
left the letter that kills, and found the spirit that gives life.[143] Let us be keen
to love that which we understand, and let us strive to imitate the drama
before us. Here I can see several devout and intelligent men who try to
relate individual sections of the narrative to Christ, as I mentioned above.[144]
But in my view there is no need for this. In a narrative there are many
details which owe their existence to the historical context and which have no
allegorical significance; it is sufficient to pick out those elements which most
clearly reflect the truth. However, we should not find fault with the pious
study of those who like to spend their time in such fruitful contemplation.
If nothing else, they certainly keep their minds occupied in holy thoughts
while busy with such things.

So I leave it to others to discover the meaning of *affectare* and *tympa-
nizare*, of falling at the doors of the gate, collapsing into arms, being carried
on his own hands, and of spittle flowing down onto the beard. But I think it
is important to investigate how David's feigning madness or epilepsy in order to escape is relevant to Christ. Pious ears would be shocked if they heard
madness or lunacy attributed to Christ, and yet this is virtually what the
psalm's heading, 'he changed his face,' is saying. They can scarcely endure
the word 'pretence,' and they can not bear 'deceit' at all. And it is not surprising that Christians shudder to hear these words applied to Christ, when
the Jews will not tolerate their application to David. They explain away the
feigned madness with the excuse that the Lord's spirit had then rushed into
him, and indeed when in former times the spirit of prophecy came upon
people, they did behave with apparent madness. Thus Saul himself was
seized by the spirit and prophesied, and elsewhere he danced naked with
the prophets.[145] In 3 Kings 20, when the prophet threatens with death the
man he ordered to wound him and who refused, and when he is wounded
by another and scatters dust over his face to avoid being recognized by the

* * * * *

142 Ps 21:7/22:6
143 Cf 2 Cor 3:6.
144 Erasmus seems to be referring to the commentaries of Pseudo-Jerome and
    Augustine and the issues discussed 291–3 above.
145 1 Sam 18:10, 10:5–6, 10 (we are not told that Saul was naked)

king,[146] he is not far removed from madness, unless we excuse him on the grounds of the working of the spirit. The pagans attribute to their prophets madness, which we prefer to call ecstasy.[147] Whenever a human instrument is activated by divine power, those who are sober think that they are seeing a kind of madness. In this way David can also be exonerated from deceit if you allow that it was true that he had left his servants hidden somewhere; his statement that he was performing the king's business can be seen as true if we take it to mean that the king sent David to do what he forced him to do. Anyone who threatens another with death is in a sense telling him to take care for his safety. Although it is clearly not right for any pious person to lie, it is permissible to use words or actions to deceive one who deserves to be deceived or who is helped by the deception. Achis deserved to be deceived, while it was expedient for Abimelech to be deceived, so that he could have a genuine excuse of ignorance in front of Saul;[148] if that did not stand him in good stead, the rightness of a plan cannot be judged by its outcome.

But whatever the historical sense may be, in attending to matters concerning mysteries let us bring ears receptive to mysteries – then there will be no stumbling block. Let us not desert the footsteps of the apostles. St Paul writes to the Corinthians: 'Because in God's wisdom the world did not know God through wisdom, it pleased God through the folly of preaching to save those who believe.'[149] If God had remained in his own wisdom, no human wisdom, however lofty, could have attained to the knowledge of God. So God descended from that wisdom which passes understanding and in a sense lowered himself to our foolishness, so that gradually, beginning with the simpler lessons, he might raise our slowness of wit to true wisdom. Similarly parents use baby talk with their babies, and the most erudite men adjust themselves to the understanding of inexperienced children – if they did not, their pupils would gain no benefit. The Apostle continues: 'We preach Christ crucified, to the Jews a stumbling-block, to the gentiles folly.'[150] You understand that in Christ perfect wisdom remained present in its entirety, but to human beings he showed an apparent foolishness. Yet

* * * * *

146 1 Kings 20:35–41
147 The key passage for 'the pagans' is Plato *Phaedrus* 265B. On ecstasy and this psalm, especially the link between the mystical sense of Scripture and prophetic madness, see Screech 223–40.
148 1 Sam 22:14–15
149 1 Cor 1:21
150 1 Cor 1:23

under this foolishness is hidden marvellous wisdom if only faith makes the mind receptive to teaching. Then he goes on: 'but to those who are called, both Jews and Greeks, Christ the power of God and the wisdom of God. For what is foolish in God is wiser than men, and what is weak in God is stronger than men.'[151] It was not in front of a random group that David changed his face, but only in front of Abimelech – that is, the Jews, who have ears but do not hear, who have eyes but do not see, who have a heart but one that has become gross so that they understand nothing except the evidence of the senses.[152] When we hear that his own relatives took chains to bind him, saying, 'He has gone mad'; when the Pharisees say, 'You are a Samaritan, and you have a devil,' and 'He has Beelzebub in him, and in Beelzebub he casts out devils,'[153] do we not seem to hear Abimelech saying, 'You saw that the man is mad: why did you bring him to me? Am I lacking in lunatics around me, that you brought this man to rave in my presence? Send him away, so he cannot enter my house.'[154]

Even today, since they have rejected him, the Jews do not have Christ in their synagogue or temple. When he taught in the synagogue in Nazareth, the followers of Abimelech expelled him from the city and took him to a mountain peak so that they could hurl him from the top.[155] In the end, he was crucified and buried outside Jerusalem. Abimelech was affronted at the sight of an epileptic, but far more serious was the affront the Jews felt at the new teaching of Christ – which is what Paul means by 'a stumbling block to the Jews.' Our Lord did not preach to the gentiles, but his teaching as conveyed by Paul seemed to them folly. When Paul preached the gospel in Athens the 'foolishly wise,'[156] that is, those who profess the wisdom of this world, which is in truth foolish, the Stoics and Epicureans, said, 'What does this sower of words' – meaning, a tub-thumper – 'want to say?' 'He seems to be a prophet of new gods.'[157] It seemed stupid to them to promise resurrection of the dead, and stupider that God should have wished to save the whole world through a man condemned and crucified. Their human wisdom had taught them that there can be no return

* * * * *

151 1 Cor 1:24–5
152 Cf Ps 113B/115:5–7.
153 Mark 3:21–2, John 8:48, Mark 3:22
154 1 Sam 21:14, slightly altered
155 Luke 4:29
156 In Greek, μωρόσοφοι. The word, deriving from Lucian *Alexander* 40, is used in a slightly different sense in the *Moria* (CWE 27 88).
157 Acts 17:18

from have-not to have, that human happiness resides in the possession of virtue, that natures which have no affinity cannot coalesce into one. It had even taught some of them that there were no gods.[158]

Now when in John's Gospel our Lord says, 'Yet a little time I am with you, and I go to him who sent me. You will seek me and you will not find me, and where I am you cannot come,' did they not think that this was madness, and say, 'Where will he go that we shall not find him? Perhaps he will go to the diaspora among the gentiles, and teach the races? What is this saying, "You will seek me and you will not find me, and where I am you cannot come?"'[159] And again, when the Lord revealed the mystery of eating and drinking his body and blood, did he not seem even to the disciples to be insane? 'This is a hard saying; who can hear it?' they said. And it is true that for those who have no understanding except that of the flesh, nothing could make less sense than this saying – but according to the Spirit, these same words are spirit and life.[160] And when he said 'Before Abraham was, I am,' they picked up stones to hurl at him as at a madman[161] – for without knowledge of the mystery, the words have no coherence nor sense. By thus changing his face, the Lord deceived even Satan, who is the real Abimelech, the king and father of unbelievers. He attacked a man, and was defeated by the God concealed in the man.

The words 'and he dismissed him, and he went away,' which occur in the heading, are actually referred by some to the fact that Christ was outraged by the Jews' lack of faith and gave the grace of the gospel to the gentiles instead.[162] But the historical context shows that David was in fact dismissed by Achis or Abimelech. In my view it seems easier to suppose that since his outward appearance was one of weakness the Jews made it possible for Christ to carry out his work of redemption. But when Christ was 'dismissed' – as no more than human, as weak, as stupid, as guilty – he 'went away' to perform the rest of his divine mission, which lasted until the moment he cried out on the cross 'It is finished.'[163] That would not have been possible had he not changed his face in front of them, for as Paul says, 'if they had known, they would never have crucified the Lord of

* * * * *

158 The most famous atheist of antiquity was Diagoras of Melos, surnamed 'the godless' (Cicero *De natura deorum* 1.1.2, 23.63).
159 John 7:33–6
160 John 6:61/60, 64/63
161 John 8:58
162 Augustine *Enarratio in psalmum* 33 1.11 PL 36 307
163 John 19:30

glory,'[164] and had Satan not been deceived by the appearance of human weakness, he would never have incited the Jews to sacrifice the victim who freed those held captive for countless ages. So the Son of Man was dismissed, that he might depart, as it was written about him.

But would that among Christians there were none like Abimelech, like Achis, who feel repugnance towards Holy Scripture, who think that Christ's teaching, far removed as it is from the wisdom of this world, is totally insane, when they hear: 'Blessed are the poor in spirit, for theirs is the kingdom of heaven. Blessed are those who mourn, those who hunger and thirst after justice; blessed are the meek, for they shall inherit the earth. Blessed are the pure in heart, for they shall see God.'[165] Love those who hate you, bless those who curse you, do good to those who speak evil of you.'[166] He who does not take up his cross is not worthy of me; he who does not deny himself cannot be my disciple.'[167] He who loves his life will lose it; he who will lose his life will find it.'[168] He who leaves his home, his fields, his wife, and his children for my sake will receive a hundredfold in this world, and everlasting life in the world to come.'[169] To strive towards these ideals is the mark of Christian faith: not always to reach them is due to human weakness, but to laugh them to scorn is a sign of pagan impiety or Jewish unbelief. And when once we have acknowledged Christ we should keep as far from that evil as we may, my dearest friends.

Now in your careful attention please notice that our history mentions three herdsmen. Saul looked after donkeys, we are told in 1 Kings 9, Doeg the Edomite pastured mules, and David was called from sheep to a kingdom.[170] The donkey is a slothful animal, full of lust and suitable for carrying loads. No load is heavier than a burden of sins; this is the woman in whose mouth was placed a talent of lead.[171] And those devoted to the pleasures of the flesh are slow in discerning the precepts of heavenly philosophy. The mule, on the other hand, setting aside the fact that it is even more tolerant of burdens, is sterile and prone to kicking, and is compounded of two species in such a way that it belongs to neither. Clearly, such are those who profess

* * * * *

164 1 Cor 2:8
165 Matt 5:3–5, 8
166 Cf Matt 5:44, Luke 6:27–8.
167 Matt 10:38, Luke 9:23, 14:27; cf Luke 14:33.
168 Matt 10:39 and 16:25, Mark 8:35, Luke 9:24
169 Matt 19:29, Mark 10:29–30, Luke 18:29–30
170 1 Sam 9:3, 21:7, 16:19
171 Zech 5:5–8

Christianity but when judged by their lives and passions are pagan, and who in fact are neither completely pagan nor completely Christian, kicking against God's grace, loaded down with riches and other greedy desires, and bearing no fruit of piety. They are mentioned in Psalm 31: 'With bit and bridle break the jaws of those who do not keep pace with you.'[172] Saul was a mule when he heard the words 'It is hard for you to kick against the goad.'[173] The reins were put on him, and from a mule he became a lamb. Peter was a donkey when he said to our Lord, 'May God favour you, let that not happen.' But the Lord put the harness on him, saying 'You know not the things that are God's; get thee behind me, Satan.'[174] When he received the harness, he was changed into a ram, the flock's leader.[175] As for us, my dear friends, we are sheep – or if we are not, let us take care that we become so, and let us flee from the harsh tyrant Saul and from the murderer Doeg, who slaughtered the priests; let us cling to the flock's shepherd, our own David. A sheep has no need of harness, rein, or spur but recognizes and follows its shepherd's voice.[176] In this way we too should obey Christ's teaching in simplicity, harbouring no doubts about his promises, for he will not deceive or abandon the little sheep that depend on him. And following David's example, let us change our face in front of Abimelech, let us seem fools to the world so that we may be wise to God, let us seem crazed, so that to God we may be sober.[177] Let us imitate St Paul, just as he imitated Jesus Christ. Paul became all things to all men, so that he might benefit all,[178] and he seemed to Festus just as David seemed to Abimelech, when Festus said to him 'Much learning, Paul, has driven you to madness.'[179] And when he asserts his authority to the Corinthians he takes on the role of a fool, saying, 'I have become foolish: you have compelled me' and, in the same epistle, 'Whether we are out of our minds, for God's sake or whether we are sane, for yours.'[180]

* * * * *

172 Ps 31/32:9
173 Acts 9:5; this Saul is not the king, but the future apostle Paul.
174 Cf Matt 16:22–3.
175 The episode immediately preceding that just mentioned relates the selection of Peter as the rock on which the church is to be built: Matt 16:13–20. On the symbolic role of the ram see *In psalmum* 22 135 above and *De bello Turcico* 218 above.
176 Cf John 10:3–5, 16.
177 Cf 1 Cor 1:27, 2 Cor 5:13.
178 Cf 1 Cor 9:19.
179 Acts 26:24
180 2 Cor 12:11, 5:13

We have spent a long time on the psalm's heading, but I hope you do not regret the delay. The field of the psalm is level, and we shall run its course quickly.

'I will bless the Lord at all times.' David speaks, overflowing with joy, as soon as he has escaped the utmost danger to his life. But what does he say? Does he grumble discontentedly at his sufferings? Does he ask 'What will ever be the end of these torments? Adversity succeeds to adversity, danger gives way to danger. I left long since my father, my friends, and kin; I was handed over to my enemies; many times I have been assailed by the king in his madness, my body has scarcely dodged his spear, I scarcely escaped his hands. Murderers were sent to my house, and I only just escaped because my wife told me of it and devised a trick, so that I slipped through the window at night. Again I faced danger in Naioth, and I should have died had not madness from the Lord come upon Saul. Then I faced starvation before Abimelech the priest, and came upon Doeg the Edomite, and then before Achis I met with certain death. When will this series of disasters come to an end?'[181] We hear nothing of this sort. But perhaps we hear words boasting of his cleverness? 'My ingenuity escaped the mad king's spear, my intelligence deceived the priest, my wit deceived king Achis.' We hear nothing like this either. But then do we hear him cursing his enemy, threatening him and planning revenge for a cruel and unjust persecution? Not at all. What do we hear then? He gives thanks to God, whose protection has brought him safely through all dangers; to him he assigns all glory, to him he renounces all vengeance. 'I will bless the Lord at all times.'

The word bless [benedicere] used in this sense is unusual in Latin authors but very frequent in the Bible. It means at once to praise, to thank, to wish well, and to hope for someone, and it may take indifferently the dative or accusative case. Here we have 'I will bless the Lord [Dominum],' but elsewhere you read 'in churches bless to the Lord [Domino].'[182] Similarly the Greeks say both 'I will do good to you [tibi]' and 'I will do you [te] good,' and also 'I bless to you [tibi]' and 'I bless you [te].' This usage was imitated by the Christians, who were not particularly careful about the niceties of diction. I thought I should point this out in passing for the 'sons of grammarians,' so that they might not interrupt us by pointing out this discrepancy.

* * * * *

181 The events are narrated in 1 Sam 18–21.
182 Cf Ps 67:27/68:26: 'In ecclesiis benedicite Deo, Domino . . .' The verb benedicere takes an accusative or a dative of the person praised (or, in biblical contexts, blessed). In classical Latin the dative is almost universal, and it is found also in the Vulgate, for example Pss 102/103:1 and 103/104:1, Daniel 3:57–90 / Song

Clearly, this is the sign that distinguishes a Christian mentality, to give thanks in the midst of afflictions and to pray that those responsible for one's sufferings may repent. You may find many who fast, who give to the poor, who pray frequently, who go about in mean attire, but very few who in the midst of a constant stream of adversities give thanks to God, who do not plot revenge, who even for evil do not return evil. These are the infallible signs by which you may recognize a mind that is truly pious and Christian. Other signs are easy to forge, but I doubt whether anyone could simulate this for long. The Lord gives us this sign in the gospel: 'Blessed are you when men shall curse you, and persecute you, and say all manner of false thing against you for my sake: rejoice and be glad' – how can you tell us to rejoice in affliction? – 'for your reward is great in heaven.'[183] Anyone who is innocent and suffers for the good deeds he has done is suffering persecution for Christ. This is the reason that he says 'false thing,' since for anyone whose bad reputation or suffering is deserved it is sufficient to endure his deserts patiently and by his troubles to learn to win a better reward. In the same way, James says, 'Brothers, think it all joy when you come upon diverse temptations, knowing that the testing of your faith produces endurance, and endurance makes the work complete.'[184] There is a similar sentiment in Paul: 'We glory in afflictions, knowing that affliction produces steadfastness, and steadfastness testing, but testing produces hope; and hope does not deceive.'[185] And again, he says to the Corinthians, 'We are cursed and we bless; we suffer persecution and we bear it; we are slandered and we try to conciliate.'[186] In his second letter to the Corinthians he runs through the list of the troubles and dangers that he had suffered for the gospel, and asserts that he would rather glory in these than in his revelations.[187]

And this is what David says when he has escaped from dreadful danger but expects still worse. He knew that Saul's anger was implacable, yet

* * * * *

of Three Children 35–68. The equivalent Greek word (εὐλογέω) almost always takes an accusative, both in classical Greek and the Greek of the Septuagint; Erasmus argues that this usage has influenced the Latin of the Vulgate, and that no arcane significance attaches to the use of the accusative in the psalm. The rhetorical phrase 'sons of grammarians' contrasts humorously with the lack of grammatical sophistication he attributes to the early Christians; cf Cicero *Ad Atticum* 1.13.1.

183 Matt 5:11–12
184 James 1:2–4
185 Rom 5:3–4
186 1 Cor 4:12–13
187 2 Cor 11:23–30

he does not say, 'Blessed is the Lord who has saved me from Abimelech' but 'I will bless the Lord at all times,' thus committing himself to praising God without ceasing, whatever kind of situation he might face. There are those who believe for a while, and who when tempted give up belief; and like them are those who give thanks to the Lord when things turn out as they hoped but in times of difficulty find fault with him, some people (I tremble to say it) actually even cursing his awesome greatness. Do we not sometimes hear such words from Christians: 'God wronged me when he took away my wife'; 'He dealt harshly with me, depriving me of my children'; 'How did I deserve God's snatching me away in the prime of life?' How different from this was Job, who when he had abundant riches, a flourishing brood of children, and countless friends gave thanks to the Lord and attributed everything to his generosity; yet when he had lost all this and his body was covered with sores, and had no one left except his scold of a wife (not the least part of his troubles) and a few friends whose wrangling increased his grief rather than soothing it, what did he say then? 'The Lord has given and the Lord has taken away; may the Lord's name be blessed.'[188] Human life goes by turns in this way and that, ebbing and flowing like a tide. There is a time for peace, a time for war; a time of plenty, a time of lack; a time for gain, a time to lose what you had gained; a time to be well, a time to be sick; a time to rejoice, a time to mourn; a time to beget children and a time to lose them; a time to marry and a time to refrain from marrying; a time for glory and a time for disgrace; a time for youth and a time for old age; a time to be born and a time to die.[189] Amid such changing situations the man of piety sings the same song: 'As the Lord decided, so it was done: may the Lord's name be blest.'[190] This is exactly the same as Paul's instructions to the Ephesians to 'give thanks to the Lord for all things.'[191] What does 'for all things' mean? For sadness and happiness equally, for all things pleasant and unpleasant. Why for happiness? Because it comes to us through the Lord's gift. Why for sadness? Because he sends it to cleanse us. For undoubtedly the Lord turns all things to good for those who fear and love him.[192] You thank the physician who gives you bitter medicine; do you not thank God who scourges you to correct you, who gives you labour so that he may give you a crown?

* * * * *

188 Job 1:21
189 Cf Eccles 3:1–8.
190 Job 1:21
191 Eph 4:20
192 Cf Rom 8:28.

If the pagans were saved from shipwreck, they gave thanks to Neptune or Venus; if they recovered from illness, they gave thanks to Apollo or Aesculapius; if they married a wife to their taste, they thanked Juno, Maker of Weddings; if they attained power, they thanked Jupiter; if they became rich, they thanked Mercury or Hercules. These blind, unhappy people thanked evil demons for the good things sent by God, and instead of singing praises to the munificence of a kind deity they praised maleficent spirits. But David shows us whom we ought to thank for everything when he says, 'I will bless the Lord.' There is one God, one Lord, whose everlasting providence governs all things. Here someone will ask what we should make of the practice of giving thanks to St Nicholas (or elsewhere St Paul or St Hieron)[193] on the recovery of lost goods, or of going to Compostela to thank St James when saved in shipwreck, or of dedicating votive offerings and a commemorative plaque to the Virgin Mother when recovered from sickness, or of honouring St George or St Barbara when returning safe from battle.[194] My view is that the mother of Christ should always be distinguished from the normal run of saints; she is his mother, and her son is all-powerful. As for the others, individuals can be excused their pious impulses if, acknowledging their own unworthiness and trembling before the greatness of the power that is above all things, they approach God through God's friends and give thanks through them, provided always that they acknowledge God as the source of everything and direct their mind's eyes to him above all. For Christ desires his members to be glorified with the head, and wishes his friends who joined him in affliction to share his honour also. It is true, however, that there is no recommendation or example of this practice in the Bible, whether you search in Old Testament or New. But anyone who thinks that any of the saints has powers which Christ lacks or that any is more ready than God to listen to prayers is in the grip of a grave superstition, not to say impiety. This is not far removed from the blindness of the pagans, who thought that there were many gods and that Apollo could do what Mars could not, Venus could do what Diana could not, and vice versa. We should tolerate human weakness but reject human impiety; and weakness should only be tolerated up to the point where it can lead to better things. But safest and

* * * * *

193 Hieron was a ninth-century Irish saint buried at Noordwijk in the Netherlands; cf *Enchiridion* CWE 66 64.
194 This statement recalls some well-known passages in Erasmus' works; see *In psalmum 85* 16 n21 above. The concessive tone adopted here, however, resembles more closely the treatment of the theme in *In psalmum 4*; see CWE 63 218 and n253.

best is the teaching of the Holy Spirit, and Christ's instructions are preferable to human importations. Christ showed us not only what we ought to
pray for, but from where we should seek it.

Now join me in looking at the examples given us by the devout. When
Moses and the Hebrews came safely through the Red Sea while the Egyptians drowned, whose greatness did he proclaim, whom did he thank? Was
it Abraham, was it Job[195] or Melchizedek? What did he sing? 'Let us sing to
the Lord, for he is magnified in his glory' are his words.[196] What of those
three holy children, when the angel made the flame grow cool? They did
not give thanks to the angel, who was simply an agent; what did they sing?
'Blessed are you, Lord, God of our fathers.'[197] When the children of Israel returned to Jerusalem from exile in Babylon, whom did they proclaim, whom
thank? 'Hymns are due to you, O God, in Zion.'[198] When Solomon had completed the temple, whom did he praise? Not the people, not the craftsmen,
not himself; instead he said, 'Blessed is the Lord God of Israel.'[199] But what
need is there to go on? The whole Book of Psalms is full of such phrases
as 'Sing to the Lord, rejoice in the Lord, bless the Lord,'[200] and all of Scripture is in agreement. What does Zechariah say in the Gospel? 'Blessed is
the Lord God of Israel.'[201] What does Mary say, pregnant both in womb
and spirit? 'My soul magnifies the Lord.'[202]

Now someone may say, 'Is it wrong to give thanks to a human being
who has deserved them? May we not praise a man endowed with exceptional qualities? If we are right to return favours to those whose kindness
has helped us, why may we not thank them?' If we speak in conformity
with religion, we praise not the man, but God's gifts in the man, which
means that we are praising God in a truer sense than we praise the man.
Similarly, we give thanks, not to the man himself, but to God who gave him
the ability and the will to help us. When Solomon saw the people coming
together to build the temple, he did not give thanks to them but spoke to
the Lord, saying, 'Lord God, strengthen this good will in them.'[203] Similarly

* * * * *

195 Job is the reading of the first and all subsequent editions, but it is clearly a
    slip for Jacob – Job lived after Moses.
196 Exod 15:1, 15:21
197 Dan 3:26, 52/Song of Three Children 3, 29
198 Ps 64:2/65:1
199 1 Kings 8:15
200 Pss 149:1, 99:2/100:1, 102/103:1–2, 20–2
201 Luke 1:68
202 Luke 1:46
203 Cf 1 Kings 8:15–61.

Paul, in 1 Corinthians 12, speaks of the differing gifts of the faithful, which are far from ordinary, and goes on to say 'But one and the same spirit works all these things, distributing them to individuals as he wishes.' A little earlier he says 'It is the same God who works all things in all people,' so that no human pride may claim responsibility for any good quality.[204] In this way St Augustine, speaking to the people on the subject of electing a successor, says, not 'I thank you for agreeing in your votes with my wishes,' but 'I thank God for your good will.'[205] It is safer to praise the dead than the living, but among the dead too whatever we praise we should attribute to God, so that God may be all things in all people.[206] Those who accept alms, also, should speak in this manner; most of them say 'I will pray for you,' but what does 'I will pray for you' mean? 'I will return a favour for your kindness.' It is pious enough to pray for someone who has helped you, but it is more restrained for one who receives alms to say 'Pray for me,' since it is more blessed to give than to receive,[207] unless of course we measure holiness by its clothing.[208] God sees what is concealed underneath. But those who belong to the ordinary crowd of the poor are often more in need of spiritual than of physical help, yet they too say, 'Give me something, and I will pray for you.' But they should give thanks in this manner: 'May the Lord who gave you your good will reward you and increase what he gave.' It is not enough that mind and behaviour are pious; Christians should show their religion in their speech also, and in everything we think, do, experience, and say we should with David bless the Lord, and his praise should be ever on our lips.

Nothing new has been said here; the sentiment sung by the psaltery is echoed by the lyre, which is done (in case anyone thinks this 'tautology'[209] is a fault) so that the saying is fixed more deeply in our minds.[210] It does happen on occasion that the same words are repeated with no fault in style, and on occasion the same idea is repeated in different words. 'Does Demipho say she is no relation of his? Is she said to be no relation by Demipho?'[211] Those

* * * * *

204 1 Cor 12:4–11; Erasmus quotes verses 11 and 6.
205 Augustine Ep 213 CSEL 2 966 / PL 33 966–8
206 1 Cor 15:28
207 Acts 20:35
208 Erasmus is thinking of his frequent target, the mendicant orders, here contrasted with the 'ordinary crowd of the poor'; compare *Exequiae seraphicae* (CWE 40 999–1013, especially 1008, 1013), also published in 1531.
209 In Greek
210 With the following discussion compare *In psalmum 1* CWE 63 55–6.
211 Terence *Phormio* 353

lines from a comedy, but one in good Latin, are thought of highly. So are the words of the most eloquent of orators, speaking of Catiline: 'He went away, left, disappeared, fled.'[212] And there are highly regarded passages from the same author where neither words nor subject matter are repeated exactly, but they are related and similar in intent, such as this: 'What, Tubero, was your drawn sword doing in the battle-line at Pharsalus? Whose body was its sharp edge seeking out? What was the purpose of your weapons? What was in your mind, your eyes, your hands, your burning spirit? What did you wish for, what desire?'[213] The man who by universal consent occupies first place among orators is using all these words for no other reason than to impress upon Caesar that Tubero was in the camp of Caesar's enemies. When similar turns of phrase occur in human writings they are praised, so when they appear in divine ones let us not think of calling them 'twice-served cabbage.'[214] Let us not say, 'It's tedious to hear the same thing over and over,' but rather let us give thanks to the divine wisdom, which adapts itself to our forgetfulness or slowness of wit. The word was made flesh for us: are we surprised that the Holy Spirit tailors his discourse to human understanding? In the same way, a mother puts food already chewed into her baby's mouth and turns the solid food she has digested into milk to give the child she is suckling. If we believe the old Greek saying that what is well said may acceptably be repeated twice or thrice,[215] then, since Scripture contains nothing not of the finest quality, no-one should find repetition irksome, even if the same thing were to be repeated twenty times.

I wanted to point this out because Holy Scripture is full of similar figures, especially in those passages which resemble poetry. It is the same Spirit who is the originator of all Scripture, but at times he changes his language. Just as the same author writes history in one style, a letter to a friend in another, and an epic poem in a third, so the language and style differ between sacred history and the psalms and canticles. The same words are repeated by David when he mourns the death of Absalom his son: 'My son, Absalom, Absalom, my son.'[216] Similarly the psalm has, 'You are my

* * * * *

212 Cicero *In Catilinam* 2.1.5. An intrusive and nonsensical *rediit* 'he returned,' which is not in the first edition, crept into the text in the Basel *Opera omnia* and is repeated in LB.
213 Cicero *Pro Ligario* 9
214 *Adagia* I v 38
215 *Adagia* I ii 49: *Bis ac ter, quod pulchrum est*
216 1 Sam 19:4

God, you are my God,'[217] and again in the Gospel we have, 'Jerusalem, Jerusalem, you who kill the prophets.'[218] Extreme grief brings about its own inspiration,[219] but the other two kinds of repetition are found everywhere. The first type is exemplified by Proverbs 16: 'Pride goes before contrition, and the spirit is raised on high before a fall.'[220] The same thing is said twice, but in different words. Of the first kind is the beginning of the psalm we are considering: 'I will bless the Lord at all times'; then, like an echo, 'his praise will be always on my lips.' We find the same in the verse 'Magnify the Lord with me, and let us exalt his name in itself.'[221] But I will not burden you by giving examples of a phenomenon that is constantly present. Of sayings composed of related sentiments the following may serve as an example: 'Wickedness is redeemed by mercy and truth, and by fear of the Lord one avoids evil'[222] – since fear of the Lord encourages one to works of mercy.

Apart from these, there is a type of statement that includes a reason, called by some *enthymema*.[223] Thus Ecclesiasticus 5: 'Do not say "I have sinned; yet what evil has befallen me?"' The reason for this is added: 'For the avenging Lord is patient in requital.'[224] Often an opposite is added, as in Proverbs 10: 'A wise son makes his father happy, but a foolish son is a sorrow to his mother.'[225] Akin to this is the type where a different sentiment is added, as in the words that follow the last example: 'The treasures of wickedness will be of no avail, but righteousness will deliver from death.'[226] And there are places where a part of the saying appears to be repeated, as here: 'And he has raised up the horn of salvation for us, in the house of David his servant.'[227]

* * * * *

217 Ps 117/118:28
218 Matt 23:27
219 *Afflatum*, translated here as 'inspiration,' is the reading of the first edition but does not quite seem to fit the context. The Basel edition reads *affectum* 'emotion,' which is not an obvious correction: *dolor* does not cause *affectus*, it is an *affectus*. Whatever the precise text, Erasmus is speaking of a kind of repetition which is the product of intense emotion.
220 Prov 16:18
221 Ps 33:4/34:3
222 Prov 16:6
223 Erasmus has considerably simplified the definitions of this figure given in Quintilian *Institutio oratoria* 5.14.1–4, but his examples are close to those at 5.14.24–6.
224 Ecclus / Sir 5:4
225 Prov 10:1
226 Prov 10:2
227 Luke 1:69; 'the house of David' is equivalent to 'us.'

If we were to keep in mind here the precise way in which ancient, especially Hebrew, music worked, we could deal with this more clearly. We read that there were several groups of musicians who took turns to sing or play on different instruments. Sometimes the voice would begin and an instrument repeat the phrase with the appropriate notes; sometimes the instrument would begin and the voice follow, while at other times voices and instruments would sound together.[228] But such music fell into disuse long ago, and only the merest traces of its existence remain for us. It is better then to return to the psalm.

'I will bless the Lord at all times; his praise shall be always in my mouth.' If we hear this with human ears, David's promise seems nonsensical. How is it possible for anyone to praise the Lord at all times and to sing his praises without ceasing, especially with his mouth? In the opinion of some, the problem can be solved by taking the passage to mean the mouth of the mind,[229] mentioned in another psalm: 'I opened my mouth and drew breath,'[230] and in a third: 'Open your mouth wide, and I will fill it.'[231] For our inner man, too, has limbs, ears, eyes, hands, feet, and mouth. Those who feed on heavenly food, who drink the blood of the Son of Man,[232] who are nourished by his flesh, eat with this mouth. Man does not live by bread alone, but by every word that comes forth from the mouth of God.[233] God's speech is food, and is eaten; it is a spring welling up to everlasting life,[234] and is drunk, but with a mouth that is spiritual.

Now I concede that all this is truly and devoutly said, but I am not convinced that it has gone to the heart of the problem. Even the mind cannot always be free for God's praise, for instance when it is occupied in other necessary activities or when it is submerged in sleep. I think rather that the knot can be cut using the same axe which solves the difficulty in the gospel.[235] Our Lord tells his disciples to 'pray constantly,' never to cease

* * * * *

228 Erasmus speculates elsewhere in his psalm commentaries on the original manner of performance of the psalms, perhaps by analogy with what he knew of Greco-Roman comedy: for instance *In psalmum 4* CWE 63 246, *De concordia* LB 488D. For his (on the whole dismissive) attitude to music in general, see J.-C. Margolin *Erasme et la musique* (Paris 1965).

229 Basil *Homilia in psalmum 33* PG 29 353B

230 Ps 118/119:131

231 Ps 80:11/81:10

232 Cf John 6:54/53.

233 Matt 4:4

234 John 4:14

235 Cf *Adagia* I ix 48: *Herculanus nodus*, also I i 16: *Nodum solvere*.

praying.[236] In the human sense this is impossible, but there is an easy solution to the problem if we take it as hyperbole – not a false hyperbole,
but one that stirs us from our apathy by the vehemence of its language.
'Always' then means 'very often.' Anyone offended by the word hyperbole
should know that this figure of speech occurs frequently in the Scriptures,
and is often pointed out by the most orthodox biblical scholars.[237] In addition, nothing could be more frequently used in common speech than this
figure.[238] One who spends most of the day in study is said to be 'constantly
at his studies,' and if we want to refer to somebody who frequently slanders us we say, 'He never ceases to revile us.' Even one of the Lord's own
parables needs this explanation: the widow did not call on the harsh and
wicked judge 'day and night,' but rather she called on him often, whenever
she had the opportunity. She did not implore his help in her sleep, while he
too slept.[239] In this way, one who prays as often as the opportunity presents
itself never ceases to pray. It is in exactly the same sense that Paul tells his
followers to pray without ceasing.[240] We may not speak about Christ, but
certainly Paul, who gives us this precept, did not always pray without ceasing. He tells married couples to agree sometimes to abstain from conjugal
activity, obviously so that they can pray, but bids them return to it lest they
experience more than they can bear, and the devil tempt them;[241] then, since
sexual intercourse precludes prayer, married couples do not always pray.
In the same way we say 'he is always present at the assembly' of one who
is present whenever an assembly is held.[242]

   This seems to me the simplest way of explaining the difficulty. But
another reverent explanation is that when someone's mind has become im-
bued with true piety, so that in everything he does or thinks or speaks he
looks only towards the glory of God, then even when eating or drinking,
even asleep, and I will go so far as to add even at play, even when he is
refreshing his mind with entertaining stories, he is praising the Lord, in

* * * * *

236 Most explicitly at Luke 18:1
237 Jerome in particular is fond of the concept; see for example *Commentarii in
    Ezechielem prophetam* 10.31 (on Ezek 31:2–10) PL 25 (1845) 299C, *Commentarii in
    epistolam ad Galatas* 2.4 (on Gal 4:15–16) PL 26 (1845) 382A.
238 This sentence itself is of course an example.
239 Cf Luke 18:3–5.
240 1 Thess 5:17
241 1 Cor 7:5; the idea is taken further at 317 below (and see n244).
242 This explanation is strikingly similar to that given by the fourteenth-century
    scholar Nicholas of Lyra in his *Postilla super psalterium*; see introductory note
    269 and n9 above.

accordance with Paul's teaching 'Do everything for the glory of God.'[243] Someone who fasts for the sake of his health, to save money, or to attract attention, or from fear of other people, or from meaningless habit, does not praise the Lord. But someone who does not fast so that his physical strength may be adequate for the work that supports his wife and children, or that gives instruction to the people, or that performs some similar work of charity, praises the Lord even when he is not fasting. Someone who sets aside his prayers to render his wife her due praises the Lord in the very action of not praying.[244]

To conclude, then, anyone whose mind is always disposed to prayer when there is time to pray 'always prays.' Just as the whole life of the faithful is a praising of God, so the whole life of the wicked is a blasphemy against God, whether eating, drinking, sleeping, or playing. But Christ, seeking in all things his Father's glory, could rightly say, 'I will bless the Lord at all times; his praise shall be ever on my lips,' and on Christ as head depends his body, the assembly of the faithful, so that it too can say, 'I will bless the Lord at all times; his praise shall be ever on my lips.' Under the natural law, under the law of Moses, under the grace of the gospel; from the world's beginning to its end, the church without ceasing blesses its Lord. Whether wounded by the persecution of rulers, reeling from the obstinacy of heretics, or enjoying an age of peace, God's praise is always on her lips, for she is convinced that however various the shifts of fortune, through him all things will turn out for her good. Each and every member of the church, so long as it remains a living member, has the capacity to say, 'I will bless the Lord at all times; his praise shall be always on my lips.' But that 'always' cannot be realized to the full in this life, which is both short and subject to innumerable tasks that interrupt our song. Only when we have returned from this exile to the heavenly Jerusalem will the Lord's praise be always on our lips. In the words of another psalm: 'Blessed are those who dwell in your house, O Lord; they will praise you for ever and ever.'[245]

The next words are: 'My soul shall be praised in the Lord; let the gentle hear and be glad.' This verse seems to have no connection with the preceding or the following words, the latter being 'Magnify the Lord with me.' Why does the psalm leap so abruptly to praise bestowed on the speaker

* * * * *

243 1 Cor 10:31. With this explanation, compare *In psalmum* 1 CWE 63 29.
244 On the important idea of conjugal debt, based on 1 Cor 7:3, see Thomas N. Tentler *Sin and Confession on the Eve of the Reformation* (Princeton 1977) 170–4.
245 Ps 83:5/84:4

when its starting point is that we should render all praise to God? Now
it says 'My soul will be praised in the Lord.' If we look at these words
more carefully, they are saying the same thing. To be praised in the Lord
is no different from boasting in the Lord, and as Paul says, 'Let him who
boasts, boast in the Lord.'[246] When thanks are given to the Lord for someone, he is praised in the Lord. In fact, some Hebrew scholars translate 'my
soul will boast in the Lord' instead of 'my soul will be praised.'[247] One's
soul is one's life. David was saved, escaping the utmost danger to his life:
those who read or hear this story should praise his soul, not for the ingenuity he showed in deceiving the people of Gath, but for the faith he had in
the Lord. One who praises David as though his own intelligence, his own
wisdom, his adaptability, his presence of mind, or even his good luck were
responsible for his escape from so many dangers, does not praise his soul
in the Lord.

What we have said about David should be applied to all the saints. If
you praise a martyr, praise him in the Lord; if you praise a virgin, praise her
in the Lord. Do not let your praise resemble that of the pagans for their outstanding men who met brave deaths in battle or otherwise deserved well
of the state. Such panegyrics contain no mention of God but glorify the
subject's country, family, riches, strength, fortune, disposition, and intelligence,[248] and in order to advertise his deeds as widely as possible and to
keep his memory alive as long as possible they celebrated them in published works and tried to pass them on to posterity with arches, columns,
and statues. In such cases it is not the soul that is praised, nor is the praise
'praise in the Lord.' The soul is the individual's inmost part, but good fortune and physical superiority lie outside the individual, and since they are
often in the possession of the most reprehensible of people, they do not in
themselves make people praiseworthy. It is mental qualities that really belong to the individual – if he acknowledges their source. Still, if we do have
physical benefits and good fortune, provided we have obtained them honestly, we should thank God for them. The blessed David wanted his deed
to be famous throughout the world through this psalm, not so that he him-

* * * * *

246 1 Cor 1:31
247 A marginal alternative in Felice da Prato's *Psalterium* 18 recto; for Erasmus'
    knowledge of this version see CWE 63 xxii and Ep 456:103.
248 Erasmus describes some of the classical topics of the encomium, as exemplified
    in Pliny's *Panegyricus* to the emperor Trajan. His own *Panegyricus*, addressed
    to Philip of Burgundy and delivered in 1504 (CWE 27 6–75), covers very similar
    ground.

self would have glory, but so that the Lord would have glory in him. He knew that all devout people in future would give thanks to God's goodness for David's miraculous escape and would heap with praises God's wisdom, which allows his own to undergo dangers, which allows the world to try all its weapons against them, so that he may make his name famous through them by showing forth his strength in vessels of clay, as Paul says,[249] by defeating the strong through the weak, by casting down the armed through the defenceless. When the achievements of Alexander the Great are extolled, not without some exaggeration, the Macedonians preen themselves. When Pericles or Themistocles is praised, the Athenians are happy; when Hannibal is celebrated, the Africans feel pride; when it is Julius Caesar's turn, the Romans are overjoyed. 'Such were our men of old,' they say. This sort of pride is doubly stupid, because people are congratulating themselves on the achievements of others and because they assign all praise to human beings. Furthermore, they admire deeds that do not deserve praise. What is it that they praise in such deeds? The destruction of cities, laying waste of fields, slaughter on both sides, a world in the grip of the madness of war; triumphs, statues, and trophies, monuments to pride and arrogance. Those who delight in bloodshed insist that their heroes shed blood, and those who enjoy cruelty in others insist that they are cruel. But David does not desire praise for such deeds or from such men. The Jews exult when Abraham or Moses or David is praised – but it is arrogance to take pride in those they do not imitate. Christian princes should be praised, but praised for Christian stratagems and praised in the Lord, so that not only the Spanish or Germans or French may be pleased, but all who love the Lord. There are those who proclaim St Francis' deeds in a competitive way, so that most in his community congratulate themselves, while the Dominicans snarl in disgust. Then again there are those who vaunt St Dominic in such a way that the heirs of Francis are full of envy, while the Dominicans congratulate themselves and say, 'Such was the man who founded our order.' It may be that some among the Benedictines, the Cistercians, and the Augustinians feel the same way. Such people are indeed praising men who are very dear to God, but they are not praising them in the Lord; neither do those who boast of them in such a manner boast of them in the Lord. Furthermore, the saints themselves take no pleasure in such praise and do not acknowledge those who praise them in this manner as their followers. How could they acknowledge those who are opposed to their principles? The purpose of

* * * * *

249 2 Cor 4:7

Francis' humility and his contempt for riches, glory, and all the world was not to let some men called by his name give free rein to savagery but to cause all to imitate him. The praise of the devout is praise of the whole church in common.

Everyone's soul, then, should boast, but boast in the Lord. They should hear praise, but not be on the lookout here, there, and everywhere for material to feed their pride and arrogance, as even today the Jews glory in David's escape; rather, as the psalm says, 'let the gentle hear and be glad.' One who is mild desires to be praised by the mild. In the literal sense, David was called a man of blood,[250] and he was such a man, even though many examples of his clemency are preserved – towards Saul, towards Absalom, towards Shimei.[251] But he whom David represents, and who says in a psalm 'Remember David, O Lord, and all his kindness'[252] was gentle without exception. Moses, too, is praised as the gentlest of all men (for what is done at God's command cannot be called harshness). But when the true Moses showed us the law of grace, when the true David brought us to the kingdom of heaven, nothing was done through cruelty. No weapons, slaughter, or bloodshed were used, but everything was accomplished with the sword of the spirit, which is the word of God.[253] This was the manner of Christ's warfare, of his victory and triumph. This is the warfare of the apostles, the martyrs, and all who were or are true disciples of Christ and who hear his words: 'Learn from me, that I am mild and lowly of heart, and you will find rest for your souls.'[254] The advice of the fierce is to create peace with war;[255] perhaps this is true of bodily peace, but the true peace of the soul comes only from patient endurance of suffering. Even in the midst of torment and death the martyrs had this peace.

When the warlike hear this, they sneer, but the gentle disciples of Christ hear it and rejoice. Lions hear it and roar, but sheep hear it and receive solace and refreshment. Why do they rejoice? Because they know that the Lord cares for them, and men's cruelty can do nothing against him.

* * * * *

250 2 Sam 16:7–8
251 1 Sam 24, 2 Sam 18:5, and 2 Sam 16:5–13, 19:16–23
252 Ps 131/132:1
253 Eph 6:17
254 Matt 11:29
255 Two slightly different topoi are reflected here. The first is the view that war may legitimately be undertaken to guarantee a lasting peace (for example Cicero *De officiis* 1.23.79); the second is the deterrence theory, expressed most familiarly in the proverbial phrase (Walther 29404a) *Si vis pacem, para bellum* 'If you want peace, prepare for war,' which is conspicuously absent from the *Adagia*.

They know that after they have endured pain for a little while, everlasting life is theirs. So Christ, received into the Father's glory through the shame of the cross, through crucifixion and death, can rightly say, 'My soul will be praised in the Lord; let all my disciples hear, and let all the mild and lowly of heart rejoice.' The victory of the head is the welfare of the members. For us the Lord underwent danger, for us he suffered, for us he emerged victorious and triumphant; so it is right that those who have become one with Christ through faith and baptism should together with him glorify God, who was in his Son, reconciling the world to himself.[256]

'Magnify the Lord with me, and let us exalt his name in itself.' The psalmist seeks a choir worthy of such a task. The most beautiful harmony is when all the members of Christ sing the same song as their head; the sweetest music is when voices differ but the intent is the same. The Hebrew sings, the Greek sings, the Scythian sings, the Thracian sings, the Indian sings, the Frenchman sings, the German sings, the Briton sings: the whole world sings, singing in harmony with Christ its shepherd, magnifying its Lord and exalting his name 'in itself' or 'in unity.'[257] Some manuscripts have the latter reading, which does not affect the sense. In a scriptural text with a mystical application, this word usually denotes the wonderful concord proper to Christ's disciples, who as they are one body so also are they animated by one spirit.[258] This concord is mentioned in another psalm in the words 'Behold how good and how pleasant it is for brothers to dwell together in unity.'[259] The world has its concords, its groups, and societies, heretics have their associations, but that 'in itself' exists nowhere except among those joined together by the spirit of Christ, and nowhere is there true peace or rest except where that 'in unity' exists. This was apparent to the man who said 'In peace, in itself, I will sleep and take my rest.'[260]

The Lord wants everyone to come to him, so that they may sing the same song he himself sings. How discordant the music is when the Arian sings one tune, the Sabellian another, the Ebionite a third, the Pelagian a

* * * * *

256 Cf 2 Cor 5:19.
257 I translate *in unum*, with the sense of coming together in one, as 'in unity.' Augustine *Enarratio in psalmum 33* 2.7 PL 36 311 states that many manuscripts have this reading. The phrase *in idipsum* 'in itself,' discussed below, is scarcely Latin; English translations of the psalm have 'together.' Compare also the discussion of the phrase in *In psalmum 4* CWE 63 270.
258 Cf Eph 4:4.
259 Ps 132/133:1
260 Ps 4:9/8. On Erasmus' use of *conglutino* 'to join together,' see *In psalmum 22* 131 n39 above.

fourth, the Donatist a fifth – but what need is there to list all the innumerable sects?[261] Each sect sings its own song, all of them out of tune with Christ and not even in agreement with each other. They have the same baptism, the same claim, the same name, but not the same mind. Would that we might all be in harmony with Christ and that even Turks and Jews might join the chorus, so that with one mouth and one spirit we might magnify the Lord: 'O magnify the Lord with me.'

The Lord is not made greater by human praise, but his glory among mankind becomes greater. He wants renown for his glory, not because this adds anything to him, but because we become better as we contemplate his sublimity, goodness, and wisdom. As we turn our mind's eye to gaze at the supreme good which is himself, everything the world admires and pursues through good and evil grows cheap and mean. It is not one who sounds the Lord's praises with his lips who magnifies the Lord completely, but rather one who turns a pure heart to the contemplation of those things that are eternal, one who becomes more self-effacing the higher he rises, and more proud in the face of the world the more he submits himself to God. No one magnifies the Lord except those who are meek and lowly of heart. The unbridled man magnifies himself; he does not glorify the Lord's name, he glorifies his own name. The Lord is magnified by those who acknowledge his sublimity and confess their own lowliness. The Lord's name is exalted by those who say with the psalmist, and say it from the heart: 'Not unto us, O Lord, not unto us, but unto thy name give glory.'[262] Then remember the song sung by the most blessed Virgin, than which nothing is more sublime and nothing more modest: 'My soul magnifies the Lord, because he has looked on the lowliness of his handmaid.' With all her virtues, all her abundant good fortune, she claims nothing for herself but disregards her own name and exalts the name of the Lord: 'For he that is mighty has done great things for me, and holy is his name.' She does not say, 'all generations will call me worthy' but 'will call me blessed.' And she does not say, 'and my glory is from generation to generation,' but 'his mercy.'[263] God alone is truly great; anything human is humble.[264] Nor is there any danger that by lowering yourself you will become less, for the only way you can be great in the Lord is by lowering yourself as much as possible. It

* * * * *

261 Varied heretical sects of the late second to fifth centuries, though Donatism survived in Africa until the eighth century

262 Ps 113B/115:1

263 Luke 1:46–50

264 There is a pun here on *humanum* and *humile*.

was thus that Christ became greatest of all and won the name that is above all names.[265] It was thus that David became great, and the apostles, and all the saints, whose names are so much revered throughout the Christian world.

It is not enough to magnify the Lord with our mouths. Everywhere we hear this song: 'Great is the Lord, and highly to be praised, and of his greatness there is no end.'[266] Magnify the Lord with your tongue, but magnify him more with your spirit. You will do this if you go down into yourself and consider how in yourself you are nothing, how lost and how wretched you are; then, turning your eyes to God, think how utterly good, utterly wise, and utterly powerful he is; think over what he has done for you, how mercifully he sought you out, how kindly he gave to you; and finally compare his goodness with your wickedness. The mind is kindled by this contemplation, so that on account of all these gifts you have been given without deserving them you magnify the Lord and exalt his name. But when you have experienced God's goodness, do not conceal it: do not dig a hole in the ground for the treasure you have discovered.[267] The secrets of kings are best kept concealed, but God receives honour when his works are revealed and celebrated. As the angel told the blessed Tobias: 'Bless the Lord of heaven, and confess before all the living that he has shown mercy to you.'[268] It is his mercy that the Lord wishes to be proclaimed, not our merits. When we add to our merits, we detract in proportion from God's great goodness, and when we praise our own worth, we denigrate in proportion his sublime glory. The man in the Gospel who was freed from legions of wicked spirits is told to return to his family and tell everyone of the great deed which God has done for him.[269] But the nine lepers receive blame: 'Were there not ten who were cleansed, and is there not one who has returned to glorify God, except this stranger?'[270] And the woman who was cured of the flow of blood when she touched the Lord's clothes, wishing to obtain so great a benefit in secret, not from any wicked motive but from shame, was compelled to acknowledge her healing.[271] Similarly St Paul continually proclaims what he had been and what through God's mercy he had

* * * * *

265 Phil 2:9
266 Ps 144/145:3
267 Cf Matt 6:19, 25:14–30.
268 Tob 12:6
269 Mark 5:19
270 Cf Luke 17:17–18.
271 Mark 5:25–34

become.[272] The physician takes a wage, and yet if the patient recovers he wants it known that he was responsible for the cure. The surgeon removes a tooth, demanding a fee and inflicting terrible pain; he keeps the tooth and shows it around, saying: 'I extracted this from his mouth.' Why are they interested in such distinction? So that their earnings may be greater. Then do we deprive the Lord of his distinction or his fee, when he has given us things that are so much greater? His wage is that more should take refuge in him and be saved; his wage is human salvation.

Then let us try with Paul to bring as many as we can as gain to Christ;[273] let us scatter abroad his benefits to us, so that we may be a sweet savour to God in every place.[274] It should not concern us if marjoram causes the death of pigs,[275] so long as the gentle rejoice. Not only in the assembly of the saints does thanksgiving resound, when all the members rejoice at the glorification of one of them, but the fragrance of God's goodness reaches even those who are outside. There too, there are those who can become gentle. Think of St Augustine's experience. The delightful fragrance of St Antony was wafted towards him, and he was healed, and made dead to the world, and began to be alive to Christ.[276]

Anyone who has found valuable treasure conceals it so that he may be the only one to benefit from it, and any man who has married a beautiful wife makes sure that he is the only one to embrace her. If treasure is shared it is lessened, and if a woman's love is distributed between many it grows cold. But the good things of the spirit have quite different properties; they rejoice in being shared among as many as possible, and anyone who shares what he has among many has more. Consequently, although David alone was saved, he calls everyone to a common thanksgiving, so that everyone may have joy in common. The shepherd in the Gospel who found the sheep that had strayed did not hide his joy but called his friends together, saying, 'Rejoice with me, for I have found the sheep that was lost'; and the woman who found the coin she had lost was not content to be glad inwardly, but invited her friends and neighbours to share her joy; and finally, when the

* * * * *

272 For instance 1 Cor 15:9–10
273 Cf 1 Cor 9:19.
274 'Sweet savour' is a stock phrase referring to sacrifice in the Old Testament; Erasmus takes its figurative use from 2 Cor 2:15.
275 A proverb (*Adagia* 1 i 38) indicating that the unworthy do not appreciate what is truly valuable
276 Augustine *Confessions* 8.12 PL 32 762

father received back his son the house echoed with congratulations and rejoicing from all within it.[277] And so David summons all mankind – those
who were then, who are now, who will be in time to come – to the shared
feast and to the same hymn of praise, saying, 'Magnify the Lord with me,
let us exalt his name in itself.'

But the chorus which the psalm has so far been summoning to praise
the Lord in concert is now here before us. What is the theme of their song?
'I sought out the Lord, and he heard me, and he rescued me from all my
troubles.' When I was utterly without protection, when every weapon was
aimed at the destruction of one weak, unarmed, and destitute victim, when
I was surrounded by fear and 'countless images of death,'[278] I did not consult the oracles, I did not resort to witchcraft; I sought out the Lord, I placed
all my hopes of salvation in him, and looked for help to him who alone is
more powerful than all. Nor did I find him deaf to my prayers: he heard
me, since I called on him with great confidence, knowing that he is utterly
faithful to his promises, and knowing that he sends afflictions to his own
only to test their faith, so that with the temptation he provides the way
of escape, and does not allow us to be tested beyond our capacity for endurance.[279] 'And he delivered me from all my tribulations': I am not sure
that anyone can truly say that in this life. When David was sent away by
king Achis, he was not freed from all his dangers, since even during his
reign he was beset by great troubles. The whole life of the faithful lies exposed to many afflictions, so who could say in their lifetime 'the Lord has
delivered me from all my tribulations?'

This problem can be solved in three ways. Firstly, the prophet's words
are true in the literal sense: referring, that is, to past dangers, which had
oppressed him in great number. St Paul employs this sense in his letters to
Timothy, when he tells him of all his sufferings in Antioch, Iconium, and
Lystra, then adds: 'And the Lord delivered me from all of them.'[280] Secondly, being certain that the Lord would be present in all dangers to come,
David declares what he knows will come to pass as though it had already
happened. The writings of the prophets quite commonly contain a figure
in which something which will happen in the remote future is spoken of
as past, because to a prophet's eyes even things which are far away are

* * * * *

277 Luke 15:6, 8–9, 22–4
278 Virgil *Aeneid* 2.369
279 1 Cor 10:13; cf Prov 3:12, Heb 12:6, Rev 3:19.
280 2 Tim 3:11

present.[281] Thus Paul to the Corinthians: 'who has delivered us and rescued us from such vast dangers; in him we place our hope, that he will
again deliver us.'[282] He rescued us by giving us a sure hope, since one who
knows for certain that in a little while he will reach a most joyous end to all
his troubles is already set free. He writes in similar vein to the Colossians:
'who delivered us from the power of darkness, and transferred us to the
kingdom of his well-beloved Son.'[283] How did he deliver you, Paul, best of
men? Did you yourself not ask the Lord three times to take Satan and his
blows away, yet received no reply but 'Sufficient for you is my grace'?[284]
Were there not among your group of widows those who went after Satan?[285]
Were there not among the Corinthians 'some gluttons, some drunkards'?[286]
Do you not declare that they are of the flesh, and make contention, and go
to law against each other?[287] Did not the Galatians apostatize to Judaism?[288]
Was not one found to be living with his father's wife?[289] And what is the
meaning of those words of yours: 'I am afraid that when I come I may find
you not as I wish, and that you may find me not as you wish; and that perhaps among you there are struggles, rivalries, hatreds, dissensions, slander,
gossip, conceit, and disturbances.'[290] Are not your epistles full of such reproaches? How then did God deliver these people from the power of darkness? How did he transfer to his Son's kingdom those who are constantly
being vanquished by Satan? There is only one possibility: he is said to have
'delivered them' because he does not allow them to suffer oppression for
ever, and he 'transferred them to the kingdom' because he gave them a
sure hope of that kingdom. If we stand firm in this hope, we have already
defeated all the dangers that beset us.

We should notice that the words of the psalm are 'from *all* tribulations.'
There are some misfortunes where no human being dares to promise help,
such as those diseases where the physician says, 'This is an incurable disease

* * * * *

281 The problem of tense in Biblical Hebrew is complex, but conventionally a
    'prophetic perfect' is recognized, in which a future event is spoken of as
    though it had already happened.
282 2 Cor 1:10
283 Col 1:13
284 2 Cor 12:7–9
285 1 Cor 7:5
286 1 Cor 11:21
287 1 Cor 3:3, 6:1–8
288 Gal 1:6
289 1 Cor 5:1
290 2 Cor 12:20

– I will not lay hands on it'; or those wounds on which the surgeons refuse to operate; or the case of those wretched captives of the Turks whom neither pope nor emperor can help.[291] But there is no misfortune from which one cannot be rescued by him who brings the dead to life, and who can summon back the souls of those long since buried.

Again, in my view one should not simply pass over the words 'I sought out the Lord.' The phrase 'I called on the Lord and he heard me' would seem more appropriate. But by the use of the word 'seek' the Holy Scriptures tell us to employ care and diligence. It is not that God is lost and we must seek him out, since he is within us. As we read of wisdom, 'If you seek her like riches, you will bury her like treasure.'[292] What will the greedy man not try in order to find treasure? But the Sixty-eighth Psalm expresses the same though in different words: 'Let the poor see and rejoice, seek the Lord and your soul shall live.'[293] The words of our psalm 'I will bless the Lord at all times, his praise will be always on my lips' there become 'I will praise God's name with song, and magnify him with praise.'[294] And again, take the sermon in the Gospel: with those three words 'ask – seek – knock,'[295] what does it commend to us but care, readiness, and vigilance? It is not enough to light a candle in broad daylight,[296] not enough to say with one's lips, 'Lord, come to my aid.'[297] David sought out the Lord and was rescued. You will ask, 'Where shall I seek the Lord?' He lies hidden in the Holy Scriptures; examine them, dig deep there, and you will find him. He lies hidden in his members; anyone who helps Christ's poor, who comforts the afflicted, who instructs those in error, is correct in his search for the Lord, and there he will find him. Go down into yourself, examine the many ways in which you have offended against the Lord, and see how mercifully he has dealt with you. Light up the lamp of faith, so that in the words of James you may 'ask in faith, hesitating not at all';[298] kindle the spark of charity, and there you will find the Lord. And do not straightaway give up hope if you fail to receive immediately what you ask for; carry on, be insistent and

* * * * *

291 *Captivi* in this context may cover subject peoples as well as prisoners of war. For Erasmus' view of life under the Ottoman empire, see *De bello Turcico* 257–9 above.

292 Prov 2:4

293 Ps 68:33/69:32

294 Ps 68:31/69:30

295 Matt 7:7

296 Cf *Moria* CWE 27 120.

297 Ps 69:2/70:1

298 James 1:6

importunate, and you will receive either what you ask for or something better.

Let us not hasten to move away from this passage. Holy Scripture is like some wonderful painting; if you look at it for a good length of time something new and delightful to contemplate is always coming into view. David knew he would be king, for he had already been anointed by Samuel, and yet he took every precaution against his murder by Saul. How then can people say, 'What good does it do me to be concerned? If I am not one of the elect my efforts will be in vain, and if I am my concern is unnecessary, since things will fall out in accordance with the decision of him whose decrees cannot be revoked.'[299] God wants his elect to be saved, but to be saved in such a manner that they unite their own efforts with the divine will. He saves us through grace, but he wants us to seek that grace through our prayers, our tears, sighs, and almsgiving. Some may dislike the phrase 'free will' because it is nowhere to be found in the Bible but entered the theologians' systems from the arrogant Stoics. But if human will is utterly ineffective, what is the meaning of the words 'I sought out the Lord and he heard me' and of the words that follow, 'Approach him and be enlightened,' especially considering that similar turns of phrase are everywhere to be found in Scripture? The Lord desires to rescue you, but to rescue you as you cry out; if you want to be rescued some other way, you will not be rescued at all.

At this point the prophet reveals to us the meaning of this great rejoicing, to share in which he summons all the gentle, so that the Lord's name may be glorified by all. But why does the Lord have need of human praise? As I have already stated, he has no need; the need is ours. What is this need? We all need hope that we may receive from the Lord what David asked for, provided we have asked the Lord in accordance with David's example. He has given the example, and adds a plea: 'Approach him and be enlightened, and your faces shall not be confounded.' All you who sit in the darkness of grief and the shadow of death, approach him who is the true light, who shines upon every one that comes into the world,[300] and the eyes of your heart will be enlightened by him, and your faces will not be

*　*　*　*　*

299 Although this parodies the consequences of the Lutheran position on *liberum arbitrium* ('free choice' is perhaps a closer translation than 'free will'), it reflects Erasmus' concern with the implications 'for piety' of that position, as expressed in the preface to *De libero arbitrio* CWE 76 8–14. Compare also *De concordia* LB V 500D–E.

300 John 1:9

confounded – that is, they will not be ashamed, for shame is manifest in the face.[301] In vain you will seek the Lord while you walk in darkness. The mind's eye is our aim and direction,[302] but this eye is defective if it sees no light; and light is faith. Now no one gives himself faith, but rather receives it from the Lord; yet no one receives it unless he approaches. What is the meaning of approach? Put nothing in the way of God's grace, but make yourselves ready for it by prayer and almsgiving. In this world the sun is available for all creatures, but it does not illumine them all. Owls are blinded by it, it is painful to those with sore eyes, and nature is no help to the blind or to those who close their eyes. To have sore eyes is a grave sin, yet one with sore eyes does see some things, after the manner of drunkards, whose eyes are weighed down by heavy drinking and who see many things in place of single ones, and moving objects instead of stationary. Such at first were the eyes of the blind man in the Gospel, who saw people as though they were walking trees.[303] But someone without faith is totally blind, though there is also a weak faith which asks of the Lord to be increased. Those without faith should pray that they may receive it, and those with only a little faith should cry, 'Lord, increase my faith.'[304] Those whose eyes are heavy because they have caught cold should purge their minds of vices and evil desires, so that their eyes may be purified and they may direct their gaze to the Lord; if they do this, their faces will not be ashamed, since it is those who fear a repulse who feel shame. 'Whatever you ask the Father in my name, he will give you.'[305] Anyone who believes this with all his heart is not abandoned in perils and put to shame, but rather the Lord will deliver him from all his anxieties and fears.

At this point a reflection on the human level may occur in some minds, that if those who are not delivered are put to shame, then all those martyrs who breathed their last amidst terrible tortures were shamed, as even today are numerous devout people whose troubles leave them only with their life. My reply is this: only the defeated are put to shame, while the victor receives glory however many weapons wound him. It is those who in their agonies deserted Christ who were really put to shame, for they in truth were defeated, even if they gained their lives. But those who in the midst of appalling martyrdoms are buoyed up by hopes of a life in

* * * * *

301 Cf *In psalmum 85* 105 above.
302 *Intentio* indicates both physical gaze and mental concentration.
303 Mark 8:24
304 Luke 17:5
305 John 14:13

heaven, and with their last words courageously confess Christ, are neither deserted nor abandoned, nor are they put to shame, but through their
glorious deaths they pass to the triumph of everlasting glory. Rather it
is the tyrants who are defeated and shamed, and in the tyrants, Satan.
The tortured gives thanks while the torturer rages: which of the two is
vanquished?

But what of the martyr who prays to be delivered from his torture
and is not rescued – is he not rejected? Let us examine the martyr's prayer:
'Lord Jesus, receive my spirit.' These are not the words of one praying
to avoid martyrdom, but of one hastening through death to his triumph.
Probably this too is what Paul had said when he wished to 'be dissolved
and be with Christ'.[306] It is, however, permissible for the faithful to pray
to God that they may be delivered from the persecution of the wicked or
from other afflictions of this life such as painful diseases, war, or pestilence. But what is the prayer of the truly devout? 'Lord, if you so will, if
it is expedient both for your glory and for my salvation, rescue me from
these troubles; if not, let that happen which is good in your sight. Only
give your servant the strength of your spirit, lest he succumb to temptation.' One who prays thus is not put to shame if he is delivered from his
troubles, and if he overcomes them he is not shamed but like a brave soldier
gains glory from his prowess in war. How could those whom our Lord himself in the gospel called 'blessed' seem to be put to shame?[307] But it is not
of much account if to some worldly people they do appear to be shamed.
True shame belongs to those who face reproaches from God, who are confounded when in that wondrous theatre, before God as judge, before all
the angels, before the whole company of the faithful, when the secrets of all
consciences are revealed, they see the righteous standing without trembling
and with fearless expressions.[308] Apparently it was Lazarus, lying in front
of the rich man's door, who was exposed to shame, but it was the rich man
who was really put to confusion when in his torment he saw the beggar re-
clining in Abraham's bosom. Lazarus received what he asked for, but the
rich man's prayer was rejected.[309] Defeat and confusion seemed to be the
lot of the lord of glory when he was bound, condemned, struck repeatedly,
spat upon, mocked with a crown of thorns, purple robe, and reed, when

* * * * *

306 Phil 1:23; on the interpretation, see Screech 139.
307 Cf Matt 5:10–12, Luke 6:22.
308 On Erasmus' use of theatrical imagery in this work, see Bietenholz *History and
    Biography* especially 26–8.
309 Luke 16:19–31

Herod sent him back to Pilate dressed in linen for dishonour,[310] when he was placed on the cross in the company of thieves. It seemed that God had utterly abandoned him when the Pharisees wagged their heads and taunted him as he hung there: 'If he is the Son of God, let his Father set him free, if he is well-disposed to him.'[311] Yet it was then that he cast down Satan and prepared for himself and for all his own the glory of immortality. So, if we do not wish our plea to be rejected, if we do not want to be put to shame, let us approach – or as others translate, let us run[312] – not to the world's defences, not to our own merits, but to the Lord, as the Son bids us, who opened the way for us, showed it to us, and fortified it.

The psalm continues: 'This poor man cried, and the Lord heard him, and delivered him from all his tribulations.' We may hope that what has first happened to the head will happen also to the members, for Christ will not abandon any part of himself, but all will be set free, all will rise again in glory. So he places himself before us as an example that we may imitate and from which we may take confidence. If you follow him who preceded you, you will reach what he has attained;[313] if you tread in his footprints, there is no doubt that you will arrive at the place which he has reached. Why turn your eyes here and there? Why gaze at those who are nothing more than man? Those who seem blessed in this world are powerful, respected, and wealthy; they enjoy perfect physical health; they have an agreeable wife, they have children, countless friends, dependants, and servants; everyone looks up to them, seeks out their company, and honours them. These, you will say, are the people whom the Lord seems to have heard, these he has rescued from all their troubles. But rather turn your gaze in the direction pointed out by the prophet, who shows you whom to imitate and where to receive sure hope: 'This poor man cried out, and the Lord heard him.' If you look at externals, according to the flesh our Lord was born of a poverty-stricken mother, and he himself was subject to greater poverty, since for the sake of the gospel he renounced even what could have been his. And if you look at the mind, no human being who ever lived was poorer than Christ, because there never has been nor will be one more free from all desire of worldly things. Now since habitual violence is often the companion of riches, the same Hebrew

*****

310 Luke 23:11, an episode reported only in this Gospel
311 Cf Matt 27:43.
312 Not in any of the standard versions of the Psalms
313 There is wordplay here on *sequor* and its compounds: *sequeris ... adsequeris ... consequuutus est.*

word has been translated by some as 'poor,' by others as 'mild';[314] and the Greek word [for 'poor'] is not πένης but πτωχός, meaning a beggar: a poor person who seeks help from others. Just as there are many who are poor in resources but plentiful in desires, so there are many destitute of virtues yet rich in a false but persuasive piety. If we wish the Lord to hear us, let us be genuinely poor, acknowledge our nakedness, and if there is anything good in us let us not claim it for our own but attribute everything to God's mercy. We should not be ashamed to admit our poverty; we should imitate the beggar's shamelessness and call on the Lord to hear us.[315]

But where does the poor man find such safety amid the dangers which are pressing on every side? From on high we are under attack by evil spirits with their fiery missiles, while the world ranges all its weapons against the faithful; Christ has left the earth, and what can give confidence to one who is poor, unprepared for war, unarmed, and devoid of resources? Christ has withdrawn his body to heaven so that from there he may help us; he has not deserted his own, but is with them till the end of time.[316] He is the king of heaven and earth. He has no need to come down to earth again; it is enough to have come down once. He has a countless host of angels through whose agency he can protect his sheep. Hear then the great help that they give: 'The angel of the Lord will send into the camp of those who fear him, and will rescue them.' The word 'send' [immittet] does not adequately convey the force of the Hebrew, which is better given in the Septuagint as παρεμβαλεῖ, a word which properly refers to fortifying a situation with a ditch and ramparts, thus making a camp as a safe base to which soldiers may retreat. The Latin word castra [camp] is in Greek παρεμβολή, meaning that it prevents the enemy's incursion. If we had a translation 'a sending in' rather than 'a camp,' I think no one would understand what was meant, yet whoever put 'send into' instead of 'fortify' was speaking no more clearly. Consequently some readers were thrown by the nonsensical-sounding words and, as Augustine tells us, corrupted the passage, translating 'The Lord will send his angel into the camp,' which

* * * * *

314 This does not appear in any of the standard versions of the psalms; probably Erasmus got the idea from Basil's commentary on this passage (*Homilia in psalmum 33* PG 29 361C), which associates the poor with the meek (or mild) by way of the beatitudes (Matt 5:3–5).

315 Erasmus discusses poverty at greater length at 338–9 and 342 below.

316 Cf Matt 28:20.

is the reading still found in the commentaries on the Psalms attributed to Jerome.[317] The prophet's meaning was better expressed by those who translated 'the angel will surround' (as St Jerome),[318] or 'the angel of the Lord will lay out the camp.' The meaning is not affected whether you take 'angel' here to mean Christ himself, who was called 'an angel of great counsel,'[319] or to mean some angel out of the number St Paul refers to in the Epistle to the Hebrews: 'Are they not all ministering spirits, sent to minister for the sake of those who will receive their birthright of salvation?'[320] These angels are mentioned also by our Lord in the Gospel, when he says, 'Their angels always see the face of the Father, who is in heaven.'[321] And in Acts it is said of Peter, 'It is his angel,'[322] and in chapter 10 of Daniel the angel Michael is a help against the Persian king.[323] And again in the Psalms: 'He will give his angels charge of you , that they may guard you in all your ways.'[324] Elisha was not afraid of the enemy's line of chariots as it bore down on them, because as a prophet he saw the defences formed by angels, and in response to his prayers the Lord opened the eyes of his servant, so that he saw the mountain covered with horses and fiery chariots, surrounding Elisha on every side; the protecting angels were greater in number than the attacking enemy, and Elisha was victorious defended by angels alone.[325] It would be pointless to enumerate the instances when angels were sent to the saints, to help them, to announce good tidings, to console them, when Scripture narrates such events in so many places.

* * * * *

317 Augustine *Enarratio in psalmum* 33 2.11 PL 36 314; Pseudo-Jerome *Breviarium in psalmos* PL 26 (1845) 920 (Migne's text has *emittit*, presumably a further corruption of *immittet*). As Augustine says, *immittet angelum Dominus* is an easy corruption of *immittet angelus Domini*, which is meaningless without a direct object.

318 Erasmus here adopts a variant reading *circumdabit* (future tense) from the *Psalterium iuxta Hebraeos*; in the following paragraph he switches to *circumdat* (present tense) as found in other manuscripts. See PL 28 (1890) 1213 and n4 (note 'f' in the first edition, 1846).

319 This is Augustine's interpretation (*Enarratio in psalmum* 33 2.11 PL 36 314), quoting Isa 9:6 in the Septuagint version.

320 Heb 1:14

321 Matt 18:10

322 Acts 12:15

323 Dan 10:13, 21

324 Ps 90/91:11

325 2 Kings 6:15–18

Nor is it a matter of great concern whether with St Basil you assume some individual angel to be so large that he can surround and protect all those who fear the Lord, or whether with St Augustine you take it that 'angel' stands for 'angels,'[326] just as we very frequently say 'soldier' for 'soldiers,' even if they are countless in number, for we are not here dealing with the number but the kind of being. The mention of an angel rules out human defences and shows that the defence is of divine origin. As for the fact that the Hebrew text has 'surrounds,' in the present tense,[327] and the Greek, like ours, 'will surround,' in the future, even this does not obstruct the sense, unless the present tense indicates that it is a constant occurrence that the angel of the Lord should guard the servants of the Lord.

But meanwhile the military expressions remind us that human life is soldier's campaigning on earth,[328] and that here we are not in our native land but in camp. It warns us not to sleep, not to give way to idle living and pleasures, but always to remain under arms, holding our shield in our left hand, our sword in our right. The angels stand guard for us, not so that we may slumber, but so that with their assistance we may fight bravely and overcome the enemy, who is constantly circling round us, looking for someone to devour.[329] If we wish to be safe from him, let us remain in camp, let us not leave the confines of the church, lest we rush into Satan's hands. If we must come to blows with the enemy, let us fight under the standards of our general, and let us fight in hope, since we have angels surrounding us with their defences – not without art either, but 'in a circle' or 'a ring.' There is no set of precautions which can completely defend a human camp so that it is nowhere open to capture. The enemy digs tunnels underneath, fires the ramparts, throws a bridge across the river, fills in the ditch, demolishes the walls with battering rams; even if none of these things happens, it certainly cannot be made safe against missiles falling from above. But the Lord, acting through his angel, has made his church sure on every side, so that there can be no entrance either for wicked men or for hostile spirits unless it is we who betray ourselves – provided that we do not abandon

* * * * *

326 Basil *Homilia in psalmum* 33 PG 29 363; but Augustine does not give the explanation attributed to him, nor is it compatible with his view that the angel is Christ. Possibly it is Erasmus' own 'commonsense,' philological suggestion, which he mistakenly credits to Augustine.

327 Erasmus deduces this from the present tense *circumdat*; see n318 above.

328 Job 7:1, a favourite quotation, alluded to in the first sentence of the *Enchiridion militis christiani* CWE 66 24

329 1 Pet 5:8

camp and provided we do not drive away by shameful behaviour the angels who are helping us. Bees are driven away by smoke and doves by evil smells,[330] but far more than these angels are driven away by shameful actions. It is only when we indulge in gluttony, drunkenness, and lust that we are really alone – or rather we are not alone, we have exchanged our band of angels for a throng of devils.

Above all, if we do not wish our defenders the angels to leave us, let us fear the Lord. The psalm's words are 'in the camp of those who fear him.' The only way in which you may fear neither men nor Satan is to fear the Lord. One who is afraid is anxious to avoid giving offence, and this fear keeps us behind the bars of innocence until we have reached the love of divine wisdom. Once we have tasted that, there is no more need for bars, and we live in the freedom of the spirit. As John puts it, 'Love casts out fear,'[331] and in Paul's words, 'Where the spirit is, there is freedom.'[332] When the Lord is so kind that he gives mankind the great honour of being everywhere protected and defended by angels, who would fear to approach him, who would hesitate to entrust himself to him? The prophet had experience of this wonderful love and care which God feels for humanity and invites all humanity to share that same experience. Similarly, Paul declares that from being a persecutor of Christ he became an apostle, and from being, as he himself admits, a sinner of the first rank he became an illustrious preacher of the gospel, all through God's mercy freely bestowed, so that no one, however gravely burdened with sin, should hesitate to approach.[333] For love is not jealous,[334] but longs to have all it possesses in common with all. I have approached and tasted, says the prophet, meaning 'I have found out by experience.' Then all of you also should approach and 'taste and (if to taste is not enough) see how sweet is the Lord.'

The word given as 'sweet' [suavis] in Latin is χρηστός in Greek, which means something more like 'kind,' 'helpful.' The same word is used in the Gospel – 'my yoke is sweet' – χρηστόν.[335] Not everyone is able to approach kings or satraps. Many are denied access, many are turned away after admission, and many receive punishment instead of the reward they

* * * * *

330 These comparisons are taken from Basil's commentary on this passage (*Homilia in psalmum* 33 PG 29 364B).
331 1 John 4:18
332 2 Cor 3:17
333 1 Tim 1:12–16
334 Cf 1 Cor 13:4.
335 Matt 11:30

had hoped for. Indeed, there are many rulers whom it is safer to avoid than to approach, as the Greek proverb 'Keep well away from Jupiter and his thunderbolt' bears witness.[336] But the Lord is not like this; his kindness exceeds that of all others as much as does his greatness. He comes to meet those who approach him; he turns to those who turn to him, as the prophet points out (speaking in the person of God): 'Turn to me, and I will turn to you'.[337] The same is conveyed by the parable of the prodigal son, whose father rushed to meet him on seeing him in the distance.[338]

Of all the senses two are the most reliable, feeling and sight. Taste is a kind of feeling peculiar to the tongue and palate, a most refined sense of feeling which distinguishes not only hard and soft, harsh and smooth, hot and cold, but thousands of different flavours. Now in the Gospel our Lord, wishing to free his disciples from any possible doubt, told them, 'Touch and see, for a spirit does not have flesh and bones.'[339] And Thomas said, 'Unless I see the traces of the nails, and put my hand into his side, I will not believe.'[340] He touched; he saw; he believed. Similarly, when John in his letter refers to faith based on certainties, he speaks of 'what we have heard, what we have seen with our own eyes, what we have looked on and what our hands have touched, concerning the word of life.'[341] But to taste signifies more than to touch, for what is tasted gives life and nourishment, while this is not true of things that are touched by hands. The Jews approached Jesus, they touched and saw him, but they did not taste him, since they chose to revile what they heard, not to believe it.

In physical terms, we see before we taste, but in spiritual concerns the opposite is true. We look at the bread that feeds our body before we put it in our mouth. But no one can look at the word of the Lord, which is bread for the soul, without first believing it. As the prophet says: 'Unless you have believed, you will not understand.'[342] Thus we seek the Lord when we turn from our sins to repentance. We approach with faith, and when we receive the first-fruits of the Spirit, like a pledge, we taste; when we enjoy his presence as we think of his extraordinary love for us and hope that we may experience the eternal bliss of gazing on his face, we see. Here

* * * * *

336 *Adagia* I iii 96: *Porro a Iove atque fulmine*
337 Zech 1:3
338 Luke 15:20
339 Luke 24:30
340 John 20:25
341 1 John 1:1
342 Adapted from Isa 7:9

we see through a glass darkly, but there we shall see him as he is.[343] Then there will be no more seeking, no more approach, since there is no faith where experience is complete. There will be no more tasting, since there is no need for a pledge to sustain hope where promises are fulfilled in their entirety. Only sight will remain, and continue for ever. The one happiness, the one pleasure of the whole army of heaven is to know – that is, to gaze on – the true God, and Jesus Christ whom he has sent.[344] Our world has dainty pleasures and distractions, but they fail to satisfy in full measure, and sometimes they bore us by their abundance. This is the only food which satisfies the soul without bloating. Every object is at rest when it achieves its end, and man is born for the purpose of knowing and of enjoying his creator. This is the bread of angels that comes down from heaven[345] to become the bread of man. The Word was made flesh[346] – that is, the Son of God became man so that he might become the food of men. Those who hunger for this bread are happy, but happier are those who eat it in the kingdom of God. Some commentators[347] interpret this passage as referring to the consumption of the Lord's body and blood, but the reference to spiritual consumption gives a reverent sense. It is true that the Lord is sweet in this way also, but as he himself says, 'The flesh is of no avail without the spirit that gives life.'[348]

'Happy is the man who hopes' (or 'trusts') 'in him.' All human happiness is illusory; the only true happiness consists in placing all one's faith and hope in the Lord. This hope does not deceive but is fulfilled after this life. In the meanwhile, we are happy because of our hope; we hold the pledge of the Spirit until the coming of that which is perfect.[349] Those who have tasted the goodness of God's word, who gaze with the eyes of faith on the good things of the world to come, which God has prepared for those who love him,[350] these are they who are truly happy.

While in human matters fear and hope are opposed, in mystical terms none have a more certain hope than those who fear the Lord. It is quite shameless to hope for a reward from a commander if you do not fear him,

* * * * *

343 Cf 1 Cor 13:12, quoted by Basil on this passage (*Homilia in psalmum* 33 PG 29 365A), who also introduces the idea of the 'pledge.'
344 Cf John 17:3.
345 Ps 77/78:25, John 6:33
346 John 1:14
347 Notably Augustine *Enarratio in psalmum* 33 2.12 PL 36 315
348 Cf John 6:64/63.
349 A reminiscence of Eph 4:13
350 1 Cor 2:9

since if you have no fear you will not obey his orders. A certain general used frequently to say that he would rather his troops feared him than the enemy.[351] Similarly, one who does not fear Christ as ruler must fear both the devil and mankind. So it is those who soldier under Christ's standards in the camp of the church that David is addressing when he says 'Fear the Lord, all his saints, since those who fear him have no lack.' Fear not only gives safety from the attacks of demons, it keeps you from every want. Sometimes through lack of supplies soldiers are forced to surrender, but once you have pledged your loyalty to Christ your general, if you fear him and obey his commandments, you need not fear that you will lack anything. It is the general's job to look to his soldiers' needs; all you need do is seek the kingdom of God and his righteousness, and all these things will be added to you[352] – through the generosity of him under whom you serve in good faith.

The case of Lazarus, who had neither house, food, nor health, is not a valid objection to this point, and neither is that of Job, who was deprived of everything that he had. One who has God has everything.[353] When Job sat naked, covered with sores, he was richer than when he had abundant possessions because he was dearer to God. To lack faith, to lack love, to lack uprightness – this is dire poverty. It is abject poverty to be rich in vices and to lack every virtue. But the one who fears God lacks nothing, at least of those things which make us truly happy. One who considers death as gain[354] suffers no lack in life when he dies. If poverty teaches one temperance and modesty, then that poverty is great wealth; it is also true, however, that those who fear the Lord and do not depart from righteousness are not generally without the food and clothing necessary to sustain life. What then are we to say when we see that the whole life of Christian people is full of deceit? What is there in the whole of nature that is not adulterated in the quest for gain? What salesman does not sell his goods for an unfair exchange, if he can hide the deception from his neighbour? How many are the methods of adulterating flour, wine, and sugar? How many are the deceptions practised in reducing the quality of cloth or of jewels? We adulterate tin with lead, bronze with copper, silver and gold in many ways. Which craft does not have its repertoire of deceits, which technique does

* * * * *

351 The fifth-century BC Spartan general Clearchus, as reported in Valerius Maximus 2.7 ext 2
352 Matt 6:33
353 Compare with this the more detailed argument in *In psalmum* 22 172–7 above.
354 Phil 1:21

not have its own ways of cheating? I need not mention the cheating that goes on among millers, bakers, tailors and coach-drivers, whose greed is so well known that it is almost an object of praise. But who is there who offers the help he owes his neighbour in an honest manner? How many people treat anything entrusted to their hands with honesty? Does not the surgeon who deliberately prolongs the healing of a wound in order to get a larger fee commit a crime that is worse than theft? And you will probably find quite a few doctors of this type as well. Then what robbery comes about from coinage, when the metal is adulterated and the weight lessened! To this we can at times add the devaluation of coin, a great disaster for the poor and a great gain for merchants. And then there are monopolies, which cause items to be sold at twelve times their former price.

In the midst of all this, where, I beg you, is the fear of the Lord? As an excuse for our misdeeds we give the fear of destitution, virtually accusing Scripture of falsehood. 'If I were to fear the Lord,' they say, 'and lived without cheating, I would go hungry,' yet while this man and that reject the fear of the Lord, how much money have they made for themselves with their fraudulent practices? Don't those words seem to belong to one who takes the words of Scripture 'Those who fear God have no want' to be false? Now hear the other side of the story: nature is content with the bare minimum, but for greed, ambition, pampered and depraved living neither earth nor sea will suffice.[355] Every day they play games of chance, every day they celebrate their drunken orgies and shell out money to their whores; then they say, 'My craft is not sufficient to keep me alive if I do not cheat a little.' You good-for-nothing! Live soberly, work steadily, and only then if you do not have enough to live on come forward and accuse the Lord.

But now we must return to the psalm. We should take notice of the words 'his saints,' which seem to imply that there are saints who do not belong to the Lord. And of course this is the case: the Turks have their saints – chaste, ascetic, unshakeable in their way of life – but these are the saints of Satan. The pagans have their divine men and women, the Jews too have their saints, and the heretics have saints whom they honour with great veneration. In fact, even in the church there are many saints in our midst who are not the saints of the Lord. There are those who fast to save expense or to attract attention, there are those who for the same reasons go around in filthy clothes, spend hours in prayer, or give alms. These are saints, but they are saints in human estimation; in God's reckoning, they

* * * * *

355 Compare *In psalmum* 4 CWE 63 195 and *In psalmum* 22 174 and n336 above.

are whitened sepulchres.[356] It is those saints whose hearts are pure, who look to nothing but Christ, whom David addresses. Those who are pure are saints, but God's saints are only those who are pure in God's sight.

There may also be a hidden meaning in the words *'all* the saints.' This may indicate that even among the saints of God there are many distinctions to be made, but that all are summoned to share in the fear of the Lord. What are these distinctions? There are saints who live in purity as priests. There are saintly rulers who govern honestly. There are saintly bishops who never cease to care for the Lord's flock. There are saintly monks, who are dead to the world and eager for the things of heaven, who are dead in flesh and who live in the spirit. There are saintly nuns who have willingly and totally devoted themselves to Christ as their husband. There are saints who keep their marriage bed unstained and preserve their vows faithfully. There are saints who earn a living for themselves and their families from a decent job honestly performed and have something left over to give those in need. A person's status in life is not so important as how much he fears the Lord. No one should say, 'I am not a monk, I am a married man and in business: how can I reach heaven?' Fear the Lord, and you will lack nothing, provided it is necessary for your salvation. Judging by the eyes of the flesh, there is no one who owns less than those who fear the Lord, and no one is better endowed with all kinds of good things than those who refuse to fear him and pursue the benefits of this world through fair means and foul. But if we judge truly, we find that those who are thought rich are the poorest of all, while the richest are those considered needy. And this is what the prophet now tells us.

'The rich were in need and hungry, but those who seek the Lord will not lose any good thing.' In the Bible, the word 'rich' is customarily used not to mean those with many possessions but those who trust in their own resources and are never satisfied even with these.[357] Thus we hear in the Gospel: 'How difficult it is for a rich man to enter into the kingdom of God.'[358] Elsewhere the Lord proclaims woe to the rich;[359] and Paul says, 'Those who want to become rich fall into temptations and into the devil's net.'[360] The antithesis in the two parts of the sentence confirms this view:

* * * * *

356 Matt 23:27
357 With what follows, compare the similar exegesis of Augustine *Enarratio in psalmum 33* 2.14–15 PL 36 315–16.
358 Mark 10:23
359 Luke 6:24
360 1 Tim 6:9

our saying is composed of opposites, and to the rich it opposes those who seek the Lord, so that we must understand that we are here dealing with those rich people who bask in their own resources and take no thought for God. There are many such among the wealthy, who have either acquired their wealth dubiously, or increased it dishonestly, or hung on to it greedily. Not without point is the well-known saying 'Every rich man is either unjust or heir to one unjust.'[361] The man who builds magnificent palaces, whose house is full of gold and silver vessels, of fabrics, of all kinds of furniture, who gives splendid dinners, who dresses like a king and goes about surrounded by crowds of servants, who keeps large numbers of horses and numerous estates, whose coffers are stuffed with gold and who has yet more out at interest, who is worth untold sums – everyone honours him as a rich man and all but worships him as a demigod. But if you turn this Silenus inside out,[362] you will find within the most appalling poverty: a mind empty of faith, devoid of charity, ungraced with any wisdom or virtue. Now compare the riches of the spirit with those owned by the wealthy, and you will see how much more pitiable is that rich man's poverty than that of a public beggar with torn clothes, empty wallet, almost no food, and no pleasures at all, but who in his inmost mind has piety, modesty, restraint, chastity, and sobriety. Wisdom is more valuable than all material riches, and whoever has wisdom surpasses all Croesuses and Crassuses.[363]

'Rich in faith' says James 'and heirs of the kingdom.'[364] Those who bewail their poverty when they have an abundance of the good things of the mind are ungrateful towards God. If the faith which justifies us and the charity which makes us rich in good works could be bought for money, would you not rush to spend unlimited sums? Yet when God has freely endowed you with such priceless gifts, you complain that you are poor because you do not have those things which are neither truly good nor permanent, since they make people no happier and are given and removed at the whim of fortune. The Stoics say that only the wise man is rich,[365] and they had seen only a shadow of true wisdom, as though in a dream: will you lament your poverty, when you know the true God, and Jesus Christ whom he has sent?[366] More, you possess God himself, in whom are all good

* * * * *

361 *Adagia* I ix 47
362 On the Silenus figure see n11 above.
363 *Adagia* I vi 74: *Croeso, Crasso ditior*
364 James 2:5
365 As reported for instance in Cicero *Paradoxa Stoicorum* 6
366 John 17:3

things! So if we are speaking of what is truly good, the words of our psalm are always true: 'The rich were poor, but those who seek the Lord will not lack any good thing.' And even if we apply it to externals, although it is not invariably true, still it is often the case that the rich are reduced to poverty through war, shipwreck, gambling, riotous living, or some other calamity. 'The third to inherit has no good from ill-gotten gains': it is not without reason that this saying has gained currency.[367] And even if none of these things happens, it is certain that death will take away everything. It is there that you can see the last degree of poverty and a complete reversal of fortune, when the rich man begs for a drop of water and is refused, while Lazarus finds refreshment in Abraham's bosom.[368] Consider also that no one is rich who desires more, who does not venture to use what he has gained, and who is always 'adding to his pile.'[369] As much as what he has not, the miser lacks what he has.[370] It is the mind that makes us rich, and not an abundance of things around us.

Where our version has 'were in need' [eguerunt] the Greek has ἐπτώχευσαν, which means 'were beggars' [mendicarunt]. Hebrew experts translate 'were made paupers' [depauperati sunt], that is, were reduced to poverty.[371] In order to make it clear that the poverty is extreme, the words 'and hungry' have been added. For a time is coming when those who ignored the goods of the spirit that they were offered here will seek them in vain. They will return at evening, they will suffer hunger like dogs, and in vain they will prowl about the city[372] – just as the unfortunate Jews for some time now have been prowling about the church, seeing it rich with so many divine gifts, seeing it refreshed with Christ's body, made drunk with his blood, and nourished by the marrow of Scripture, while they themselves are dying of hunger and thirst.

Again, where we read 'the rich,' Jerome translates 'lions,' and another version has 'lion cubs.'[373] These variations present no obstacle to our understanding but rather give a fuller explanation. As we have said, the subject

* * * * *

367 Proverbial; see Walther 5081.

368 Luke 16:19–31

369 Horace Satires 1.1.34

370 Publilius Syrus 684, Otto 225; Erasmus' source was probably Jerome Ep 53.10 PL 22 549.

371 This is a marginal alternative given in the Psalterium of Felice da Prato 18 recto.

372 Cf Ps 58:7/59:6.

373 Jerome Psalterium iuxta Hebraeos PL 28 (1890) 1213 and Felice da Prato Psalterium 18 recto; compare the various English renderings.

of the verse is not any person who happens to be well off, but those who are rich in this world, whose reliance on their wealth makes them proud and cruel, who increase their riches by robbing and plundering the poor, who oppress the weak, who keep the merchandise of the needy for themselves, and who exhaust the supplies of the lowly by usury and monopolies. These are flesh-eating lions, and their children are lion cubs, or else they themselves are the cubs of that lion which is always prowling about snatching at someone to devour him.[374] It is to rich people of this sort that James announces imminent poverty: 'Come now, you rich, weep and lament for the misery that is coming to you. Your riches have turned rotten,' and so on.[375] Miserable riches! The truly rich are those who have laid up their treasure in heaven, where thieves do not dig, nor moths make holes, nor mould corrupt.[376]

Some take this passage to refer to the Jews and gentiles, and this too makes good sense.[377]The Jews thought they were rich in righteous works, and spurned Christ, who had true riches to offer. The gentiles, on the other hand, had no law, no synagogue, no knowledge of God, nor indeed anything which satisfied them, yet they were made rich through faith, while the Jews were reduced to utter poverty, having now no city, no temple, no sacrifices, no God and no Christ – for whoever denies the Son has denied the Father. And so the Lord has filled the gentiles, who thirsted after righteousness,[378] with good things, and the rich he has sent empty away.[379] Those who felt nausea on seeing the bread of heaven,[380] who made excuses when invited to the great feast,[381] deserve to go hungry. Those who filled in with earth the veins of living water opened by Isaac deserve to thirst.[382] And so while they go hungry, the weak, the blind, and the lame recline at the Lord's table.

What befell the Jews through long usage will happen also to Judaizing Christians, who are inwardly devoid of faith and love and boast of their diet, their fasts, the observances, and like formalities, saying, 'We are rich and lack nothing; we have such a huge supply of good works that

* * * * *

374 Cf 1 Pet 5:8.
375 James 5:1–2
376 Cf Matt 6:19–20.
377 Thus Basil *Homilia in psalmum* 33 PG 29 368A–B
378 Matt 5:6
379 Luke 1:53
380 Possibly an allusion to Num 11:4–7, or to 1 Cor 11:29
381 Luke 14:16–24
382 Cf Gen 26:15–22.

we can enrich others with them.' But what does the Holy Spirit say in the Apocalypse to one who is rich in this way? 'You do not know that you are wretched, miserable, poor, naked, and blind.' Then how will such a one become truly rich? 'I advise you to buy from me gold refined by fire,' and so on.[383] Anyone who wants to become rich through his own resources actually becomes poor, but one who truly wishes to become rich should buy from him who is rich for the benefit of all and admit that whatever good thing he has comes from him. 'Those who seek such treasures will not lack any good thing.' 'But these people who search do not have gold, ivory, jewels, or fine cloth.' If they do not have them, they are not good. 'But they do not have beauty or strength or good health.' Even these are not really good, and for those who are lacking in them, it is better not to have them. The word 'to seek' is used once more when Solomon tells us to be diligent and vigilant: 'If you seek wisdom like money and bury it like treasure, then you will understand the fear of the Lord, and you will find the knowledge of God.'[384] Heavenly wisdom has inexhaustible veins of water, which must be tapped continuously as long as we remain in this life. The Jews seek this treasure on the surface – the letter – and in dietary prescriptions, but the riches of the spirit are hidden deeper than this. What expense, what labour is spared when people dig deep into the earth in order to find at last some gold in the dust? Then how can we be too lazy to search through so priceless a treasure in order to find God?

Now that the prophet has used such splendid promises to make all of us eager to fear the Lord and to seek him out, someone may ask what is the fear of the Lord, or how is the Lord to be sought out? Those who speak thus show that they can be taught, because they are eager to learn. So the Holy Spirit is pleased with these words, and says, 'Come, you sons, listen to me, I will teach you the fear of the Lord.' There you hear the voice of a most loving and most gentle teacher, if only we offer ourselves as ready pupils. One who moulds the soul is more of a father than one who begets the body,[385] and a pupil owes more to a good teacher than to a parent: from one he gains life, from the other the ability to live well, and life is in

* * * * *

383 Rev 3:17–18
384 Prov 2:4–5
385 Basil here comments (*Homilia in psalmum* 33 PG 29 369A) that 'the pupil is the teacher's spiritual child.' Erasmus goes further: the teacher is a truer parent than are the biological mother and father. This sentiment recurs in, for example, *Concio de puero Iesu* (CWE 29 66) and as a topic heading in *Ecclesiastes* (LB V 1086B).

vain unless it is well lived. But what does the teacher say to the Jews who stopped up their ears against this philosophy? 'You brood of vipers, how can you speak good when you are evil?'[386] They were serpents who had closed their ears to the voice of the cunning enchanter.[387] So if we want to be children of God, we must offer ears that are both teachable and eager; teachable because of faith, eager because of hope. If we have been God's good disciples, we shall be his children also. Let us not say with the Jews, 'Go away from us, we want no knowledge of your ways,' for this is the sin against the Holy Spirit, which will not be forgiven either in this world or in the world to come.[388] Let us rather receive the word of the Lord, for to all who received him he gave power to become the children of God, believing in the name of Jesus.[389] So James says 'He brought us forth by the word of truth, so that we might be a kind of first-fruits of his creation.'[390] And our Lord in the Gospel calls his disciples 'my children';[391] he had given birth to them, and like a careful mother he held them in his lap, loving them more tenderly the more weaknesses they revealed. And Paul uses these words to the Corinthians: 'I became your father in Christ Jesus through the gospel,'[392] and these to the Galatians: 'My little children, to whom I give birth once more, until Christ is formed in you.'[393] The seed is the word of God,[394] and if faith is added to it, it produces a new creation. And so our heavenly Father calls to us from his seat 'Come, you sons.'

Let us give ear to him who calls us so lovingly, let us go to him, since he has not consented to come first to us: 'Come to me, make your heart ready.' Some scholars, using a Hebrew reading, translate 'make yourselves ready' instead of 'come.'[395] One who presents himself to be taught has made himself ready, and one who has simple trust is fit to be taught. A professor of human philosophy will say that one who learns must feel trust. It is not always safe to trust a human being, however learned, yet it is entirely

* * * * *

386 Matt 12:34
387 Ps 57:5–6/58:4–5
388 Matt 12:32
389 John 1:12
390 James 1:18
391 Mark 10:24, John 13:33
392 1 Cor 4:15
393 Gal 4:19
394 Luke 8:11
395 This is a marginal alternative given by Felice da Prato *Psalterium* 18 recto, and according to Chomarat *Grammaire et rhétorique* 669 a distorted echo of a rabbinical tradition.

safe to trust God, who cannot be deceived and knows not deceit. Be sons, and come – not to the Jews, not to the philosophers, the astrologers, or the magicians, but to me, of whom the Father said, 'This is my beloved Son: hear him.'[396] Why listen to the uninspiring stories of the Jews? Why listen to the Pharisees, who teach only human teachings? Why listen to the Stoics or the Peripatetics, who set forth what they do not understand?[397] Hear me; I teach a philosophy that belongs to heaven, I teach what is certain and assured, what I have seen with my Father. In the same way, according to Solomon, wisdom calls out in the busy street and offers her words at the city gates: 'How long, little ones, will you love your childhood? Turn and give heed to my reproof.'[398]

There can be no doubt that so great a teacher, who calls us so lovingly, has something important to offer: so what is it? 'I will teach you the fear of the Lord.' He has already commended the fear of the Lord to us in glowing terms. What are these terms? That those who fear the Lord are protected by angels from all dangers. And further? That those who fear God are untouched by any kind of want. The rewards are outstanding, but in order to fear the Lord in the correct way you need instruction. How many rules must you learn to become skilled in dialectic? – yet dialecticians do not immediately gain happiness.[399] How many precepts do you need to learn the art of painting? – but how slender are the wages. How much more studious, then, we should be in learning the art of fearing the Lord. Let us approach eagerly, for this teacher gives us the very thing that he commends. Teach us, then, best of teachers, we are attentive.

This, then, is what our eloquent teacher says to all mortals: Whoever is affected by the fear of human beings cannot properly fear the Lord. Not every kind of fear of the Lord immediately makes a person happy; evil spirits quiver and tremble at the day of the Last Judgment,[400] and wicked men fear the Lord as he sends thunder and lightning, shakes the earth, sends pestilence, or threatens shipwreck. Then even the wicked fall on their knees,

* * * * *

396 Matt 17:5
397 Erasmus picks two of the most influential of the ancient schools of philosophy and implies that they had an inkling of (Christian) truth without the revelation to put it in context; study of them by Christians is therefore superfluous. The Stoic school was founded by Zeno of Citium (335–263 BC); the Peripatetics were the followers of Aristotle.
398 Prov 1:22–3
399 In the medieval arts course, dialectic was virtually equivalent to logic; Erasmus treats it dismissively as a branch of the scholastic philosophy he despises.
400 Cf James 2:19.

raise their hands to heaven, beseech God with prayers, shout aloud, and implore his help. But their fear of the Lord is like fear of a robber or an evil spirit: they are afraid that they will be hurt, and when the danger passes the fear disappears as well. This is a slavish sort of fear, a temporary and barren one also; but the fear of the Lord is fertile and brings hope to birth in us, as Isaiah writes: From your fear 'we have conceived, O Lord, and as it were laboured in travail, and we have given birth to the spirit' of salvation.[401] No different from this is Solomon's saying, that 'the fear of the Lord is the beginning of wisdom.'[402] You hear of fertility and abundance; now hear of constancy: 'The fear of the Lord is holy; it remains throughout all ages.'[403] If you are a servant, be an honest servant, do not serve appearances, and fear your master – not because he may in anger send you poverty, sickness, or some other bodily ill, but fear him who will judge the living and the dead, fear him who will say to those who did not obey him, 'Go, accursed ones, into the eternal fire, which is prepared for the devil and his angels.'[404] A man's slave can escape his master's notice, he can evade punishment, but you, where can you run to escape? Where will you hide to avoid his notice? Then if you are a servant possessed of hope, fear this punishment, and if you are a son, honour the Father who so loves you, who deserves so well of you; honour him so much that even if there were no hell your love would still make you wish not to offend him in anything. But anyone who says that he fears God and still perseveres in his sins and fails to keep the Lord's commandments, should be aware that he does not fear the Lord correctly.

Listen, all the world, as our heavenly teacher calls out: 'Who is there that wishes for life, who desires to see good days?' Surely in reply to this no one hesitates to call out: 'We wish, we desire.' But if you like the reward, fulfil your obligations: 'Keep your tongue from evil,' and so on. And when you hear the word 'life,' do not think of bodily life, which is more truly death than life, since we hold it in common not only with those who lack faith but even with brute beasts. The words are not addressed to animals, but to man, who shares in reason. A human life is something special, which beasts cannot know; this is the life lived by those who are animated by the spirit of God, by those who live devout lives. The soul is the life of the body, and God is the life of the soul; after this life comes blessed immortality.

* * * * *

401 Isa 26:17–18; the evident sense has been altered by Erasmus' additions.
402 Ecclus 1:16 / Sir 1:14
403 Ps 18:10/19:9
404 Matt 25:41

Who then is there who longs for this life, who wishes to see good days? Those days when one's whims are indulged and when one makes a handsome profit are usually called good, but there is no true enjoyment where there is a bad conscience, and there is no true gain where good sense is lost. Someone may quote, 'Who follows me must take up his cross'[405] – those who wish to live faithfully in Christ Jesus will suffer persecution – and ask how this relates to the 'good days' promised here? Our sufferings in this world last for an instant; the fulfilment of the Lord's promises made through his prophet lasts for ever. And yet any true enjoyment, any true rejoicing, is found only in the minds of those who fear the Lord. A mind free from worries, as Solomon says, is like a continual feast.[406] Who is there who had greater experience of every kind of trouble than Paul, yet how he rejoices everywhere in his epistles! He writes to the Corinthians: 'I am filled with comfort, I have superabundant joy in each of my afflictions.'[407] It was not sufficient to write 'abundant': he writes 'superabundant,' trying to express almost a kind of drunkenness of joy.

In slave auctions, the auctioneer calls out, 'Who is there who wants to buy a slave with musical and linguistic skills?' He offers anyone the chance to buy if he pays the price. Similarly Christ excludes no one from the sale of such happiness, but calls out, 'Who is the man who wishes for life, who desires to see good days?' Everyone replies for himself, 'I wish, I desire' ('desiring' is rather more than 'wishing'). If you wish, here are the goods ready for you; now you hand over the money. What is the price? 'Keep your tongue from evil, and let not your lips speak deceit.' Next, this sentiment is repeated in different words. Is it sufficient not to sin with the tongue? Certainly not, and straightway 'Turn from evil' is added, meaning 'depart from every kind of wicked deed.' Even that is not enough, for there follows 'and do good.' These actions prove that we have the true fear of the Lord. But why pick only the tongue, out of all the parts of the body?[408] Because no part is more useful if it is used properly, and none more harmful if it is not controlled in the correct manner. For this reason Solomon says, 'Death and life are in the hands of the tongue. Who guards his tongue, guards his

* * * * *

405 Matt 16:24
406 Prov 15:15
407 2 Cor 7:4
408 Basil too discusses the evils of the tongue at this point (*Homilia in psalmum 33* PG 29 373B–D), but Erasmus himself had already exhaustively explored the themes that follow in the *Lingua* of 1525 (CWE 29 250–412).

soul.'[409] And according to St James, 'If anyone thinks himself religious and does not restrain his tongue, his religion is in vain. And anyone who does not err in his words is a perfect man.'[410] Since the tongue is by nature slippery and volatile, we are told to use the fear of the Lord like a bridle to restrain it. The first step in virtue is to be silent, not only with our mouth but in our thoughts, so that in silence and hope may be our strength,[411] for where there is much talking sin cannot be far away.[412] Pythagoras demanded five years' silence of his disciples:[413] can we wonder if Christ asks those who learn the heavenly philosophy to restrain their tongues? Be slow to speak, quick to hear, and in sacred matters be long in learning before you teach. Pythagoras wanted his disciples to be silent, but for Christ it is enough to keep the tongue from evil, under this name including vice of every kind.

The opening lines of this psalm were 'I will bless the Lord at all times; his praise shall be ever on my lips.' It was for this purpose above all that human beings were given a tongue, and its next most important use is to teach, advise, and comfort our neighbour. The third use of the tongue is as a sword, when we stand up bravely to defend Christ's glory, in order to ward off and strike down the enemy. But the utmost form of evil is to spew out blasphemies against God, and the most destructive is to slander one's neighbour and speak against him, for that is a kind of murder. Those who knowingly commit perjury are only a short step from blasphemy against God, and even closer are those who either from wickedness or bad habit take horrible oaths. When the French happen to mention their king, they take off their hats and add a worthy prayer, 'May God give him a good life' – but Christians, with a complete lack of respect, continually mention God or Christ with filthy lips. There are some who are unable to tell a foolish or obscene joke without adding 'by God' at every other word. I wish that this vicious habit was heard only in Germany. But the custom has reached the point where it seems almost the proper practice of court and city to keep repeating 'by God.' What do these words sound like in the mouth of a young girl, or in the mouth of a priest or monk? Yet we are so accustomed to it that we see no disgrace and no sin. Children learn it from their parents and

* * * * *

409 Prov 18:21, 19:16 (the latter passage altered)
410 James 1:26, 3:2
411 Isa 30:15
412 Cf Prov 10:19.
413 Diogenes Laertius *Lives of the Philosophers* 8.10

nurses, and a child hears another child swearing by God. I repeat, this is very close to blasphemy, but closer still are those who swear by Christ's passion, by the five wounds, by Christ's head, by his brain, by his hair, by his belly, his navel, his bowels, by God's feet and shoes. But all blasphemy is surpassed by those – the mind shrinks from recording this – who swear 'by God's harlot' or 'by God's mother's private parts.' The same is true of those who cannot promise to do anything for certain unless they say 'I will do this even if God is unwilling' or 'in God's despite.' And they do not say these things only in terrible misfortune, when sometimes an unbearable grief forces shocking words out of us, but in the most trivial circumstances, when they have a bad throw at dice or when they miss a catch at ball. Tongues infected with Gehenna's poison! Even for such loathsome evil they advance the excuse of custom. That might go some way towards excusing less serious faults, but general habit can be no more an exculpation of blasphemy than of sacrilege or murder.

Now what sort of good wishes do these people who blaspheme against God give to their neighbour? I am not now speaking of the curses an angry man heaps on another, but the curses friend gives to friend by way of pleasantness. In some regions someone who wants to seem friendly will greet a friend he has not seen for some time with: 'God give you a hundred lumps! (meaning the plague) – where have you been all this time?' And in another part of the world they say 'God send you epilepsy, when can we get together for a drink?' Custom makes this nonsense seem a sophisticated way of speaking. More tolerable are the curses some people inflict on themselves when they want to be believed: 'May a huge devil carry me off if I've ever seen anyone play ball better' they say. And how many ways we have of cursing someone when we are angry: 'Devil break your neck,' 'Get pleurisy,' 'Get Lazarus' scabs' (meaning leprosy), 'Hope you have a flow of blood.' How can those who cannot keep their tongues from such wicked sayings believe that they fear the Lord? Can the same person fear and blaspheme against the same object? Once the punishment for cursing a father or mother was death, so what punishment is appropriate for blasphemies against God? And yet whoever curses his neighbour curses God, for we help and harm Christ in his members. When someone insults the king's insignia or his statues, he is punished as one who does violence to the king's majesty; should not then one who curses another person, created in God's image and redeemed by Christ's blood, have cause to fear God? In a former time we blasphemed against God when we gave the honour due to him to evil spirits. That was the old tongue, but now that the Lord has given us a new tongue with which we have now confessed the true God and his Son with the Holy Spirit, let blasphemy be far from our mouths. Let us not misuse an organ dedicated to blessing by employing it to curse either God or man, but let us heed the Apostle's warning: 'Let no wicked speech come from your mouths, but any speech that is good to build up faith, so that it may give grace to those who hear.' And in order to convey that an evil-speaking tongue injures not only our neighbour but God, he adds: 'And do not grieve God's Holy Spirit, in whom you have been sealed for the day of redemption.'[414] From this you gather that the spirit of God dwells in the faithful, but that he is grieved in the blasphemer, the perjurer, the giver of curses, the disobedient, the speaker of shame.

How great is the sword that pierces the mind of one who truly loves and fears God when he hears a Christian uttering blasphemous phrases such as I have listed above. So that your tongue can be pure, make sure that you have a pure heart, for it is here that all the sins of the tongue well up as though from a spring. For this reason Paul continues, 'All bitterness and anger and resentment' – that is, the spring, what follows is the fruit – 'disturbance and blasphemy must be taken from your midst.' Is it enough to have a heart free from bitterness, anger, and resentment?' By no means, and so he adds, 'with all evildoing.'[415] he gives similar instructions to the Colossians: 'Now put away all of these from your mouths: anger, resentment, evildoing, blasphemy and shameful speech. Do not deceive one another.'[416] Why does he include the word 'now'? Previously, being pagans, you spoke like pagans, but now your mouth is consecrated to Christ: let it do nothing but serve his glory. 'For the rest, whatever is true, whatever is chaste, whatever is upright, whatever is holy, whatever is lovely, whatever is auspicious, if there be any goodness, if there be any praise for teaching, think on these things.'[417] Let these things pass through your mind, and then let your tongue speak out.

'And let not your lips speak deceit.' The first part of the verse seemed to be directed primarily at blasphemy, while this second part is aimed against deceiving one's neighbour. One who hurls unrestrained abuse at his neighbour wounds him openly, not by tricks or deceit; one who uses guile like poison is even more destructive. Such tricks are the use of perjury for deceit, the telling of lies, defamatory stories whispered in secret, the spoiling of a reputation by putting out scandal sheets under a pseudonym, corruption by flattery, leading people into evil traps through ingenious

* * * * *

414 Eph 4:29–30
415 Eph 4:31
416 Col 3:8–9
417 Phil 4:8

and wicked plans, spreading false teaching, and misleading by hypocrisy: in fact, anything that uses skill for a harmful purpose is deceit. Since it is here that the majority of evils are born, a holy tongue is numbered among a good person's chief praises: 'Who speaks truth in his heart, who does not work deceit with his tongue.'[418] If the tongue is restrained and the mind pure, there automatically follow the next words of both psalms, the one giving praise: 'nor does wrong to his neighbour,'[419] the other giving instruction: 'Turn from evil and do good.' When through baptism or penance we cast off the old man with his acts and put on the new, who is renewed in the knowledge of God, according to the image of his creator, we are turning from evil. When we have been cleansed from our sins and we adorn the empty house that is our mind with works of goodness – with sobriety, modesty, restraint, sincerity, almsgiving, prayer, thanksgiving, sacred studies, and contemplation of the holy – then we are doing good. The first steps in piety are to move away from wrongdoing and to offer a pure heart to the Holy Spirit as fit material for his actions.

It is not in vain that the Holy Spirit has added these last words. Today, too, you will see people who think they are perfectly good if they refrain from injury, fraud, and theft but keep what they have to themselves. They quarrel with none and they slander none, but they fail to teach or advise or rebuke their neighbour. They do not indulge in drunken excess, but they give no help to those who are dying of hunger. They speak no blasphemy, but they make no resistance to blasphemous actions. Enough examples: they live without committing offences, but they live for themselves and think only of their own peace of mind. This is not the way of St Paul, who weeps with those who weep,[420] who burns with every sin committed, who shares the sicknesses of any and everyone, and who endures infamy and scorn to secure the salvation of individuals.

Since there are many different kinds of evil, why does our text say, 'turn from evil,' in the singular? The reason is that this form is the clearest way to express the whole and entire body of sins, just like the words of John the Baptist about Christ: 'Behold him who takes away the sin of the world.'[421] In the same way the psalm has earlier said, 'Keep your tongue from evil,' so that no kind of evil can be excluded. There are those who say,

* * * * *

418 Ps 14:3/15:2–3
419 Ps 14/15:3
420 Rom 12:15; the rest of the sentence is not a quotation, but a description of Paul's concern with individuals shown in many of the epistles.
421 John 1:29

'I keep my tongue from blasphemy, but it's not necessary to keep it from slander – that's a universal failing' or 'I don't perjure myself, but speaking lies and obscenity is another matter.' And we hear from some quarters, 'I don't indulge in adultery or incest, just in simple fornication,' and 'I restrain myself from theft, but I can't restrain myself from drunkenness.' It was in order to prevent such sentiments from being heard that the psalmist said simply 'Turn from evil.'

Perhaps we may also note that he says, 'turn from evil' rather than 'avoid evil.' In this life everything is full of evils, and so no one can avoid evil; but one may turn aside from it to avoid injury. One turns aside to avoid a weapon by bending one's body; so whenever an opportunity for sin is hurled and evil rushes down upon us, let us turn aside and move our thoughts in another direction. If you ask where, the answer is to prayer, to charitable gifts, to reading the Bible, to the torments of hell and the reward of eternal life. But if we are to turn aside from evil whenever it seeks us out, what can we hope for those who deliberately acquire the raw material of sin for themselves?

Again, one might ask at this point, what is evil and what is good? The obvious evils are demonstrated by the law ingrained in everyone's mind, 'Do not do to another what you would not like done to you.'[422] But further, whatever is forbidden in the Bible is evil, and whatever is advised and commended there is good. And here I may also refer to another reason why mystical writings attribute chief responsibility to the tongue. Everyone can see that both the belly and the parts beneath it are responsible for many evils and that numerous sins are committed by the eyes and the hands, but the tongue alone does more harm than all these put together. But what in fact is this other reason? Just as the origins of every evil began with the tongue, so the beginnings of all salvation came also through the tongue. It was the serpent's tongue, both lying and blasphemous, that led Eve into error. God had said, 'If you eat, you will die,' but the serpent says, 'You will not die, but your eyes will be opened, and you will be like gods.'[423] This is deceit, giving false promises in order to mislead, and it is blasphemy, attributing untruthfulness to God. Doubtless then Eve seduced her husband with soft words, for 'evil talk corrupts good ways.'[424] You see how much evil the first authors of the human race brought upon themselves from this

* * * * *

422 Cf Matt 7:12; but Erasmus' wording suggests that he thinks of this principle as part of the 'natural' law, accessible to all without Christian revelation.
423 Cf Gen 3:4–5.
424 1 Cor 15:33; *Adagia* I x 74

brief conversation. They hid themselves – a typical ploy of one who wants to use deception if he can. They were called to acknowledge their sin, for in the tongue lay the remedy for the evil. But the tongue was already poisoned with deceit; Adam concealed his crime, and when he could not hide he advanced a false excuse: 'I was afraid because I was naked.'[425] If he had really been afraid, he would not have touched the tree forbidden to him. 'Because I was naked' – here he tacitly accuses God of not giving clothing to his settler. He heard God relate his sin: 'You ate from the tree which I forbade you to taste; now, poor wretch, only keep your tongue from evil and confess your sin.' But he refused, and adding evil to evil he threw the blame on the woman, or rather indirectly on God himself, for giving her as companion to him. What of the woman? She blamed the serpent. This is not speaking the truth, it is an attempt to deceive even God himself, who sees all hearts.[426] And hence came that whole regiment of evils among which mortals now spend their lives.

From the tongue came the sickness; from the tongue came also healing. In place of the serpent's blasphemy and lying tongue came the Word of God, in whose mouth is found no falsehood, but who gave glory to God in all things and offered words of life to the human race. He carried out his own teachings and fulfilled his promises. Eve heard the serpent and rushed to death through the devil's guile; the church heard Christ and was restored to life through Christ's spirit. The woman held converse with the serpent and learned to make excuses for sin, so deserving a curse; the church listened to Christ and learned to confess sins, so gaining a blessing: for blessed is the man who trusts in the Lord.[427] Those who are transformed on the model of the blessed one themselves become blessed. They attain righteousness by believing in their hearts, and they achieve salvation by confessing with their mouths. Anyone who renounces the devil and all his vain displays thus keeps his tongue from evil, and anyone who confesses that Jesus is the Son of God and the only author of all salvation speaks with a new tongue, magnifying God and helping his neighbour. The old man is cast off, and faith works through love in the new.[428] Is anything else needed? Nothing, other than to progress in the way of the Lord with-

* * * * *

425 Gen 3:10
426 Cf Acts 1:24, 15:8.
427 Jer 17:7. The parallels contrasting Adam with Christ and Eve with the church are traditional, though Erasmus omits the popular contrast of Eve and Mary.
428 Cf Gal 5:6.

out ceasing, 'until we reach the perfect man and the measure of Christ's fullness.'[429]

'Seek out peace and pursue it.' 'There is no peace for the wicked, says the Lord.'[430] Only piety gives true peace – a threefold peace. It causes man to be freed from his sins and to be at peace with God; in the apostle's words: 'Justified through faith, we have peace with God.'[431] But where does this peace come from – from our own merits? Certainly not; it comes from our Lord Jesus Christ. When our conscience does not trouble us about anything, we are at peace with ourselves, since nothing is more restive and ill-tempered than a bad conscience. And we shall have no difficulty in being at peace with our fellows if we speak ill of no one and take advantage of no one but speak good and do good for everyone to the best of our ability, and further, if we do not curse those who curse us and do not take vengeance on those who hurt us but return good for injuries. This is what Paul says in his Epistle to the Romans: 'If it is possible, having peace with all in so far as depends on us.' How can this be achieved? 'Not by defending yourselves,' or, more clearly, by avenging yourselves, 'but leave it to [God's] anger: for it is written, "Vengeance is mine, says the Lord, and I will repay."'[432]

This injunction, you will say, is extremely hard to follow, but still more difficult are the words earlier in the same chapter: 'Bless those who persecute you, bless them and do not curse them.'[433] The apostles did this, and so did Paul, yet they did not have peace with all men; for this reason he prefaces his advice with 'if it is possible,' and certainly the apostles had peace even with Jews and with pagans in so far as it lay in their power.

This is the chief fruit of a good tree,[434] not to allow injuries inflicted by anyone to remove us from peace of mind and not to allow any insults to keep us from the desire to do good. Other fruits we can easily imitate, or they can deceive us. We read of monks in the desert of old who would compete with each other in prayer, fasting, ragged clothes, and poor food, in nights spent on the bare ground, and in extremes of heat and cold. Some

* * * * *

429 Eph 4:13
430 Isa 48:22
431 Rom 5:1
432 Rom 12:18–19, quoting Deut 32:35
433 Rom 12:14
434 Cf Matt 7:17; also see *In psalmum 1*, where the tree is a central motif, especially CWE 63 44–5.

would take no food for three days, some for six, some even longer; we read of some with worms in their mouths because of their starvation. All of this gave them a great reputation for sanctity with the uneducated, but when those among these saints who became bishops were maligned and injured, it was immediately plain, as Chrysostom says, that they were madmen, incapable of bearing even the slightest wrong.[435] Trees of this sort have a diseased root; they have leaves in abundance but bear none of the fruit of true piety. It is likely that Satan gains quite as much from contests of this kind as he does from the dissolute behaviour of others: I refer to such as indulge in these pursuits with no sense of measure or from some purely human motive. Possibly even today you will find people whose use of such practices gives them a reputation of great holiness both with others and with themselves, and yet who need not receive even a blow – hurtful words will suffice – for them to summon the whole world to vengeance, so that their actions proclaim how far they are from real piety.

Let us all fear the Lord, and let us all become children of peace, forgiving each other in the love of God, so that together we may follow those things that are of peace and together guard those things that contribute to our spiritual formation.[436] There are many things in life that weaken the foundations of peace and harmony, and consequently the prophet wants us to be vigilant and careful in preserving peace: 'Seek out peace and pursue it.' If you have a quarrel with your neighbour, make sure that you become friendly with him once more; make it up to him if you have offended, heal if you have wounded. If he injures you without provocation, forgive him from your heart, drive out his anger by kind words, shower him with benefits; if you do this, you will heap burning coals on his head.[437] There are those, however, who respond to kindness by growing more harsh. What can you do with such people? They are not human beings, they are more savage than wild beasts, which may be savage by nature but are still tamed by kindness. But you have played the part of a human being, you have sought peace; it remains for you to pursue it.

We pursue those things which elude us, and we pursue things which are in the process of completion. Complete and perfect peace does not occur in this life, but we must still strive towards perfection as far as our human weakness will allow, since if we do not seek out and pursue peace while we are here, we will not reach that blessed peace of the kingdom of heaven.

* * * * *

435 Chrysostom *De sacerdotio* 3.13 PG 48 649. Erasmus had edited this work in 1525.
436 Rom 14:19
437 Rom 12:20

Meanwhile, the peace of God that passes all understanding will keep our hearts and minds in Christ Jesus,[438] until the coming of that which is perfect in every part, when we shall be no more mixed with impurities, but God will be all in all.[439] But before that time, it might seem that the faithful face two dangers if they never retaliate: firstly, amid such a crowd of the wicked there might be no good people left; and secondly, if they go unpunished the wicked might be moved to greater extremes of daring and wrongdoing. Both objections are met by the prophet in two verses, in which he tells us that the faithful will never lack a defence, however hard pressed they may be, and that the wicked will not go unpunished for their evil deeds. 'The eyes of the Lord,' he says, 'are upon the righteous, and his ears are towards their prayers. But the face of the Lord is upon those who do evil, to cut off their memory from the earth.' What can anyone fear, whom can he fear, if the Lord's favouring eye is always upon him? He allows his own to suffer affliction for a while, it pleases him to watch the struggles of the faithful; but while he watches them he gives them strength to keep them from going under and increases their power so that they prevail. One weak, defenceless man is conspired against by the masses, by savage hordes of men in armour, who attack him with trickery, wickedness, poisoned tongues, bribery, and above all with the pretence that they have weapons. They run up and down, all over the world; there is nowhere untouched by the serpents' poison of their lips as they blow the trumpet of Allecto.[440] 'Come, everybody; let no one refuse to join this campaign. Let us oppress the righteous poor man, let us not spare him, let us lie in wait for him, because he is inconvenient to us and opposes our actions. He reproaches us for sins against the Law, and accuses us of sins against our training. He claims to have knowledge of God and calls himself son of God. He became to us a reproof of our thoughts; the very sight of him is a burden to us, because he is unlike others in his ways, and his ways are strange. We are considered by him as something base, and he keeps himself from our ways. Let us condemn him to a shameful death.'[441] Here the conspiracy of the Scribes, Pharisees, and priests against

* * * * *

438 Phil 4:7; Erasmus adopts the reading of the Greek text 'will keep' as against most manuscripts of the Vulgate, which have 'may it keep.'
439 1 Cor 15:28
440 One of the Furies; Erasmus has in mind the episode in Virgil *Aeneid* 7.323–539, where as agent of Juno Allecto stirs up fear and hatred of the Trojan newcomers among the Italians and then herself blows the trumpet that summons to war.
441 Cf Wisd 2:10–20; the passage has been shortened and slightly altered.

the poor man Christ is so plainly depicted that if the church's judgment was not different I might suspect that this book was written after Christ's resurrection.[442]

The actions of the Pharisees towards Christ are repeated today against Christ's sheep by those like the Pharisees, who are afraid for their power, who fear lest their tricks be revealed, who are anxious for their bellies and their pleasures. Now how great do you suppose that poor man's courage will be? What will he do, surrounded by so many lions, dogs, and vipers? What else will he do but turn his eyes to the Lord and commit himself to him who though one is more powerful than all evil spirits and all the legions of the wicked? Then, trusting in his defence, he will say with the prophet 'The Lord is my salvation, whom shall I fear? The Lord is the protector of my life, of whom shall I be afraid?'[443] And again, 'I shall not fear the people in their thousands who surround me.'[444] 'Whether I live or die, I live or die to the Lord.'[445]

The conspirators think: 'If he keeps his eyes trained on the upright, he will not see our plans, and we shall do what we do without punishment.' But this is not the case. Why so? 'And the face of the Lord is upon those who do evil.' Hebrew scholars tell us that the word used here means not simply 'face' but 'terrible' and 'angry' face.[446] God does not change his face, but the same face brings comfort to one, fear to another. When soldiers who have fought well look at their leader they are happy, expecting a prize, while when deserters look at the same leader they are filled with horror, expecting to be punished. In the same way, at the coming of the Son of Man, how great will be the joy of those who endured shame, captivity, torture, fire, and death in his name, as they look on his face; but

* * * * *

442 This is certainly the assumption of most modern biblical scholars. But Erasmus' personal view will have depended partly on Jerome, who judged that the books now known as deuterocanonical or apocryphal did not belong to the true canon of the Old Testament (*Praefatio in libros Samuel et Malachim* PL 28 [1846] 556).

443 Ps 26/27:1

444 Ps 3:7/6

445 Cf Rom 14:8.

446 Chomarat (*Grammaire et rhétorique* 668) suggests that Erasmus simply guesses this from the context, but his starting point was more likely Basil, who states his opinion (*Homilia in psalmum 33* PG 377A) that the reference is to God's openly hostile face at the Day of Judgment, and Pseudo-Jerome (*Breviarium in psalmos* PL 26 [1845] 922): 'by *face* we understand *anger*.' If Erasmus also used Nicholas of Lyra, he would have found at this verse the incorrect statement made here about the Hebrew text.

how great the fear and trembling of those who dealt cruelly with his members. So as you wage war here against the ruses of the wicked, do not let yourselves become downcast, for you are fighting under the gaze of your everlasting leader, and he who slumbers not nor sleeps[447] never takes his eyes from you. If human resources fail, straightaway there is one with you to bring help if you will only send him messengers – your prayers, made with confidence. His ears are as ready and attentive as his eyes are friendly, so you have no need to work retaliation: the enemy's strategy, their plots and machinations, do not escape him, and his gaze is trained on them as well, not in order to crown them, but to make their memory vanish from the earth. When even the memory of someone has disappeared, that person has perished utterly. Clearly all the wicked are removed from the earth by death, but how is their memory removed? Surely the names of Caligula, Nero, Annas, and Caiaphas are well known today? We must take 'name' in the sense of a good reputation. Those men strove for praise, and they received it from vast numbers of people by killing Christ as a blasphemer and Christians as criminals, and they tried numerous ways of ensuring their glory among later generations. But all their glory was turned into utmost disgrace by the Lord. Those they killed as criminals are now honoured throughout the world as saints, while the name of those who killed them is universally abhorred, and if their memory survives it survives only to their shame. The memory happily endures of those whose names are written in heaven, where there will be no mention of the wicked; but those whose names are erased from the land of the living are wretchedly consigned to eternal oblivion, and are not recorded with the just.[448] This is the land which our Lord promises to the gentle in the gospel: 'Blessed are the meek, for they shall inherit the earth.'[449] This miserable earth of ours may be held, occupied, and possessed for a little while by lions, so long as that other and most happy land falls to the sheep in perpetuity.

As the psalmist earlier gave his own experience as an example, so now to strengthen further the trust felt by the devout he brings many righteous men before our eyes, so that we may hope for ourselves what we have seen befall others if we only imitate their righteousness. 'The righteous cried out,' he says, 'and the Lord heard them, and rescued them from all their afflictions.' The Hebrews in Egypt cried to the Lord, and the Lord set them free. They cried out in their exile in Babylon, and the Lord rescued

* * * * *

447 Cf Ps 120/121:4, Isa 5:27.
448 Cf Ps 68:29/69:28.
449 Matt 5:4

them. When persecuted by countless rulers they cried out, and the Lord delivered them. The three children in the burning furnace cried out, and they
were set free. Jonah cried out from the whale's belly, and the Lord saved
him. Elisha cried out, and those sent to kill him were blinded. Elkanah's
wife Hannah cried out and was freed from the reproach of barrenness.
If I were to enumerate all those who cried to the Lord and were heard, I
should run out of time sooner than of names. But we must ask whether
he always rescues those who cry out, and whether he saves them from
all their troubles. He snatched the three children from the fiery furnace,
but he did not rescue the Maccabees from their dreadful torments. He rescued Daniel from the lion's den, but he consented to the slaughter of innumerable prophets. He sent his angel to free Peter from chains, but when
Paul called on him three times he did not free him from Satan's goads.[450]
There are some martyrs whom the Lord rescued temporarily but later allowed to be killed. I have given an answer to this problem on two previous
occasions:[451] firstly, they are rescued in accordance with their request. A devout cry for help is not a demand for release if it is better for him who
calls not to be released or if it conduces more to the glory of God. Consequently, whether they are delivered from torture or whether they die, they
have what they asked for. Secondly, anyone who is victorious has been delivered; so when the Lord gives the righteous sufficient spiritual strength
to place them above all evils, he has delivered them by ensuring that they
are unconquered. And finally, death rescues the righteous from all their
troubles and places them where there is no pain but rather eternal joys –
so the righteous man who escapes evils by dying is more truly delivered
than one who is rescued temporarily, only to be saved for other and more
bitter struggles. Indeed, leaving the question of persecution to one side,
our whole mortal life brings countless miseries in its train. Swimming to
land is a more real escape from shipwreck than remaining on board, escaping the storm, and expecting another one – or a whirlpool, or a Charybdis,
or rocks, or some other danger. So if we follow the second argument, one
who though assailed by many hardships can be overcome by none because
he is protected by God's grace is rescued from all evils even in this life.

* * * * *

450 Biblical references for the named examples given are, in order: Exod 2:23–
    5, Jeremiah 50, Dan 3:24–94 / Song of Three Children 1–68 and Dan 3:24–7,
    Jon 2:2–11, 2 Kings 6:18, 1 Sam 1:10–20, 2 Macc 7, Dan 6:20–3, Acts 12:7–17, 2
    Cor 12:7–9. The contrast between the three holy children and the Maccabees
    is from Augustine on this passage (*Enarratio in psalmum* 33 2.22 PL 36 320).
451 Cf 325–6 and 329–31 above, the commentary on verses 5 and 6.

If we follow the third, death sets us free even from those inconveniences which inevitably accompany this mortal life, even for those who seem most fortunate in this world.

'The Lord is near to those whose heart is troubled, and he will save the humble in spirit.' Some render the Hebrew as 'The Lord is very near to those with contrite heart, and he will preserve those who are broken in spirit.'[452] The prophet brings many points together to strengthen our confidence. If the Lord is so close to us, why do we so often find the word 'cry'? Is God like a deaf man, so that even when he is next to us we have to shout? God is in your heart, and there is no need to shout in order to make him hear. He heard Hannah, though she did not speak aloud.[453] But anyone who asks the Lord for something with a lively faith and ardent love is calling on him with a loud voice, even if he is silent; it is for the followers of Baal to open their mouths as wide as possible and bellow.[454] Ours is a cry of the heart, not of the mouth. Faith and love have an inward voice that reaches the ears of God. In the human sense, God is nowhere, in that he is confined by no place, just as he is confined by no time; or if he is anywhere, he is equally everywhere, without location, as he is always, without a situation in time. But in the mystical language of Scripture, he is close to some and looks on others from a distance, as he gazes intently on some and keeps his face from others. When we look from on high, we see things less clearly the lower they are, but God – the highest of all things – looks most intently with his eyes of mercy on the very lowest. As another psalm puts it: 'God is on high, and regards things that are low; he knows things that are lofty from afar.'[455] What is the sense in raising yourself on high and placing yourself against God? If you want him to see and hear you, lower yourself – with your heart, not your body.[456] He loves a gentle heart, a humble heart, a heart that is contrite and broken. On whom will my spirit rest, he asks, if not on the humble, the peaceful, on one who fears my words? 'God resists the proud, but to the humble he gives grace.'[457] And another psalm says 'A contrite and humbled heart you will not despise.'[458]

* * * * *

452 This is Erasmus' variation on the text of the *Psalterium iuxta Hebraeos* PL 28 (1890) 1213, retaining the words *contritis* and *confractos* (where the Vulgate has *tribulato, humiles*).
453 1 Sam 1:13
454 Cf 1 Kings 18:26–8.
455 Ps 137/138:6
456 Cf Augustine *Enarratio in psalmum 33* 2.23 PL 36 320.
457 1 Pet 5:5
458 Ps 50:19/51:17

So what is a broken heart and a contrite spirit? It is a heart which places no faith in its own strength, and distrusting all the resources of human nature commits itself utterly to God's will, so that from it, as from clay, he may mould whatever he wishes.[459] What else is man but an earthen vessel – however rich, however powerful, however strong, however learned, however prudent he may be? If the clay grows hard, it cannot be shaped by the spirit but resists the grace that would mould it. Then shatter this pot with your rod, O Lord, and break it into pieces like a potter's vase,[460] so that when it is moistened again by your mercy it may obey your spirit, which fashions it anew. No one can be a vessel of honour, fit for every service in the great house of the Lord, unless he is refashioned by the heavenly potter, who asks of us nothing but a medium that obeys the fingers of the spirit. It was because they had grown hard through trust in their own works that the Jews always resisted Christ's teaching. But a contrite heart cannot resist anything; it does not raise itself up or plan retaliation, it simply awaits the hand of the Lord. Do not sculptors either look for dust or make their own, as fine and powdery as possible, in order to make their works as expressive as they can? This is the sort of heart we should show to the craftsman Spirit.

Speaking through Isaiah, the Lord says this to the Judaizer, the man who trusts in his own strength: 'But I will proclaim your righteousness, and your works will not help you. When you cry out, let your collection of idols set you free. The wind will carry them all away, and the breeze will bear them off.'[461] That is what he says to the hardened clay; now hear about the contrite heart. 'He who has faith in me shall inherit the earth. For the high and lofty one says this, he who dwells in eternity and whose name is holy: he dwells in a high and holy place, and in a contrite and humble spirit, so that he may give life to the spirit of the humble, and to the heart of the contrite.'[462] You hear of a Lord who dwells on high, but also of the same Lord who lives in a heart that is contrite, humble, and broken. So if we want the Lord to be close to us, we should prepare for him the dwelling place of our heart, so that he may make his power complete in our lowliness. He may fashion and refashion us, but nothing entrusted to his hands can perish.

The world gives us promises of delights which sound appealing, but it deceives us; it offers food, and in it places the executioner's instruments.

* * * * *

459 Cf Rom 9:21.
460 Ps 2:9
461 Isa 57:12–13
462 Isa 57:13, 15

But the Lord prophesies trouble, so that we may be forewarned and thus more easily bear what comes. Which is preferable, to move from temporary difficulties to everlasting joys or to go from fleeting comforts and the pleasures of the moment to the torments of hell? It was decreed by God that those who live a good life should suffer various tribulations in this world, so that their crown in the world to come might be the more glorious. 'Many are the tribulations of the righteous, but the Lord will deliver them from all of these.' It would be hard to hear that the afflictions of the righteous will be so many, if it did not go on to say 'but the Lord will deliver them from all of these.' The soldiers have much to endure, but a guaranteed victory is close at hand. If a human general could give such a certain promise to his troops, how eager and responsive his soldiers would be in the face of every peril! What does an Epaminondas[463] or some other such general promise to his men? If they are victorious, they will share in the plunder; if defeated, they will gain renown for their courage – a renown soon to be forgotten. But our general, Christ, promises his soldiers the wages of a good conscience while they remain here and in time to come an everlasting glory. Since he brings his promises to pass with no less ease than he makes them, why are we not there at the fight, in all eagerness?

To find out how much distress the Christian soldier must endure, it suffices to read St Paul's account of his campaigns: 'In many labours, in more imprisonments, with countless beatings, and frequently at death's door. Five times I have received from the Jews forty lashes minus one. Three times I have been beaten with rods, once I have been stoned, three times shipwrecked. I have spent a day and a night adrift at sea; on frequent journeys I have been in danger from rivers, in danger from bandits, in danger from my own people, in danger from the gentiles, in danger in the city, in danger in the wilderness, in danger in the sea, in danger from false brethren; in toil and hardship, in many wakeful nights, in hunger and thirst, in much fasting, in cold and without clothing. And besides those external perils, I am tortured inwardly by a pressing anxiety for all the churches.'[464] What a vast army of misfortunes – he has not described their sum total, or each individually. Yet he glories in all of them, because he realizes that they are only the material for greater glory. 'In the world you will have troubles,' says the Lord, 'but be confident, I have conquered the

* * * * *

463 The famous fourth-century Theban general who was largely responsible for the downfall of Sparta's influence in Greece; his sayings are recorded by Plutarch *Moralia* 192C–194C (*Regum et imperatorum apophthegmata*).
464 2 Cor 11:23–8, the last verse slightly altered

world.'[465] Trust in me, and you will conquer through me. If you trust in yourselves, you will be cast down; trust in me, and he who has rescued me will rescue you also if you are joined to me.

There are many afflictions that are not those of the righteous: war, plague, quarrels, lawsuits, and above all the torments of an uneasy conscience. But the afflictions peculiar to the righteous are those which they suffer on account of their righteousness. Robbers and brigands have their share of afflictions, even if they escape punishment, but only those are blessed who 'suffer many things for the sake of righteousness.'[466] The experience of hunger, thirst, cold, heat, illness, old age, and death only marks us out as human beings; yet they too can be changed into potential for our blessedness, if we wholeheartedly seek the kingdom of God and his righteousness. But what of those who have committed a crime and are punished by law? They too, if they truly repent, can change their affliction into good. There is a certain degree of righteousness in acknowledging one's lack of righteousness and patiently enduring the punishment one has deserved.

But supposing one were to ask for what reason the Lord wished those whom he has destined to inherit his kingdom to be put through so many trials here, when he could have let them live a pleasant life in this world and then translate them to immortality. 'O man, who art thou to reply to God?'[467] This was the Lord's decision. Is a disciple greater than his teacher, or a servant than his master?[468] Christ took that way to his glory; are you asking to be moved from pleasures to pleasures? If you ask why the righteous suffer afflictions in this world, what you are saying is like asking why soldiers attack an enemy, or why athletes oppose each other in competition. Obviously, the answer is so that their qualities may be universally apparent. Who would admire the patience of Job if he had not been pitted against Satan? Who would know of the greatness of David had his virtues not been thrown into relief by the wickedness of Saul? And if it is permissible here to introduce an example from secular literature, Hercules would have remained in obscurity if he had not been made famous by the dangers to which Juno's hatred exposed him.[469] The terrors that the Lord throws in

* * * * *

465 John 16:33
466 Cf Matt 5:10.
467 Rom 9:20
468 Cf Matt 10:24.
469 In the most usual version, Hercules performs his heroic labours because of the machinations of Juno, who was consumed by hatred for the son of her husband Jupiter by a mortal woman.

our path are of no account when he who sends us into danger is the same who bestows victory on us and who frees from all evils the soldier who has been tried and tested.

In order to fix this hope more firmly in our hearts, the psalm repeats the same sentiment four times. First, 'I sought out the Lord, and he heard me, and rescued me from all my afflictions.' Shortly following this we have 'This poor man cried out, and the Lord heard him, and saved him from all his troubles.' Then, in more general terms, 'The righteous cried out, and the Lord heard them, and rescued them from all their afflictions.' The fourth occurrence is here: 'Many are the tribulations of the righteous, and the Lord has delivered them from all of these.'[470] And the same is repeated at the end, 'The Lord will redeem the souls of his servants.' This is not mere human repetitiousness; the words are repeated so many times so that they stimulate our deafness, make our forgetfulness attentive, and turn our lack of faith into strength.

'The Lord guards all their bones, not one of them shall be broken.' This can be simply accepted as a parallel to our Lord's saying to the apostles in the Gospel: 'Not a hair of your heads shall be lost.'[471] This hyperbole is a promise that the whole man will rise again, even though on this earth the body may perish by fire or by sword. How many hairs fall from our head in our lifetime? They have nothing to do with our resurrection, any more than our nail-clippings have. But perhaps the word 'bones' conceals some more inward sense. In Exodus we come across the prohibition on breaking the bones of the passover lamb,[472] and the Evangelist shows that this is a prophecy referring to the Lord, since in historical fact the bones of Christ were not broken on the cross – even though it is remarkable that his hands and feet should have been pierced by nails without breaking any bones.[473] So let us grant that in Christ's body no bone was broken – but this very fact shows us a higher truth which bears out the figure, since it is not plausible that no bone was broken among those who were thrown to lions and leopards and torn to pieces, or sawn in half, cut with axes, stoned to death, or thrown off cliffs. Rather, just as our inner man has his own eyes and ears, his head and face, his belly, feet, and hands, so he also

* * * * *

470 The version given by Erasmus earlier, in accordance with the Septuagint and Vulgate, has 'the Lord *will* deliver them'; here, influenced no doubt by the past tenses in the verses just quoted, he gives instead '*has* delivered them.'
471 Luke 21:18
472 Exod 12:46
473 John 19:33–6

has his bones. When you hear 'The wise man's eyes are in his head,'[474] obviously you take this to mean his mental powers, and when you hear 'The
Lord's law is clear, and lights up the eyes,'[475] you think of the intellect.
When you hear 'I opened my mouth and drew breath,'[476] you interpret it
as the mouth of a soul which has faith. It is just the same with 'He who
has ears to hear, let him hear,'[477] and 'You have broken their teeth,'[478] and
'I will keep your law in the midst of my belly,'[479] and 'Your hands are full
of blood,'[480] and 'The righteous man's foot does not stumble'[481] – you take
these to be parts of the mind, not parts of the body. So what do 'bones'
mean? In the body of a living creature there is nothing more solid than the
bones. They are connected with each other by sinews and thus support and
move the body's whole bulk, and in their inmost parts, like a precious store
of treasure, nature has hidden the marrow. If you inquire what it is that
most strengthens human beings in every temptation, you will know what
the bones of the righteous are. Without prejudice to those devout people
who have spent much ingenuity on this passage – or who might have done
so – it seems to me that bones indicate the strength of faith:[482] as Peter says,
'Resist him, being strong in faith.'[483] As long as faith remains in us, complete and unimpaired, our enemy cannot defeat us, and if it should ever
happen that we lose our footing and come crashing down, we can easily
right ourselves again and return more keenly to the battle. But when the
bones are broken, no one can rise up and fight.

Growth of faith in an individual is matched by an equal growth in
strength of mind, just as babies are both small and weak, because their

* * * * *

474 Eccles 2:14; this and the following examples are taken from Basil on this pas-
     sage (*Homilia in psalmum 33* PG 29 383A–C).
475 Ps 18:9/19:8
476 Ps 118/119:131
477 Mark 4:23 and 7:16
478 Ps 3:8
479 Cf Ps 39:9/40:8 (*Psalterium iuxta Hebraeos* PL 28 [1890] 1219).
480 Isa 1:15
481 This example is puzzling, but may be an impressionistic reminiscence of Ps
     90/91:12 (= Matt 4:6, Luke 4:11).
482 The most usual interpretation of 'bones' here is 'virtues' in general; Augustine
     Enarratio in psalmum 33 2.24 PL 36 320 takes it to mean specifically faith. But
     Erasmus is perhaps signalling his preference for a tropological interpretation
     over one that examines such questions as how to square this passage with the
     breaking of the bones of the martyrs (365 above and Basil *Homilia in psalmum
     33* PG 29 381) or the just thief (Augustine ibidem 321).
483 1 Pet 5:9

bones are soft and continue gradually to grow until they harden. This is why Paul calls those who are weak in faith 'little ones in Christ,'[484] as were the Galatians whom the devil had cast down into Judaism.[485] So whenever we feel our faith is hesitant, let us cry out with the prophet: 'Heal me, Lord, for all my bones are troubled,'[486] let us cry with the apostles: 'Lord, increase our faith.'[487]

If bones are faith, what are sinews and flesh? The sinews are love, which links member to member, so that each can perform its proper function. The flesh is good works, which are inseparable from faith and love and also form its ornament and safeguard. But since the faith of all pious people is one, how does it happen that it says: 'He guards all their bones, not one of them shall be broken'? Faith is indeed one, but you could say that there are as many faiths as there are articles of faith. Someone whose legs are whole can still have a broken arm. Heretics seem to have some bones which are not broken, since there are many articles of faith that they profess with piety along with us. The Jews, too, agree with us in acknowledging one God, creator of heaven and earth. It is a large bone, but the only one. Yet the Lord safeguards all the bones of the righteous; he does not allow the righteous to depart from the truth of the Catholic faith in any point, for no one can be saved if even one of his bones is broken. It does not help the Jew that he believes in one God if he denies the Son and the Holy Spirit. It is useless to admit that Christ suffered for our sake if one denies the resurrection of the body. So what are we to say of those who died in some heretical error? Irenaeus became a chiliast, Cyprian thought that those baptized by heretics were in need of rebaptism, while St Jerome condemned as heretical the opinion that a bishop who, once baptized, remarried after the death of a wife he had married before his baptism should be removed from office. Augustine constantly proclaims that unless baptized children have received the Lord's body and blood they are lost eternally, their baptism benefiting them not at all, and it is clear that almost the whole western church was of this opinion, and probably the eastern church as well.[488] Now if these men were

* * * * *

484 1 Cor 3:1
485 Cf Gal 4:1–11.
486 Cf Ps 6:3/2.
487 Luke 17:5
488 The Chiliasts or millenarians believed that Christ would rule on earth for a thousand years before the Last Judgment; it appears that this belief was never formally declared heretical. See J. Lawson *The Biblical Theology of St Irenaeus* (London 1948) 279–91. Cyprian's opinion is stated in Ep 71 *ad Quintum* PL 4 (1844) 408–11, for example, and put in context in *De unitate* 11 PL 4 (1844)

saints, why did the Lord not guard all their bones? And if they were not saints, why does the church honour them as such? A wounded or dislocated bone is one thing, but a broken bone quite another. A wounded bone can be healed, a bone out of joint can be put back in place, but a broken bone is scarcely curable. There are very few examples of a confirmed heretic's return to the church. But those whose error is a merely intellectual one and whose emotions have not been seduced are easily brought back to the path.[489] This was the case with Paul, and so when he received a warning he at once returned to the path.[490] Consequently, if the church had admonished those devout men, they would immediately have rejected their erroneous beliefs.[491]

But it is simpler to explain this verse in connection with the resurrection of the dead, like the prophecy of Ezekiel, speaking to dry bones which receive breath and join together once more.[492] Good men had been burned, their bones reduced to ashes and scattered to the wind and waves, so that there might be no possibility of restoring them. But Almighty God does not allow one bone to be broken in such a way that it may not rise again at the time of judgment. Thus the prospect of resurrection makes the death of the upright both happy and enviable, since they will rise again to everlasting life; but equally, it causes the death of the wicked to be terrible, since whether they will or no they will rise to the torments of hell, though they would be better off if the individual perished utterly at death. As John says, 'Blessed are those who die in the Lord,'[493] and those who die in the Lord are those who die with a clear hope of resurrection. So it is not death that

* * * * *

507–8; see P. Hinchcliff *Cyprian of Carthage and the Unity of the Christian Church* (London 1974), especially 98–118. For Jerome's view see Ep 69 PL 22 653–64. Augustine's opinion can be found, for instance, in *De peccatorum meritis et remissione* 1.20.27 PL 44 124.

489 The distinction made here is an important one for Erasmus: 'merely intellectual' error implies some unintentional inadequacy in the formulation of doctrine; by contrast the 'emotions' or inner disposition (*affectus*) constitute the subjective self which directs our actions. Cf *In psalmum* 22 185 and n399 above, and further CWE 63 Introduction xxxii.

490 Acts 9:3–18; cf Acts 22:2–16 ('the path').

491 Erasmus gives a much fuller treatment of the heterodox opinions of the Fathers in *In psalmum* 38 LB V 432B–435B; on his appeal to the doctrinal fluidity of the Fathers, a key strand in his efforts to promote toleration among contemporary Christians, see Irene Backus 'Erasmus and the Spirituality of the Early Church' in *Erasmus' Vision of the Church* ed H.M. Pabel (Kirksville, MO 1995) 95–114.

492 Ezek 37:1–14

493 Rev 14:13

is miserable, but a bad death, just as life is not good in itself, but only a life well lived. Things are turned upside down when the wicked say, 'Let us condemn him to a dreadful death';[494] Scripture says 'The death of sinners is terrible.'

But if the death of sinners is terrible, and no one's life is free from sin, who will be saved?[495] The prophet does not here mean any and every sin, for not every sin leads to hell. So what kind of sin is he talking about? Anticipating the question, he makes this clear: 'And those who hate the righteous man will do wrong.' But whom does he mean by the righteous man? Primarily, he means him who through faith makes righteous everyone who comes into this world.[496] Those who reject him and refused to believe him hear the words 'You will die in your sins.'[497] Such a death is terrible. But the verse can also correctly be understood to refer to anyone at all. 'Do not be surprised if the world hates you, since it hated me before you.'[498] Anyone full of the spirit of this world will hate all those in whom they see the image of Christ. There is scarcely hope for such people; but those who sin from time to time, who hate themselves for it, but who love the modesty in others which they themselves lack, who love the restraint which they do not possess, who give their resources to help the righteous when in need, and who ask for their prayers – for them, if they do these things without hypocrisy, there is hope, since they have not gone so far in sin as to hate the righteous man, but rather hate themselves for their lack of righteousness. We must pray that such people make progress, since to love another's righteousness and to hate one's own lack of it is already a step on the road to righteousness.

Now if the death of the wicked is terrible, that of the devout must be enviable. But we are not here talking about what the general run of people call good and bad. Most people say that those who are rich, respected, and healthy, who experience no hardship and no catastrophes, have a good life. It is the same if they come across someone who has reached a ripe old age with all his faculties intact, who leaves flourishing offspring, who breathes his last in the company of high-ranking friends, in the arms of the wife who will close his eyes, especially if his last illness was neither serious nor prolonged and his death was not painful – 'euthanasia' as Augustus

* * * * *

494 Cf Wisd 2:20, quoted at 357 above.
495 The argument that follows is from Augustine *Enarratio in psalmum* 33 2.26 PL 36 322.
496 The phraseology recalls John 1:9.
497 John 8:24
498 Cf John 15:18.

called it.[499] If there follows a funeral on a grand scale, with huge crowds of mourners, great lamentations, vast ranks of torch-bearers, ostentatious bells tolling, solemn requiems chanted, and a tomb adorned with marble, ivory, silver, and gold, next to the high altar of course, then the world says 'How happy he was in his death!'[500] But if he dies in sin, then according to the prophet his death was terrible. Such was the death and burial of the rich man in the gospel, while Lazarus seemed to die in great misery, although his death was precious in the sight of the Lord.[501] The rich man's death took him to eternal torment, while Lazarus was given everlasting rest. He died in the filth, among the dogs, in poverty, with no friend, relative, or wife by his side, and yet this death was a happy one, while that of the rich man was terrible. What use is it for a corpse to rot in church, if the soul is buried in hell?

We should put more trust in Scripture than we do in common opinion. Some people observe a person wasting away with a slow disease, who makes his confession, is absolved, and receives all the church's sacraments at his sickbed, and who dies amidst a crowd of people praying for him, and say 'What a good death!' But when someone dies of apoplexy or a stroke or some other instantaneous failure of the body, without confession or sacraments, they say 'His death was a dreadful one,' and 'God keep me from a sudden death.'[502] But why do we judge our neighbour, when we do not know in what state of faith he died? There are many kinds of death, and we cannot choose whether we die in one way or another. In my view, many who perished by the hangman's noose, or the executioner's sword, or by fire, died a holier death than some rich people who displayed every virtue that could be placed on public view. Only God knows what lies hidden in the heart.

So the cruel should take heed that the death of sinners is terrible, and turn back from their evil ways. The humble who are wronged should also take heed, and cease to think of revenge. If there is any comfort in vengeance (as another psalm has it, 'the righteous man will rejoice when he sees the vengeance'),[503] then there is no more weighty vengeance than that which awaits the wicked: a terrible death in sin, an everlasting punishment.

* * * * *

499 Suetonius *Lives of the Caesars: Augustus* 99. Erasmus calls Augustus by his pre-imperial name Octavian.

500 This attitude is satirized in the Colloquy *Funus* CWE 40 764–79.

501 Luke 16:19–31; for the phrasing cf Ps 115/116:15.

502 Compare the prayer in the Litany of the Saints: 'A subitanea et improvisa morte libera nos, Domine.' Erasmus also criticizes this request in *De praeparatione ad mortem* (1534) CWE 70 416–7.

503 Ps 57:11/58:10

In days gone by, the saints took pleasure in contemplating God's truthfulness and justice, since thus he fulfilled his promises and gave evil its just deserts. From the universal perspective, even the horrors of hell increase what is fitting and harmonious. But let it never happen in this life that one human being rejoices in the death of another. It is true that in the writings of the prophets we frequently come across prayers asking that the enemy should be 'put to confusion' and 'perish,' but it is our part here to understand a different kind of vengeance – that is, that they should be put to the confusion of repentance, and that the wicked personality in them should be put to death while the good begins to live. Everyone beset by sin should wish for such an end: that he may repent and feel shame and put to death whatever lives a bad life in him. Let him feel shame for his adultery; let him kill the adulterer and give life to the lover of modesty and restraint.

Those who have investigated the Hebrew sources give another reading of this verse: 'Evil will kill the wicked man, and those who hate the righteous man will be deserted (or, destroyed).'[504] This shows that those who hate piety and who torment the devout will get no advantage from it; even though no one takes vengeance on them, they bring about their own death through their wrongdoing. For sin is actually the death of the soul, and so all those who hate Christ, and who persecute him in his members, are dead even in this life, and whatever evil they plan against others will rebound on themselves. Their plan is to destroy the righteous man, but the result will be that they themselves are destroyed for all eternity and deprived of God's mercy. Conversely, the evil that they plotted against the righteous will turn to the righteous' benefit, since the size of their crowns is increased by the magnitude of their struggles. The Jews tried everything in their power to get rid of Christ and his teachings completely, but all their evil attempts redounded to Christ's glory. Wicked rulers unleashed every possible assault on Christ's followers, but in trying to destroy them they glorified them, in labouring to extinguish religion they increased its strength and scope, and in attempting to secure their own rule they secured their own destruction. Why did they perish, why were they deserted? Because their own evil caused their deaths, when in their madness they hurled themselves against that stone which yields to none.[505] And why did the stubborn and

* * * * *

504 The reading of Jerome's *Psalterium iuxta Hebraeos* PL 28 (1890) 1214, with a few synonyms substituted by Erasmus; for 'deserted,' see n507 below.
505 The stone is the rock of Christ, the foundation of the church; (Matt 16:18, 1 Cor 10:4); cf *In psalmum* 3 CWE 63 166. The wording also suggests Erasmus' personal motto, *Concedo nulli*, 'I yield to none'; see J.K. McConica, 'The riddle of Terminus' *Erasmus in English* 2 (1971) 2–7.

misguided plans of the wicked against the good avail them nothing? Because the Lord redeems them. The original Hebrew has the present tense
here, indicating that the promise is valid for all time.[506] If it happens sometimes that the Lord does not redeem the bodies of his own, he certainly
redeems their souls, which he keeps from that real death which is sin. For
this reason the text continues 'and none who trusts in him will do wrong.'
When faith no longer exists, sin leads to death, but however great the sin, as
long as a spark of faith is alive, it is a sickness rather than death. So no one
who continues to trust in the Lord commits a sin which leads to death. Peter was soon restored because he had not abandoned his faith, while Judas
was lost for ever because he had cast away hope.

Instead of our reading, 'they will not do wrong,' some render the Hebrew as 'they will not be deserted':[507] different words, but the same meaning. To be truly deserted is to be abandoned by God's mercy, which sin
drives away from us – not all sins, but persistent mortal sin. Thus they
will not be deserted, because they will not sin, and they have not sinned
because God's grace has not left them.

But why, when previously he had spoken of sons ('Come, you sons,
listen to me') does he now call the same people his servants? 'Son' is a title of love, 'servant,' of obedience. God's love came first, and when he had
freely made us righteous he adopted us among his sons. So long as we
keep his commandments in holy fear and perform whatever he orders us,
obedient even to death, we are his servants, and the more we are servants,
the more we are sons. In human society it conveys esteem to be called a
son, while low status is indicated by the title of servant; but to be called
a servant of God is a title of honour. We are called sons because we return God's love who loves us, because we are heirs to his kingdom, and

* * * * *

506 In fact both Jerome's versions give the future tense *redimet* 'will redeem'; Erasmus, who is anxious to stress the present tense (see n327 above), may have
taken *redimit* 'redeems' from Pseudo-Jerome *Breviarium in psalmos* PL 26 (1845)
923B, where it is used to express Christ's continuing act of redemption through
time. For Erasmus' view of the *Breviarium* see *In psalmum 85* introductory note
6 n19 above. The quotation of this verse is unusual in that it is not complete;
the full text, referred to but not quoted just below and again in the final paragraph, is 'the Lord will redeem the souls of his servants.'

507 Erasmus' textual acumen deserts him here; *non derelinquet omnes* 'he will not
desert all those,' found in some manuscripts, is clearly a corruption of *non
delinquent omnes* 'all those ... will not do wrong,' not an independent translation of the Hebrew. But his emphasis here is on what is appropriate, not on
philological correctness.

because we are grafted onto Christ[508] through the waters of rebirth.[509] We are servants inasmuch as we have been redeemed from Satan's tyranny by Christ's precious blood, and now following his teaching we walk in newness of life.[510] A father will care for his children, a redeemer will protect those he has set free. When in his compassion he calls us to the grace of the gospel, he uses the word 'son' almost to please and flatter us. But when he prevents the wicked and the agents of the devil from tormenting the faithful, he calls them servants, since he has rescued them from Satan and placed them under his own authority and protection. Clearly it is madness to plot the destruction of those who have such a loving father and such a powerful master. Under the sway of such a shepherd, there is nothing for us, his sheep, to fear, provided that we are simple and humble, that our heart is contrite, and that we do not trust in our own strength but place all our hope in him. We can be certain that amid this world's storms he has saved our souls from mortal sin and that his mercy will not abandon us, but at the resurrection he will restore us complete to the company of his kingdom, where with all the saints we will bless and magnify him at all times, and his praise will be ever in our mouths; to whom is due all honour and glory for ever. Amen.

* * * * *

508 The metaphor is from Rom 11:17–21.
509 Titus 3:5
510 Rom 6:4

WORKS FREQUENTLY CITED

SHORT-TITLE FORMS FOR ERASMUS' WORKS

INDEX OF BIBLICAL AND
APOCRYPHAL REFERENCES

GENERAL INDEX

WORKS FREQUENTLY CITED

This list provides bibliographical information for works referred to in short-title form in this volume. For Erasmus' writings see the short-title list following.

Allen — *Opus Epistolarum Des. Erasmi Roterodami* ed P.S. Allen, H.M. Allen, and H.W. Garrod (Oxford 1906–58) 11 vols and index

ASD — *Opera Omnia Desiderii Erasmi Roterodami* (Amsterdam 1969–)

Bietenholz *History and Biography* — Peter G. Bietenholz *History and Biography in the Work of Erasmus of Rotterdam* (Geneva 1966)

CCL — *Corpus Christianorum*, series Latina (Turnhout 1954–)

CEBR — *Contemporaries of Erasmus: A Biographical Register of the Renaissance and Reformation* ed Peter G. Bietenholz and Thomas B. Deutscher (Toronto 1985–7) 3 vols

Chomarat *Grammaire et rhétorique* — Jacques Chomarat *Grammaire et rhétorique chez Erasme* (Paris 1981) 2 vols

Cochlaeus *Dialogus* — Joannes Cochlaeus *Dialogus de bello contra Turcas in Antilogias Lutheri* (Leipzig 1529)

CSEL — *Corpus Scriptorum Ecclesiasticorum Latinorum* (Vienna and Leipzig 1866–)

CWE — *Collected Works of Erasmus* (Toronto 1964–)

Eck *Enchiridion* — Johannes Maier of Eck *Enchiridion locorum communium adversus Lutheranos* (Landshut 1525)

ERSY — Erasmus of Rotterdam Society Yearbook

Felice da Prato *Psalterium* — Felice da Prato (Felix Pratensis) *Psalterium ex Hebraice Latine redditum* (Venice: D. Bomberg 1515)

Heath CC — M.J. Heath *Crusading Commonplaces: La Noue, Lucinge and Rhetoric Against the Turks* (Geneva 1986)

Heath 'Renaissance Scholars' — M.J. Heath 'Renaissance Scholars and the Origins of the Turks' *Bibliothèque d'Humanisme et Renaissance* 41 (1979) 453–71

Housley *Later Crusades* — Norman Housley *The Later Crusades 1274–1580: From Lyons to Alcazar* (Oxford 1992)

LB   *Desiderii Erasmi Roterodami opera omnia* ed J. Leclerc (Leiden 1703–6) 10 vols

Luther *Confutatio*   Martin Luther *Confutatio determinationis doctorum parrhisiensium* (Basel 1523)

Luther *Works*   Martin Luther *Works* (Philadelphia 1955–   )

Otto   A. Otto *Die Sprichwörter ... der Romer* (Leipzig 1890)

Pius II *Opera*   Pius II (Aeneas Sylvius Piccolomini) *Opera quae extant omnia* (Basel 1551)

PG   *Patrologiae cursus completus ... series Graeca* ed J.-P. Migne (Paris 1857–66; repr Turnhout) 162 vols

PL   *Patrologiae cursus completus ... series Latina* ed J.-P. Migne (Paris 1844–55, 1862–5; repr Turnhout) 217 vols and 4 vols indexes. *Patrologia Latina Database* (ProQuest Information and Learning Company 1996–2005) available by subscription online (http://pld.chadwyck.com [January 2005]) and on CD-ROM (proquest.co.uk). In the notes, references to volumes of PL in which column numbers are different in the first edition and in later editions or reprints include the date of the edition cited.

Screech   M.A. Screech *Ecstasy and the Praise of Folly* (London 1980)

Schwoebel *Shadow of the Crescent*   R. Schwoebel *The Shadow of the Crescent: The Renaissance Image of the Turk (1453–1517)* (Nieuwkoop 1967)

Tracy *Politics*   J.D. Tracy *The Politics of Erasmus: A Pacifist Intellectual and His Political Milieu* (Toronto 1978)

Vives *De conditione*   Juan Luis Vives *De conditione vitae christianorum sub Turca* (Antwerp 1529) / *Opera omnia* ed G. Majansius (Valencia 1782–90; repr London 1964) 8 vols, V 447–60

WA   *D. Martin Luthers Werke, Kritische Gesamtausgabe* (Weimar 1883–   )

Walther   Hans Walther *Proverbia sententiaeque Latinitatis medii aevi* (Gottingen 1963–9) 6 vols

Williams *Radical Reformation*   G.H. Williams *The Radical Reformation* (Philadelphia 1962)

Titles following colons are longer versions of the same, or are alternative titles. Items entirely enclosed in square brackets are of doubtful authorship. For abbreviations, see Works Frequently Cited.

Acta: Acta Academiae Lovaniensis contra Lutherum *Opuscula* / CWE 71

Adagia: Adagiorum chiliades 1508, etc (Adagiorum collectanea for the primitive form, when required) LB II / ASD II-1, 4, 5, 6 / CWE 30–6

Admonitio adversus mendacium: Admonitio adversus mendacium et obtrectationem LB X

Annotationes in Novum Testamentum LB VI / CWE 51–60

Antibarbari LB X / ASD I-1 / CWE 23

Apologia ad Caranzam: Apologia ad Sanctium Caranzam, or Apologia de tribus locis, or Responsio ad annotationem Stunicae ... a Sanctio Caranza defensam LB IX

Apologia ad Fabrum: Apologia ad Iacobum Fabrum Stapulensem LB IX / ASD IX-3 / CWE 83

Apologia adversus monachos: Apologia adversus monachos quosdam Hispanos LB IX

Apologia adversus Petrum Sutorem: Apologia adversus debacchationes Petri Sutoris LB IX

Apologia adversus rhapsodias Alberti Pii: Apologia ad viginti et quattuor libros A. Pii LB IX / CWE 84

Apologia contra Latomi dialogum: Apologia contra Iacobi Latomi dialogum de tribus linguis LB IX / CWE 71

Apologia de 'In principio erat sermo' LB IX

Apologia de laude matrimonii: Apologia pro declamatione de laude matrimonii LB IX / CWE 71

Apologia de loco 'Omnes quidem': Apologia de loco 'Omnes quidem resurgemus' LB IX

Apologiae contra Stunicam: Apologiae contra Lopidem Stunicam LB IX: (1) Apologia respondens ad ea quae Iacobus Lopis Stunica taxaverat in prima duntaxat Novi Testamenti aeditione ASD IX-2; (2) Apologia adversus libellum Stunicae cui titulum fecit Blasphemiae et impietates Erasmi; (3) Apologia ad prodromon Stunicae; (4) Apologia ad Stunicae conclusiones; (5) Epistola apologetica adversus Stunicam [= Ep 2172]

Apologia qua respondet invectivis Lei: Apologia qua respondet duabus invectivis Eduardi Lei *Opuscula*

Apophthegmata LB IV

Appendix de scriptis Clithovei LB IX / CWE 83

Appendix respondens ad Sutorem LB IX

Argumenta: Argumenta in omnes epistolas apostolicas nova (with Paraphrases)

Axiomata pro causa Lutheri: Axiomata pro causa Martini Lutheri *Opuscula* / CWE 71

Brevissima scholia: In Elenchum Alberti Pii brevissima scholia per eundem Erasmum Roterodamum CWE 84

Carmina LB I, IV, V, VIII / ASD I-7 / CWE 85–6

Catalogus lucubrationum LB I / CWE 9 (Ep 1341A)

Ciceronianus: Dialogus Ciceronianus LB I / ASD I-2 / CWE 28

Colloquia LB I / ASD I-3 / CWE 39–40

Compendium vitae Allen I / CWE 4

Concionalis interpretatio (in Psalmi)

Conflictus: Conflictus Thaliae et Barbariei LB I

[Consilium: Consilium cuiusdam ex animo cupientis esse consultum] *Opuscula* /
 CWE 71

De bello Turcico: Consultatio de bello Turcico (in Psalmi)

De civilitate: De civilitate morum puerilium LB I / CWE 25

Declamatio de morte LB IV

Declamatiuncula LB IV

Declarationes ad censuras Lutetiae vulgatas: Declarationes ad censuras Lutetiae
 vulgatas sub nomine facultatis theologiae Parisiensis LB IX

De concordia: De sarcienda ecclesiae concordia, or De amabili ecclesiae concordia
 (in Psalmi)

De conscribendis epistolis LB I / ASD I-2 / CWE 25

De constructione: De constructione octo partium orationis, or Syntaxis LB I /
 ASD I-4

De contemptu mundi: Epistola de contemptu mundi LB V / ASD V-1 / CWE 66

De copia: De duplici copia verborum ac rerum LB I / ASD I-6 / CWE 24

De esu carnium: Epistola apologetica ad Christophorum episcopum Basiliensem de
 interdicto esu carnium LB IX / ASD IX-1

De immensa Dei misericordia: Concio de immensa Dei misericordia LB V / CWE 70

De libero arbitrio: De libero arbitrio diatribe LB IX / CWE 76

De praeparatione: De praeparatione ad mortem LB V / ASD V-1 / CWE 70

De pueris instituendis: De pueris statim ac liberaliter instituendis LB I / ASD I-2 /
 CWE 26

De puero Iesu: Concio de puero Iesu LB V / CWE 29

De puritate tabernaculi: De puritate tabernaculi sive ecclesiae christianae (in
 Psalmi)

De ratione studii LB I / ASD I-2 / CWE 24

De recta pronuntiatione: De recta latini graecique sermonis pronuntiatione LB I /
 ASD I-4 / CWE 26

De taedio Iesu: Disputatiuncula de taedio, pavore, tristicia Iesu LB V / CWE 70

Detectio praestigiarum: Detectio praestigiarum cuiusdam libelli germanice
 scripti LB X / ASD IX-1

De vidua christiana LB V / CWE 66

De virtute amplectenda: Oratio de virtute amplectenda LB V / CWE 29

[Dialogus bilinguium ac trilinguium: Chonradi Nastadiensis dialogus bilinguium
 ac trilinguium] *Opuscula* / CWE 7

Dilutio: Dilutio eorum quae Iodocus Clithoveus scripsit adversus declamationem
 suasoriam matrimonii / *Dilutio eorum quae Iodocus Clithoveus scripsit* ed Emile V.
 Telle (Paris 1968) / CWE 83

Divinationes ad notata Bedae LB IX

Ecclesiastes: Ecclesiastes sive de ratione concionandi LB V / ASD V-4, 5
Elenchus in N. Bedae censuras LB IX
Enchiridion: Enchiridion militis christiani LB V / CWE 66
Encomium matrimonii (in De conscribendis epistolis)
Encomium medicinae: Declamatio in laudem artis medicae LB I / ASD I-4 / CWE 29
Epistola ad Dorpium LB IX / CWE 3 / CWE 71
Epistola ad fratres Inferioris Germaniae: Responsio ad fratres Germaniae Inferioris
    ad epistolam apologeticam incerto autore proditam LB X / ASD IX-1
Epistola ad graculos: Epistola ad quosdam imprudentissimos graculos LB X
Epistola apologetica de Termino LB X
Epistola consolatoria: Epistola consolatoria virginibus sacris, or Epistola consolato-
    ria in adversis LB V / CWE 69
Epistola contra pseudevangelicos: Epistola contra quosdam qui se falso iactant
    evangelicos LB X / ASD IX-1
Euripidis Hecuba LB I / ASD I-1
Euripidis Iphigenia in Aulide LB I / ASD I-1
Exomologesis: Exomologesis sive modus confitendi LB V
Explanatio symboli: Explanatio symboli apostolorum sive catechismus LB V /
    ASD V-1 / CWE 70
Ex Plutarcho versa LB IV / ASD IV-2

Formula: Conficiendarum epistolarum formula (see De conscribendis epistolis)

Hyperaspistes LB X / CWE 76–7

In Nucem Ovidii commentarius LB I / ASD I-1 / CWE 29
In Prudentium: Commentarius in duos hymnos Prudentii LB V / CWE 29
Institutio christiani matrimonii LB V / CWE 69
Institutio principis christiani LB IV / ASD IV-1 / CWE 27

[Julius exclusus: Dialogus Julius exclusus e coelis] Opuscula / CWE 27

Lingua LB IV / ASD IV-1A / CWE 29
Liturgia Virginis Matris: Virginis Matris apud Lauretum cultae liturgia LB V /
    ASD V-1 / CWE 69
Luciani dialogi LB I / ASD I-1

Manifesta mendacia CWE 71
Methodus (see Ratio)
Modus orandi Deum LB V / ASD V-1 / CWE 70
Moria: Moriae encomium LB IV / ASD IV-3 / CWE 27

Novum Testamentum: Novum Testamentum 1519 and later (Novum instrumentum
    for the first edition, 1516, when required) LB VI

Obsecratio ad Virginem Mariam: Obsecratio sive oratio ad Virginem Mariam in rebus
adversis, or Obsecratio ad Virginem Matrem Mariam in rebus adversis LB V / CWE 69
Oratio de pace: Oratio de pace et discordia LB VIII

Oratio funebris: Oratio funebris in funere Bertae de Heyen LB VIII / CWE 29

Paean Virgini Matri: Paean Virgini Matri dicendus LB V / CWE 69
Panegyricus: Panegyricus ad Philippum Austriae ducem LB IV / ASD IV-1 / CWE 27
Parabolae: Parabolae sive similia LB I / ASD I-5 / CWE 23
Paraclesis LB V, VI
Paraphrasis in Elegantias Vallae: Paraphrasis in Elegantias Laurentii Vallae LB I / ASD I-4
Paraphrasis in Matthaeum, etc (in Paraphrasis in Novum Testamentum)
Paraphrasis in Novum Testamentum LB VII / CWE 42–50
Peregrinatio apostolorum: Peregrinatio apostolorum Petri et Pauli LB VI, VII
Precatio ad Virginis filium Iesum LB V / CWE 69
Precatio dominica LB V / CWE 69
Precationes: Precationes aliquot novae LB V / CWE 69
Precatio pro pace ecclesiae: Precatio ad Dominum Iesum pro pace ecclesiae LB IV, V / CWE 69
Psalmi: Psalmi, or Enarrationes sive commentarii in psalmos LB V / ASD V-2, 3 / CWE 63–5
Purgatio adversus epistolam Lutheri: Purgatio adversus epistolam non sobriam Lutheri LB X / ASD IX-1

Querela pacis LB IV / ASD IV-2 / CWE 27

Ratio: Ratio seu Methodus compendio perveniendi ad veram theologiam (Methodus for the shorter version originally published in the Novum instrumentum of 1516) LB V, VI
Responsio ad annotationes Lei: Liber quo respondet annotationibus Lei LB IX
Responsio ad collationes: Responsio ad collationes cuiusdam iuvenis geronto didascali LB IX
Responsio ad disputationem de divortio: Responsio ad disputationem cuiusdam Phimostomi de divortio LB IX / CWE 83
Responsio ad epistolam Alberti Pii: Responsio ad epistolam paraeneticam Alberti Pii, or Responsio ad exhortationem Pii LB IX / CWE 84
Responsio ad notulas Bedaicas LB X
Responsio ad Petri Cursii defensionem: Epistola de apologia Cursii LB X / Allen Ep 3032
Responsio adversus febricitantis libellum: Apologia monasticae religionis LB X

Spongia: Spongia adversus aspergines Hutteni LB X / ASD IX-1
Supputatio: Supputatio calumniarum Natalis Bedae LB IX

Tyrannicida: Tyrannicida, declamatio Lucianicae respondens LB I / ASD I-1 / CWE 29

Virginis et martyris comparatio LB V / CWE 69
Vita Hieronymi: Vita divi Hieronymi Stridonensis Opuscula / CWE 61

Index of Biblical and Apocryphal References

General Index

Aaron 164–5
Abel 21, 48, 155, 287
Abiathar 291, 294–6
Abimelech 269, 275, 276–8, 287–91, 293–9, 302–6, 307, 309
Abraham 19, 24, 41, 84, 102, 147, 173, 297, 298–9, 304, 311, 319, 330, 342; sons of 284
Absalom 292, 313, 320
Achan, cause of Israel's defeat 249
Achias 294. *See also* Achis
Achimelech 288, 291
Achis 276, 278, 287, 291, 294, 296–9, 302, 307, 325
Achitob 294
Adam 108, 152 and n193, 179, 353–4 and n427
Adrianople (Edirne), Ottoman capital 224–5
Adrian vi, Pope 248
Aesculapius 163, 310
Africans 319
Agamemnon 135
Agar 71
Agrippa von Nettesheim *De occulta philosophia* 245 n183
Ahab deceived by prophecy 244–5
Ahaz 102
Aias (variant of Achias) 295
Albania, Ottoman conquest of 225–6
Alcmene 163 n266
Aldhelm *De laudibus virginitatis* 114 n551
Alexander the Great 176 n353, 264, 319
Alexander vi, Pope 177 n357, 232, 247

Alger of Liège *De veritate corporis et sanguinis Domini* 239 n155
Allecto 357 and n440
allegory 147–8 n148, 163 and n263; in Scripture 127, 141, 280–5, 301
Allophylli (Philistines), opponents of the Hebrews 235
Alp Arslan ('Asanus'), Seljuk prince 222
Amadeo of Savoy 224 n78
Amalekites, opponents of the Hebrews 255
Ambrose, St, and Theodosius 236, 252
– *Commentarium in epistolam ad Romanos* 154 n208
– *De obitu Theodosii* 236 n142, 265 n270
– *De officiis* 236 n143
– *Expositio evangelii secundum Lucam* 216 n37, 239 n156
– Sermon 62 *De bellico tumultu* 236 n143
Amelech 71
Amerbach, Bonifacius 203, 205
Ammon 71
Anabaptists, oppose resistance to the Turks 205, 206, 233 n129, 257 n234, 258 n236
Anaxagoras 283 and n38
Andrew (apostle), called by Christ 136
Andronikos iv, Byzantine emperor 224 n78
angels 19–20, 34, 63, 332–5
Annas 62, 88–90, 110, 181, 359
annates, abuse of 250
Antioch 325

This book

was designed by

VAL COOKE

based on the series design by

ALLAN FLEMING

and was printed by

University

of Toronto

Press